Doing Time

Doing Time

An Introduction to the Sociology of Imprisonment

Second edition

Roger Matthews
London South Bank University, UK

palgrave
macmillan

First published 1999 by
MACMILLAN PRESS LTD
This edition published 2009 by
PALGRAVE MACMILLAN

Palgrave Macmillan in the UK is an imprint of Macmillan Publishers Limited,
registered in England, company number 785998, of Houndmills, Basingstoke,
Hampshire RG21 6XS.

Palgrave Macmillan in the US is a division of St Martin's Press LLC,
175 Fifth Avenue, New York, NY 10010.

Palgrave Macmillan is the global academic imprint of the above companies
and has companies and representatives throughout the world.

Palgrave® and Macmillan® are registered trademarks in the United States,
the United Kingdom, Europe and other countries.

ISBN-13:   978–0–230–23551–9   hardback
ISBN-13:   978–0–230–23552–6   paperback

This book is printed on paper suitable for recycling and made from fully
managed and sustained forest sources. Logging, pulping and manufacturing
processes are expected to conform to the environmental regulations of the
country of origin.

A catalogue record for this book is available from the British Library.

A catalog record for this book is available from the Library of Congress.

10   9   8   7   6   5   4   3   2   1
18   17   16   15   14   13   12   11   10   09

Printed and bound in Great Britain by
CPI Antony Rowe, Chippenham and Eastbourne

Contents

List of Tables and Figures

Tables

Figures

Introduction

Since the publication of the first edition of this book in 1999 the debates around imprisonment have changed considerably and a great deal of literature on the subject has been produced. Probably the most significant change has been the increasing focus on the growth of imprisonment on both sides of the Atlantic in a period in which recorded crime is decreasing. Addressing this development has prompted the writing of three new chapters for the second edition, which critically examine the role of economics, politics and culture in shaping the use and scale of imprisonment, as well as looking at the role of crime and sentencing.

In the course of re-examining these processes it is suggested that much of the available literature fails to adequately conceptualise or analyse recent developments in penal policy. It also appears to be the case that most of the current explanations do not fit very well with the empirical evidence. Thus the three new chapters in this book, while attempting to remain expositional, take issue with a number of widely accepted claims concerning the growth of imprisonment. Alternative explanations are presented and discussed.

Most of the other chapters have also been revised and updated to incorporate changing debates and more recent literature. In some cases these revisions have been considerable. The literature and debates, particularly in relation to women's imprisonment and youth custody, have moved on significantly over the last decade and the revised nature of these chapters in this volume is designed to reflect these developments.

The basic format and approach of the book, however, remains much the same as the first edition; that is, the aim is not only to introduce the reader to some of the key debates associated with imprisonment, but also to engage in sociological theorisation and analysis. Each chapter takes up different theoretical, conceptual, methodological and empirical issues. In this way it is designed to go beyond a straightforward description of the prison system or the cataloguing of 'facts' about imprisonment. Instead, it emphasises the primacy of theory and the need to critically engage with the subject matter.

The discerning reader will note that there are a number of sub-texts running through the book. Although the book is largely expositional it does not mean that it is theoretically or politically neutral. The first edition involved in part an attempt to provide something of a defence of Rusche and Kirchheimer's path-breaking book *Punishment and Social Structure* against the critiques that their work was reductionist because it focused on economic relations or that it was a book about the relation between unemployment, the labour market and punishment. In this edition of *Doing Time* I have tried to shore up this defence a little more by suggesting that it is more appropriate and instructive to see recent developments in the nature of punishment in relation to post-Fordism rather than postmodernism. That is, the aim is to suggest that it is the changing nature of productive relations with their effect on space and time that provides a better understanding of the causal dynamics involved.

By the same token, more weight is given to socio-economic and cultural processes, rather than political processes, in explaining the changing nature of imprisonment. The current debate on imprisonment tends to be dominated by an emphasis on politics and the ways in which 'populist punitiveness' is driving up the prison population. Attributing the changing nature and scale of imprisonment to the will and interests of punitive politicians or an intolerant public is not only a theoretically and empirically weak form of explanation, but one that veers towards voluntarism, rather than seeing developments in the nature of imprisonment as part of a wider dynamic.

Another theme running through the book is the attempt to reconnect crime and imprisonment. One of the strange features of criminology is the way in which scholars and researchers conveniently separate the study of crime from the use of imprisonment and try hard to disassociate these aspects of the criminal justice process. The result is that one half of the criminological community concentrates on crime and victimisation, while the other half focuses on aspects of social control, punishment and imprisonment. Thus one group concentrates on the actions and motivations of offenders and victims, while the other is mainly concerned with the process of reaction and the labelling of deviant behaviour.

One of the main tasks of realist criminology is to reconnect crime and punishment and to argue that 'crime' itself is the product of a complex process of action and reaction. Realists developed the 'square of crime' to try to capture the process of crime creation and to show that crime itself could not be reduced to an act or to the motivation of individual offenders. Reference is made to realist literature throughout the book, and the perspective that informs this book will become more apparent if these references are followed up.

My involvement with critical realism in the last few years has increased my awareness of methodological issues and in particular the limits of empiricism. Empiricism, which involves the examination of covariance between two phenomena, is rife within criminology. In some cases this covariance is presented in the form of statistical correlations, in other forms the simultaneous movement of two social phenomena is presented as evidence that they are causally linked. In opposition to these often spurious connections critical realists argue that the causal relations between phenomena has nothing to do with their degree of covariance or the number of times that they are seen to occur together. The aim is to identify the causal processes involved and in particular to try to understand the process of change.

It soon becomes apparent that this book has been deeply influenced by two classic texts – Michel Foucault's *Discipline and Punish* and George Rusche and Otto Kirchheimer's *Punishment and Social Structure*. These two publications share three important attributes. The first is that like all great books they have a transformative effect. That is, having read them it is difficult if not impossible to view the processes of prisons and punishment in the same way as before. Second, that they locate the changing nature of prisons and punishment in changing socio-economic developments, rather than limiting their attention to the penal sphere. Third, they do not descend into a moralism in which their analysis of imprisonment is conditioned by their views on the desirability or otherwise of imprisonment. Instead, they offer a form of analysis that aims to understand the dynamics and effects of imprisonment in a theoretically informed and analytical way. It is therefore, strongly recommended that these two texts are read in conjunction with this new edition of *Doing Time*.

Drawing on these and other key authors the book provides an overview of the historical developments of incarceration and an introduction to key debates. The first two chapters should be read together. They cover the history of imprisonment and examine the three key elements that distinguish and shape the modern prison – space, time and labour. Drawing on the theoretically informed history that Foucault develops in *Discipline and Punish* the second chapter explores the concepts of space, time and labour and identifies the various contributions that these three elements make to the use, size and development of the prison. Chapter 3 examines some of the key sociological contributions to the literature on imprisonment. Dating back to the 1940s and 1950s there is a rich vein of sociological literature that aims to theorise the role of 'total institutions' like the prison and the way in which different groups of people adapt to and deal with imprisonment. The chapter looks in particular at the issues of order and control in prisons and discusses the way in which these objectives are achieved.

Chapters 4, 5 and 6 are closely related since they focus on the current explanations for the increase in penal populations in Britain and America. It is suggested in relation to these increases in the prison population that it may be less to do with political shifts or sentencing policies and more to do with the level of recorded serious crime combined with cultural variations between different countries. Chapters 7, 8 and 9 also form a related group. They look, in turn, at juvenile incarceration, women and imprisonment and race and imprisonment. The recent increases in the number of women incarcerated in America, Canada, Australia and in the UK has raised questions about whether women's involvement in crime – particularly serious crime – is a function of the changing status of women in these countries, a greater involvement in crime or changes in sentencing practices. The chapter traces through the movement of women from arrest to incarceration in order to try to answer these questions. Similar issues have arisen in relation to juvenile incarceration and the racial disparity in the use of imprisonment. The final chapter looks at the future of imprisonment and raises the question of whether the prison population is likely to continue to expand in countries like Britain and America in the future or whether the significant, socio-economic and political changes that are currently taking place will lead to decrease in the use of imprisonment.

In each chapter there are a number of key themes and concepts that are explored and there are a number of up to date references that readers can consult. The book also includes a list of relevant web addresses for many key agencies and institutions around the world that have a connection to imprisonment as it is recognised that students and researchers increasingly use web sites to access and download information.

1
The Emergence of the Modern Prison

Introduction

The seventeenth century marked a watershed in the history of punishment across northern Europe. During this period thousands of the poor, the destitute, the vagrant, the insane and the deviant found themselves segregated and confined in special institutions designed to remove them either temporarily or permanently from mainstream society. This period has been described as 'The Great Confinement' (Foucault, 1977). It marked an era in which the main forms of punishment began to shift from public executions, whippings and floggings, as well as the widespread use of forms of public shaming in the pillory or the stocks, to one in which institutions such as bridewells, workhouses, asylums and jails became the preferred response to the management of 'problem populations'.

These developments, until relatively recently, have been poorly documented. Until the 1970s the few available books on the history of imprisonment tended to present the prison as a naturally evolving institution which developed out of the local jails that were widely used in the medieval period. Although these historical accounts provide useful descriptions of the administrative and institutional changes that have occurred, they tend to ignore the specific historical characteristics of the modern prison, and to overlook the wider social context in which it emerged. These 'administrative' or 'traditional' histories lack an analysis of 'passion, power and conflict' (Howe, 1994), and are generally 'long on facts and short on interpretation' (Rothman, 1971). In particular, they fail to examine the differences between medieval jails and fortresses – which were primarily places where prisoners were held while awaiting trial, execution or deportation – and the modern prison – in which the deprivation of liberty itself for a specified period of time becomes the dominant mode of punishment.

The new histories of incarceration that emerged in the 1970s and 1980s were also generally critical of the earlier Whig histories, which attempted to explain the shift from one type of punishment to another as a product of humanism, involving a shift from barbarism to civilisation. Such explanations, it was argued, failed to recognise that the new forms of incarceration were, by and large, directed at significantly different populations, and that it was not so much a case of less punishment or more benign punishment, but a different *form* of punishment. The crucial question for the new 'revisionist' histories was: 'Why prison?' That is, why it was this particular form of confinement rather than any other type of punishment that came to dominate in the seventeenth and eighteenth centuries. There was also a related question of how this change in the form of punishment was connected to changing social and economic conditions.

The spectacle of suffering

In the introduction to *Discipline and Punish*, Michel Foucault (1977) provides a vivid and gruesome description of the processes by which Robert François Damiens was hanged, drawn and quartered in Paris in 1757 for attempting to take the life of King Louis XV. As a consequence of Damiens's unusual strength and because the horses were not accustomed to drawing, his execution was a long and painful spectacle, involving the severing of his legs at the joints and 'the same was done to the arms, the shoulders, the arm pits and the four limbs; the flesh had to be cut almost to the bone, the horses pulling hard carried off the right arm first and the other afterwards' (Foucault, 1977: 5).

Spectacles of this kind, involving offenders being hanged, drawn and quartered, were relatively rare events in the eighteenth century. Foucault, however, uses this particular case to exemplify how, despite the gruesome nature of these public executions, they were an accepted form of punishment; and how this particular sanction, involving the infliction of severe physical pain and ultimately death, formed an essential part of the formal response to particular types of transgression in this period. The spectacle of suffering was intended to put the crowd in mind of the vastly greater terrors of hell. Culprits were expected to show repentance and to confess their crimes before the assembled crowd. Public confessions were often the route to a quick and relatively painless death.

In England, death by hanging was widely practised throughout the seventeenth and eighteenth centuries. There were eight hanging days in every year. In London, hangings were carried out at Tyburn (now Marble Arch) until 1783, after which time they were conducted at Newgate prison. These events were well attended by local populations and attracted, among others, the vagabond population of London, who were often referred to as the 'London Mob':

> On the morning of a hanging day the bells of the churches of London were rung buffeted. The cries of hawkers selling ballads and 'Last Dying Speeches' filled the streets. The last preparations for death in the chapel at Newgate were open to those able to pay the gaoler his fee. The malefactor's chains were struck off in the press yard in front of friends and relations, the curious, the gaping and onlookers at the prison gate. The route of the hanging procession crossed the busiest axis of the town at Smithfield, passed through one of the most heavily populated districts in St. Giles's and St. Andrews, Holborn and followed the most-trafficked road, Tyburn Road, to the gallows. There the assembled people on foot, upon horseback, in coaches, crowding nearby houses, filling the adjoining roads, climbing ladders, sitting on the wall enclosing Hyde Park and standing on its contiguous cow pastures, gathered to witness the hanging. (Linebaugh, 1977: 67)

Public support for hangings, however, began to wane in the eighteenth century, and the 'hanging match', as it was called, increasingly became a focus of disturbances, brawls and riots. As the century progressed, these public executions rested less on spontaneous public support and more on the force of arms. On a number of occasions, individuals were plucked from the jaws of death by members of the crowd. Hangmen were jeered and attacked, and increasingly public hangings became uncertain, precarious events, particularly in cases in which those to be hanged were seen as the victims of injustice or were popular characters. One point of concern was the snatching of bodies by the surgeons, who paid high prices for fresh corpses on which to practise their medical skills (Linebaugh, 1977).

But the fading support for public executions went much deeper than the activities of the surgeons or the saving of particular souls from the scaffold. Among the social elite, public executions were viewed with increased scepticism, and hangings were seen as being more likely to undermine public order than to reinforce social norms. In short, towards the end of the eighteenth century public forms of punishment lost their legitimacy in England as well as other parts of Europe (Spierenburg, 1984).

Influential writers and social commentators, including Daniel Defoe (1728), Bernard de Mandeville (1725) and Henry Fielding (1751), advocated the removal of hangings from public view. Alongside those calling for the cessation of public hangings were those who advocated the use of imprisonment, particularly in the form of solitary confinement, as a more effective and more appropriate form of punishment.

A just measure of pain

Throughout Europe in the seventeenth and eighteenth centuries there were major changes taking place in the nature of social and economic relations. The old feudal order was breaking down, and the predominantly agricultural economy was gradually being replaced by new forms of production and government. During this period, there was an increasing concern with vagrants, rogues and beggars, and particularly with the increased levels of theft, which were seen by some commentators to be a consequence of the instigation of absolute private property and the growing number of goods that had become available (Marx and Engels, 1975).

Bound up with these changes was the introduction of new penal codes. Old laws appeared crude and ineffective and pressure for reform came from both inside and outside the legal profession. The traditional forms of legality were seen to lead to injustices and as being unable to provide adequate protection for the new forms of property (Thompson, 1975). These changes were accompanied by the emergence of the nation-state, which claimed monopoly of the use of coercive force. These developments had two important consequences. First, the right to punish shifted from the vengeance of the sovereign to the defence of society. Second, these new penal codes were characterised by the separation of illegality from the protection of rights and the protection of private property. The aim was to introduce a new penal code in which there would be a clearer codification of penalties and which would lay down new principals for administering punishment. In contrast to the variable and personalised system of penalties which was prevalent prior to the eighteenth century, the new penal system was charged with the task of administering the criminal law in a more rigorous, certain and efficient manner.

A key figure in this process was Cesare Beccaria, whose book *An Essay on Crimes and Punishment* (1764) was translated into a number of European languages and whose writings deeply influenced the formulation of new penal codes and strategies across Europe. Central to Beccaria's approach is the assumption that crime is a rational activity in which individuals assess the benefits and consequences of their action and that the pains of punishment should be just enough to outweigh the potential advantages of engaging in crime. In this way he sought to maximise the deterrent effects of punishment, while minimising cost and effort. Punishment, he maintained, should be certain and firm, without being unnecessarily brutal or prolonged. In outlining this 'classicist' approach Beccaria emphasised that punishment should be applied equally and should be linked to the seriousness of the offence (Roshier, 1989). The major focus should be on the proportionality of punishment, which in turn requires a precise calibration of offences on a scale of seriousness. Among many reformers the objective was to develop a system which was able to dispense punishment equally to all those engaged in illegalities and thereby to provide a just measure of pain.

Crime, in the new order, came to be seen as a transgression not against the sovereign but against society. The offender, having broken the 'social contract', is not to be brutalised or ridiculed, but rather should be allowed to repay society in a way which would regenerate respect for property, liberty and the freedom of others. As formally free and equal citizens, the perpetrators of crimes require a form of punishment which treats them equally, and which deprives them of the one thing they have in common: individual liberty. From this perspective the emphasis is upon the act, and not the motivation or background of the offender. The aim was to promote formal equality, which meant that all offenders should be treated the same, irrespective of personal or social circumstances. Consequently, the rich and the poor, young and old, males and females should receive equal punishment, whatever their substantive differences.

The roots of the prison system lay in mercantilism, and its promotion and elaboration was the task of the Enlightenment. The dual aspiration of Enlightenment thinkers was that prison could perform the function of reforming the individual offender, while simultaneously improving society. It could make the idle poor industrious and thereby turn a social deficit into something productive. Through the application of scientific and rational principles, it should aim to produce useful obedient subjects. These modernising influences found expression in the prison (Morrison, 1996). Imprisonment provided a form of punishment which could be based on precise calculations of time. By removing people from the contaminating influences of the community, the prison promised to provide an environment in which the prisoner could be reformed. At the same time, the deprivation of liberty would serve as a continuous reminder to others of the consequences of non-conformity. Through the combination of these different forces, imprisonment became widely seen as an obvious and almost irresistible option.

Jails, workhouses and houses of correction

The modern prison did not emerge at the end of the eighteenth century fully formed and functioning. In fact, it was the combination of a number of institutions which had been used for holding captives. The modern prison grew on one side out of the local jails which had been used as places of detention, and on the other from the houses of correction which had emerged from the old bridewells. Thus the term 'prison' is often used generically to cover a number of different institutions (McConville, 1995).

In order to distinguish between previous forms of confinement and the modern prison which arose at the end of the eighteenth century, and which appeared fully formed in England and Wales during the 1840s with the opening of Pentonville, it is necessary to examine briefly the development of the various forms of confinement that were in use between the beginning of the seventeenth century and the end of the eighteenth century.

From as early as 1556, bridewells were established in England in order to suppress idleness and vagrancy, in light of the apparent inefficacy of the traditional remedies for begging and moral offences. By the law of James I passed in 1609 it became obligatory for all English counties to provide bridewells, or 'houses of correction' as they became widely known. The other major institution for dealing with the poor was the workhouse, which was established throughout England in the seventeenth and eighteenth centuries. Workhouses, which operated as a form of surrogate 'household', were often family-run enterprises, providing basic relief and employment for the poor, vagrants and the destitute. They were originally established as institutions designed to deter the poor from making applications for public relief. In the eighteenth century the aim of workhouses became more focused on setting the poor to work. Children tended to predominate among the inmates of workhouses and meagre wages were paid to those who stayed there. There was some overlap between the workhouses and the bridewells, based upon the often arbitrary distinction between the 'deserving' and 'undeserving' poor. Workhouses and bridewells can be seen as providing a complementary approach to the same problem. With the threat of the workhouse or the bridewell hanging over their heads, the local poor might be driven to work, while vagabonds from elsewhere might be scared away (Innes, 1987).

Since the fourteenth century local jails had been used for a number of purposes apart from holding those awaiting trial or transportation. They had been widely used to hold debtors until they were able to pay their debts. In the debtors' prisons, friends and the curious were generally admitted, and in prisons like the Fleet and the Marshalsea in London, members of the family could be accommodated within the institution (Byrne, 1992). These establishments were privately run, and jailers could make a profit from the sale of ale and other goods, or through the provision of services. The experience of confinement was largely conditioned by the ability of prisoners to pay for the available goods and services. Disorder and neglect were the dominant features of the eighteenth-century prison, in which different categories of prisoners mingled together:

> On entering the jail one was confronted with the noise and smell of the place. It was seldom easy to distinguish those who belonged to the prison from those who did not. Only the presence of irons differentiated the felons from the visitors or the debtors from their families. The jail appeared to be a particular type of lodging house with a mixed clientele. Some of its inhabitants lived in ease while others suffered in squalor. There was little evidence of authority. Some prisoners gambled while others stood drinking at the prison tap. (McGowan, 1995: 79)

Squalor and corruption, which were both widespread in these eighteenth-century houses of correction, became a cause of concern among prison visitors. A number of prison reformers, including John Howard (1777) and Elizabeth Fry (1827), campaigned to rid the prison of these abuses. Howard, Fry and other evangelically-minded reformers wanted prisons to operate as healthy and efficient institutions. They were opposed to the indiscriminate mixing of inhabitants and placed great emphasis upon the benefits of solitude and isolation in order to remove individuals from the corrupting influence of other prisoners. Confinement, in the eyes of the reformers, should be coupled with a religious purpose. Prisoners, it was felt, should not be able to drink, gamble or spend their time in idleness. Thus, in contrast to the disordered and profligate nature of the eighteenth-century penal institution, penal reformers wanted to introduce the 'well-ordered prison', which would stand as a counterpoint to the disorder from which crime and other social problems sprang. In his survey of prisons in the 1770s, John Howard (1777) estimated that the prison population was just over 4,000, of which over half of those imprisoned were debtors (59.7 per cent), while felons awaiting trial, execution or transportation made up approximately a quarter (24.3 per cent), and petty offenders made up the rest of the population.

The Prison Act of 1865 formally amalgamated the jail and the house of correction and the resulting institution became known as a prison. Local prisons remained in operation but only served as places of punishment for those sentenced for terms of up to two years. Thus, by the mid nineteenth century, imprisonment had become more centralised and more firmly established as a disciplinary institution. Although confinement in its various forms had become the dominant form of punishment by the eighteenth century, other forms of punishment also prevailed: notably transportation.

Transportation and the hulks

From the early eighteenth century onward, transportation overseas was used for felons, and some 30,000 people were transported to the American colonies between 1718 and 1775. The reported rising tide of crime and overcrowding in prisons overcame the reservations which certain critics had concerning the effects of transportation and made it a relatively attractive option. However, the abrupt interruption of transportation in 1775 caused a crisis in the prison system. This was resolved in 1776 by the use of old vessels which became known as hulks. These were used as places of temporary confinement. Prisoners were set to work during the day clearing the Thames and other seaports, returning to the vessels at night to eat and sleep. This form of punishment was generally viewed with disfavour and there was widespread criticism of the conditions on these vessels.

After the curtailment of transportation to the American colonies following the American Revolution, the focus turned to Australia as an alternative destination. In 1787 the first fleet of eleven ships set sail for Botany Bay. In some of the early voyages the death rates on convict ships were as high as 25 per cent (Hirst, 1995; Hughes, 1987). By the 1840s transportation was abolished to New South Wales, and all transported convicts were sent to Van Diemen's Land (Tasmania). Charges of inefficiency, corruption and the decreased demand for labour made the task of finding work for convict gangs more difficult. These problems were compounded by the discovery of gold in New South Wales and Victoria, which made punishment in exile to these places appear an absurdity, while the rapid rise in prices during the gold rush made the whole process of transportation and exile more expensive to the British government. In 1852 transportation to Van Diemen's Land was abandoned. In place of transportation the government implemented the Australian 'ticket of leave' scheme, which was a precursor to parole.

Labour, discipline and punishment

In their pioneering work *Punishment and Social Structure* (1939 [2003]), which was first published in 1939, Georg Rusche and Otto Kirchheimer argued that the nature of punishment is determined by the form of productive relations in any period. There are two basic methodological principles which inform the text: (1) 'every system of production tends to discover punishments which correspond to its productive relationships'; and (2) 'punishments as such do not exist, only concrete systems of punishment and specific criminal practices exist'.

For them, the use of transportation, for example, was primarily motivated not so much by the humanitarian impulse to give convicts a fresh start in a new country as by the need to overcome the shortage of free labour in the colonies in a period in which there was a surplus of labour in England. Although decisions to adopt or abandon a particular mode of punishment may be couched in terms of humanism, these decisions, Rusche and Kirchheimer argue, are underpinned by material interests (Weiss, 1987). Therefore, they suggest that one should be careful in simply attributing penal change to the activities of reformers, as historians like David Rothman (1971) tend to do. Instead, there is a need to look behind the rhetoric of reformers and ask why it should be that in any particular period certain arguments should find an attentive audience. At the same time, the manner and speed with which prison reform takes place, Rusche and Kirchheimer argue, is not only a function of the weight of the arguments for change but is also dependent upon wider social conflicts and struggles between classes (Ignatieff, 1981). Rusche and Kirchheimer maintain that prisons are part of a disciplinary network for regulating the poor and for imposing discipline. For these reasons, they argue that conditions in prisons are governed by the principle of 'less eligibility', such that conditions in prisons must be no better than those experienced by the poorest sections of the working classes, otherwise members of the lowest social strata will not be deterred from committing crimes (Melossi and Pavarini, 1981).

But although Rusche and Kirchheimer (1939 [2003]) recognise the role of the prisons in encouraging time and work discipline in industrial capitalism, their explanation of the emergence of the modern prison is tied more specifically to the system of productive relations. Their basic axiom that 'Every system of production tends to discover punishments which *correspond* to its productive relationships' (emphasis added) clearly expresses their view that it was the changing form of production and associated changes in the organisation of labour which were the main determinants of the prison. A close reading of Rusche and Kirchheimer, however, makes it clear that the *correspondence* between the emergence of industrial capitalism and the prison is far more complex than the disciplining of 'free labour'. They were abundantly aware, as was Marx, that all systems of production are systems of 'social production', and that there is a complex dynamic relation between agency and structure. Along with Marx they would no doubt recognise that 'people make the world but not under conditions of their own choosing'. It is also evident to Rusche and Kirchheimer that the formal equality which operates in the sphere of consumption and distribution in capitalist societies is an essential element in the development of a form of punishment which incorporates the principal of equivalence.

Also, like Pashukanis, Rusche and Kirchheimer recognised that the commodification of time was an essential component in the development of the modern prison:

> Deprivation of freedom for a period stipulated in the court sentence is the specific form in which modern, that is to say, bourgeois capitalist, criminal law embodies the principal of equivalent recompense. This form is unconsciously yet deeply linked with the conception of man in the abstract and abstract human labour measurable in time. (Pashukanis, 1978: 180–1)

Thus for Rusche and Kirchheimer the emergence of the modern prison was seen to be 'overdetermined', in that it was the product of a number of overlapping and mutually reinforcing determinations. But they were also aware that political movements too could influence the use of imprisonment. The development of Fascism throughout Europe in the 1930s, which affected both these authors personally, had a number of direct effects on the nature of law, the administration of sanctions and the direction of penal reform. In Germany new laws were passed or were interpreted within a racist framework, while judicial independence diminished and 'special courts' were introduced. There was a return to capital punishment and prison conditions deteriorated rapidly.

Although *Punishment and Social Structure* has been highly influential in changing the way in which the history of imprisonment has been conceived, it has been criticised by some commentators for being too economistic and reductionist, despite the fact that it offers a number of different levels of social and political analysis. Other commentators have criticised it for not being economistic enough (Garland, 1990; Howe, 1994; Melossi, 1978; Weiss, 1987; Zimring and Hawkins, 1991a). Strangely, a number of critics who accuse Rusche and Kirchheimer of reductionism themselves engage in reductionist analysis, usually in the form of sociological or political reductionism, or alternatively offer an unmitigated eclecticism with no identifiable determinants or causal process. In fact, the majority of critics demonstrate a consistent failure to address what has been called 'the problem of determinations', which raises the question of the relationship between the economic, political, social and cultural 'levels' and the (relative) autonomy of each (Barrett, 1991). Needless to say, as members of the renowned Frankfurt School, Rusche and Kirchheimer would have been only too aware of the problems of reductionism and economism, since these issues were central to the work of the School in the 1930s (Jay, 1973).

The two key terms in Rusche and Kirchheimer's analysis which have been the basis of much discussion and confusion are 'determines' and 'corresponds'. The term 'determines' may be used in a hard or a soft form (Williams, 1980). In the soft form it means 'setting limits on' or 'exerting pressure'. It is in this way that it is used by Rusche and Kirchheimer. The term 'corresponds' expresses the ways in which these pressures are exerted in different social formations, recognising that there may be variations in the 'fit' between the dominant forms of social production and the forms of state, law and systems of punishment. At the same time, as Rusche and Kirchheimer themselves note, to say that a form of punishment 'corresponds' to the system of productive relations is itself a tautology. However, they use the term 'correspond' to signify that there is a definite relationship which is of a causal rather than contingent nature.

One writer who clearly recognises the significance of Rusche and Kirchheimer's work is Michel Foucault. Although Foucault (1977) addresses a different problematic from that covered by Rusche and Kirchheimer, he recognises the need to analyse 'concrete systems of punishment', and acknowledges that the writings of Rusche and Kirchheimer 'provide a number of essential reference points' (1977: 24). In fact, it is arguably the case that Foucault's account of *The Birth of the Prison* is underpinned by the same type of materialist analysis as is presented by Rusche and Kirchheimer (see Smart, 1983). Like Rusche and Kirchheimer, Foucault emphasises that the role of the emerging forms of punishment in the eighteenth and nineteenth centuries was not necessarily more humanitarian than previous forms of public torture and humiliation.

Indeed, the aim was not to punish less, but to punish better. Punishment was required to be more universal and to penetrate more deeply into the social body if it was to create a docile and responsive workforce.

The new forms of disciplinary punishment which were developed in the prison were not simply repressive, but were also designed to be positive and productive. In Foucault's account, prisons produced new techniques for controlling individuals through systems of surveillance, classification and examination. The forms of discipline implemented in the prison were the embodiment of new modalities of power. Whereas sovereign power, which had been dominant in the Middle Ages, promoted public forms of punishment aimed at the body, the emerging forms of juridical power in the eighteenth century were aimed primarily at the soul. These new power relations found expression in a number of different institutions, often involving similar techniques for managing individuals and groups. Is it any wonder, Foucault asks, that prisons resemble factories, schools, barracks, hospitals, which all in turn resemble prisons?

Foucault is particularly interested in the ways in which power is crystallised in institutions such as the prison, and in how such institutions, once established, generate their own knowledges, discourses, practices and effects. He outlines the ways in which the prison created a new institutional space in which offenders could be studied and analysed. It was within this space that the 'delinquent' was born and accredited with a biography and a personality which was held to exist outside and beyond the commission of a specific act. Thus it was not, Foucault maintains, the scientific study of crime that created the possibility of the prison. On the contrary, it was the invention of the prison that created the possibility for the scientific study of crime. The enduring legacy of the prison, whatever its failures and limitations as a site of reform or deterrence, is that it gave birth to a new form of scientific knowledge – criminology.

It is through the analysis of power that Foucault aims to explode the self-evident character of the prison, and explain its apparent naturalness and how we have come almost unthinkingly to associate prison and punishment in contemporary society. The task of enquiry, Foucault maintains, is to explain the 'obvious', the taken-for-granted aspects, and to reveal the underlying processes and assumptions upon which the modern prison rests. His work has been highly influential in relation not only to how we think about imprisonment but also to more general contemporary debates on punishment, social control and power (Dreyfus and Rabinow, 1982; Garland, 1990; McNay, 1992).

Foucault's work, however, like that of many of his predecessors, has been criticised for not examining the application of discipline and punishment to women. The masculinist bias of many of the 'histories' of imprisonment, it has been argued, fails to consider the specific role of women's prisons. A consideration of 'herstory', it has been suggested, could potentially throw some new light on, or even force a rethinking of, the role and development of imprisonment.

Women's imprisonment

An examination of the development of the confinement and imprisonment of women raises a number of questions for historians. Even a cursory review of the subject reveals that there are major differences in the pace and processes of development of women's prisons. There are also noticeable differences in the organisation and functioning of women's prisons, and the types of offences for which women were incarcerated. More generally, the history of women's confinement raises issues about the relationship between the labour market and imprisonment, and also the value of 'social contract' theories, since women did not become fully enfranchised citizens until the twentieth century.

Women prisoners have been counted and discounted. However, women have a long history of confinement, as Sherrill Cohen points out:

> From the sixteenth century onwards more and more women were subject to some form of institutionalisation in poorhouses, bridewells and asylums. In earlier periods women had been confined to convents and Magdalene homes and consequently the ideology of the institutional segregation of women either as a form of punishment or as a sanctuary was well established by the seventeenth century. (Cohen, 1992: 17)

Women made up a considerable percentage of the population of bridewells. In fact, in London during the seventeenth and eighteenth centuries the number of women confined in bridewells was often greater than the number of men. Although bridewells were used mostly for vagabonds and thieves, they were also used for offences against public morals and disturbing the peace, with the result that prostitution and other forms of sexual immorality were favoured targets. By the beginning of the eighteenth century, women could be confined to bridewells for a range of moral offences, including 'bearing bastard children', 'lewdness', or 'failure to maintain their families':

> Surviving 'calenders' of commitments from the Westminster bridewell show men and women being committed at a rate of forty to fifty

a month, women being committed as frequently as men. Most commitments seem to have arisen from street offences. Common grounds for commitment include 'idle and disorderly' or 'lewd, idle and disorderly' behaviour, 'nightwalking' and 'pilfering'. Some of the chattier entries reveal to us people taken by the watch in the middle of the night from a suspected bawdy house; taken endeavouring to break open a goldsmiths' show glass; giving great abuse to Their Majesties' people; threatening to burn houses; keeping a disorderly house and disturbing the neighbours; pilfering linen from a poor washerwoman's room and pilfering a bunch of sausages. (Innes, 1987: 84–5)

In many bridewells work was irregular, menial and yielded little profit. The work available often involved such tasks as the crushing of hemp or flax, which were the preliminary stages in the manufacture of textiles. The available bridewell records indicate that women were more productive in this work and this may be part of the reason why the 'Master' of the bridewells might have been more willing to refer women to these institutions. A further reason why women might have been welcomed into certain bridewells is that there were reports of these institutions becoming highly profitable brothels (Zedner, 1995). Within these mixed institutions there were numerous examples of women being encouraged or coerced to provide sexual services. It was the visibility of this 'immorality' and 'lewdness' which evangelical reformers found so distasteful and which motivated them to campaign for separate prisons for women. Separate prisons, it was argued, could reduce exploitation, improve morals and be tailored to gender-specific needs.

In Britain, the Jail Act of 1823 required that women be held separately from men, that they be supervised only by women, and that men were only to be allowed to visit the female part of the prison if they were accompanied by a female officer. In the nineteenth century a limited number of prisons were established specifically for women, but in most cases women were in segregated wards or wings of men's prisons.

There were, however, separate institutions for women in existence in the seventeenth and eighteenth century, in the form of Magdalen houses for 'repentant' prostitutes. In these institutions, which sprang up across Europe in this period, the emphasis was upon penitence and religious instruction. Work was designed to be educational, reformative and 'cleansing'. And consequently the principal tasks tended to include textile manufacture, handicrafts and domestic service, as well as cleaning and laundering. In this way these 'fallen women' could be reformed and returned to their 'proper' female role.

For many reformers, separate prison establishments was seen as a more effective way of controlling women. It was widely felt in the nineteenth century that women required different treatment from men, while it was the case that a system of silence and separation was thought to be particularly suitable for women, since they were held to be more impressionable and needed more protection from contaminating influences than men. The role of labour, however, was felt to be less important for women. They were not subjected to the treadmill and were excused from some of the more onerous tasks. However, they had to endure regimes of greater tedium, and were subjected to more intrusive forms of surveillance (Dobash *et al.*, 1986).

As women were placed in adapted buildings or the wings of the men's prisons, the influence of architecture was less evident and a greater emphasis was placed upon personal influences. That is, while the emphasis in men's prisons was on impersonal disciplinary techniques of reform, women's prisons were regulated primarily through interpersonal relations and the power of religion, as well as through forms of 'medicalisation'.

Towards the end of the nineteenth century women were often given short sentences for trivial offences such as theft, drunkenness and disorderly conduct. Prostitutes still filled the prisons (but a significant percentage were confined in hospitals for the treatment of syphilis and other sexually transmitted diseases) and there was a growing number of habitual offenders who were regularly recycled through the prison system. By 1872 there were three women's prisons – Millbank, Fulham and Woking – which between them had just under 1,400 places. But in the last two decades of the century the number of women imprisoned began to decrease at a faster rate than the male population (Zedner, 1991). This declining rate of imprisonment continued throughout the twentieth century. The reasons for this seem to be a combination of a number of factors, including the increasingly widespread view which surfaced in the last decades of the nineteenth century that prisons are not suitable places for the vast majority of female offenders. There was also a change in the perceived nature of female criminality in this period, as well as the development of a number of alternatives to custody which were designed to divert certain types of women away from custodial institutions.

The well-ordered prison

The limits of transportation and the growing concerns about crime and disorder at the end of the eighteenth century encouraged the development of new and more effective forms of punishment. The mounting critiques of the existing penal institutions, with all their abuses and inadequacies, persuaded the authorities that a well-ordered, disciplined, clean and properly managed form of confinement was required. These new and refurbished prisons were developed in the first half of the nineteenth century. They introduced new codes of discipline, more bureaucratic forms of organisation and management and changes in prison design.

Prisoners were to be differentiated and new systems of classification were introduced. The aim was to develop a system based on solitary confinement, silence, religious instruction and labour discipline. The 'moral architecture' of the prison was to express and incorporate these aims, while improving order, health and conditions. The ultimate aim was to turn incorrigible prisoners into model citizens. Prisons would be a mechanism, as Bentham put it, 'for grinding rogues honest'. Through specially designed institutions it would be possible, reformers believed, to produce a rationally organised space which would foster the development of reason and the self-regulation of inmates. Importantly, these redesigned prisons had to deal with what was perceived as the contagious nature of crime. The threat of contagion was dealt with by separating the young from the old, men from women and the vulnerable from the predatory. In contrast to the eighteenth-century penal institutions in which prisoners were allowed to congregate freely, the new nineteenth-century prisons were built with separate cells of a uniform size. Rules of silence were imposed upon prisoners, and in some prisons inmates were made to wear masks, to ensure that they would not be recognised either in the prison or when they left.

The design and layout of the new nineteenth-century prisons was a hotly contested issue. The central debate among reformers concerned the degree and type of segregation that should be imposed and there was considerable discussion in the 1820s in America and Europe about the merits of segregating prisoners. While many of those engaged in this debate agreed upon the fundamental principles of individual containment and separation, the central issue was whether or not prisoners should remain totally isolated or be allowed to work together during the day. This debate crystallised around the competing systems in the Auburn and Pennsylvania prisons in America.

The Auburn State Prison in New York, which was established in 1823, adopted a regime in which prisoners were to sleep alone in their cells at night and labour together in the workshop during the day. In the Pennsylvania prison, which was built in 1829, the prisoners were kept totally separate, in order to reduce the possibility of 'contamination'. Left in total solitude and divorced from evil influences, the prisoners would have the opportunity to reflect on the error of their ways and to examine their consciences. Inmates remained in solitary cells for eating, sleeping and working. 'They saw and spoke only to carefully selected visitors and read only morally uplifting literature – the Bible' (Rothman, 1971: 85). It was felt that this strategy, if rigorously pursued, would allow the prisoner to be cured of vice and idleness through a combination of hard labour and contemplation.

After a prolonged debate and much soul-searching the Auburn system won out. Advocates of the Auburn system argued that total isolation was unnatural and that it bred insanity. The case in favour of the Auburn system was enhanced by the fact that it cost less to run and potentially brought greater returns from convict labour. Consequently, the Auburn system came to be widely adopted both in America and in most of Europe.

Underlying these debates was the shared premise that incarceration was the proper response to criminal behaviour and that there should operate a silent system with a minimal diet and strict discipline. Prisons became more militaristic in style and although they contained a considerable percentage of vagrants, poachers, petty thieves and public drunkards, a strict regime of prison discipline was vigorously enforced. Alongside the introduction of military practices and military personnel, there was a growing presence of other professionals in the form of medical doctors and psychiatrists, who were introduced to diagnose, treat and cure offenders. Crime, like madness, was seen by many medical professionals as arising from a lack of self-control, and as a deviation from the path of reason. According to one influential medical practitioner, writing in 1806, 'criminal habits and aberrations of reason are always accompanied by certain organic peculiarities manifested in the external form of the body, or in the features of the physiognomy' (Cabanis, quoted in Ignatieff, 1978: 68). It was a short step from this assertion to the measuring of skull shapes and sizes, which is often associated with the founding father of criminology, Cesare Lombroso, and the development of the science of phrenology.

This vision of the criminal as a pathological subject stood in stark contrast to the classicist conception of the rational citizen choosing between good and evil, maximising pleasure and avoiding pain. The apparent contradiction between free will and determinism, and between the utilitarianism and reformative theory, was overcome in the neo-classicist doctrines through a reformulation of the relation between guilt and punishment. Thus:

Reformative theory presented punishment to offenders as being in their own interests while utilitarian theory cast it as an impartial act of social necessity. In rejecting retributive theory, the reformers sought to take the anger out of punishment. As it was legitimised by the prisoner, punishment was no longer to be in Bentham's words 'an act of wrath and vengeance' but an act of calculation, disciplined by consideration of the social good and the offenders needs. (Ignatieff, 1978: 75)

In many respects these new ideas of prison design and the stress on silence and solitude were realised in the construction of Pentonville Prison in London in 1842. Pentonville itself quickly became a model for prison architecture and discipline, not only in England but also across Europe. The prison held 520 prisoners in separate cells. Four wings radiated out from a central point from which each cell door could be observed. Both the prisoners and the guards were forbidden to talk and the thick walls and individual cells ensured that other forms of communication between prisoners would be kept to a minimum.

Between the 1830s and 1870s the average daily prison population in England climbed steadily, partly as a result of the decline in the use of transportation. Also between 1848 and 1863, prison was transformed from an institution which was used mainly for summary offences and petty felonies into the predominant form of punishment for all major crimes, except murder.

According to the prison rules, 'Every prisoner shall be required to engage in useful work for not more than ten hours a day, of which so far as it is practicable, at least eight hours shall be spent in associated or other work outside the cells.' The principal forms of work available were sewing mailbags, rag-stripping, mat-making, tailoring, cleaning and basket-making (Morris and Morris, 1963). The commitment to work discipline was evident in those prisons where productive and useful labour was not available. In these prisons the treadmill was widely used. Its attraction to the prison authorities was that it provided a form of exercise that could be used by the uneducated, while the pace and resistance of the wheel could be controlled.

One of the major problems in providing useful work for prisoners was that many prisoners were unskilled and the period of time which the average prisoner spent in prison was relatively short by current standards. Nearly two-thirds of those sentenced by magistrates in the 1860s were given terms of a month or less, while in the higher courts over half were sentenced for six months or less. Approximately 20 per cent of those convicted were sentenced to the harshest penalty, penal servitude

(McGowan, 1995). There was a growing disparity between the aspirations and ideals of reformers and the reality of prison experience. Increasingly, towards the end of the nineteenth century, critics were claiming that prisons were failing in relation to the twin objectives of reforming and punishing offenders.

The demise of the prison?

The possibility of prisons achieving the objective of turning unruly offenders into law-abiding citizens was always somewhat utopian. Even if the nineteenth-century prisons had not suffered from overcrowding, corruption and cruelty, the degree of individual transformation which could be expected in short periods of confinement was always likely to be limited. The objective of designing out malicious influences within the prison was undermined by the fact that the prisoners found ways to communicate and there were obvious limitations to the enforcement of rules of silence in shared cells. The cells themselves were small, and confinement in these restricted spaces for long periods of time was increasingly seen as being detrimental to the physical and psychological well-being of inmates. Reports of brutality were widespread, although there was evidence of greater professionalism and accountability among prison staff. Many prisons were dirty and the food was poor. There were breakdowns of security and control, with repeated escapes and riots. In the word of the Gladstone Committee in 1895, the evidence of the operation of the prison system was that it had demonstrably failed, and that 'a sweeping indictment had been laid against the whole of the prison administration'.

Prison, it appeared, had little apparent effect on criminal behaviour: recidivism was rampant and there was a reported increase in violent crime. The emerging Eugenics movement raised concerns about whether imprisonment was the proper response for the 'feebleminded' and the 'degenerate'. On another level, various radical reformers pointed to the fact that very few prisoners were drawn from the middle and upper classes, and that prison appeared as a form of punishment which was reserved almost exclusively for the poor and the destitute. The claim of the doctors and the psychiatrists that they could 'cure' offenders were also seen as being largely exaggerated.

Given these limitations, the question which historians have asked is: why did the prison persist into the twentieth century? Was it the case, as David Rothman (1980) has suggested, that good intentions went wrong and the ideals of 'conscience' were undermined by 'convenience'? Or was it that prisons were performing other less visible functions? As Michael Ignatieff (1978) has argued, the prison had to offer something to justify the enormous expense. The persistent support for the penitentiary, he suggests, 'is inexplicable so long as we assume that its appeal rested on its functional capacity to control crime'. Rather, support for the prison rested on its role as part of 'a larger strategy of political, social and legal reform designed to re-establish order on a new foundation'.

Michel Foucault (1977), in contrast, argues that it was the general deterrent effect of recycling the same offenders through the penal system which became the main rationale of incarceration. Thus for him recidivism was not so much a failure as a method of producing what he calls an 'enclosed illegality' of petty criminals who can be held up to the 'respectable' poor as an example of the dangers of nonconformity, and also a vehicle for gathering information and engaging in the surveillance of certain populations. Foucault asks:

> Can we not see here a consequence rather than a contradiction? If so, one would be forced to suppose that the prison, and no doubt punishment in general, is not intended to eliminate offences, but rather to distinguish them, to distribute them, to use them; that it is not so much that they render docile those who are liable to transgress the law, but that they tend to assimilate the transgression of the laws in a general tactics of subjection. Penality would therefore appear to be a way of handling illegalities, of laying down the limits of tolerance, of giving free rein to some, of putting pressure on others, of excluding a particular section, of making another useful, of neutralising certain individuals and profiting from others. In short, penality does not simply 'check' illegalities; it 'differentiates' them, it provides them with a general 'economy'. And, if one can speak of justice, it is not only because the law itself or the way of applying it serves the interests of a class, it is also because the differential administration of illegalities through the mediation of penality forms part of those mechanisms of domination. Legal punishments are to be resituated in an overall strategy of illegalities. The 'failure' of the prison is to be understood on this basis. (Foucault, 1977: 272)

Although the prison persists, it is clear, as Rusche and Kirchheimer (1939 [2003]) point out, that throughout Europe and North America the use of imprisonment decreased from the end of the nineteenth century until the beginning of the Second World War. The decline of the prison population, they suggest, is bound up with the changing nature of productive relations involving new forms of manufacture: namely Fordism and Taylorism. In this form of production-line manufacture the discipline of the worker is contained *within* the production process itself (Lea, 1979; Melossi, 1979). Moreover, the shift in this period towards 'welfare capitalism' produced other regulatory mechanisms, with the consequence that the prison shifted from being a punishment of first resort to a backup sanction serving as a punishment of last resort.

The welfare sanction

Towards the end of the nineteenth century a new modality of punishment emerged, in which the dominant forms of segregative control were supplanted by new forms of regulation centred around social integration and inclusion. For whole sections of the population, particularly the young and the vulnerable, forms of welfare intervention arose which aimed to deal with 'social problems' and 'problem populations' within the family and the 'community'. Intervention hinged on the perceived needs of certain individuals and involved a shift of emphasis from legal control to normalisation (Garland, 1985).

If it were the case that the nineteenth-century prison had been concerned with disciplining labour and regulating production, the emerging forms of welfare intervention appeared to be more concerned with the process of reproduction and the quality of labour power. The family became a central focus of intervention, and the establishment of a range of new agencies and institutions, particularly social work, probation, the borstal and the juvenile reformatory, signified the emergence of a new welfare complex.

The important characteristics of the shift towards the 'welfare sanction', in which welfare interventions were always conditional on compliance, was that they marked a shift away from the act to the offender. The aim of sanctions was not so much to address guilt but to identify needs and inadequacies (Garland, 1981). Sanctions therefore needed to be flexible, personalised and, where appropriate, continuous. The emphasis upon continuity can be critical, since repairing the perceived damage to the individuals requires not their removal from the locality, but working with families in the community in order to improve the process of socialisation and thereby to produce less-damaged subjects.

Social work is a key element in this process. The new forms of state-sponsored social work replaced the Victorian emphasis on personal charity and philanthropy to meet the needs of the poor. Instead professional social workers could deal with 'cases', and if necessary the whole family, since deviancy in one member might signify the breakdown or malfunctioning of the family as a whole. As part of the development of these normalising strategies, newly-developed agencies such as probation were able to provide more continuous forms of supervision and surveillance, either as an alternative to custody or as part of a post-release strategy. The Probation Act 1907 encouraged the development of non-custodial penalities, while the establishment of a separate system of juvenile justice in 1908 directed the newly-formed juvenile court to take account of the child's welfare in making disposals. From the outset the remit of the juvenile court extended beyond criminal offences, and was to include cases where children were deemed to be 'in need of care and protection'. Juvenile reformatories and borstals were designed both for punishment for wayward juveniles and as 'child-saving' institutions providing education and training. Sentences in relation to these institutions tended to be indeterminate; release was decided not only by the judge but also by the Prison Commissioners, and was dependent upon an individual's progress and reformation. The development of various interventions and the availability of alternatives to custody, as well as the removal of certain categories of offenders from prisons, meant that the 'welfare sanction' had a significant impact upon the composition of the prison population and the role which the prison was deemed to serve.

Conclusion

This brief overview of the emergence of the modern prison has been necessarily schematic and selective. The histories which emerged during the 1970s and 1980s have moved us a long way forward from the administrative and technical accounts that were previously available. They have also encouraged us to think more critically about the assumed humanitarian impulses which were once widely assumed to lie behind the development of the prison. However reassuring we might find such accounts, they do not square very well with the evidence. By the same token, 'revisionist' histories have forced us to rethink the claim that prisons arose as a direct response to the growth of crime and disorder. The critical questions which the revisionist historians raise are: why did punishment come to take the specific form of imprisonment in a certain period and what were the social determinants which produced and shaped this response in different countries? Similar questions arise in relation to the emergence of the 'welfare sanction' at the end of the nineteenth century. The relative decrease in the use of imprisonment in many Western countries during the first half of the twentieth century raises the question of the factors which affect the scale of imprisonment, as does the subsequent increase in the use of imprisonment in recent years.

In attempting to explain these historical changes, we are drawn ineluctably into the central debates over structure and agency, and by implication into questions about the sources and exercise of power. Few historians, with one or two notable exceptions, believe that these developments are either simply a reflection of the 'needs of capitalism', or are purely the product of the campaigns of well-meaning reformers.

1556	The first Bridewell opened in the City of London.
1717	The Transportation Act provided for transportation to the American Colonies.
1776	The hulks were introduced.
1779	The Penitentiary Act included proposals for improved diet and paid labour in prisons.
1783	Public hangings moved from Tyburn to Newgate Prison.
1787	The first fleet of convicts set out for Botany Bay.
1823	The Gaol Act imposed new systems of classification involving the separation of male and female prisoners.
1835	The Penal Servitude Act was passed under which women were to be governed by the same rules and regulations as applied to male prisoners.
1838	A separate juvenile prison was established in Parkhurst.
1840	Transportation to New South Wales ended.
1842	Pentonville Prison in London opened.
1853	A separate wing for women prisoners was established at Brixton.
1857	The last prison hulk taken out of service.
1861	The Whipping Act abolished whipping for virtually all offences.
1863	The Carnavon Committee was appointed to re-examine discipline in local jails.
1865	The Prison Act formally amalgamated the jail and the house of correction.
1867	Transportation ended.
1868	Public ceremonies of execution ceased.
1877	The Prison Act transferred control of local jails to central government.
1895	The Gladstone Committee on Prisons reported.
1898	The Prison Act introduced new categories of imprisonment based on the characteristics of the offender.
1901	A borstal scheme was established in Rochester Prison.
1907	The Probation Officers' Act created the professional probation officer.
1908	The Children's Act created a separate system of juvenile justice.

Figure 1.1   Some key dates in the history of imprisonment in England and Wales

However, even if we avoid the twin excesses of functionalism and voluntarism, there are a number of unanswered questions and contested issues which require serious consideration. Michael Ignatieff (1981), in a critique of revisionist histories in which he includes the work of David Rothman and Michel Foucault as well as his own, argues that these authors incorporated three major misconceptions in their work: 'that the state controls a monopoly over punitive regulation of behaviour, that the state's moral authority and practical power are the major sources of social order, and that all social relations can be described in terms of power and subordination'. Ignatieff is particularly critical of those forms of overly conspiratorial class analysis which see the prison as a response to class fear or as a form of punishment imposed by the ruling class on the poor. Instead, he argues that though the development of the prison may have important class dimensions, the conspiratorial view presents ruling-class views as being too unified, while paying little attention to the genuine support for incarceration among sections of the working class. Also, such accounts tend to play down how the prison relates to other forms of regulation, both formal and informal. Consequently he has called for a substantial reassessment of these revisionist histories and the ways in which they deal with the critical issues of the state, power and class. Other historians have also accused the revisionists of an endemic masculinist bias, and of underestimating the significance of race in the development of imprisonment. Nevertheless, revisionist histories have provided some important conceptual tools for uncovering the conditions which made the emergence of the modern prison possible, and have identified some of the critical processes which shaped its development. These processes, however, require further investigation.

2
Space, Time and Labour

Introduction

An examination of the conditions which underlay the emergence of the modern prison reveals that its development was bound up with the changing nature of three essential elements – space, time and labour. The particular forms in which these elements combined gave the prison its specific characteristics and differentiated it from other forms of punishment. Although a number of contemporary and historical studies have alluded to the significance of one or more of these factors, their triangulated and interdependent nature has not, as yet, been fully explored. The seminal writings of Michel Foucault (1977), Rusche and Kirchheimer (1939 [2003]), and Henri Lefebvre (1991) and Anthony Giddens (1984), as well as a number of other sociological thinkers, have begun to examine how these elements have developed historically and in particular how they have conditioned the organisation and the functioning of social institutions such as the prison.

Space

The coercive segregation of offenders in designated institutions is one of the main hallmarks of the modern prison as a form of punishment. The separation of prisoners from the rest of society represents a clear statement that physical and social exclusion is the price of nonconformity. High exterior walls and reinforced doors which divide the rows of cells of uniform dimensions from the designated areas of work and recreation are familiar characteristics of many of our prisons. Dispersal prisons, for example, are secured by very high perimeter walls that allow for areas of open space within the prison and a freedom of movement which is normally unavailable in local prisons. In open prisons, on the other hand, the thick, high walls are replaced with wire mesh and metal gates so that the separation from the outside world is less clearly demarcated, both physically and ideologically.

Within the prison itself space is used to differentiate between different types of prisoners, and to set boundaries on disciplining practices.

Whether prisoners are held on normal location, in segregation units, or in hospital units, they will be subject to different forms of control and different sets of rules. By the same token, being moved from one space to another, or alternatively being placed in isolation or segregation, is routinely used in prison as a method of control and as part of a repertoire of rewards and punishments. Thus, selected prisoners may be moved without warning from one location to another if they are deemed 'troublesome' or 'at risk' of engaging in some form of disruption, while others may be moved to more open prisons as a reward for good behaviour.

Prisons epitomise the ambiguous nature of notions of 'public' and 'private' space. Prisons are 'public' institutions in that they are run by or on behalf of the state, but they are 'private' in as much as they involve exclusion from the 'public' domain. The distinction between private and public space carries its own messages of difference, and provides the material basis for the construction of ideologies which portray the prison population as a unique and distinct group of people. Significantly, in Britain at least, there is no 'private' space as such within prison, since prisons are 'public' institutions. This means, for example, that all acts of homosexuality, although they may involve acts between consenting adults, are by definition illegal, since they cannot be carried out in 'private'. In contrast, in some European countries areas of private space have been constructed in prisons in order to allow conjugal visits. Thus within the prison various activities which may be legitimate or normal on the 'outside' become redefined on the 'inside' (Rose, 1987).

Space is, therefore, never neutral. It establishes social divisions. It defines and redefines behaviour. It sends out messages. It provides the basis for the construction and dissemination of ideologies. It is a mechanism through which the distribution and circulation of bodies is achieved. It reflects and defines social relations and finally, it is a mechanism through which order is realised.

Henri Lefebvre (1991) makes a distinction between 'real' and 'ideal' space. Real space refers to material phenomena such as buildings, rooms, and furniture. Ideal space, on the other hand, is more abstract, referring to different forms of social ordering produced through the formulation of mental categories which involve, for example, different architectural designs and forms of organisation. Prisons are complex social constructions which embody a mixture of real and ideal space.

They are at once material, functional and ideological. The organisation of space in the modern prison allows for the supervision and control of prisoners, while providing a means for differentiating and mapping them. It also provides for the routine supervision of inmates, the monitoring of dangerous communications and the possibility of achieving subjection through detailed and regular inspection.

In the development of the modern prison a new consciousness of space was realised. The design of the prison was widely seen as critically important to the formulation of different objectives. Issues concerning the design and layout of prisons in the eighteenth and nineteenth centuries were debated with great fervour among reformers and social commentators. Which distribution of space would be most effective in minimising the risk of contagion, allowing self-reflection and facilitating the maximum degree of surveillance? How could the distribution of space help to achieve these different objectives? Did the existing structures create the right rhythms, allow appropriate movements and foster desirable relations? How could prisons be designed to achieve the reform of the prisoner? These were the questions posed by penal reformers.

The proper ordering of space, it was recognised, could produce better communications, and allow easier movement and a better use of time. The proper use of space should, according to Michel Foucault (1977), 'eliminate the efforts of imprecise distributions, the uncontrolled disappearance of individuals, their diffuse circulation, their unusable and dangerous coagulation'. The same spatial logic has been applied historically to other institutions, such as schools and hospitals. According to Foucault, the construction of these institutions is designed to effect the most profitable distribution of bodies and simultaneously to facilitate the processes of examination and inspection. Institutions such as schools and hospitals resemble the prison not only in that they look like them physically, but also because they are designed to allow the deployment of certain forms of discipline. Thus for Foucault the strategies and objectives of regulation are, as it were, built into the very bricks and mortar of institutions; once materialised in this form, they have definite effects, although these effects are not always those which were anticipated.

As Robin Evans argues (1982), the construction of the modern prison was conditioned by a number of different objectives: security, ventilation, reformation, classification, inspection and labour. Security was to be achieved by high, thick walls and regular surveillance. The preoccupation with ventilation was a product of the widespread belief that jail (typhus) fever was generated and disseminated in the atmosphere, and that good ventilation was required to encourage the continuous flow of air. Reformation was seen to require the separation of prisoners, and it was felt that prison design was potentially the most effective way of creating and enforcing demarcations and divisions between prisoners. The aim of prison architecture was to segregate prisoners from the wider community and to keep them, as far as possible, from each other. Closely related to the aims of reform was the formulation of ever more detailed systems of classification which divided prisoners up into different types. At the beginning of the nineteenth century the Society for the Improvement of Prison Discipline had created 20 categories of prisoners: 6 for houses of correction and 14 for jails. The formulation of these categories and the more detailed separation of prisoners was designed to limit the spread of wickedness and corruption. Significantly, by 1818 the Society for the Improvement of Prison Discipline decided that it was not the *crime* that prison punished but what they described as the 'habits and inclination of prisoners'. The objective of segregation had, however, to be balanced against the growing emphasis upon the need for inspection. From 1800 onwards inspection became an increasingly dominant theme in prison. Providing space for different forms of labour has been a continual preoccupation for prison architects. A major focus of the debate which took place in the mid nineteenth century concerning the relative advantages and disadvantages of the Auburn and Pennsylvania systems was centred around the arrangements for work in the prison. The introduction of the treadwheel, the crank and other imaginative devices designated to replicate 'hard labour' placed new pressures on the distribution of space within prisons. Each of the six imperatives that Evans identified helped to influence the design of the modern prison. Each, however, had different requirements in relation to design. Some required enclosure and compartmentalisation, others required exposure and association. The competing models that were proposed provided various responses to these imperatives and those which gained political favour were those which were seen to combine the designated aims in the most economical and effective ways. Historically, the architectural design of the prison has been conditioned by the dominant views of human nature and criminality in any period, combined with the changing objectives associated with the process of imprisonment. A review of the changing design of prisons since the beginning of the nineteenth century indicates that four main styles have been developed in different periods: radial, Panopticon, 'telegraph pole', and the 'new generation' prisons, which incorporate a podular design.

The radial design

The dominant style of prison architecture in Europe in the nineteenth century was the radial design. This construction, which involves a number of wings panning out from a central point, was seen to be the most appropriate way to divide prisoners into different groups located in their respective wings, while allowing control and co-ordination to be located at the pivotal point. Thus, in a period in which prisoners spent virtually all their time confined to their cells, a single officer could, by standing at the centre, observe each of the various wings in turn by simply turning his head through 180 degrees.

A classic example of a radial design is to be found in Pentonville Prison in North London. Pentonville was run on the principles of non-communication and strict separation, which it was held would encourage meditation and self-reflection while reducing the possibility of contamination by limiting the spread of bad habits. It was felt that these silent and austere institutions would maximise the deterrent effects of incarceration, although this aim had to be balanced against growing demands for improvements in diet and hygiene. Reformers like John Howard, however, emphasised that there was no necessary contradiction between improving conditions in prisons and maintaining their deterrent value, since 'confinement in a prison, though it may cease to be destructive to health and morals, will not fail to be sufficiently irksome and disagreeable, especially to the idle and the profligate' (Howard, 1777: 44).

When it was opened in 1842, Pentonville held 450 male prisoners who were housed in cells of a uniform size, spaced along tiers within the three wings which radiated out from a central point (see Figure 2.1). Within each cell there was the necessary equipment to carry out work and the basic requirements for daily living:

> His cell was thirteen-and-a-half feet from barred window to bolted door, seven-and-a-half feet from wall to wall, and nine feet from floor to ceiling. Its contents were sparse; a table, a chair, a cobbler's bench, hammock, broom, bucket, and a corner shelf. On the shelf stood a pewter mug and a dish, a bar of soap, a towel and a Bible. Except for exercise and chapel, every minute of his day was spent in this space amongst these objects. When the prison opened in 1842 convicts spent eighteen months in solitude. As the authorities became familiar with its effects, the period of solitude was reduced, first to twelve and then to nine months. (Ignatieff, 1978: 4)

Spatial segregation involving solitary confinement produced a series of negative effects over and above those which might have resulted from segregation from the wider society. Total segregation within the prison produced disturbingly high rates of death, insanity and suicide. Although the system of solitary confinement eventually fell into disfavour, the radial design used in the majority of Victorian prisons still remains in evidence.

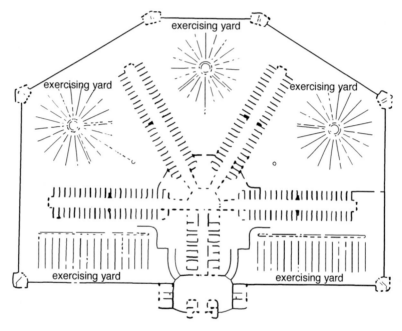

Figure 2.1 Radial design prison

The Panopticon

Michel Foucault (1977) has suggested that the design which provided the most efficient system of surveillance and regulation was the Panopticon, developed by Jeremy Bentham (1791). Bentham's aim was to develop a design for the prison which would maximise surveillance. The Panopticon, he felt, provided the ideal structure, since a guard positioned in the tall, central control tower could exert continuous surveillance around the prison. Narrow viewpoints in the tower would make it impossible for prisoners to see the guard and to know at any one particular moment whether or not they were actually being watched.

For Bentham, the dual attraction of the Panopticon lay, first, in the possibility that regulation could operate independently of any particular controller and, second, in that those upon whom control was exercised were caught up in a power relation in which they themselves were the bearers. Panoptic power, therefore, has the essential characteristic that it is unverifiable, continuous, and brings both those who exercise it, and those who are subject to it, into a relation in which parties are complicit, although not necessarily actively engaged. It is the way in which the Panopticon appears to transcend the traditional opposition of coercion and consent, and the way in which this depersonalised form of regulation is built into the structure and design of the institution, which fascinates Foucault. Much to Bentham's disappointment, however, the

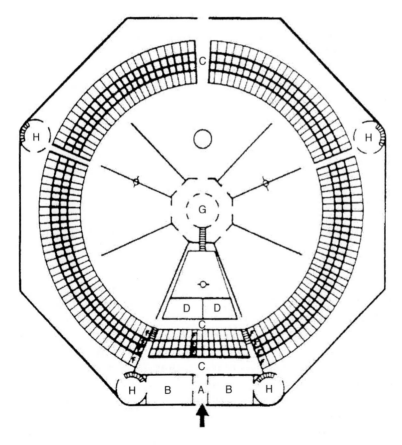

Figure 2.2 Panopticon

Panopticon was never widely used as a basis for prison design, or for that matter as a model for other types of institution. Two of the few prisons which were built upon this design were Stateville Prison in Louisiana, built in 1919, and the Western Penitentiary in Pittsburgh. Both prisons incorporate the central features of the Panopticon, with a tall central tower overlooking circular rows of cells (see Figure 2.2). However, the fact that Bentham's model has not been widely adopted suggests that the primary functions it was designed to achieve did not accord with the objectives of prison administrators in the nineteenth century. By implication, this raises the issue of just how significant the Panopticon is as the ideal model of control in contemporary society (Shearing and Stenning, 1985).

The 'telegraph pole' model

Victorian prisons, which were built largely on the radial design, continued to operate and dominate the prison estate into the twentieth century, despite the fact that the theories and attitudes around which they had been constructed had fallen into disfavour. It was not until the 1930s in America that a new principle of construction emerged. This involved a number of individual oblong cell blocks arranged either side of a linking control corridor or hallway. This design, which has become known as the 'telegraph pole' model, was adapted from various pioneering prisons, such as that built at Fresnes in France in 1898, and the separate block plan which had been used some years earlier at Wormwood Scrubs in London.

The emergence of the telegraph pole model reflected the demise of the separatist philosophy. Rather than focusing on the separation and isolation of prisoners, prisons became designed to allow a greater degree of inmate socialisation, movement and activity. In this model the use of the central point, which had been a dominant feature of radial and Panopticon-type constructions, was rejected in favour of the separate control of each block (see Figure 2.3). To some extent the development of prisons with separate blocks reflected changes in the system of prisoner classification in relation to the perceived risk to security that different types of prisoners were seen to pose. It was also felt, particularly by American prison administrators, that separate blocks joined by short corridors made administration and supervision easier, while improving the conditions in which prisoners lived.

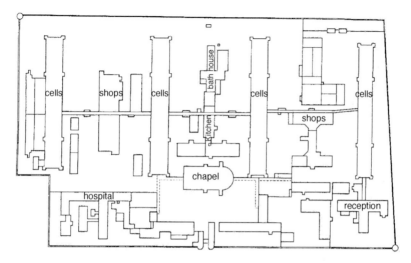

Figure 2.3   'Telegraph pole' model

The podular design

The trend towards the construction of a number of units, each containing a relatively small number of inmates, has been developed into the podular design, in which prisons are divided into a number of small buildings that open onto a central multi-use area, enabling staff to observe both the living and recreational activities more easily (see Figure 2.4). These 'new generation' prisons, as they are often called, extend the principles of classification of different types of prisoner, and reflect changes in the form of organisation towards a more decentralised system of unit management, which aims simultaneously to reduce the levels of staffing and to allow the more effective transfer of prisoners within the between institutions (Home Office, 1985).

In these new generation prisons the emphasis is upon the provision of accommodation and association rather than employment. There is less evidence of the traditional cells, bars and doors, and a greater emphasis upon improved circulation and movement. They involve a simultaneous shift towards normalisation and increased surveillance. A central aim is to provide improved security both for staff and inmates. The construction of these prisons, which incorporate new forms of 'soft architecture' by using bright colours and less hardware, has raised questions about whether they are able to achieve an environment which is simultaneously more secure and less damaging (Canter, 1987; King, 1987).

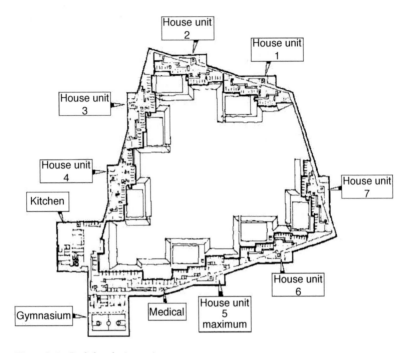

Figure 2.4   Podular design prison

In an examination of Oak Park Heights, an American 'new generation' maximum security prison, Roy King (1991) points to differences in the systems of surveillance, the movement of staff and prisoners, and the levels of internal and external security which this type of prison displays in comparison to those employed in a typical dispersal prison in England and Wales, such as Gartree. The organisation of new generation prisons tends to be centred around a control 'bubble', in which video and other surveillance equipment is placed, and from which the guards are able to co-ordinate the movement of prisoners. A distinguishing feature of this form of prison design is that areas of work are built directly above the prisoners' rooms, and the construction of separate corridors and stairways for staff and prisoners allows inmates to move more freely from one section to another, while the staff are able to gain access quickly to certain strategic areas that are denied to the prisoners. The net result, King concludes, is that Oak Park Heights is 'perceived to be safer, more secure, and more trouble-free', offering 'a fuller and more highly rated programme of treatment, industry, and education, and better contact with the outside world'. The important distinction between these new design prisons and dispersal prisons is that the security is shifted from the design of the buildings themselves to the perimeter, the corridors and to the more extensive use of technology.

These four designs have historically reflected the changing attitudes and objectives of imprisonment, and demonstrate how space has been employed in different periods. Thus, it is evident that the deployment of spatial divisions in the prison is conditioned by theories of human nature, concepts of criminality, the changing objectives of imprisonment, forms of classification, management practices, and principles of control and surveillance. The fact that various prison designs have mirrored the social relations and attitudes which gave rise to them in particular periods has resulted in an ongoing tension between what prisons were designed to achieve and what they are commonly used for. This tension is most pronounced in relation to the competing objectives of deterrence and rehabilitation. Just as the early separatist designs were seen in practice largely to negate any rehabilitative role that was assigned to prisons, so the new podular design prisons based on a number of small units were built to promote rehabilitation rather than deterrence. However, by the time the podular design prisons became established, the rehabilitative ideal had fallen into disfavour with prison administrators and was widely replaced by a warehousing strategy, for which these small, low buildings were particularly unsuitable.

In this context a number of critical questions about the design of prisons have arisen. These questions concern the possibility of combining improved levels of control and surveillance with the realisation of rehabilitative goals, including the provision of training and education. They also raise the linked question of the relationship between the external security of the prison and the internal safety of prisoners. As John Ditchfield has noted:

> With the disappearance of separation (which itself had made escape rather difficult) and the growth of social regimes, the need of internal control and external security was expressed more functionally (and less aesthetically) by an increase in the amount of internal hardware in prisons and by an increase in perimeter security, both physically and in the sense of separating it from the rest of the prison. The result – in America at least – has been a tendency to 'over-build' prisons both physically and technically, largely because it has been much easier to design for escape proof security than to design and build for good regimes. (Ditchfield, 1990: 94)

The tendency to 'over-build' has also been evident in Britain, particularly following a number of celebrated escapes in the 1960s and 1970s, as well as more recent incidents at Gartree, Parkhurst and Whitemoor, which have all served to increase the emphasis upon the external security of the prison (Home Office, 1995).

The sociological focus on the use of space as an instrument for producing order and facilitating control within prisons draws attention to the relatively subtle but effective ways in which social regulation is achieved. Just as in other areas of daily life, the most effective forms of regulation in prisons tend to be those which are less visible and less dramatic. Overt forms of coercion and brutality, although not absent from the prison, always carry the danger of generating resistance. In recent years a growing number of criminologists have come to realise that spatial forms of control are generally more subtle, less controversial and often more effective ways of regulating different populations (Clarke, 1992). This is not to suggest that spatial divisions are not contested, or that forms of spatial control are not resisted. The fact that riots in prisons involve the objective of controlling certain spaces and redefining their use underlines the fact that spatial control is critical to the exercise of power (Adams, 1990).

Time

Space and time have historically been closely linked. But at a certain juncture social space and time became disconnected and appeared increasingly unrelated. This separation occurred at a point in which time itself became commodified and functionally specialised. In the transition to industrial capitalism, lived time loses its form and its interest, except for the time spent working. Time from this point on is recorded primarily on measuring instruments – clocks and watches – that are as isolated and functionally specialised as time itself. The expulsion of 'lived' time Henri Lefebvre (1991) suggests, is one of the hallmarks of modernity. He argues that time, 'which is the greatest of all goods is no longer visible to us, no longer intelligible. It cannot be constructed. It is consumed, exhausted, and that is all.'

In a similar vein, Anthony Giddens has argued that the commodification of time is one of the most significant developments associated with the emergence of capitalism. He states that:

> Time as lived time, as the substance of lived experience of durée of Being, becomes 'formless duration' with the expansion of capitalism,

this is what time seems to be, just as money seems to be the standard value of all things. Time as pure duration, as disconnected from the rationality of existence, comes to be perceived in direct opposition to the actual state of things, as real 'objective' time, because like money it is expressed in a universal and public mode. This universal and public mode, again like money, is nothing less than its own quantification as a measure of standing at the axis of a host of transformation/mediation relations. The commodification of time, and its differentiation from further processes of the commodification of space, hold the key to the deepest transformations of day-to-day social life that are brought about by the emergence of capitalism. (Giddens, 1981: 131)

E. P. Thompson (1967) has argued that the Industrial Revolution not only brought about a change in the form of production but also promoted the tyranny of the clock. With the rise of industrial capitalism time was no longer 'passed' but 'spent'. The changes in manufacturing technique demanded a greater synchronisation of labour as well as a greater degree of punctuality and exactitude in the routine of work. The twin processes of the social dislocation of time and its technical calibration provided the basis on which labour time could more easily be calculated, while non-work time became seen as 'spare' or 'free' time. Importantly, time itself became compartmentalised in space, and took on a linear quality which superseded the cyclical forms of time that had dominated in pre-capitalistic periods. Linear time became an established feature of modernity, underpinning notions of progress and individual transformation. These two notions were in turn associated with the conception of prison as a mechanism for reforming offenders.

As an institution which could enforce the deprivation of liberty for a designated period of time, the prison appeared as a 'natural' form of punishment. This occurred for a number of reasons. The first important attribute of a time-centred mode of punishment was that it appeared universal and independent of each individual. Time and liberty, it was held, were commodities which all citizens possessed in equal amounts and could dispose of freely. In fact time was one of the few attributes which both the rich and the poor were seen to possess in roughly equal quantities. What, therefore, could be more reasonable than that those who transgressed the law should be given a form of punishment whose effects would be experienced equally by all?

The second major attribute of time-based punishments is that they have an objectivity and solidity not found in those forms of punishment that were widely used in the Middle Ages, such as shaming and the expression of remorse. The length of sentence can be calibrated directly in relation to the seriousness of the offence, and the severity of punishment can be tied to the principle of proportionality in clear and precise ways.

The third attribute of time-based punishments is that because time itself is essentially a social construct it confers on imprisonment a quality which is truly social. The prison may therefore appear as the consequence of human endeavour, or as the outcome of a 'civilising' process standing in contrast to the 'barbaric' forms of punishment which were prevalent in previous periods (Franke, 1992; Spierenburg, 1984).

The fourth attribute of time-based punishments is that as time becomes commodified it can be 'traded', 'gained' or 'lost'; that is, the period of time served can be adjusted and linked to the performance of the prisoner. Good behaviour, hard work and reform can all, in principle, be traded off against the length of sentence.

In reality, however, time inside prison was never the same as time on the outside. Institutional confinement changes the ways in which time is experienced. Time served in prison is not so much 'spent' as 'wasted'. The process of imprisonment, rather than channelling and redistributing time, involves the negation of time. Individuals removed from the workplace and the labour market – the principal sphere of 'lived' time – and simultaneously removed from their families and communities, are no longer able to spend 'free' time. Thus, although imprisonment is in essence about time, it is experienced as a form of timelessness, with prison terms often being described as 'doing' or 'killing' time. This paradoxical relation between time and imprisonment is explicable to some extent by identifying the different forms of time that are experienced both inside prison and in the wider society. There is a need to make a distinction between physical, mental and social time (Lefebvre, 1991).

Physical time is the duration taken to perform certain tasks, and is gauged essentially in terms of the activities and experiences of the body. This is linked to biological rhythms and to the natural movements involved in seasonal change. In the prison setting the daily rhythms of the body are often influenced by the change of daily routine, while the seasonal changes are muted and less relevant. Mental time or 'inner' time refers to the processes of reflection or imagination. These are the subjective processes which nineteenth-century prison reformers felt were critical to the processes of introspection and personal reform. But, as the experience of solitary confinement showed, the preoccupation with introspection can lead to depression, insanity and suicide, rather than rehabilitation.

Social time involves the continuous movement between the past, the present and the future. Although a complex process, the construction of social time is an everyday activity by which individuals try to understand the process of change. For the prisoner, however, because the present is placed in suspension, the ability to link the past to the future is limited, since the meaning of time itself is 'lost'. For some long-term prisoners for whom the future is an unthinkable and terrifying prospect, time is reduced to a continuous present and therefore lacks any proper chronology. These prisoners are in danger of losing a sense of personal development or purpose (Cohen and Taylor, 1972).

Paradoxically, the more time you have, the more it decreases in value. Therefore a recurring problem of linking imprisonment to the principle of proportionality is that the 'value' of an eight-year sentence is not necessarily twice that of a four-year sentence. By the same token, the effect which the period of confinement has on each prisoner will be a function of the individual's own mental and social time scales, and these in turn will dramatically affect the ways in which imprisonment is conceptualised and experienced (von Hirsch, 1992).

As the world speeds up and social time is accelerating, physical time appears to slow down. Thus a five-year sentence given in 1950 would tend to be experienced as a significantly longer sentence in 2000. Therefore the overall increase in the average length of sentence in real terms in recent years has an even greater significance than might at first appear. As social time continues to accelerate and physical time slows down in relation to the past, and as the present and future lose their continuity, it is probably not surprising to find that many prisoners turn to 'inner time' and become more involved with their own inner experiences. In this context, drug-taking, particularly of hallucinatory drugs, is likely to become particularly attractive, since it is able to place time into further suspension and thereby release the prisoner, albeit temporarily, from the apparent timelessness of prison life. Drugs do more than tranquillise or anaesthetise the prisoner: they readjust time. For those who were regular drug users before entering prison, drugs normalise time, in that its passing corresponds to those forms of social time which were previously experienced on the outside. By the same token, the drug subculture that has been found to be prevalent in many prisons also provides a way of organising daily life and giving meaning to the prison routine that for some approximates to the normal routines of life outside the confines of the prison. Thus by engaging in an activity whose objective is to create what we might call 'fantasy' time, prisoners can spend their days involved in activities – buying, trading, hustling, scoring – which correspond to familiar 'real time' activities conducted on the outside (Devlin, 1998). Thus physical, mental and social time can be conceptually differentiated and analysed by specialists in different fields – principally sociologists and psychologists – but the prisoner cannot afford the luxury of such strict divisions. Instead, he or she must move constantly between these levels and explore their implications and live their contradictions.

A central feature of prison life is the timetable which provides a regular programme of activities and a semblance of structure and order to the day. But, as Foucault (1977) has argued, the timetable is an essentially negative and limiting device designed primarily to eradicate idleness. Modern systems of discipline require, he argues, forms of regulation which are also positive and which involve inducements and incentives. For Foucault, the prison is not just an institution of punishment but is also designed for the production of discipline, and one of the aims of discipline is to increase speed and efficiency. The objective is to make the use of time as productive as possible, extracting from every hour and every moment the maximum utility.

So for Foucault discipline is a way of capitalising on time. This is achieved through graduated processes of training such that individuals can learn tasks of ever greater complexity and perform them with increased proficiency and dexterity. He suggests that these processes allow new forms of regulation:

> The 'seriation' of successive activities makes possible a whole investment of duration by power; the possibility of a detailed control and a regular intervention (of differentiation, correction, punishment, elimination) in each moment of time: the possibility of characterizing, and therefore of using individuals according to the levels in the series that they are moving through; the possibility of accumulating time and activity, of rediscovering them, totalised and usable in a final result, which is the ultimate capacity of an individual. Temporal dispersal is brought together to produce a profit, thus mastering a duration that would otherwise elude one's grasp. Power is articulated directly onto time, it assures its control and guarantees its use. (Foucault, 1977: 160)

Thus, as Foucault explains, the distribution of time is usefully associated with both training and the development of certain skills and competences in prison. The organisation of time, like space, is inextricably bound up with the establishment of order and control, and both are linked, directly and indirectly, with the organisation of labour within prisons.

The nature of time-based punishments changed, however, around the end of the nineteenth century, with the greater use of indeterminate sentences. In place of fixed penalties greater flexibility was introduced into the sentencing process by setting maximum and minimum periods of confinement. The growing emphasis on treatment and rehabilitation encouraged the use of more open-ended forms of sentencing which would allow greater discretion in the release of prisoners. This development increased the powers of prison administrators and provided a useful control mechanism within the prison itself. It also increased the demand for more information on prisoners, since clearly the provision of proper treatment required detailed knowledge not only of their offending but also of their personal and social characteristics. The therapeutic encounter, as David Rothman (1981) has argued, works to a different clock from industrial or even medical time. Overcoming resistance, trauma, or more simply denial can take a long time. A proper 'cure', psychiatrists insist, is never quick.

The 'stretching' of time through the use of indeterminate sentencing became particularly pronounced in America in the first half of the twentieth century. However, over the last three decades it has come under repeated attack for inadvertently extending the average length of sentences – creating unnecessary anxiety for prisoners, who remain uncertain about their release date; injecting considerable discretion into the penal system, and creating injustices by exacerbating discrepancies in time actually served (Bottoms, 1980; Rotman, 1990). Over the past two decades the relation between time and punishment has been reappraised, with a consequent shift back towards forms of determinate sentencing.

Labour

Labour is tied to the process of imprisonment on two interrelated levels. On one level, labour has historically been a core feature of imprisonment, oscillating between productive and commercialised forms of industry on the one hand, and training and rehabilitative strategies on the other. On another level, the significance of labour relates to the nature of work outside the prison and particularly to free wage labour as well as the operation of the labour market. The operation of labour both inside and outside the prison has shaped the nature of imprisonment in different historical periods.

Inside the prison, prison labour performs a number of functions. It provides goods and is a source of revenue. It provides training and the possibility of rehabilitation through work. It provides a vehicle for instilling time and work discipline in those who were unable or unwilling to find proper paid employment and it is a mechanism of control, providing a way of ordering time and keeping prisoners occupied (Simon, 1993).

In the eighteenth and early nineteenth centuries prisons were often run as profit-making institutions and a number of establishments paid for themselves through the goods produced by prisoners, while some even made a profit. However, the profit-making capacities of prisons were always limited. During the nineteenth century there was growing opposition to prison-made goods because they could undercut the price of commercially-made goods, and entrepreneurs complained of unfair competition. Objections to the exploitation of prison labour came from free labour too, particularly in periods of recession or unemployment. They argued that the employment of prisoners restricted available employment and pushed down wages. Objections also arose from various prison reformers, who disliked the fact that certain prisoners were receiving a wage which approximated commercial rates. Indeed, the prospect of prisoners earning significant sums of money was seen as transgressing the principle of 'less eligibility' by some commentators, who were concerned that prison labour might be better paid than free wage labour. They were also concerned that the living conditions of prison labour exceeded those of the poorest worker, with the consequence that the deterrent effect of imprisonment would be undermined (Melossi and Pavarini 1981; Rusche and Kirchheimer, 1939 [2003]).

It was also the case, as Rusche and Kirchheimer (1939 [2003]) point out, that prison labour was itself anomalous, in that forced labour has no economic justification in a capitalist system of production. In consequence prison labour can only be fully justified in relation to its educative and rehabilitative roles. Moreover, the ability of prison managers to sell goods at less than the market price undermines the exchange value of commodities, and simultaneously breaks the critical connection between time, production and price. Time is the mediating link between labour and exchange value, since it is the units of time that make values of commodities divisible and quantifiable and permit their common existence as interchangeable items.

The organisation of prisons militates against efficient production. However fundamental the relationship between labour and imprisonment might be, prisons are not factories. The different forms of spatial distribution within prisons have not always easily accommodated manufacture. Indeed the historic trends in the design and construction of prisons have to some extent been away from a preoccupation with manufacture and towards other concerns.

Prison labour suffers from a disadvantage, in that it lacks the type of co-operation that has been an important feature of free labour. As Marx (1970) pointed out, free labour working in co-operation with others acquires an increased productive power. In short, Marx is arguing that the combination of social labour working in a factory produces more than the sum of its parts. Prison labour, on the other hand, it could be argued, produces less than the sum of its parts. Because prisons are not factories, and because prisoners are not part of the organised working class, the productive potential among prison labour is organisationally limited. To put it another way, production and manufacture in prison is likely to be inefficient and in many respects is 'primitive' and 'pre-capitalist'. Thus if the forms of labour which are prevalent in prison are pre-capitalist, they are unlikely to embody the forms of 'discipline' that are required for a capitalist form of production. Prisoners may work side-by-side, but they do not work in 'co-operation' as in factory production, or within an organisation whose prime purpose is the extraction of the maximum amount of surplus value.

The combined effect of these restrictions on the use of prison labour historically has been to limit the range of goods which could be profitably produced. These restrictions made it virtually impossible for prisons to be run as commercial, profit-making institutions, particularly as there are other impediments which have served to limit the quality and quantity of goods that can be produced. One major impediment to the use and profitability of prison labour is that the majority of those incarcerated enter the prison with few skills and low educational levels. The general removal of financial incentives and the repetitive and monotonous nature of prison work provide little intrinsic interest. Consequently, attitudes towards work and prisoners' motives for engaging in work in prison are different from what they would be on the outside. The concept of 'job satisfaction' is fairly alien to prisoners, and the interest in work is often associated with the perks, mobility and autonomy which different tasks offer. Given that the majority of prisoners are imprisoned for relatively short periods of time, the interest in a 'career' of employment within the prison is likely to be of limited relevance to the average prisoner (Hawkins, 1983).

One innovative response to the limited productiveness of prison labour was developed in the mid nineteenth century by Alexander Moconochie, who was the governor of Birmingham Prison. He suggested that, instead of paying prisoners wages, it would be preferable to instigate a system of credit, which he called the 'mark' system, by which the productiveness of prisoners could be linked to the acquisition of 'marks', which could then be used to 'purchase' reductions in the length of sentence. He explained:

> I think that ... time sentences are the root of very nearly all the demor-
> alisation which exists in prisons. A man under a time sentence thinks
> only how he can cheat that time, and while it away: he evades labour
> because he has no interest in it whatever, and he has no desire to please
> the officer under whom he is placed, because they cannot serve him
> essentially; they cannot in any way promote his liberation. Besides
> this, in his desire to while away his time, he conjures up in his mind,
> and indulges, when he has the opportunity, in every sort of prurient
> and stimulative thought, and word, and where he can act ... Now
> the whole of these evils would be remedied by introducing a system
> of task sentences. A man under a task sentence would strip his coat
> to work, he would set a proper value upon time, which under a time
> sentence is hated, and he would exert himself in such a way that he
> could not but improve, *he must improve*. (Moconochie, 1850, quoted
> in Webb and Webb, 1963: 167)

The conception of the mark system, involving a 'task sentence', can be seen as the precursor to the policies of early release for good behaviour and to what Americans call 'good time' laws. However, the actual implementation of the mark system in the mid nineteenth century was associated with scandal and abuse, particularly in Birmingham and Leicester Prisons, following reports that various acts of cruelty as well as illegal methods of inducement were applied in order to persuade prisoners to engage in more demanding forms of labour.

The limitations on the use of productive labour in prisons resulted in the short term in the widespread introduction of modes of unproductive labour in the form of the treadwheel and the crank, and in the longer term in a shift in emphasis towards the training and possible rehabilitative value of prison work. The adoption of the treadwheel and crank was at first met with widespread enthusiasm among reformers because it was felt that the drudgery and monotony of this form of labour would enhance the deterrent value of prison, while the physical exertion involved would keep prisoners occupied. After a few years, however, the negative consequences of the treadwheel became apparent to observers, since long periods on the 'everlasting staircase', as it was known, caused serious physical damage to both men and women, and it was seen as a depressing and degrading form of punishment which did little to stimulate the mental capacities of inmates or encourage any kind of emotional regeneration.

The longer-term shift towards training, and a growing emphasis upon preparing the prisoner for employment after leaving prison, was more positive and less destructive. In the Departmental Home Office Inquiry of 1933 it was stated that 'The main object of prison employment should not be the exploitation of prison labour so as to secure a return to the State, but the rehabilitation of the prisoner.' The problem with this objective is that it assumes employment is a major cause of crime and that offenders engage in crime because they do not have the necessary skills to undertake legitimate forms of employment. It is also the case that the types of skill which can normally be acquired in prison are of limited utility. In conjunction with these limitations, the costs of proper training are considerable, particularly given the uncertainty of the outcome (Cooper and King, 1965).

There have been in the postwar period a number of attempts to run prisons as commercial and profitable institutions. In America in the 1970s, attention shifted towards the introduction of 'Free Venture Prisons', while in England and Wales there were similar attempts to move back towards the creation of industrial prisons, or 'factories with fences' as they have been called (Weiss, 1986). The general aim was to introduce a full working day for prisoners, increase financial and other incentives, and exercise a 'hire and fire' policy in order to remove unproductive prisoners, while using the profits to offset the costs of incarceration and to contribute towards the cost of supporting dependants and compensating victims.

Although there was a surge of activity in England in Wales in the 1970s, and despite the fact that on both sides of the Atlantic a range of new occupations have been introduced, productive work in prisons has been in general decline in recent years (King and McDermott, 1989). Apart from the problems of low skill and educational levels among prisoners, the continuous turnover of inmates, the general lack of motivation and incentives has made competitive and commercial forms of production difficult to sustain. Moreover, in those prisons in which a more commercially-orientated wage structure has been introduced, the established nature of staff–prisoner relations has been brought under pressure and the subcultural relations which were in place have been undermined by the development of a sub-economy in which divisions of wealth may change the balance of power within the prison, leading to new forms of instability.

A continuing constraint on the recommercialisation of prison industries is the spatial dimensions of the prison. The old Victorian prisons have cramped workshops and the new generation prisons are not designed for large-scale production. The type of work which is probably most viable in contemporary prisons is low-skill service work, but although this is potentially profitable, it offers little in the way of training and carries limited rehabilitative value.

Thus the history of labour in prison is plagued with apparently unresolvable tensions. The very prospect of forced labour within prisons appears as an anomaly in a capitalist society, while the spectre of idleness is viewed as an unnecessary waste. Work in prisons is not fully 'disciplinary' in the sense that it lacks normal incentives, proper training, and the experience of co-operation and collectivism which has been a characteristic of free labour. When work is at its most commercial and profitable it tends to have a low rehabilitative or educational value; and when the training and rehabilitation are emphasised, prison labour is at its least productive and efficient. It may be the case, however, as a number of commentators have argued, that the real significance of the relation between work and imprisonment is more to do with the relation between imprisonment and the wider labour market.

It was Rusche and Kirchheimer's (1939 [2003]) central contention that the form of punishment is conditioned by the changing nature of productive relationships and the organisation of labour. Thus for them it was the creation of free wage labour and the changing nature of the labour market which shaped the use of imprisonment and gave it its historical specificity. From this vantage point, they suggest that prison acts as an institution for absorbing and ideally recycling those who are unable or unwilling to participate in the labour market, while providing a general deterrent for those who are tempted to engage in illegitimate activities. The crux of this argument is that with the development of industrial capitalism the traditional ties of support and dependence are broken down, and the worker becomes separated from the means of production. The increasingly atomised individual is then free to sell his or her labour on the market, but is nevertheless forced to sell his or her labour power or starve. It is this atomisation and consequent vulnerability in the face of the market which Marx identified as the central locus of social control in capitalist societies. As labour appeared in its 'pure' form in the nineteenth century through its separation from the household and from private property, the significance of the labour market as a regulatory mechanism became even more pronounced (Offe, 1985).

The control exercised by the labour market has a number of similarities to the type of ideal system of control developed by Jeremy Bentham and presented by Michel Foucault. It is impersonal. It involves a form of continuous surveillance. It is both a cause and an effect of the atomisation and differentiation of individuals; and finally, it incorporates a form of power which is not simply excised *on* individuals but also *through* them. It is the knowledge that each worker is potentially replaceable and that the value of labour power is constructed independently of each individual that constitutes the 'invisible threads' of control in capitalist societies (Lea, 1979). The experience of imprisonment has a dual effect on the individual in relation to the labour market: one immediate and the other long term. The immediate effect is the deprivation of liberty and a loss of certain rights for a specified period of time. The longer-term effect involves a changed relationship to the labour market itself, since the sanction of imprisonment carries a certain stigmatisation which affects the individual's future marketability.

Thus, in general, the prison serves three related roles in relation to the labour market: (1) it compensates for the imperfections of the market mechanism by increasing incentives to participate in a legitimate occupation, even at low rates; (2) it reinforces the division between the respectable and non-respectable working class by pointing to the potential dangers of non-participation in the labour market; and (3) it serves the market by absorbing some of those who are socially or economically marginalised or are unable to compete effectively, thus increasing the overall competitiveness and quality of available labour power. However, the more effective imprisonment is in reducing the marketability of individuals in relation to the labour market, the more unlikely it is to be successful in imposing labour discipline on those who are incarcerated.

The changing nature of labour at the end of the nineteenth century and the development of welfare capitalism persuaded Rusche and Kirchheimer (1939 [2003]) that the social and regulatory roles of the prison would diminish throughout the twentieth century and that the fine would become more widely used as a form of punishment. The advent of Fordism and its associated forms of work discipline, they believed, would render the established forms of prison discipline anachronistic. The evidence that the prison was increasingly becoming an institution of 'last resort', with a consequent overall decline in prison populations in both Europe and America, suggested that the use of imprisonment would continue to decline during the twentieth century. In the postwar period, however, the rate of decline has been halted, and in some countries reversed. In response to Rusche and Kirchheimer, Ivan Jancovic (1977) argues that there are two critical questions which have now to be answered. These are: (1) In what ways do the changing forms of custodial and non-custodial forms of punishment correspond to contemporary productive relationships?, and (2) What functions does the prison perform in advanced capitalist society?

Conclusion

The modern prison emerged at a point of intersection between three changing lines of force – space, time and labour. This development, however, should not be read as the bringing together of three 'variables' which just happened to combine in an accidental and contingent fashion. Rather, the modern prison was a product of a particular historical configuration which involved the commodification of all three elements, the separation of space and time, the simultaneous technical quantification of time and the formation of a capitalist labour market that involved new forms of freedom and unfreedom.

As Anthony Giddens (1990) has argued, the buying and selling of labour time is one of the most distinctive features of modern capitalism, while the 'dynamism of modernity derives from the separation of time and space and their recombination in forms which permit the precise time–space "zoning" of social life'. The implications of these observations is that it is the precise seriation of time and its compartmentalisation which makes the possibility of 'doing time' as a form of punishment possible, while the development of time in evolutionary and linear terms underpins notions of progress and an associated belief in the possibility of individual reform through the application of scientific knowledge and disciplinary techniques. Based upon these conventional distinctions between time and space, the prison takes on a naturalness and appears as an 'obvious' form of punishment. And what could have been more natural during the rise of industrial capitalism than subjecting aberrant populations to the rigours of labour discipline?

Just as these three elements combined to give imprisonment its unique historical character, by an extension of the same processes and an application of the same logic, space, time and labour became the central organising principles of the prison and an intrinsic part of its regulatory mechanisms. But its functioning has never been harmonious. The very construction of the prison was underpinned by a number of competing and at times incompatible objectives. The determinants of design, the organisation of time, and the attempts to engage in productive labour came into continuous conflict, with each one placing constraints upon the realisation of the others.

3
Order, Control and Adaptation in Prison

Introduction

It is normally only when a major disturbance or riot occurs in a prison that the issues of order and control become an object of concern. At these times the response is predictably to enhance physical security, to identify and remove 'troublemakers' or to impose a tougher system of control. The fact that, despite the frequent use of these familiar practices, the number of disturbances and riots in prisons continues to take place in England and Wales suggests that, individually or in combination, they have a limited effectiveness or may even be counterproductive. There is, no doubt, always a pressure at the moment of conflict to repair the damage as quickly as possible and to return to 'business as usual'. But the reliance on immediate and pragmatic responses often represents a failure to examine the more deep-seated and enduring processes which generate disorder. Consequently, these forms of crisis management only tend to work in the short term, if at all. Thus the problem of penal pragmatism is that it often turns out not to be very practical.

In contrast to penal pragmatism, sociologists have emphasised that, just as social order is sustained through a complex process of human interaction, so order in the prison is a social and practical accomplishment (Wrong, 1994). Studies of imprisonment, however, have the distinct advantage that the prison involves a more contained and manageable object of analysis. The prison has a number of characteristics that makes it a unique social institution. As we have seen, it has been historically shaped through the key elements of space, time and labour, and these have also played a critical role in its internal control and organisation. But alongside these processes there are other factors that serve to affect the nature of order in prisons. Identifying these various processes has been a central task of the sociology of imprisonment. Many of the earlier contributors in this tradition focused primarily on the processes of subcultural formation and adjustment to imprisonment (McCleary, 1961).

Early sociologies of imprisonment

The starting point of enquiry for much of the early sociological literature on imprisonment was the question of why prisons which contain large numbers of people who are detained against their will are not the sites of continuous hostility and conflict. Why is it the case that, in an alien environment in which the number of prisoners at any one time will outnumber the guards, they do not overthrow their captors? Particularly in those situations in which guards are unarmed, or where prisoners live in overcrowded conditions and are subject to extreme deprivations, it might reasonably be expected that they would make strenuous efforts to free themselves.

Among the early sociologies of imprisonment, the aim was to address these issues by analysing the changing patterns of authority within the prison, as well as through an examination of the relation between the prison and wider social and cultural movements (Bowker, 1977). The focus upon these changing social relations was stimulated by the fact that imprisonment itself was undergoing some marked changes in America during the period between 1940 and 1960, when much of this work was being produced. These studies constituted both a contribution to and a reflection of these developments.

The major changes which took place during this period involved first a transition from authoritarian styles of management towards a more open 'bureaucratic–lawful' system (Barak-Glantz, 1981). That is, towards a style of management which is less reliant on the authority of a single prison governor and operates with a more differentiated, flexible and bureaucratic form of organisation, which is able to administer a growing number of treatment and training programmes within an expanding prison system. This process of opening up the prison and providing more flexible, and in many cases more liberal, regimes was accompanied paradoxically by an increase in the number of riots and disturbances in prisons. There were also a change in the types of prisoners who were entering the prison system in the 1950s and 1960s. They became increasingly younger, and were drawn disproportionately from ethnic minority groups, and certain prisons became dominated by offenders who had strong allegiances to particular gangs (Jacobs, 1977).

In his study of a maximum security prison in Menard, Illinois, Donald Clemmer (1940) attempted to show that the social organisation of prison subcultures was based on the 'wishes, ambitions, drives and habits' which inmates had acquired before entering the prison.

Clemmer claimed that despite the regular turnover of inmates there was considerable continuity in the internal culture of prison, and that this was a function of the social groupings from which the prison population was drawn. He claimed that the inmate subculture was largely 'imported', that it reflected the predominantly male, lower class, and poorly educated nature of the prison population, and that these inmates operated an 'inmate code' which embodied the norms and values of these particular social groups. This inmate code involved an emphasis on loyalty among inmates and provided a set of guidelines about how they should ideally behave towards each other and to staff. This code of conduct, Clemmer argued, provided a degree of cohesion within the prison and, though the code was formally pro-inmate and anti-authority, it was also conducive to the securing of order. Moreover, just as prisoners developed an inmate subculture, the guards also developed an occupational culture which reflected their background and value systems and which provided a stable point of reference for the development of a system of informal controls, within which working practices could operate with some predictability and coherence.

The prison, according to Gresham Sykes (1958), is to be viewed as a microcosm of the wider society, except that the 'threat of force lies close, beneath the surface', and also that control lies in the 'hands of the ruling few'. However, he notes that the requirements of prison labour, and the emphasis on treatment and on individual reform, place limits on the exercise of this power. As a result, rather than the custodians being omnipotent, they are engaged in a continuous struggle to maintain order. Constraints on the exercise of power are also produced by the bureaucratic nature of the system, such that its exercise needs to be based on legitimate authority and consequently must operate in accord with social norms, laws and sensibilities. In this context the use of physical force is both inappropriate and may be counterproductive. Thus, rather than rely on crude forms of coercion, prisons employ systems of rewards and punishments, although the 'rewards' that are available in the segregative world of the prison are necessarily limited.

For guards to carry out their work, Sykes argues, they require some degree of co-operation from the inmates. Evaluations of the guards' performance will be measured by the activities and attitudes of the prisoners. Guards are therefore compelled within this 'society of captives' to tolerate minor infractions and to exercise considerable discretion in the enforcement of prison rules. At the same time prisoners have an interest in maintaining some level of predictability and stability in their daily lives and in maintaining a reasonable degree of personal security.

According to Sykes, all prisoners are subject to a number of basic deprivations. These include the deprivation of liberty, the deprivation of goods and services, the deprivation of heterosexual relationships, the deprivation of autonomy and the deprivation of security. To this list could be added other deprivations, including the loss of certain rights. The 'pains of imprisonment', as he calls them, are not necessarily experienced by all prisoners in the same way. They are all to some degree negotiable, and implementing these forms of deprivation provides some of the 'sticks and carrots' available to prison authorities. Things which are taken for granted in the outside world can become perks and privileges in the prison.

Prisoners are seen to develop a system of norms and a variety of roles which are aimed at mitigating the 'pains of imprisonment'. Alongside these roles a special language or argot is developed in order to generate an effective system of communication within the inmate social system. A framework of formal and informal codes develops, which not only provides a philosophy for doing time, but also establishes patterns of interaction and stabilises staff–inmate relations.

One of the dominant themes in the early sociologies of imprisonment was the relationship between the outside culture from which prisoners were drawn and the prison subculture itself. This form of enquiry paralleled the development of subcultural theory within criminology and the growing number of studies which analysed how subcultures arise in response to collectively experienced problems and situations (Downes, 1966; Hebdidge, 1979). The process of 'prisonisation', as Clemmer called it, involves the adaptation by different social groups to imprisonment. This 'importation' model challenged the 'deprivation' model, which claimed that it was the restrictive nature of imprisonment that was the dominant factor in inmate adjustment. Within the sociological literature on imprisonment these two models have been cast as competing alternative explanations, but, as Thomas (1977) has demonstrated, they are not theoretically incompatible, since it is likely that the prisoner's social and cultural background will provide the conceptual framework through which the deprivations of imprisonment will be perceived and experienced. However, there still remains some disagreement over the explanatory power of both these models, and the priority which should be accorded to each in accounting for the processes of adjustment.

Within the various contributions to the literature on the sociology of imprisonment different forms of individual and collective adaptation have been identified. Although various authors place a different emphasis on different types of adaptation, most agree that modes of adaptation are not static and that different individuals and groups may move between them during their period of confinement. There are considerable variations in the modes of adaptation which sociologists have identified, but they tend to boil down to three essential types.

1. *Co-operation or colonisation* In this mode of adaptation prisoners will aim to keep out of trouble and do their time with the minimum degree of conflict and stress, and with the intention of working towards their earliest release date.
2. *Withdrawal* This can take a number of different forms, including physical separation from other inmates, engaging in minimum degrees of communication, depression, or self-mutilation and suicide.
3. *Rebellion and resistance* This may involve engaging in riots or disturbances at one extreme, and forms of non-cooperation at the other. The form which rebellion or resistance takes will depend upon the pressures placed on offenders, their background and experiences and the extent to which they feel that their confinement or treatment in prison is fair and just.

Studies on women's prisons suggest that women tend to adapt to imprisonment in significantly different ways from men (Devlin, 1998; Bosworth, 1999). Their removal from their family and children and their greater geographical dispersal and consequent isolation often means that the experience of confinement can be particularly difficult for women. Women exhibit different forms of adaptation and resistance than men. The range and nature of roles which women adopt in prison are different from those evident in men's prisons.

Other authors examining the ways in which different groups deal with imprisonment have argued that the growing number of black prisoners in America experience imprisonment differently from their white counterparts. In some of the early literature it was strongly suggested that black prisoners would be more resilient to the 'pains of imprisonment' because of their experience in the urban ghettos and because of their greater levels of solidarity. Ghetto life is held to harden the individual, while the hostile environment of the streets is seen to make the experience of imprisonment less painful (Irwin, 1970; Wright, 1989). The evidence to support these contentions is mixed. Taking reports of aggressive behaviour, the propensity to self-mutilation, depression and suicide as indicators of 'adjustment', studies have shown inconsistent results. Some of the discrepancies in the findings are a product of the different definitions of the key terms that have been used, such as 'aggressive' and 'anxiety', as well as the adoption of different statistical techniques and sampling strategies. In one recent study, which set out to test 'deprivation' and 'importation' models of adjustment, Miles Harer and Darrell Steffensmeier (1996) found in a survey of 58 federal prisons that black inmates have significantly higher rates of violent behaviour but lower levels of alcohol and drug misconduct than white inmates. They interpret their findings as lending support to the 'importation' model of prison adjustment.

James Jacobs (1979), examined the changing racial composition of the American prison population during the 1970s, and found that prison subcultures were characterised by racial polarisation and conflict. Up until the 1960s a system of segregation by race was in operation in American prisons. In Attica, for example, in the early 1970s, there were black sports teams, different barbers for blacks and whites, and separate ice buckets for black and white inmates on 4 July. Black protests against segregation and discrimination in prison was actively proselytised by the Black Muslims, who provided the organisational and conceptual tools for challenging the existing structures of the prison system. At Stateville penitentiary in Illinois the growing politicisation of black prisoners under the influence of the Black Muslims during the 1970s challenged the authority of the prison guards and the legitimacy of the prison system itself. Consequently there developed a greater solidarity among black prisoners (Jacobs, 1977). Jacobs claims that by the end of the decade race had become the most important determinant of the individual's prison experience. The greater solidarity of black inmates, according to Jacobs, served to tilt the balance of power within the prison and posed new problems of control for prison authorities, as the established individualised forms of control became increasingly difficult to mobilise. The Black Muslims rejected the notion that all prisoners should be treated the same or that prisoners should 'do their own time'. In opposition to some of the earlier sociological studies of prison subcultures, Jacobs suggests that:

> The view of prison as a primitive society governed by its own norms and inhabited by its own distinctive social types, was always somewhat exaggerated. Racial divisions are not the only changes that exist within the prisoner subculture, but in many contemporary prisons racial politics set the background against which all prisoner activities are

played out. Taking race relations into account will help correct the overemphasis on the uniqueness of prisons and will lead to a fuller understanding of the prison's role as an institution of social control. No prison study of any kind can afford to overlook the fact that minorities are over-represented in the prisoner population by a factor of five, and that prison, ironically, may be the one institution in American society which blacks 'control'. (Jacobs, 1979: 24)

Thus, although the early sociologists of imprisonment had made the important observation that relations in prison are linked to wider social processes, there was a tendency to emphasise the cohesion and conformity of the inmate subculture rather than to identify divisions and antagonisms. At the same time they provided an overly rational conception of inmate adjustment, which made critical appraisal of prison subcultures difficult to formulate. The emphasis upon the authenticity of adaptations, the rationality and the functional role of subcultures left little room for critical comment. This was 'zookeeper' sociology with a vengeance: many sociologists were content to describe and admire their subjects (Gouldner, 1968; Young, 1970).

These descriptions of subcultural adaptation, as Ward and Kassebaum (1965) noted, tended to overestimate the level of inmate solidarity, while presenting men's prisons as the norm. The exaggerated levels of solidarity painted a picture of the prison population as a homogenous group and the social system in prison as being in a stable state of equilibrium. From this functionalist perspective, the processes of conflict and change within the prison system became difficult to explain, as did the growing number of riots and disturbances which occurred throughout the 1970s. The increasing politicisation and polarisation in prison, as well as the growing emphasis upon prisoner rights in the 1970s and 1980s, shifted attention away from the examination of prisoner subcultures and modes of adaptation to the more general issues of discipline and control.

Stanley Cohen and Laurie Taylor (1972) have argued that in the early sociological accounts of adjustment to imprisonment routine forms of resistance engaged in by prisoners are played down in favour of an undue stress on the passivity and adaptability of inmates. Resistance, they argue, can take a number of forms: self-protection, campaigning, escaping, striking and confronting. They also argue that forms of adaptation will be dependent on prisoners' ongoing links with the outside world, as well as on the social class and background of offenders. They quote Bettelheim's (1960) study of concentration camps, in which he showed that political prisoners managed to endure the camps much better than non-political middle-class groups, who were unable to cope with the shock of incarceration. Upper-middle-class prisoners, on the other hand, who segregated themselves from the rest of the prison population, were unable to accept what was happening, being convinced that they would soon be released because of their importance.

John Dilulio (1987) has argued that the level of abstraction at which many of these early sociological accounts were pitched meant that they were not very informative about the precise mechanisms by which riots and disorder might occur in prisons. His rejection of these sociological approaches, however, does not lead him to argue for a more sophisticated form of theorisation. Like other 'right realists', he is sceptical of the analysis of 'deep structures' and prefers a more pragmatic approach, focusing on the more immediate situational factors which may lead up to breakdown of control. In this way he aims to promote more effective forms of managerialism and to represent a growing body of criminologists, practitioners and policy-makers who have little time for theorising, and have instead gravitated towards more administrative and technical responses (Currie, 1998; Feeley and Simon, 1992; Matthews and Young, 1992). However, it has been suggested that this managerialist approach is of limited utility and is far less 'realistic' than its advocates claim. A more productive approach to the problem of social order in prisons is provided by a number of more recent sociological contributions that have turned their attention to the analysis of 'total institutions', bureaucracies and power.

Total institutions, bureaucracy and power

Alongside the literature on prison subcultures and forms of adaptation to imprisonment, there is another strand of sociological theorising that has focused on the prison as a particular type of state-regulated bureaucratic institution. This body of literature, which became increasingly influential in the 1970s, was generally more critical and reflexive than the earlier writings. The investigation into the bureaucratic nature of the modern prison has led in turn towards a more detailed consideration of the nature of power relations operating both inside and outside the prison.

Gresham Sykes (1958) pointed out, in *The Society of Captives*, that 'The prison is not an autonomous system of power, rather it is an instrument of the State, shaped by its social environment, and we must keep this simple truth in mind if we are to understand the prison.' Sykes, however, failed to develop this insight fully, although he was clearly more aware than most that the prison, along with the school, the asylum and the hospital, represented a new type of state institution which had its origins in the nineteenth century.

According to Max Weber (1948), the growing division of labour and the increasing differentiation of tasks in modern society called for a new type of bureaucratic institution that could handle complex tasks in a rational and co-ordinated way. The perceived advantage of this type of organisation lay in its capacity to carry out a range of tasks in a way which was impersonal, but nevertheless subject to legal controls and public scrutiny. The degree of legitimation the prison commands will affect the ways in which control is exercised in prisons and how it is responded to by prisoners. Power can be seen to be legitimate to the extent that: (1) it conforms to established rules; (2) the rules can be justified with reference to beliefs shared by both the dominant and subordinate parties; and (3) there is evidence of consent by the subordinate party to the particular power relation (Beetham, 1991). Thus the legitimacy of the prison may be called into question either by changes in the nature of wider social political and economic developments or by the failure of prisons to adhere to established rules and procedures. Thus:

> [E]very instance of brutality in prisons, every casual racist joke and demeaning remark, every ignored petition, every unwarranted bureaucratic delay, every inedible meal, every arbitrary decision to segregate and transfer without giving clear and well founded reasons, every petty miscarriage of justice, every futile and inactive period of time is delegitimising. (Sparks and Bottoms, 1995: 607)

Although Weber saw the development of bureaucracies as inevitable because of their technical superiority over other forms of organisation, he was highly sceptical of this impersonal form of organisation, since he believed that the discipline of bureaucracy would eventually encroach into every sphere of life. Indeed, it was the administrative and organisational techniques that were developed in bureaucratic institutions like the prison which later spread into the private sector. Thus it was not the organisation of the prison that was in this sense derived from the factory, but rather it was the factory which came to adopt the bureaucratic and administrative strategies that were originally 'perfected' in state institutions (Clegg, 1990; Melossi and Pavarini, 1981).

The defining characteristics of modern bureaucracies, according to Weber (1948), are that they are impersonal, rule-governed organisations with a hierarchical command which allows 'precision, speed, unambiguity, knowledge of the files, continuity, discretion, unity, strict subordination, reduction of friction and of material and personal costs; these are raised to the optimum point in the strictly bureaucratic administration and especially in its monocratic form'. These characteristics are embodied in the modern prison in its hierarchical organisation, separation of tasks, rules and procedures, impersonality, development of surveillance techniques and systematic gathering of information on prisoners. But the question which was raised by Blau and Scott (1963) is, Who benefits from the operation of these bureaucratic institutions? They suggest that there are basically four possible beneficiaries: the owners and managers; the employers in the organisation; the clients, customers or inmates within the organisation; or the general public. An assessment of the benefits and effectiveness of a bureaucratic institution like the prison needs to consider these options. Correspondingly, when asked the question, 'Does prison work?', the answer must necessarily be, 'Work for whom?'

Other writers have questioned the presumed efficiency and effectiveness of bureaucracies. Robert Merton (1957), for example, demonstrated how executive pressure for reliability and predictability in the actions of organisational members can lead to formalisation and standardisation. In a similar vein, Alvin Gouldner (1954) pointed out that the rules which are supposed to guide bureaucratic decision-making always have to be interpreted and implemented by members of the organisation if they are to have any meaning. In doing so, he made an important distinction between the issuing of rules and their enactment, and by implication between formal and informal rule-following processes.

One powerful example of the ways in which bureaucracies can work in one particular, albeit extreme, context involving mass confinement is provided by Zygmunt Bauman (1989) in his analysis of the Holocaust. Bauman argues that the Holocaust and the atrocities which were carried out in concentration camps were not just a consequence of the activities of a few psychopathic Nazis, but were made possible by a developed bureaucracy and its associated forms of rationalisation. Behind every camp commander was a body of bureaucrats gathering information, collating files and making decisions. It was the breakdown of the overall process into a multiplicity of discrete tasks that created a form of 'moral blindness', such that the outcome was not attributable to any specific agent, as all agents could rationalise their specific contribution. If the SS strategy had relied on direct force, it would have required more troops and more time, involved more expense and might well have generated more resistance. It was, however, the collection of detailed information, the production of incentives and disincentives, the formulation of systems of classification and prioritisation, as well as the forging of co-operation with the Jewish organisations themselves, which made the Holocaust possible.

Thus, in many respects, the Holocaust represents the 'dark side' of modernity, but it is not an irrational aberration or deviation. It was, Bauman suggests, disturbingly 'normal':

> Considered as a complex purposeful operation, the Holocaust may serve as a paradigm of modern bureaucratic rationality. Almost everything was done to achieve maximum results with minimum costs and efforts. Almost everything (within the realm of the possible) was done to display the skills and resources of everybody involved, including those who were to become the victims of the successful operation. Almost all the pressures irrelevant or adversary to the purpose of the operation were neutralised or put out of action altogether. Indeed, the story of the organisation of the Holocaust could be made into a textbook of scientific management. Were it not for the moral and political condemnation of its purpose imposed on the world by the military defeat of its perpetrators it would have been made into a textbook. There would be no shortage of distinguished scholars vying to research and generalise its experience for the benefit of an advanced organisation of human affairs. (Bauman, 1989: 149–50)

The suggestion that rationalised bureaucratic organisations have a propensity to produce undesirable and unanticipated effects was imaginatively developed by Erving Goffman (1968) in his classic account of 'total institutions' such as the asylum and the prison. Goffman defined a 'total institution' as a 'social hybrid, part residential community, part formal organisation'. These institutions he describes as 'forcing houses for changing persons, each is a rational experiment in what can be done to the self'. Within those institutions which claim that their objective is to rehabilitate or cure individuals, the actual effects of institutionalisation is more likely to result in debilitation and to produce what he calls the 'mortification of the self'.

Goffman argues that the specific effects of confinement in these establishments derives from the separation of work and home, the distance between inmates and staff, limited opportunities and restricted communication, combined with a lack of personal security. On entering the total institution inmates are stripped of their familiar social and cultural supports, around which their personal identity had previously been centred. The implication of this process is that any programme of rehabilitation within prisons must first overcome these negative and debilitating processes. Within this 'egalitarian community of fate', as he calls it, a fundamental revaluation of the self and others takes place which provides a basis for solidarity, sympathy and support between inmates. In this situation the criteria by which inmates judge each other may have less to do with the offences they have committed and more to do with the personal qualities of each individual. At the same time the forms of protection which might have been available in the outside world are increasingly absent within the total institution, and the prisoner may experience new forms of vulnerability and victimisation.

However, Goffman's powerful analysis failed to differentiate clearly between different 'total institutions' and the different dynamics that operated in each. Clearly there are marked differences between the processes of degradation and adaptation in prison and those in mental institutions. Moreover, it was precisely at the point when prisons were becoming less 'total' and were beginning to become open that Goffman's writings began to circulate. The important implication of Goffman's analysis is that the newly-developed inmate 'self' will be constructed through interaction with other people in prison and by engaging in the daily rituals which operate in these institutions. However, on leaving the prison, ex-prisoners are likely to revert to their previous selves in as much as they engage with the same significant others and become involved in the same type of activities that occupied their time before they entered prison. These transformations of the 'self' may go some way to explain the apparent paradox that the behaviour and attitudes of people in prison is a poor predictor of their post-prison attitudes and activities (Ditchfield, 1990).

The difficulty of achieving the rehabilitation of offenders within the confines of the prison was advanced by Norval Morris (1974), who questioned the means by which the reform of individuals was being attempted in different prisons. Morris's critique was both theoretical and practical. On the theoretical level he challenged the 'medical model' that was circulating in the penal sphere at that time, which considered rehabilitation in terms of 'curing' offenders. On the practical level, he was critical of many of the methods being used, such as tranquillising drugs and behaviour modification techniques. In general, he argued that you cannot effectively rehabilitate people by force, and that within the confines of the prison it was necessary to move away from what he called 'coercive cure' towards 'facilitated change'. That is, rehabilitation programmes should be made available and inmates should be made aware of the possible benefits of engaging in these programmes, but participation should, as far as possible, be voluntary and should not be linked to incentives such as early release.

Although Morris's contribution almost certainly encouraged greater accountability in relation to the use of certain forms of treatment in prisons, there remains an unresolved tension in his critique. If it is the case that the medical model is badly flawed, and the very notion that prisons can serve rehabilitative purposes constitutes what David Rothman (1973) calls 'the noble lie', then it is difficult to see why Morris would endorse prisoners engaging in rehabilitative programmes at all – even on a voluntary basis. Thus what appears at first sight to be a 'liberal' and humanistic critique of the use of unwarranted forms of 'treatment' in prisons and of employing illegitimate means to achieve certain ends, turns out to be a thinly veiled anti-humanism which questions the possibility and desirability of offering rehabilitation programmes in prisons at all (Cullen and Gilbert, 1982; Rotman, 1990). The dilemma is that offenders are unlikely to have a spontaneous interest in engaging in rehabilitative programmes which aim to reduce their propensity to offend, unless they are given incentives to do so. At the same time the state and the general public have a vested interest in prisoners leaving prison no more of a social burden than they went in. Reducing the period of time served is one of an array of incentives prison authorities regularly use to encourage or persuade prisoners to engage in the available rehabilitative programmes and co-operate in other ways. By posing these available options in terms of a strict duality of coercion or consent, Morris creates a dichotomy which is neither theoretically tenable nor practically applicable. There is clearly a considerable array of options which lie between the extremes of coercion and consent.

The prospect of going beyond the identification of control strategies, either within the crude oppositions of coercion and consent or as deliberate conscious strategies, has been opened up by Michel Foucault (1977) in his analysis of power. It was Foucault's consideration of space and time in relation to the development of the modern prison that, as we have seen, played a critical role in the development of his analysis of power. Like Goffman, Foucault is interested in the ways in which power relations in society become crystallised in its institutions – particularly state institutions – and how, once having taken shape, institutions act back upon society and the populations they were designed to regulate. Thus, in his analysis of prisons, hospitals and asylums, he traces out how different institutional structures emerge and how they then come to define, differentiate and even create 'individuals'.

Foucault's approach is similar to Weber's in a number of ways. Like Weber (1948), Foucault examines in detail how bureaucratic and administrative processes operate within these segregative institutions and how they sustain order and secure compliance. Foucault also focuses on the way in which a bureaucratic institution can become an 'iron cage' which eventually constrains its creators. A further feature of Foucault's approach which draws on the work of Weber is his examination of the processes by which bureaucracies dominate through the gathering of information, the development of surveillance techniques and the formulation of specific knowledge(s). Foucault (1982) is also interested in the process of rationalisation but, unlike Weber, he argues that the aim of investigation should be the analysis of specific rationalities as applied to madness, medicine, sexuality or crime, rather than rationalisation in general.

In analysing the process through which order and discipline is routinely achieved in prison, Foucault is drawn into a wider examination of power. Although the analysis of power that he develops in *Discipline and Punish* was later modified and subjected to a degree of self-criticism, the conceptual schema he presents and the processes he identifies provide an invaluable starting point for understanding the dynamics of control within segregative institutions (Foucault, 1979, 1982). In opposition to those accounts which see power as something 'possessed' by one group and directed at others who are 'powerless', Foucault argues that, even within settings such as the prison, power is not a thing which is possessed, but a strategy whose effects are realised through a network of relations and tactics. This network is in a constant state of tension, since its effects are never certain and the exercise of power is always subject to the possibility of resistance. For Foucault, then, power is always 'in play' and even prisoners and captives are 'inside' power relations. In the same way as Gresham Sykes (1958) identifies order in prisons as the product of a process of negotiation between staff and inmates, Foucault sees guards and prisoners in a power relation which is mutually defining and constraining. This does not mean that these power relations are symmetrical, but that it is never a zero-sum game.

The analysis of these power relations, Foucault came to realise, is central not only to any appreciation of how order is achieved and maintained in prison, but also to an understanding of the role of the prison in wider society. The exercise of disciplinary power since the end of the eighteenth century, he argues, has been concerned with reforming, educating and moulding individuals. These strategies, however, have not necessarily made individuals more obedient. Rather, they have sought to construct a better invigilitated process of adjustment (Dreyfus and Rabinow, 1982).

What is important about Foucault's analysis of power is that it operates on a number of levels and aims to link micro and macro processes. At one level he analyses the changing power relations in society in general, involving the control of groups and populations. At another level he examines how the pursuit of order in institutions is bound up with the detailed regulation of the body. Taking the body as the target of power and discipline, Foucault argues that, unlike previous forms of sovereign power which aimed at the mutilation of the body, modern 'disciplinary power' is productive, in that it aims to train and discipline the body in order to prepare it to carry out tasks, increase its capacities and improve its efficiency.

Drawing on Foucault's work and subsequent critical commentary, as well as the insights from the literature on the sociology of imprisonment, it is possible to begin to construct a composite picture of the diverse processes through which order is maintained in prisons. Some of these processes, as we have seen, are linked to a wider set of power relations, and are tied to issues of legitimacy – not only of the prison itself, but also of the wider political processes. Within the prison we can distinguish between the operation of direct and indirect control strategies. Indirect control strategies involve the use and distribution of space and time and the deployment of work and other activities involving the differentiation and organisation of prisoners. It is these forms of control, which are built into the very structure and organisation of the prison, that are most pervasive and, although they are in many respects hidden, they remain central to the construction of order.

It is in relation to these indirect forms of control that we should consider the effects of overcrowding in prison. From a control perspective, overcrowding undermines the established spatial and temporal structures of control within the prison by interfering with the distribution of bodies and the organisation of activities. Overcrowding has a domino effect in that it has a propensity to upset routines, to create bottlenecks, and to reduce the flexibility of decision-making. The combined effect of these impediments is to render some of the more pervasive but less visible forms of control inoperable. The degree of bureaucracy and styles of administration which operate in this context will also have an effect on control strategies, through the separation and ordering of tasks, the degree of impersonal rule-following behaviour and the ways in which formal and informal rules are interpreted and implemented.

Direct control strategies can be seen to operate in relation to two related oppositions: incentives and disincentives; privileges and punishments. These oppositions, although overlapping, are not identical. Systems of incentives and disincentives tend to be more informal and discretionary and involve, for example, decisions regarding the allocation of work or lengths of visits. Privileges and punishments, on the other hand, involve a more formalised set of options, such as the granting of early release or the imposition of disciplinary procedures.

The recurring questions which have been raised by sociologists and policy-makers are how these different control strategies relate to each other and how they link to different models of adaptation for different populations. One method of addressing this question is to construct a matrix with control strategies on one axis and different types of prison, or prison regime, on the other (see Cohen and Taylor, 1972; Sparks *et al.*, 1996). Typologies of this kind are based on the underlying assumption that forms of adaptation within prisons are structured and patterned and that this patterning is a function of different prison regimes. It is also assumed that there tends to be an 'elective affinity' between different types of regime and the control strategies which they are most likely to adopt. Thus more authoritarian regimes are normally associated with a greater reliance on physical security, rigid adherence to timetables, and extensive use of internal disciplinary procedures, including the use of segregation and isolation of 'difficult' prisoners. At the other extreme those prisons which involve a considerable degree of self-management rely on forms of dynamic security, shaming and forms of collective responsibility (Parker, 2007). The clustering of these various elements in different types of prison raises the further question of whether particular regimes and their associated strategies of control are more likely to encourage particular forms of adaptation and discourage others.

It is possible to explore these questions by taking two modes of adaptation, or rather maladaptation – suicide and riots – and examining the extent to which they are likely to occur in particular types of prison employing particular control strategies. These issues have practical as well as theoretical significance and consequently they are of interest to a number of prison reform groups and prison administrators. Taking Foucault's suggestion that a useful point of departure in analysing power relations and the processes of control is through the identification of points of conflict and resistance, suicides and riots appear to be suitable starting points for investigation.

Modes of adaptation to imprisonment

Suicide

Is there any discernible pattern to the incidence of suicides in prison? Is there a relationship between the personal and social characteristics of those who commit suicide and the ways in which they experience different regimes? In answering these questions we must begin from a recognition that what appears to be the ultimate expression of individualism is, as Durkheim pointed out (1952) in his classic study, *Suicide*, a profoundly social act. People, according to Durkheim, attempt or commit suicide because the social conditions in which they live and when the social relationships in which they are enmeshed become 'anomic'.

Various sociologists following Durkheim have, however, pointed to the methodological difficulties in identifying suicides and attempted suicides both in society in general and in prisons in particular (Liebling, 1999; Liebling and Ward, 1994). A distinction is made in the official literature, for example, between suicides and 'probable' suicides, which include those cases in which suicide seemed on inspection to be the likely cause of death but which might have been recorded by the coroner as 'accidental death' (Home Office, 1984). Bearing these definitional problems in mind, there does appear to be some forms of patterning, since suicide is more common per capita among the male population (although self-injury appears more prevalent per capita among the female population) and among those under 21 years of age, while it tends to occur early in the sentence and is more prevalent among remand prisoners living in poor conditions. Significantly, in 2007, 20 per cent of self-inflicted deaths occurred within the first seven days of prison. Interestingly, the type of offence or length of sentence has not been found to have a significant effect on the incidence of suicide. There is, however, a tendency to attempt to explain the incidence of suicide in prison as a function of the mental instability of some prisoners with histories of psychiatric disorder. The Report of the Working Party on Suicide in Prison (Home Office, 1986), for example, concluded that suicide was more prevalent in the remand population because there was a 'higher proportion of prisoners exhibiting factors known to be associated with suicide risks such as mental disorder'. But even in those cases where a clear link between mental disorder and suicide can be demonstrated, this would account for only about 30 per cent of the suicides which occur in prison. As Alison Liebling (1992) has shown, those committing suicide in prison are less likely to have a history of psychiatric disorder than those committing suicide among the general population. Whereas some 90 per cent of the recorded suicides in the community have a history of psychiatric disorder, only a third of those who commit suicide in prison have similar histories.

The tendency to 'explain' suicides in prison in purely individualistic terms means much less attention has been paid to the effects of regime factors or the role of control strategies. One consequence of these predominantly psychological accounts of suicides in prison is that forms of prediction based on them have been relatively unsuccessful (Lloyd, 1990). At the same time, one unfortunate consequence of the limited ability to identify the patterning and processes leading to suicide has been a steady increase in the number of recorded suicides in prison in England and Wales, rising from 65 in 1997 to 92 in 2007 (Prison Reform Trust, 2008).

The research which has considered regime factors has pointed mainly to the nature of depersonalisation in prison, the range of available activities and the degree of social stimulus. Regimes which are smaller and which allow regular contacts with family, friends and members of the community all seem to be less likely to have a high incidence of suicide. There is evidence of an 'isolation effect', both physical and social, which appears to be related to suicide. Strangely, however, the isolation or transfer of prisoners deemed 'at risk' of suicide are among the main strategies to have been adopted by prison authorities (Home Office, 1986). Research on suicides among young prisoners has found that they tend to cluster in particular institutions, and involve the more vulnerable sections of the prison population. Many of those who have attempted suicide have reported that they had been provoked by threats, teasing or bullying (Liebling, 1992). Typically, those most likely to attempt suicide are those who are physically and socially isolated in prisons with few activities and with little contact with home and family.

The reluctance in the past to address these social, institutional and regime factors can be seen as the result of the adoption of a number of 'techniques of neutralisation' among prison administrators by which they distance themselves from these acts and minimise responsibility (Sykes and Matza, 1957). These 'techniques' have taken the following form:

1. denying the role of incarceration by focusing predominantly on the biological and psychological backgrounds of those concerned;
2. denying the 'rationality' of suicide or attempted suicide, thus keeping the 'rationality' of the institution intact;
3. claiming that the suicide or self-injury was merely a manipulative strategy aimed at drawing attention or gaining advantage;

4. 'blaming the victim' by claiming that the suicide occurred because the person did not know how to cope or respond;
5. refusing to discuss the problem openly, with an emphasis upon secrecy and security in order not to promote the idea among the prison population in general;
6. presenting suicides as random and impulsive events with no discernible pattern; and
7. claiming that suicides are the outcome of a number of factors and there are no identifiable causes.

These rationales for distancing the problem, outlined by Simon Page in his study of suicide and self-injury in Armley Prison (1993), could be extended. His analysis demonstrates the ways in which these discourses have provided an obstacle to a fuller understanding of the causes and processes which promote suicides in prison. A recent official report points out that while there had been some improvement in recent years:

> However, inspections still found gaps and deficiencies in suicide prevention work, particularly among residential staff. Most establishments had safer custody managers, but there was often insufficient dedicated facility time or cross-deployment, which left little time to improve the quality or effectiveness of suicide and self-harm procedures, and sometimes left gaps in the care of vulnerable prisoners. There was no full-time suicide prevention post in two immigration removal centres, despite a large number of 'self-harm at risk' forms being opened for an increasingly vulnerable population.
>
> However, ACCT procedures alone do not create a safe environment. As inspection and other reports have often shown, it is the whole environment – including relationships and activities – that contributes to wellbeing. (HM Chief Inspector of Prisons, 2009)

Dame Anne Owers, the Chief Inspector of Prisons, also pointed out in the same report that many prisons are still routinely using strip conditions and body belts as a response to self-harming rather than addressing the underlying problems. She has called for a more integrated and comprehensive approach to these issues that places them in context, if suicide and self-harm in prisons is to be effectively addressed.

Violence, riots and disturbances

It is necessary at the outset to make a conceptual distinction between riots, disturbances and violent incidents in prison: whereas riots and disturbances are collective actions, violent incidents involve individuals. Levels of interpersonal violence in prisons are notoriously high. King and McDermott (1989), for example, found in their survey of five adult prisons that 12.5 per cent of their sample had been assaulted at some time, 6.8 per cent had been sexually attacked and 33 per cent said that they had been threatened with violence. A more recent study conducted by Edgar *et al.* (2003) found that 30 per cent of young offenders had been assaulted and that 44 per cent had been threatened with violence. These studies suggest that violence is part of the normal routine in prison and that it does not represent so much a breakdown in order, but is rather one of the mechanisms through which order is maintained (Bottoms, 1999). As Table 3.1 indicates, the number of inmate-on-inmate assaults and inmate-on-staff assaults are extremely high in prisons in England and Wales (although no figures are given for staff-on-inmate violence) as is damage to prison property. The most frequently used punishments are forfeiture of privileges, confinement to a cell and stoppage or reduction of earnings.

Although these individual and collective actions are not totally unrelated, it is the case that there is no necessary or direct relation between these two levels. Riots and disturbances may also be differentiated from each other in that, though both riots and disturbances involve collective protests, riots involve the attempt to take command over certain areas of the prison through the use or threat of force. A disturbance, therefore, may involve a collective protest over conditions, in which prisoners refuse to eat the food or decide to stop work, whereas a riot will typically involve the attempt to capture and control space. These distinctions are important, although there may well be an overlap both strategically and organisationally between disturbances and riots.

There has been a long history of riots and disturbances in prison, but since the 1950s in America and the 1960s in Britain they have become much more prevalent. In his review of riots in Britain and the US, Robert Adams (1992) has usefully periodised the recent history of riots in both countries. In the immediate postwar period, although prisons were run in a generally authoritarian manner, with a personalised and centralised system of command and general polarisation of guards and prisoners, there was little room for riots and other forms of conflict. Paradoxically, it was during the 1950s and 1960s, when prisons were becoming more open and more facilities and programmes were being made available, that the number of riots increased, many of which were centred around a growing dissatisfaction with prison conditions. From the end of the 1960s through to the end of the 1970s, during what has been referred to as the

Table 3.1 Selected offences punished and punishments in prison, 2007 (England and Wales)

	Confinement to cell or room	Forfeiture of privileges	Stoppage or reduction of earnings	Type of Punishment Caution	Other	Additional days	All punishments	All offences
Violence	**3,304**	**16,594**	**8,210**	**614**	**824**	**1,028**	**30,574**	**17,677**
Assault	1,959	5,906	3,079	162	478	946	12,530	7,165
On staff	*860*	*2,033*	*1,087*	*53*	*163*	*600*	*4,796*	*2,837*
On a prisoner	*803*	*3,026*	*1,607*	*86*	*273*	*225*	*6,020*	*3,319*
Fights with any person	1,337	10,668	5,124	451	345	70	17,995	10,475
Escape Abscond	**12**	**23**	**18**	**1**	**2**	**93**	**149**	**119**
Escapes from prison or legal custody	6	16	11	1	0	88	122	103
Attempted escape	6	7	7	0	2	5	27	16
Disobedience/Disrespect	**10,073**	**37,079**	**22,546**	**2,828**	**1,527**	**2,462**	**76,515**	**45,064**
Threats/abusive words/behaviour	2,998	14,009	8,077	639	629	313	26,665	15,211
Disobeys any lawful order	6,599	18,814	11,351	1,722	724	2,074	41,284	24,699
Wilful Damage	**1,395**	**6,091**	**4,657**	**227**	**447**	**558**	**13,375**	**7,536**
Sets fire to prison or property	111	324	208	9	36	71	759	428
Destroys/damages prison or property	1,284	5,767	4,449	218	411	487	12,616	7,108
Unauthorised transactions	**5,247**	**18,949**	**13,066**	**891**	**708**	**8,742**	**47,603**	**28,858**
Drugs offences:	2,253	5,571	3,805	76	200	4,025	15,930	9,780
Unauthorised use of a controlled drug	*1,704*	*4,409*	*3,255*	*55*	*152*	*3,253*	*12,828*	*7,827*
Has in his possession:	2,898	12,837	8,864	778	492	4,632	30,501	18,410
Other offences	**1,409**	**7,787**	**5,302**	**781**	**414**	**577**	**16,270**	**9,873**
Denies access to any part of the prison to an officer	151	331	198	10	29	129	848	496

Source: Adapted from *Offender Management Caseload Statistics 2007* (Table 8.4), Ministry of Justice (2008b).

post-rehabilitation era, riots and disturbances became more frequently associated with demands for rights and took a more political character. These riots raised issues of legitimacy and treatment in prisons. Riots in Folson and Attica Prisons, in 1970 and 1971 respectively, were among the most violent in American penal history. The Attica Prison riot, which left 43 men dead and more than 80 wounded, was seen as the result of a combination of poor conditions, understaffing, a sense of injustices and the brutal methods adopted by the guards to deal with the rioting prisoners. In the UK the riot in Albany Prison in 1972 was widely seen as a turning point, since it involved a level of violence not previously seen in British prisons. The decline of the rehabilitative ideal was marked by a series of 'crises' and the increasing polarisation of staff–inmate relations. In the recent period riots appear to have become more diverse in their location and in the populations involved, although their frequency has continued to increase. In some cases riots themselves do not have clearly articulated objectives but may be a way of drawing attention to, or halting, certain practices within the prison. Alternatively, they may be aimed at undefined 'improvements', although these may not be clearly identified at the time. This does not necessarily make them any less rational or purposeful activities. Significantly, the recording of riots and disturbances in official publications in England and Wales has become increasingly restricted and obfuscated over the last two decades. During the 1990s riots and disturbances were increasingly referred to by the term 'concerted indisciplines'. Over the past decade, however, this term has itself disappeared from the official statistics. At the same time the table presenting the number of riots and disturbances that take place in prisons in England and Wales has been withdrawn and the incidents of riots and disturbances have been subsumed within the general figures on violence, assaults and wilful damage in a way that makes them impossible to distinguish from interpersonal acts. Thus the only way currently to find out about the occurrence of riots and disturbances in prison is through the occasional reports that appear in the media.

In many respects the 'techniques of neutralisation' adopted in official discourse in relation to suicide up to the end of the 1980s have been paralleled by the official views on the nature and significance of riots in prison. These take the following form:

1. a denial of the existence of prison 'riots' and a willingness to acknowledge only incidence of violence or wilful damage;
2. claims that there is no pattern to these disturbances and that they are random, spontaneous or contingent events;

3. claims that all riots and disturbances over the past few decades have been resolved without any major damage occurring;
4. the assertion that riots and disturbances are isolated incidents and are limited to certain parts of the prison system;
5. the repeated claim that riots and disturbances are the outcome of the activities of a few troublemakers or a particular 'toxic mix' of prisoners'; and
6. claims that riots and disturbances occur mainly as a result of overcrowding or a lapse in security, or both.

Events during the 1980s and 1990s rendered these 'techniques of neutralisation' largely redundant. The growing incidence of riots in different types of prisons, including those without overcrowding and even newly-built prisons, revealed the transparency of these official explanations. The apparent limitations and increasing costs involved in adopting 'get tough' policies has prompted an exploration of different types of regime, particularly those in which prisoners take more responsibility for their actions and engage in forms of self-regulation. One notable example of this development is the Barlinnie Special Unit in Glasgow.

In 1973 a small number of the most disturbed, disruptive and violent offenders in Scotland were decanted into a Special Unit in Barlinnie Prison. The unit was run as a 'therapeutic community', in which prisoners participated in decision-making and were responsible for their own behaviour and for that of their peers. Prisoners who did not co-operate could be transferred by the community meeting of staff and inmates to other prisons. Prisoners were given some extra privileges and greater responsibility for the internal day-to-day running of the unit (Whatmore, 1987). Between 1973 and 1989 only two assaults and seven serious incidents occurred. This extremely low level of interpersonal violence has been attributed to the features of the regime, and particularly to the quality of staff–prisoner communication (Cooke, 1989). Despite this success, the Barlinnie Special Unit was closed down in 1996, following a report which, while noting the merit of prisoners taking more responsibility for their actions and being more directly involved in collective forms of decision-making, suggested that in this case 'liberalism had been taken too far', and objected to what was seen as a lack of 'physical and mental stimulus' in the unit (Scottish Office, 1993).

It was, however, not until the eruption in Strangeways Prison in Manchester in 1990 that a major re-examination of the possible causes and conditions that might lead to riot in prisons occurred. The Woolf Report (1991) provided one of the most comprehensive reviews of this issue which has ever been carried out in Britain. It examined the causes, conditions and the processes which led up to the riot in Manchester, and concluded that, if riots were to be avoided, there needed to be a proper balance between 'security, control and justice' within prisons, although it emphasised the primacy of control and made it clear that the delivery of 'justice' was dependant upon the maintenance of an adequate level of security. Lord Justice Woolf made a number of recommendations, including the improvement of conditions, the creation of smaller and more local 'community prisons', a revised judicial process in prison and the formulation of 'contracts' for each prisoner, setting out expectations and responsibilities.

The recommendations of the Woolf Report were only partly acted upon, while the number of riots in prisons in England and Wales has continued to increase since 1991. These developments have raised the question of whether these riots could have been prevented if the recommendations of the Woolf Inquiry had been fully implemented; or alternatively, whether it was the limitations of the inquiry in terms of the way it conceptualised these processes that prevented it from being adopted (Morgan, 1991; Sim, 1994).

The precise causal processes which produce riots have as yet not been identified, and clearly monocausal explanations are unlikely to account for the complex processes through which riots occur. At the same time multifactor explanations in which different variables are seen to combine in apparently accidental ways are also of little explanatory value. Moreover, explanations which account for riots purely in terms of absolute deprivation and poor conditions appear to be undermined by the fact that in many cases riots appear to occur during periods in which conditions are improving. It would seem that it is often the degree of 'relative' rather than 'absolute' deprivation that is critical. In the same way, responses which simply call for more physical security, improved environmental conditions, the removal of 'troublemakers' and the like tend to conflate 'triggers' with causes, and focus predominantly on observable events rather than the underlying generative mechanisms which produce these outcomes (Pawson and Tilley, 1997). Explanations of riots, like explanations of suicide, need to begin from a recognition of the social, structural and institutional contexts in which they take place, the causal mechanisms which underpin them and the 'triggers' which set these mechanisms off.

One recent explanation of prison riots which goes beyond monocausal and forms of explanation based on absolute deprivation and poor conditions has been presented by Arjen Boin and William Rattray (2004). Drawing on the work of Useem and Kimball (1989), they argue that prison riots take place when prisons go into systemic crisis, which involves the inability of the prison administration, on one hand, to contain tensions and disturbances, combined with a sense amongst inmates that conditions are unjust, on the other. In this process the presumption of legitimacy is shattered and there is a weakening of administrative authority. In this context a single event or a lapse of security can lead to riot. As Boin and Rattray argue, in prisons where conditions do not give rise to grievances and in which security is tight, a riot is an unlikely event. Thus they aim to explain three of the perplexing problems associated with prison riots. First, why riots occur following a relative minor incident. Second, why riots may occur even when prison conditions are improving. Third, why a significant number of prisoners decide to join in with the riot once it begins (Carrabine, 2005, Crewe, 2007).

In developing this form of explanation Boin and Rattray (2004) suggest that a 'vicious cycle' can occur which is similar to the 'disorder amplification spiral' outlined by Rod Morgan (1997), in which the aim is to understand disorder not as an event but as the outcome of a process (see Lea and Young, 1984). Within this model the established control strategies become problematic. This can occur for a number of reasons, including problems of legitimacy, change of organisation, and a sense of worsening conditions or of unfair treatment. Once this dynamic is set in motion, it is likely to create greater polarisation between staff and inmates, a growing sense of antagonism and insecurity and a decreased level of tolerance on both sides. At this point any number of 'triggers' may serve to turn anger and frustration into a riot. This model can be expressed diagrammatically (see Figure 3.1).

This amplification spiral can also be applied to suicides and self-injury, although it would take a slightly different form. The major difference between the two general processes is that in the case of suicide and self-injury the untenability of control strategies produces a growing sense of anomie and insecurity among inmates, which results in stronger prisoners exercising more control over the vulnerable and weaker prisoners, rather than directing their hostilities towards the staff. In response to these developments, the staff engage in a series of interventions, ranging from isolating and moving prisoners, to reducing prisoner activities and visits. All these responses may encourage certain vulnerable prisoners to escape from the sense of normlessness and isolation in the only way that seems available. These two processes exemplify the ways in which a breakdown of the existing system of control may occur, and how certain dynamics can set in motion a series of self-reinforcing processes which appear to have their own momentum and logic.

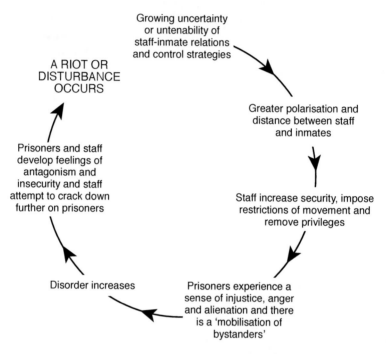

Figure 3.1   Disorder amplification spiral: riots and disturbances

Conclusion

Order in prisons does not arise *sui generis*. Like social order in general, it is achieved through a complex interplay of forces and a variety of control strategies which work in combination, but whose effects are never certain. We have learned from the early sociologies of imprisonment that there is an important relationship between the social and cultural backgrounds of those who enter prison, and that these backgrounds provide a framework that mediates the ways in which the deprivations, or 'pains of imprisonment', are experienced. The work of Erving Goffman (1968) and Norval Morris (1974) has sensitised us to the role of 'total institutions', the relation between ends and means and the importance of accountability. The work of Michel Foucault (1977) and Zygmunt

Bauman (1989) has drawn our attention to the problems of bureaucracies and the complex and often subtle ways in which power relations operate. They both emphasise that if segregative institutions were to attempt to operate around a simple dichotomy of coercion and consent, they would have limited effectiveness, require more staff and be more expensive to run. Understanding something about the modern prison, they point out, requires a more detailed examination of the 'analytics' of power and the combination of direct and indirect, conscious and unconscious strategies through which control is exercised and order is achieved. In particular, they emphasise the ways in which forms of 'moral blindness' can be achieved through the separation of tasks in bureaucratic institutions such as the prison, with the consequence that no one appears responsible for the outcomes.

Through an examination of two modes of (mal)adaptation – suicide and riots – it is evident that, although disorder can take a number of forms, it is patterned. Disorder may occur as a result of a breakdown in controls, their limited acceptability or their perceived inappropriateness in certain prisons at certain times. This may involve acts of refusal and rebellion or an unwillingness to tolerate injustices or, in some cases, 'rioting for rights'. However, the experience of disorder and a breakdown of controls are not in themselves necessarily progressive or liberating, as the evidence of suicide and victimisation in prisons testifies.

Thus the official response to many of these critical issues has, in Britain at least, involved a mixture of denial and distancing, with the consequence that there has been a growing reliance on penal pragmatism. As we have seen, however, pragmatic responses are often of limited utility, mainly because they are unable to grapple with the more deep-seated and less visible causes of disorder. Sociological approaches, in contrast, offer little in the way of instant solutions, but they do serve to alert us to the various dimensions of the processes of control in prison, while sensitising us to the different types of power relations. They have also usefully drawn our attention to the wider issues of legitimacy. Finally, they have made us aware of the interplay between control and adaptation in prison, and their relation to the wider network of power relations, which circulate in the social, political and economic arenas.

4
The Political Economy of Imprisonment

It's the economy, stupid

It is widely reported that during Bill Clinton's election campaign in 1992 a large sign was placed on the wall in Clinton's campaign office saying 'The economy, stupid' to remind campaign workers of the need to address issues related to the economy. Subsequently, the phrase 'It's the economy, stupid' has become part of the political and cultural lexicon. It would probably be appropriate to place such a notice on the walls of criminology departments, since the majority of criminologists either only pay lip service to the role of the economy in shaping crime and punishment, or ignore it completely. On those occasions when criminologists do introduce some consideration of the economy, they often engage in a crude reductionism or economism involving references to poverty, unemployment, deprivation and the like, as the unmediated determinants of crime and punishment. Instead of seeing economic relations as part of a complex set of forces that serve to generate certain pressures or place constraints on social relations, the 'economic' is seen as a separate autonomous sphere that dictates a particular set of responses. Some of the more useful contributions to the 'economic' literature tend to talk in terms of social formations, epochs, assemblages, and other forms of periodisation in order to indicate that different periods have a certain unity, and this may be generally expressed as 'industrial capitalism', 'welfare capitalism', or in terms of 'Fordism' and 'post-Fordism'. The significance of these forms of periodisation is that they aim to capture a set of interrelated relations which involve particular forms of discipline which, by implication, promote different forms of punishment.

This was precisely the project that Rusche and Kirchheimer (1939 [2003]) pursued. Their aim was to examine the impact that different systems of productive relations had on the nature of punishment, with the aim of explaining not only the quantity of the intensity of punishment but also the *form* of punishment. Their task was to try to explain why punishment took a specific form, such as transportation or imprisonment. Their answer was that the changing forms of punishment *corresponded* to the dominant productive relations in different periods. As members of the Frankfurt School, Rusche and Kirchheimer worked alongside writers such as Herbert Marcuse and Theodore Adorno, who were deeply critical of economic reductionism and stressed the role of politics, class struggle, ideology and culture in shaping 'productive relations' (Jay, 1973; Melossi, 2003b).

As noted above, Foucault (1977), himself a member of the Communist Party for 25 years, was deeply embedded in the Marxist tradition and recognised the enormous and original contribution that Rusche and Kirchheimer made to the understanding of the history of punishment in general and imprisonment in particular (Smart 1983). The task, as Foucault acknowledged, was to build on this base and further elaborate the processes involved. Rusche and Kirchheimer and Michel Foucault agree that the two fundamental characteristics of the modern prison are that it is intimately bound up with labour discipline and is an essentially class-based form of punishment. The failure to grasp these fundamental attributes makes the significance of imprisonment difficult to comprehend, although all these authors recognise that there are a range of other forces that can shape the operation of the prison, including political, religious and social determinants (see Rothman, 1971).

Criminological reviews of Rusche and Kirchheimer's work, however 'even-handed' they claim to be, tend to be either ambivalent or dismissive. Thus David Garland (1990) accuses Rusche and Kirchheimer of 'materialist reductionism' and argues that *Punishment and Social Structure* 'seriously overestimates the effective role of economic forces in shaping penal practice', and claims that they 'grossly underestimate the importance of regional and political forces', despite the fact that Rusche and Kirchheimer spend a whole chapter discussing Fascism and the role of authoritarian political regimes in shaping punishment. Garland, like so may other criminologists, has little problem with other forms of reductionism – political, social and cultural – and generally bases his critique on what is not covered in the book rather than appreciating the enormous contribution that the book makes to an understanding of the subject.

There are, however, other examples of how criminologists overlook or play down the role of the 'economy' and productive relations in addressing issues of crime and punishment. In a recent article, Cavadino and Dignan (2006), claim to address the issue of 'political economy', and in doing so they divide the twelve advanced capitalist countries that they have selected into four groups on the basis of their political orientation – neo-liberal, conservative, capitalist and social democratic. That is, rather than identify these countries in relation to their productive relations, employment patterns, the relation between the manufacturing and service sectors, level of deprivation, and other features that might be referred to as 'economic', they define them principally in terms of their political makeup. However, the way in which these countries are grouped is questionable, and the US, England and Wales, Australia and New Zealand, for example, are lumped together and presented as examples of 'neo-liberal' countries, obscuring significant differences between them, and in particular playing down American exceptionalism. Thus this discussion of 'political economy' contains some very questionable 'politics' and is almost devoid of any reference to the 'economy'.

Despite these limitations, there is an ongoing body of academic work that has looked from various vantage points at the relationship between economic relations, the labour market and crime and punishment. One line of enquiry has examined the relationship between business cycles and changing levels of crime and incarceration. This work is often premised on the assumption that in periods of recession and economic downturn that property crime and imprisonment rates will increase (Witt *et al.*, 1999).

Crime, imprisonment and the business cycle

In his pioneering work *Recession, Crime and Punishment*, Steven Box (1987) explored the relationship between changes in forms of unemployment and inequality on the level of crime and imprisonment. He noted that while there was some evidence of a link between unemployment and crime, the relationship was inconsistent. The lack of a direct correspondence between unemployment and crime amongst the different studies that Box surveyed was, he noted, partly a consequence of the different measures of both crime and unemployment adopted by different researchers. Some used police data, some drew on victimisation studies, while others used arrest or conviction data. Significantly, many of these studies did not address the question of whether it was the recently unemployed who were actually involved in committing crime. The concept of 'unemployment' itself has become widely contested in recent years and it has become repeatedly redefined. Indeed, the way that unemployment has been counted has changed in the UK more than 30 times over the past three decades (Levitas, 1996).

Steven Box's novel contribution to the unemployment, crime and imprisonment debate, was that while it might be the case that unemployment will directly or indirectly exercise some pressure on property crime, that imprisonment rates are just as likely to be pushed up by the belief amongst politicians, the judiciary, the police, the probation services, as well as sections of the general public, that an increase in unemployment *will* cause an increase in crime. It was, however, Box's contention that while unemployment had some impact on crime, the increase in the prison population was largely a consequence of government attempts to restructure and control the labour force, while noting that the increase in prison numbers can serve to reduce the official level of unemployment since it removes, temporarily at least, a number of people from the unemployment pool. Employing Spitzer's (1975) division of 'problem populations' into 'social junk' (mentally ill, sick, disabled) who have to be *managed* and 'social dynamite' (the unemployed and unemployable, the 'underclass') who have to be *controlled*, Box suggests that the growth of imprisonment is in part a function of its capacity to both manage and control both groups, particularly in periods of recession (Pyle and Deadman, 1994). However, the uncertain and inconsistent nature of the relationship between unemployment, crime and imprisonment has led researchers to pursue two alternative directions of enquiry. The first involves a focus on consumption patterns as a predictor of changing rates of crime. The second involves an examination of the role of inequality.

One of the most influential accounts of the role of consumption on crime has been presented by Simon Field (1990, 1999) a Home Office researcher. Although his approach suffers from the same deficiencies as the research studies on unemployment in relation to the measurement of the key variables, his study has attracted considerable attention because it has been credited with offering what appears to be a more imaginative and rigorous approach. Making a distinction between personal crime and property crime, Field, in his initial formulation, attempts to demonstrate that property crime has an inverse relationship to personal consumption such that when personal consumption increases, the rate of change of property crime decreases, and vice versa. He produces a number of graphs that show a strong correlation between consumption levels and crime rates and he claims to distinguish between purely coincidental connections and causal relations. He also draws on routine activities theory in order to try to explain differences between short- and long-term developments.

Despite these claims, Field's explanation collapses into a-theoretical empiricism. It is the identification of the covariance of consumption and crime that persuades Field and his followers about the nature of the relationship, rather any demonstration of a causal connection. Routine activities theory is in fact used as an *ex post facto* form of rationalisation to account for the 'facts'. However, the adoption of routine activities theory is appropriate since it is not so much a 'theory' as a set of fairly vague and ultimately unverifiable propositions which can be readily adapted to fit a wide range of explanations (Ekblom and Tilley, 2000).

In reviewing his account of the link between crime and the business cycle, Field (1999) has recognised some theoretical and conceptual limitations of the original formulation. Most significantly, Field's model does not explain the downturn in property crime during the period 1992–96. Also, a related study carried out by the same author in Europe and America found that different dynamics applied and that the predictability of the original formulation was, at best, limited (Field, 1995; Hale, 1998). The litmus test, however, for contributions of this type is their predictive capacity for the future. Field predicts, on the basis of his revised 'equilibrium' model published in 1999, that theft and burglary in the UK will increase in the coming years, partly as a result of increasing consumption and an increase in the number of young males. However, the crime statistics show that between 1999 and 2006, domestic burglary and vehicle theft have continued to decrease (Farrington and Jolliffe, 2005; Nicholas *et al.*, 2008).

Clearly, if there are causal connections between changes in the business cycle and the levels of crime and imprisonment, empiricist approaches are unlikely to detect them. There is a common-sense belief that patterns of crime and punishment will be affected by periods of recession and prosperity, although the type of methodology adopted by Field and others has been unable to identify the key mechanisms in play or capture the changing social *meaning* of consumption patterns or unemployment.

A more promising approach to this issue is an examination of the role of inequality in affecting crime and punishment. The focus on inequality rather than unemployment arises mainly from the recognition that it is not always absolute deprivation that propels people into crime, but rather a sense of *relative deprivation* that arises from inequalities. The notion of relative deprivation has the additional advantage that it can apply to a number of different forms of inequality and therefore potentially makes a contribution to explanations of white-collar and corporate crime. It is suggested that it is the disjunction between aspirations and opportunities that provides the motivation to engage in crime, and this can happen at every level of the social structure (Young, 1992).

Drawing on strain theory and notions of anomie, criminologists have argued that both property and violent crime can be stimulated by greed, the desire for wealth, personal advancement and in some cases the pursuit of luxuries. It is often argued that the resolution of the problem of relative deprivation is to try to develop a more inclusive and integrated society, but paradoxically it tends to be in situations of near proximity to others that differences of income, wealth and quality of life become more visible. It is typically second-generation immigrants, rather than first-generation, who feel more resentful about differences of income and opportunities between themselves and indigenous populations (Lea and Young, 1984; Martens, 1997)). The effects of relative deprivation appear to be compounded in societies where there is a strong sense of individualism and a weak capacity for collective responses to inequality (Sutton, 2004). More strategically, the reduction of relative deprivation is more likely to be achieved through the redistribution of wealth and opening up the opportunity structure.

The recognition of the capacity of relative deprivation to explain the basis for the motivation to engage in crime is linked to the analysis of inequality, both economic and social, in providing a context that stimulates crime and which, in turn, may contribute to the growth of imprisonment. Studies of inequality in different countries have indicated that in those countries in which the gap between the rich and poor are smaller, there is a greater level of trust, less violence, lower levels of homicide, and life expectancy in general tends to be higher. Indeed, some writers claim that while inequality may not be the only source of crime and social ills, it makes a major contribution to the prevalence of social problems, particularly where there are sharp class differences and high levels of relative deprivation (Wilkinson and Pickett, 2007). It is where we stand in relation to others in our own society that is important.

It is the high level of inequality and relative deprivation which are therefore often seen to account for the relatively high homicide, teenage pregnancy and imprisonment rates in America. In contrast, countries like Japan, Sweden and Norway, although not as rich as the US, all have smaller income differences and do well in relation to these measures. These issues, it is argued, tend to be compounded in countries with limited social mobility and greater residential segregation between the rich and poor. It may be not so much deprivation but the insecurity generated in economically and socially divided societies as well as the creation of different subcultures with their own particular set of values and norms that affect crime rates. The gap between the different social groups and social classes can contribute to the process of 'othering', by which criminologists mean the objectification and distancing of others who consequently receive less empathy, sympathy and tolerance (Young, 2003). It is not surprising, therefore, to find that although crime is mainly intraclass rather than interclass, the rich tend to harbour the most punitive attitudes towards offenders (Brillon, 1988).

In a review of the various models and explanations of the relationship between imprisonment and the labour market, unemployment, and business cycles, John Sutton (2004) found that higher income inequality was associated with higher imprisonment rates, while more generous spending in unemployment insurance and benefits appeared to reduce imprisonment rates. Strong union activity and strong social democratic parties contribute, he suggests, to lower rates of incarceration, by promoting collective solutions to social problems and generating less punitive responses to crime. In short, Sutton claims that while imprisonment rates are not overly responsive to fluctuations in labour *supply*, they are sensitive to variations in labour market *structure*. In this way Sutton believes that he is both refining and extending Rusche and Kirchheimer's (1939 [2003]) thesis that one of the major functions of prisons in capitalist societies is to manage surplus labour.

Sutton's (2004) analysis, while raising important issues about the nature of the labour market and the role of politics in structuring employment and security, suffers from the problem of using aggregate figures in making cross-national comparisons and, as he acknowledges, a definitive analysis of the relationships between the business cycle, the labour market and imprisonment would require a more finely grained mode of analysis. In particular, an examination of these issues would require a more detailed examination of different sub-populations, particularly ethnic minorities and migrant populations.

Overall, it would seem that the literature on the effects of the business cycle, relative deprivation and inequality on crime and imprisonment remain suggestive but inconclusive. This is in part because studies tend to be one-dimensional, focusing exclusively on deprivation or consumption patterns rather than linking movements in the economy and the labour market to wider social and political processes.

The costs of imprisonment

Prison, it is often said, can be an expensive way of making bad people worse. The costs of imprisonment are growing in many countries as the number of prisons and prisoners increase. These costs involve not only the direct costs of building and running prisons, but also the costs incurred in funding ancillary agencies that provide backup or support for the Prison Service, as well as for the families and dependants of those incarcerated. The costs associated with prisons in England and Wales has increased from £2.8 billion in 1995 to £4.3 billion in 2005 (Carter Report, 2007). The average cost per prisoner in a state-run prison was estimated to be £37,500 in 2005. At that time there were 76,000 people in prison. This number reached 83,000 at the end of 2008. Alongside these costs are the costs of building and maintaining new prisons. England and Wales has recently embarked on a new prison-building programme which was originally planned to cost £1.2 billion to provide an additional 10,000 prison places by 2014, but revised estimates suggest that this figure will more than double, and the revised estimate is £2.3 billion (Ford, 2005). In America, the costs of corrections have increased fivefold over the last 20 years, from $13.5 billion to $65 billion (Bureau of Justice, 2007; Stephan, 2004).

Despite the growing concern about rising costs of incarceration in many countries there are a handful of criminologists who claim that 'prison pays'. By calculating the number of offences prisoners might have committed if they had not been in prison and placing a value on each of these offences, an assessment is made of the cost-benefit of incarceration. Marvell (1994), for example, calculated that every state prisoner committed approximately 20 crimes a year on average and that, when broken down by crime type, every additional prisoner leads to an average of 0.06 fewer rapes, 0.63 fewer robberies, 6.10 fewer burglaries, 12.65 fewer larcenies and 1.11 fewer vehicle thefts. He adds that there is no discernable impact on homicides and assaults. Marvell calculates that the combination of the costs of imprisonment and the monetary loss to victims appears to be roughly equal and he concludes that reducing crime by expanding prisons is unlikely to be very cost effective.

A further study by Piehl, Useem and Dilulio (1999) developed a cost-benefit analysis of imprisonment and found that many people currently in prison do not pass a cost-benefit test, and that this was particularly the case for those convicted of drug-only offences. Based on inmate accounts of their offending histories, the study compared the social costs associated with different types of offenders and compared this to the costs of incarceration per inmate. Their conclusion is that if the aim is to maximise the cost-benefit of incarceration then it would be preferable to concentrate on high-rate property and violent offenders.

A review of Home Office research conducted by Civitas (2004), an influential think tank, claimed that if prisons could be used to incapacitate the most persistent and prolific offenders, they could be cost-effective. Drawing on the Halliday Report, *Making Punishments Work* (Home Office, 2001a) and David Farrington *et al.*'s (2000) examination of the cost-effectiveness of youth custody, the Civitas publication concludes that incarcerating persistent offenders is not only 'good value for money', but also that 'it's a bargain!'

There are a number of problems with this form of analysis. Critics have queried the mathematics on which these calculations of cost savings are based, as there are major problems about how the costs, particularly the 'social' and 'indirect' costs of imprisonment, are calculated. In many of these cost-benefit studies only the direct costs of accommodating prisoners are considered. Second, a significant population of offenders are imprisoned when they are at the peak of their offending and therefore basing cost savings on assessments of their most recent offending histories may overestimate any potential savings. Also, offending patterns change with age, and as those imprisoned grow older it is likely that their level of offending would decline (Currie, 1998).

It is the case, however, that imprisonment is more than a crime-reducing mechanism and that its function cannot be reduced to calculations of cost-benefit analysis. Although the cost of imprisonment is important, and while this type of analysis may provide further justification for dealing with low-level offenders in other ways, there are core issues of justice and punishment that for many override financial considerations. However, as the costs of incarceration escalate, prison administrators are making more efforts to save money on prison expenditure, while community groups are debating the benefits of building prisons rather than schools and other public amenities. Indicatively, as a result of budget constraints in the US in 2002, 25 states have reduced their spending on prisons in recent years; half have cut their capacity by closing prisons or otherwise eliminating prison beds (Jacobson, 2006).

Attempts to save money by contracting out services to private prison providers have in general proved unsuccessful. Although the number of privately run prisons continues to increase and private prison contractors such as Wackenhut Corrections Corporation and the Correctional Corporation of America reported profits of $135 million and $238 million in 2000 respectively, various evaluations in America have found that there are no significant cost savings by using private rather than public prisons (Pratt and Maahs, 1999; Perrone and Pratt, 2003). Similar conclusions have been reached in the UK. A survey carried out by the Home Office found that there was a steady convergence between public and private sector costs during the 1990s, and concluded that private prisons offered little or no saving to the taxpayer (Park, 2000).

The labour market and imprisonment

The relationship between the labour market and imprisonment is both critical and complex. There are at least four significant dimensions to this relationship. The first, which Rusche and Kirchheimer emphasised, is the changes in the form of productive relations which has been discussed above. Second is the level of unemployment and the size of the marginalized population. Third is the impact that imprisonment has on worsening the position of ex-prisoners in relation to the labour market. Fourth is the impact that imprisonment can have on families and neighbourhoods in terms of creating and sustaining economic dependency and cycles of disadvantage.

As Katherine Beckett and Bruce Western (1997; Western, 2006) have shown, the US prison population accounts for approximately 2 per cent of the male labour force. Consequently the exclusion of these prisoners from the statistics on male employment has reduced the official counts of unemployment by between 30 per cent and 40 per cent since the mid 1990s. Ironically it is this unemployment figure that is frequently cited on both sides of the Atlantic as a major indicator of the success of the deregulated economy of the US compared with the more corporatist economies of Western Europe.

One of the major effects of imprisonment on individuals is that it seriously affects their employment prospects on release. For individuals whose relation to the legitimate labour market has in many cases been tenuous, a period of imprisonment significantly reduces the likelihood of securing meaningful employment. Where jobs are available to ex-prisoners, they tend to be low paid. The high levels of recidivism for ex-prisoners are testimony to the low levels of individual reform and rehabilitation achieved in prisons and the tendency to recycle the same people through the criminal justice system again and again (Western *et al.*, 2001).

However damaging and depressing the effects of imprisonment on individual offenders may be, there is a wider issue of the impact that imprisonment can have on families and dependants and, in some cases, neighbourhoods. Recent studies have drawn attention to the 'collateral damage' of imprisonment and the ways in which the effects of incarceration go far beyond the prison walls (Mauer and Chesney-Lind,

2002). The immediate effect of imprisonment for those with children is that their partner becomes a single parent for a period of time and is often 'sentenced to welfare dependency' in order to support their children. In these predominantly poor households children are more likely to fail at school, have poor health and engage in delinquency. In short, there is a tendency to create cycles of disadvantage, which decrease the life chances of dependants, particularly if one or both parents spend long periods of time in prison. American research shows that the total number of children with incarcerated fathers increased sixfold from about 340,000 to 2.1 million between 1980 and 2000. Thus in 2000 nearly 3 per cent of all children in America had fathers who were incarcerated (Western, 2006).

In situations in which a significant number of prisoners are drawn from certain areas and neighbourhoods there may be other collateral consequences. These can include a breakdown of informal controls, a disinvestment in schools and a decrease in the number of firms willing to invest in the area with a consequent loss of legitimate employment opportunities (Hagan and Dinovitzer, 1999). In neighbourhoods with a particularly high concentration of people in prison it is suggested that incarceration can destabilise communities and undermine the building blocks of social order. Imprisonment in these cases serves to further undermine vulnerable and disadvantaged neighbourhoods and helps to sustain the conditions for high rates of crime and disorder and predictably supply future prison populations. In this way the concentration of prison populations tends to diminish both *human capital* – the talents that a person brings to social life – and *social capital* – the capacity of a person to accomplish important personal aims through the development of connections with others (Clear, 2002).

One of the consequences of high levels of incarceration in the US is the disenfranchisement of millions of Americans with a felony conviction. Most states in America deny the right to vote for persons while incarcerated, while some 14 states impose a lifetime ban on voting. Based on these figures, an estimated 3.9 million Americans – including 1.4 million African American men – are unable to vote. In some states as many as 40 per cent of African Americans are likely to be permanently disenfranchised (Austin *et al.*, 2001; Fellner and Mauer, 1998). In England and Wales all prisoners are barred from voting under the Representation of People Act (1983) except those held on remand. However, in 2005 the European Court of Human Rights ruled that a blanket ban breaches prisoners' human rights. The issue is now under review, although the response from the Lord Chancellor indicates that the government does not favour a change of policy, but there is a possibility of a constitutional crisis arising from this issue (Campbell, 2008).

Globalisation and crime control

The development of globalisation has made a major impact not only on national economies and forms of production but also on the nature of the national state as well as social and cultural lives (Aas, 2007; Mallory, 2006). Significantly, from the vantage point of criminology it has fostered new forms of morality and new forms of transgression. The effects of globalisation are evident not only in the reorganisation of world markets in commodities but also in relation to its impact on local neighbour-hoods and communities. For this reason, sociologists often use the term 'glocalisation' to express the simultaneous global and local effects of this development (Bauman, 1998; Robertson, 1995). Globalisation is associated with a widening of income differentials, increasing uncertainty and discontent as a consequence of an increasing sense of relative deprivation across the social spectrum which in turn places stress on family life and is held responsible for creating a widespread crisis of identity (Young, 2003; Fraser, 2003). It is also held responsible for creating new and modified forms of transgression and adaptation, while affecting formal and informal reactions to crime. As Jock Young has pointed out, globalisation involves not only changes in the movement of labour but also changing cultural configurations, creating new alliances and new social divisions:

Globalisation means nothing if it does not imply transgression: of a world brought closer together and the diminishing of cultural differences where the barriers are daily breached by the mobility of labour and the all-pervasive penetration of the mass media. The values of the majority constitute the normative life of the minority and generate the bulimia that fuels their discontent. The very similarity of the underclass, indeed its over identification with the values of consumerism and hedonism, sets itself up almost like an unwitting target for the resentment of the included. Each facet of their behaviour mocks the daily constraints of the included. Yet there is a fascination here as well as a disliking and a fear. The culture of the underclass with its compensatory masculinity, resorts to violence and rampant individualism – all over accentuations of the wider culture and then in turn influences film, fashion and popular music. The street scripts the screen and the screen scripts the streets. The borders are transgressed, the boundaries are criss-crossed, and the centre begins to resemble the margins just as the margins the centre. (Young, 2003: 410-11)

In terms of crime control, probably the most significant development has been the increased focus on the activities of migrant populations, on one hand, and organised crime, particularly in relation to human trafficking and drug dealing, on the other. Although both groups are held to be more actively involved in crime and arguably the seriousness and impact of international organised crime networks is more socially and economically damaging, it is the migrant population who across the world are increasingly becoming embroiled in criminal justice systems and imprisonment (Tonry, 1997; Weber and Bowling, 2008). The vulnerability and visibility of migrant populations, language problems, lack of understanding of the operation of the criminal justice system and limited access to good-quality legal representation all contribute to the growing number of non-nationals in European prisons. The concentration of migrant populations in deprived inner-city neighbourhoods with limited access to resources or work opportunities also tends to produce high crime areas.

Indeed, in Europe one of the most significant developments over the last two decades has been the dramatic increase in the number of non-nationals in prison. The population of foreigners in prison varies between different countries, with Luxemburg and Switzerland having over 50 per cent, Austria, Belgium and Greece having over 40 per cent and Italy and the Netherlands having in excess of 30 per cent. Across Europe, approximately 20 per cent of prisoners are foreigners (Kalmthout and Hofstee-van der Meulen, 2007; Melossi, 2003a; Wacquant, 1999). Some criminologists have tried to explain the high proportion of foreigners in prison in Europe as a result of the high level of criminal activities engaged in by non-nationals, while others see it as an outcome of more intense policing and discriminatory practices by criminal justice agents. However, the available evidence suggests that neither of these views fully explains these developments. It would seem that there are a significant number of foreigners kept in pre-trial detention because they do not enjoy the safeguards provided to citizens, for whom pre-trial detention may only be imposed in exceptional circumstances (Tomasevski, 1994). In contrast to citizens, foreigners are often held in custody on charges related to migration rather than on criminal justice grounds. They may be detained when entering the country or may be held as 'illegal immigrants'. As non-citizens they may be denied rights and freedoms that apply only to citizens.

The experience of imprisonment for migrants tends to be particularly harsh. Often removed from family and friends they lack support and protection. There are also significant limitations in the ability of national and international organisations to uphold the human rights of foreign prisoners. Although the conditions and treatment of non-nationals in prison has become a target of international concern, and in some cases condemnation, the existing level of official monitoring and regulation is extremely limited. (Spinellis *et al.*, 1996)

Apart from the legislation in most countries protecting human rights and formal prison rules, there are a number of international bodies and agreements designed to protect the rights of all prisoners and to regulate the conditions of confinement. There are also the European Prison Rules (1987), which contain explicit provisions for foreign prisoners, while the United Nations Committee on Crime Prevention and Control (1984) adopted recommendations for the treatment of foreign prisoners, particularly relating to health care. Also, the European Committee for the Prevention of Torture (CPT) carries out inspections and visits to prisons across Europe and publishes its findings. However, there are major limitations to the enforcement of the 'rules' proposed by these bodies since they serve mainly as guidelines and recommendations.

In the US similar problems are reported. The growing concerns during the 1990s with drugs and terrorism have increased the focus on immigrants and resulted in passing new legislation aimed at detaining 'aliens' and asylum-seekers. As a result the average daily detention population more than tripled between 1994 and 2001. The immigration agency in the US detains approximately 200,000 people annually, and detainees are held in processing centres, local jails, private custodial facilities and federal penitentiaries. These are 'administrative detainees' and they are not serving a sentence. Reports of the experiences and conditions under which many of these people are kept makes sombre reading. As in Europe, the detainees are vulnerable and isolated, lacking effective protective legislation (Dow, 2004).

Orchestrating these changes in the use of custody are changes in the nature of the state itself. The development of globalisation has resulted, it has been argued, in a 'hollowing out' of the state as well as a shift from 'rowing' to 'steering'. That is, the growing internationalisation of trade and the power of multinational companies has restricted the power of the national state. At the same time, state agencies are increasingly expected to harmonise their policies at the transnational and international levels. The endless comparisons of incarceration rates around the world are evidence of the growing emphasis on harmonisation. The transnational flows of capital, it is argued, have undermined the national state's ability to steer the economy resulting in a tendency towards deregulation and privatisation (Garland, 1996).

It would appear, however, that while state forms may be changing to some extent in the ways that critics suggest, in relation to crime control, the national state, in the UK at least, is taking a more direct and interventionist role and the provision of domestic security is one of the ways in which the reorientated state can claim to serve its citizens. Thus, rather than deregulation, we have seen, as John Braithwaite (2000) has argued, the development of new forms of regulation extending to new areas of civil society based on innovative forms of 'contractual governance' (Crawford, 2003, 2006). There has also been a significant increase in the amount of crime-related legislation passed in England and Wales between 1997 and 2005. These changing forms of state intervention have impacted upon the penal sphere in a number of different ways. On one side, we have seen the development of 'get tough' policies including mandatory and determinate sentencing and the growth of the prison population in both the UK and the US. However, on the other side, we have witnessed the development of restorative justice, community-based sanctions, and a growing emphasis on rehabilitation in prisons. As Pat O'Malley (1999) has pointed out, crime control policy over the last decade or so has been volatile and contradictory.

In sum, the impact of globalisation has been uneven and inconsistent. The belief that globalisation would lead to the convergence of policy across the Western world has not materialised. There has no doubt been an element of policy transfer and the establishment of international bodies proposing policies making recommendations, but national differences persist, while globalisation itself has created a plurality of development and responses in different countries. As John Muncie (2005) has argued, globalisation does not produce uniform or homogenising outcomes, rather it produces differentiation, segmentation and contestation. Thus it is important not to overstate the impact of globalisation on national penal policies while recognising that there are developing international movements and pressures that impact in diverse and contradictory ways on national economies, social relations, political geographies and the nature of state control.

From Fordist to post-Fordist discipline

Following Foucault, many criminologists have associated the development of the prison with modernity and have attributed recent changes in the use and function of imprisonment as a function of 'late modernity' or postmodernism (Hallsworth, 2002: Penna and Yar, 2003). However, this approach does not allow us to properly examine the contours of the historical development of social control, particularly towards the end of the nineteenth century, or to fully comprehend recent developments in the use and nature of imprisonment. Rather, seeing these historical movements in relation to the transition from Fordist to post-Fordist modes of regulation provides a more promising analytic framework. Fordism is associated with the process of mass production which developed at the end of the nineteenth century and is associated with the development of the modern 'cornflake' family, compulsory education and the emergence of the Keynesian welfare state designed to support working communities. Thus, during the first 70 years of the twentieth century, the development of Fordism was not just a system of mass production, but rather instigated a diverse and totalising set of relations that ushered in new forms of discipline and regulation.

The Fordist project aimed to rationalise not only factory production but also family and community life within a national framework involving an emphasis on self-regulation. Fordism created what Foucauldian's refer to as 'the social' – a network of overlapping apparatuses in which diverse institutions of social control became interconnected, providing both support and constraint (Donzelot, 1979). The fields of industrial relations, social work, criminal justice, public health, education, community corrections, and to some extent custodial institutions, became mutually permeable. In Foucault's terms, Fordist discipline involved a form of bio-power. It was systematic and capillary. It operated, according to Nancy Fraser (2003), through individual self-regulation, which is the original meaning of the term 'social control' (Innis, 2003). Considerable emphasis was placed on educational and socialising practices, and a proliferation of experts – psychologists, doctors, marriage guidance counsellors, social workers and the like – who contributed to the process of socialisation by promoting autonomy and aiming to increase the individual's capacity for self-regulation. Post-Fordism, in contrast, Fraser argues, is a product of globalising tendencies that transform the role of the national state and call for alternative modes of regulation and control (Amin, 1994). In the post-Fordist mode of subjectification the individual becomes an actively responsible agent obligated to enhance his or her quality of life through his/her own efforts and own decisions. Post-Fordism is equated with the emergence of 'post-disciplinary' society involving new forms of flexible control directed at groups and collectivities rather than individual legal subjects to be managed and contained (Feeley and Simon, 1992). The relations between work, the family and the community are transformed as workers become more mobile and the organisation of labour becomes more segmented (Di Giorgi, 2006; Lea, 1998). Post-Fordism is destructive of traditional 'communities' while breaking down the collective national project developed under Fordism. Thus:

> [Rather] postfordist regulation establishes new forms of [transnational] segmentation. Working largely through population profiling, it separates and tracks individuals for the sake of efficiency and risk prevention. Sorting the capable and competitive wheat from the incapable and uncompetitive chaff, postfordist welfare policy constructs different life courses for each. The result is a new kind of segmented governmentality: responsibilised self-regulation for some, brute repression for others. In this 'dual society' a hypercompetitive fully networked zone coexists with a marginal sector of excluded low achievers. (Fraser, 2003: 69)

Developing a Foucauldian analysis, Fraser sees the emergence of the 'prison industrial complex' as a feature of post-Fordist forms of regulation, and she sees the expansion of the prison in countries like America and Britain as a direct consequence of the bifurcated control strategy she outlines.

The prison industrial complex

The term 'prison industrial complex' is a parody of the notion of a 'military industrial complex' in which the American economy was seen as linked to a war economy. Christian Parenti (1999) suggests that there are three ways in which corporate interests can be seen as driving criminal justice policy and fostering penal expansion. These include the aim of building new prisons in areas of deindustrialisation or high unemployment, privatising the prisons industry and the use and exploitation of prison labour (Lapido, 2001; Smith and Hattery, 2006; Wray, 2000). It has been widely reported in America that many run-down areas have competed for the right to build new prisons in the hope of providing employment for local workers. New prisons are seen as anchor industries, which can serve to bring other businesses and service organisations into the locality.

The privatisation of prisons is seen as a way of private interests making a profit out of the prison boom while claiming to save the state money, improve conditions and increase transparency. Despite the fact that private prisons have not realised any of these objectives, they now account for 6.5 per cent of prisoners in America and 11 per cent in

England and Wales (Nathan, 2005; Prison Reform Trust, 2008). In England and Wales all new prisons are currently either privately financed, privately designed, privately built or privately run. Although companies like the Corrections Corporation of America and Wackenhut Corporation have made handsome profits over the past two decades, the promised benefits seem to have eluded the taxpayer. Their major achievement appears to have been in influencing the design of new prisons and creating a more diverse and less transparent penal system (Harding, 1997). In the US and the UK there is increasing resistance to the spread of private prisons by the prison officers' union, who feel threatened by the anti-union ethos of these private companies.

In addition to contracting out the design and management of prisons to private companies, there is a growing array of services and resources provided by a wide range of business interests within the expanding prisons industry. A growing number of commercial businesses are becoming involved in supplying goods to prisons. A review of prison magazines and trade publications reveals that a wide range of companies are interested in selling their products to prison departments, both nationally and internationally (Lilly and Deflem, 1996).

The third dimension of the prison industrial complex is the use and exploitation of prison labour by private and state-owned companies. The aim is to turn prisons into centres of manufacturing and preferably into profit-making establishments. The low cost of labour has encouraged entrepreneurs and businesses to set up 'joint ventures' with the prison authorities to establish a range of industries within the prison estate. As Parenti explains:

> Already American convicts toil for private firms making copper faucets, blue jeans, circuit breakers for nuclear power plants, and stretch limousines. In San Diego prisoners working for CMT Blues were employed tearing 'Made in Honduras' labels off t-shirts and replacing them with labels reading 'Made in USA'. Other convicts take reservations for TWA, work at telemarketing and data entry, and slaughter ostriches for export to Europe. (Parenti, 1999: 230)

In conjunction with these 'joint ventures' there are state-owned prison industries as well as federal prison industries that sell products to other federal agencies. Although a significant number of prisoners are employed in these forms of activity, prison labour is in fact, according to Parenti, a 'side show'. That is, many of these industries either lose money or break even and therefore it is difficult to see how the industrialisation and commercialisation of prison labour has served to stimulate prison expansion. At best, prison labour serves a largely ideological role stressing the desirability of employment. Prison labour tends to lack motivation, and be poorly skilled and generally inefficient. In reviewing the notion of a 'prison industrial complex' Parenti argues that we need to move away from an explanation based upon a narrow interest group model and move towards a 'more holistic class analysis that looks at the needs of the class system and class society in general'. Prisons and criminal justice, he argues, are about managing the surplus population created through economic and political disruption.

Parenti's attempt to link the use of imprisonment with the changing of production, capitalist crisis, growing inequalities and the changing nature of class relations represents a powerful and erudite account of the development of penal change in America over the past three decades. However, the links between the changes in class relations are not fully explored and the shift to the 'American Gulag' appears as much as a rationalisation as an explanation. In many respects changes in class relations and political organisation seem to provide the necessary but not sufficient conditions for explaining prison expansion and why militarised forms of policing emerged at precisely the time they did rather than earlier or later.

A more radical version of the concept of the prison industrial complex thesis is provided by Julia Sudbury (2002, 2004), who attempts to link what she sees as the militarisation of penal control in America with militarisation abroad in the form of the war against Iraq. On one side, she claims that the development of the prison industrial complex has led to prison expansion in order to control the marginalised and the poor, particularly African Americans and women, through the generation of a multi-billion dollar market for private operators. In line with Parenti, she links the shift towards militarisation and security in America with the military aggression abroad. The aim, she argues, is to control surplus populations – namely, black, Latino, immigrant and other marginalised and disadvantaged populations. She sees a blurring of the distinction between criminals and terrorists, and this is reflected in the building of 'superjails' serving as warehouses for thousands of prisoners in both America and Iraq. These 'superjails' are characterised by and have an emphasis on incapacitation rather than rehabilitation. They are austere, 'no frills' institutions which aim to reduce the cost per prisoner through the use of video surveillance in order to reduce staffing levels. In response, she calls for penal abolition and the formulation of a broad-based coalition in the US and globally to campaign against 'the perpetual prison machine' (Dyer, 2000).

The underclass debate

The premise of those who have contributed to the literature on the prison industrial complex is that the prison is increasingly being used to contain and neutralise the growing surplus population or 'underclass'. In addition, Malcolm Feeley and Jonathan Simon (1992), in their influential depiction of the 'New Penology', claim that one of the major shifts in incarceration is towards the management of the underclass, whom they describe as 'a segment of society that is viewed as permanently excluded from social mobility and economic integration'. In America, they claim the term 'underclass' is used mainly to refer to black and Hispanic populations living in zones of poverty in the inner cities. Thus:

> In contrast to groups whose members are deemed employable, even if they are temporarily out of work, the underclass is understood as a permanently marginal population, without literacy, without skills and without hope; a self-perpetuating and pathological segment of society that is not integrated into the larger whole, even as a reserve labor pool. Conceived in this way, the underclass is also a dangerous class, not only for what any particular member may or may not do, but also more generally for potential misbehaviour. It is treated as a high-risk group that must be managed for the protection of the rest of society. Indeed, it is this managerial task that provides one of the most powerful sources for the imperative of preventative management in the new penology. (Feeley and Simon, 1992: 467–8)

The depiction of the underclass presented by Feeley and Simon is in many respects similar to that given by the conservative writer Charles Murray (1990, 1994; IEA, 1996). For Murray, the indicators of an emerging underclass are the growth of long-term unemployment, the increase in the number of single-parent households, the social and geographic concentration of crime and the level of spatial segregation. A review of the available evidence, however, only lends limited support for the underclass thesis (Crowther, 2000). Thus, although the level of unemployment in Britain and America over the past decade has been relatively low, America has experienced a considerable increase in the number of long-term unemployed. This appears to be largely due to structural changes in the economy and increased productivity so that companies can achieve higher output with fewer workers and 'no longer need to dip into the pool of displaced workers' (Uchitelle, 2005).

In contrast, in the UK, the number of long-term unemployed increased in the early 1990s but has fallen ever since (Begum, 2004). It is the case that long-term unemployment is concentrated geographically, with parts of the North of England in particular having very high rates. Research conducted by the Social Exclusion Unit (2002) in the UK has found that two-thirds of those admitted to prison were unemployed at the time of arrest. The same research reported that one in seven of those admitted to prison had never been employed. Prisoners tend to have a history of intermittent employment, usually in temporary jobs. Most have limited skills and few academic qualifications. It has also been estimated in the UK that 3 million working-age households had no adult members in work (Walling, 2004). In America, official labor statistics exclude persons not looking for work. On this basis the unemployment rate for state prison inmates at admission in 2003 was 16.8 per cent, while it has been estimated that almost half of inmates in state prisons reported that they had received welfare or lived in publicly supported housing. Half of the parents in prison have a family member who has been incarcerated, and the majority of state (62 per cent) and federal (63 per cent) prisoners reported having at least one child under the age of 18 (Harlow, 2003). According to Bureau of Justice figures, 31 per cent of jail inmates had grown up with a parent or guardian who abused alcohol or drugs, while about 12 per cent had lived in a foster home or an institution. Approximately one in four state and federal inmates reported having a child (Glaze and Maruschak, 2008). The clear message that comes out of these prisoner profiles is that the majority of prisoners come from what are referred to as dysfunctional families or have been in local authority care.

Taking victimisation surveys as a proxy for crime, the evidence suggests that victimisation in the UK has become increasingly socially and geographically concentrated. Trickett *et al.* (1995) showed that the increase of victimisation during the 1980s in England and Wales was not widely distributed amongst the general population but became more heavily concentrated amongst certain social groups living in specific areas. Similarly, American research has shown that in large urban centres like New York, a disproportionate number of those sent to prison are drawn from a very limited number of neighbourhoods. When prisoners return to these neighbourhoods after leaving prison they tend to contribute to the continued increase in the level of offending, resulting in a growing concentration of crime and victimisation. (Fagan, 2004; Lawrence and Travis, 2004).

The fourth criterion that Murray presents is the level of spatial segregation. The ghettoisation of the poor is a well-noted feature of American society. Even in generally affluent cities like Los Angeles and Washington there exist significant ghetto populations composed mainly of different ethnic minority groups. Mike Davis (1990) has vividly described how new forms of spatial segregation and control developing in cities like Los Angeles are fostering new social and geographic divisions in American society. In the UK, however, this form of ghettoisation is not so much in evidence. Society in general appears to be more ethnically integrated and multiracial. It is not that the spatial segregation of the poor is absent from the UK, but the boundaries are more permeable than they are in the US.

Thus it would seem that new social divisions and new forms of marginalisation and social exclusion are developing, while in some areas long-term unemployment is increasing. Although a significant proportion of prisoners come from single-parent households, the majority are brought up in what are currently referred to as dysfunctional families or institutions. At the same time, some of the level of hyperghettoisation that was evident in America in the 1980s and 1990s seems to be in decline, and there is evidence of a growing black middle class in America (Mingione, 1996; Wilson, 1993).

The contention that there is an 'underclass' that are socially and economically excluded from mainstream society plays down the ways in which social, cultural and moral processes overlap in contemporary society (Hayward and Yar, 2006). Thus, rather than embrace an oppositional set of values, members of the so-called 'underclass' are found to embrace the ideals of consumerism, money wealth and status – in fact, most of the components of the American Dream (Young, 2003). Spatial segregation, in certain areas at least, is not as strict as is often suggested, while physical and moral boundaries are regularly crossed. The language of exclusion overstates the divisions and overlooks the fluidity and movement of contemporary urban life.

Second, and relatedly, the suggestion by Feeley and Simon that a central feature of the 'New Penology' is the management of the poor and the marginalised hardly distinguishes it from the 'Old Penology'. The modern history of crime and punishment centres around the regulation of what were referred to in the nineteenth century as the 'criminal classes' or the 'dangerous classes'. The style of management may have changed, but not the object. A key feature of the modern criminal justice system, and a source of some confusion, is that while it operates with an individualised system of justice centred around the processing of legal subjects, its ultimate objective is the regulation of collectivities and aggregate populations.

Third, if we look at who gets sent to prison we find that it includes a significant percentage of the population that goes beyond the 'underclass'. In America it is estimated that approximately 5 per cent of all persons in the US will be imprisoned during their lifetime. For men it is 9 per cent; for African Americans it is 16.2 per cent, and for Hispanics it is 9.4 per cent (Bonczar and Beck, 1997). At current levels of incarceration, an African Caribbean male has a one in four chance of going to prison during his lifetime, while a Hispanic male has roughly a one in six chance and a white male has a one in twenty-three chance. In England and Wales it is estimated that 7.5 per cent of males and 0.5 per cent of females born in 1953 will have been given at least one prison sentence before the age of 46 (Prime *et al.*, 2001). These figures suggest that while imprisonment is reserved largely for the poor and the powerless, it includes social groups that to some extent cut across the divisions between the marginalised and mainstream society.

Conclusion

As we have seen, there is a limited and variable interest in examining the political economy of imprisonment. The available studies tend to suffer either from a one-sided focus on the 'economy' as if it were an autonomous realm that determines the use of imprisonment in some unmediated way, or alternatively they operate with crude models of unemployment and consumption as primary or sole determinants of crime and punishment. The process of globalisation, however, has increased the need to engage with economic issues at both the national and the international level and to consider the impact of these developments on the state, migration and changing attitudes towards crime and punishment. Understanding the causal processes involved in these shifts is one of the major challenges that faces criminology, and responding to this challenge will require moving beyond the forms of empiricism that permeate the subject.

It has been suggested that it is more instructive to examine the changing use of imprisonment in relation to the shift from Fordism to post-Fordism and the attendant changes in the form of discipline and punishment, rather than seeing these developments purely in terms of a shift from modernity to postmodernity. In the process of engaging with these complexities we need to examine in more detail the primary function of imprisonment and decide whether it is to incapacitate and manage the marginalised 'underclass' in order to remove them from the labour market, or whether the main function of the prison is to act as a deterrent to the respectable working class while affording them a semblance of protection and security.

5
The Politics and Culture of Imprisonment

Introduction

It was Rusche and Kirchheimer's (1939 [2003]) expectation that the steady but continuous decline in the number of people incarcerated across Europe that had occurred between the end of the nineteenth century and the 1930s would continue. The prison, they argued, had become an anachronistic institution and would in due course be replaced as the dominant form of punishment by the fine. The decrease in the prison population in England from just under 33,000 in 1880 to just over 14,000 in 1930 suggested that prison use was in general decline, and as this trend was replicated in other European countries it suggested that this change was structural and linked, they argued, to the changing nature of productive relations.

In the postwar period, however, prison populations in most European countries have grown and the number imprisoned in England and Wales has increased from 45,000 in 1985 to over 80,000 in 2008. In the US, the prison population has increased fourfold over the last two decades and is currently in excess of 2 million. The re-expansion of the prison raises important questions for penologists concerning the use and function of imprisonment in contemporary society (Jankovic, 1977). In particular, the shift towards what has been termed 'mass incarceration' over the past three decades in the US where imprisonment has increasingly been used as a punishment of first rather than last resort, represents not only a major quantitative but also qualitative change in the use of imprisonment. Further, the continued increase in prison populations in both the US and the UK, despite a substantial decrease in crime, has problematised the relation between incarceration and crime and called for more sophisticated explanations of the changing use of imprisonment.

Few writers following Rusche and Kirchheimer and Foucault have focused on the changing nature of productive and power relations to explain these developments, but have rather focused on the more immediate social and political processes that may affect the scale of imprisonment. These attempts to explain penal developments tend to focus on a range of determinants that can be divided into 'exterior' processes, which operate largely outside of the criminal justice process, and 'interior' processes, which operate within the criminal justice system. In the previous chapter we looked at some of these exterior processes such as changes in the labour market and other socio-economic processes and their association with imprisonment. In this chapter we focus on demographic shifts, political movements including the ascendancy of neo-liberalism, the demise of the welfare state, the surge in 'populist punitiveness' as well as cultural variations. Amongst the interior processes are included changes in the nature of crime, sentencing policies and the use of non-custodial sanctions, and these issues will be the focus of the following chapter. Although it is conceptually possible to treat each of these processes separately as if they were autonomous realms, we should not lose sight of the reality that these interior and exterior processes are often interrelated and that the wider social and political processes are necessarily mediated by a number of complex mechanisms which combine in different ways to produce specific and at times unexpected and contradictory outcomes. It is for this reason that it is always necessary to engage in detailed empirical investigation in each case, and why we need to be extremely cautious about generalising across countries and continents (Pawson and Tilley, 1997; Matthews, 1987).

Analysing the changing scale of imprisonment, and identifying the specific reasons for its expansion or contraction, is critical for the development of reforms. A number of competing explanations have been put forward to account for the changing size of the prison, and a central objective of much of the analysis is to identify the main determinants of change in order that some form of intervention can be devised to adjust the prison population to a desired level, although there is little consensus over exactly what this level should be.

The point of drawing attention at the outset to these various complex and at times, conflicting processes is that it is necessary to attempt to develop forms of analysis which are capable of grasping the *causal* processes involved in determining changes in the scale of imprisonment (Pawson and Tilley, 1997; Sayer, 1992). Thus it is apparent that those forms of explanation which employ linear, one-dimensional or single-factor models are likely to be of limited utility at best, or seriously misleading at worst (Zimring and Hawkins, 1991b). The task is to identify the causal mechanisms in play, while recognising that these may involve counter-vailing forces that pull simultaneously in different directions.

When measuring the scale of imprisonment, it is sensible to attempt to explain not only the changing numbers of people in prison or sent to prison, but also changes in the composition of the prison population, particularly in relation to age, race and gender, as well as differentiating between the types of offences for which offenders are imprisoned (see Chapters 7, 8 and 9). This is not only because the types of offences for which people have been imprisoned has varied historically, but also because changes in the composition of the prison population may provide important clues about the changing role of the prison in contemporary society. It is also necessary to distinguish between changes in the remand and general prison population, while the analysis of the changing scale of imprisonment in the US requires an appreciation of the variation between different states and the relation between state, federal prisons and local jails (Lawrence and Travis, 2004).

If the conceptual and methodological issues that have been identified so far did not in themselves present a daunting enough task, there are problems arising from the interpretation of the data which are no less formidable. These are related in particular to the available data on the changing use of imprisonment. The majority of studies, for example, take as their point of reference the average daily population (ADP), while some others refer to the number of receptions into custody (RIC) in any given period. These two forms of measurement allow us to distinguish between the *stock* and *flow* of the prison population. Although there is, of course, a relationship between the number of receptions into custody and the average daily population, this relationship is not invariant, since the changing lengths of prison sentences will condition the period of incarceration served. The period of time served will, in turn, be subject to the use of early release mechanisms such as parole. Thus in some periods the number of people sent to prison can level off or decrease while the average daily population increases because the average length of sentences and/or time served is increasing.

The timeframe over which the changes in the scale of imprisonment is measured is also critical, since the period over which developments are examined can radically affect the picture of change which is produced and the questions that are asked. Depending on the measures used and the timeframe taken, different researchers can produce conflicting accounts of changes in the scale and use of imprisonment. For example, if we take the period between 1970 and 1990 in England and Wales, different commentators have variously identified this period as being one of overall increase, relative stability, and even for short periods a decrease in the scale of imprisonment (Nuttall and Pease, 1994; Rutherford, 1986).

One of the fundamental determinants that can affect the nature and level of crime and imprisonment is socio-demographic shifts. Changes in the size, composition and distribution of different sub-populations can make significant differences in the numbers available for imprisonment. Although there is little evidence of a consistent correlation between changes in the general population and imprisonment rates, this does not mean that there are not more or less direct links between these two phenomena.

Demographic changes

Predictions of the changing scale of imprisonment based on changes in the size of the general population are unlikely to be very accurate (Zimring and Hawkins, 1991b). However, it is widely recognised that changes in the prison population need at least to be seen in relation to the overall changes in the population, particularly when comparing the number of people in prison over a relatively long period of time, or when making comparisons between imprisonment rates in different countries. Thus criminologists and official bodies tend to present prison numbers in relation to 100,000 of the general population (see Pease, 1994). Typically, surveys of imprisonment rates in different countries have found that, while most Western European countries have an incarceration rate of 60–150 per 100,000, England and Wales has a rate of 142 per 100,000, while the US has the highest prison population in the world with over 700 per 100,000 (Walmsley, 2005).

Although analysing shifts in penal populations as a function of changes in the overall size of the general population provides a more meaningful approach, it is often necessary to examine the makeup of the population in more detail. This is because there are some groups in the general population that are more likely to go to prison than others. Just as we know that crime and victimisation is concentrated socially and geo-graphically, so the population who are most likely to go to prison are the marginalised groups living in poor urban neighbourhoods (Young, 1988). Changes in the composition and distribution of these specific groups, criminologists have come to realise, can have a significant effect both on the level of crime and on the use of imprisonment. Thus any meaningful discussion of the demographic effects on prison populations needs to begin from changes in the numbers of those who may be described as 'crime-prone', 'victim-prone' and 'prison-prone'. Thus a significant decrease in the number of juveniles in the general population during the 1980s in England and Wales resulted in delinquency becoming a 'scarce resource' (Pratt, 1985). It is not only that the population of the most crime-prone group decreased significantly during the 1980s, but also that juveniles experience relatively high levels of victimisation, and their reduced numbers had a depressing effect on crime and victimisation rates in this period. It is also likely that the resulting decrease in juvenile custody rates was mediated by a sense that juvenile crime was becoming less of a problem and that more inclusive welfare strategies constituted a more appropriate response to this group (see Chapter 7).

In the US, however, the ageing of the baby-boomers was expected to lead to a decrease in the prison population in the 1990s, but this did not occur. Despite the changing age structure, prison admission rates grew for all age groups during this period. However, rather than the 11 per cent increase that might have been predicted on the basis of demographic changes, the prison population increased by a dramatic 235 per cent between 1979 and 1994. A number of factors seem to have produced this substantial increase, according to Marvell and Moody (1997), including the greater emphasis on incapacitation, the impact of the 'war on drugs', and the fact that imprisonment rates increased for older age groups in this period.

The significance of looking at social demographic changes is that it raises the critical question, 'Who goes to prison?', and reminds us that the selection process is socially structured and that prison is a punishment that is reserved mainly for the poor and marginalised. There is also a second and related question concerning the impact of imprisonment on the lives of individual offenders, their families and their neighbourhoods. In general, prisoners have few academic qualifications, poor work histories and limited skills. They also tend to have a background of social and economic exclusion, and around 70 per cent suffer from two or more mental disorders (see Table 5.1).

Jeffery Reiman, in his classic publication *The Rich Get Richer and the Poor Get Prison* (2004), argues that the criminal justice system conspicuously fails to eliminate crime but instead creates an identifiable group of 'criminals' drawn predominantly from poor and marginalised groups whose incarceration serves an ideological as well as repressive function. The ideological function, he maintains, is to reassure 'respectable' society that they are being protected while reinforcing the notion that crime is mainly an activity engaged in by the poor, thereby diverting attention away from the transgressions of the rich and powerful. At every stage

Table 5.1 Characteristics of the prison population in England and Wales

Characteristic	General population	Prisoners
Ran away from home as a child	11%	47% of male sentenced prisoners and 50% of female sentenced prisoners
Taken into care as a child	2%	27% (those who had been in care also had longer criminal careers on average)
Has a family member convicted of a criminal offence	16%	43% (35% had actually been in prison)
Regularly truanted from school	3%	30%
Excluded from school	2%	49% male and 33% of female sentenced prisoners excluded from school
Left school at 16 or younger	32%	89% of men and 84% of women
Attended a special school	1%	23% of male and 11% female sentenced prisoners
Have no qualifications	15%	52% men and 71% women
Numeracy at or below Level 1 (the level expected of an 11-year-old)	23%	65%
Reading ability at or below Level 1	21–23%	48%
Writing ability at or below Level 1	No direct comparison	82%
Suffer from two or more mental disorders	5% men 2% women	72% male sentenced prisoners 70% female sentenced prisoners
Suffer from three or more mental disorders	1% men 0% women	44% male sentenced prisoners 62% female sentenced prisoners
Drug use in previous year	13% men 8% women	66% male sentenced prisoners 55% female sentenced prisoners (in year before imprisonment)
Hazardous drinking	38% men 15% women	63% male sentenced prisoners 39% female sentenced prisoners (in year before imprisonment)

Source: Social Exclusion Unit (2002).

of the process, Reiman argues, the criminal justice and prison system targets the poor while weeding out the rich. From framing the laws, to the use of police discretion, to the quality of legal representation and the decision-making of the judiciary, the activities of the poor and powerless are more systematically and intensely regulated. At the same time, the 'crimes of the powerful', which are often more socially damaging, are largely ignored or dealt with outside of the criminal justice system. The repressive function of imprisonment is achieved through the segregation of a selected group of offenders, which serves as a reminder to the working class of the potential consequences of non-conformity.

Reiman also points to the significance of race when addressing the question of who goes to prison. The fact that over 40 per cent of inmates in state and federal prisons in the US are African Americans and 20 per cent are Hispanic suggests that, alongside class, race forms part of the explanation of prison growth. Although it is often difficult to disentangle class and race, since a significant proportion of African Americans and Hispanics come from the poorer and more marginalised sectors of society, there does appear to be a significant racial dynamic operating in relation to the criminal justice system (see Chapter 9). There is also a considerable body of research that suggests that different forms of racial discrimination operate at the various stages in the criminal justice process, while at the sentencing stage, racial discrimination operates to the disadvantage of certain ethnic minority groups (Austin *et al.*, 2001; Bowling and Phillips, 2002; Bright, 2003; Hood, 1992; Tonry, 1995). In England and Wales, African Caribbeans currently account for one in six of all inmates, and one in a hundred black British adults were in prison in 2003.

In Europe, a disproportionate number of foreign nationals are incarcerated. In countries like France, Greece, Germany and Italy, around 20–30 per cent of the prison population is made up of foreign nationals. Significantly, in Switzerland it is estimated that around 70 per cent of prisoners do not have a residence permit. Indicatively, foreign prisoners tend to serve their time in high-security prisons because of the 'flight risk', while Swiss prisoners are more likely to serve their time in open prisons (Stephens, 2006). Although the numbers of foreign prisoners incarcerated in England and Wales is lower than in most other European countries, the numbers are steadily rising. Between 1994 and 2004 there was a 55 per cent increase in the number of British nationals in prison and a 152 per cent increase in foreign nationals, with the consequence that one in eight of the people in prison in England and Wales are foreign nationals (Lyon, 2006).

In recent years, attention has turned from questions about the general population to a focus on the spatial distribution of certain groups. US research has found that in some neighbourhoods, up to 25 per cent of adult male residents are locked up on any given day (Clear *et al.*, 2001). Eric Cadora has mapped locations in Brooklyn, New York, to identify where prisoners come from (Dobkin, 2005: Wagner, 2005). He found that the locations that prisoners were drawn from are highly concentrated, and calculated that on the basis that each prisoner cost the state $30,000 a year to incarcerate, that there were 35 blocks with at least 33 people who had been sent to prison over a period of a year, and consequently he has called these the 'million dollar blocks'. Related research, also based in New York, has shown that in the 1980s some seven community board districts accounted for over 70 per cent of the state's prisoners. In the period 1990–96, the rates of incarceration in these locations either increased or remained stable (Fagan, 2004). There is, it would seem, an area effect on incarceration levels through a combination of a number of factors, including poverty, lack of legitimate opportunities, poor education and training, and a breakdown of informal controls.

The demise of the welfare state?

For the most part, the twentieth century involved an essentially bifurcated system of crime control. This involved exclusionary strategies, on one hand, in the form of incarceration, and more inclusive community-based welfare-orientated strategies, on the other. In the postwar period, however, the Keynesian welfare state has come under attack from all sides. It was deemed to be too expensive and too intrusive, and that, rather than addressing crime and other social problems, it was accused of creating dependency and fostering pathologies. As a consequence, the Keynesian welfare state, which once proudly boasted that it would look after people from 'the cradle to the grave', has been subject to reorganisation and review. In light of these changes, some criminologists, such as Loic Wacquant (2001a), have argued that the re-expansion of the prison is a more or less direct consequence of the retrenchment of the 'welfare state', which is rapidly being replaced by a 'penal state'.

One such account is presented by Katherine Beckett and Bruce Western (2001), who claim that welfare and incarceration operate as two sides of the same 'policy regime' aimed at the governance of social marginality. To test this hypothesis they examine changing levels of welfare expenditure in different states and compare them to changing imprisonment rates. Their findings, with certain qualifications, appear to confirm their hypothesis, and they claim that, based on 1990s evidence, those states with less generous welfare programmes feature significantly higher incarceration rates, while those with more generous programmes incarcerate a smaller share of their residents.

While it is the case that a significant proportion of people in prison have slipped through the social welfare net or have been subject to the inadequacy of welfare provision, as in the case of closing of mental hospitals (Davies, 2004; Human Rights Watch, 2003), the analysis presented by Beckett and Western and others falls into the twin traps of empiricism and functionalism. Empiricists assume that because two phenomena co-vary, they can demonstrate or imply causation. Thus the research task involves gathering data on regularities and repeated occurrences. However, as critical realists argue, what causes something to happen has nothing to do with the number of times it has been observed happening or the degree of covariance (Sayer, 2000).

Closely related to the deficiencies of empiricism are the limitations of functionalism. The suggestion by Wacquant (2005), for example, that the welfare state is gradually being replaced by a penal state is based on a hydraulic model of social change where a decrease in the pressure on one side is seen to result in an increase in pressure on the other. As with empiricism, this form of mechanical functionalism ignores or downplays the causal connections involved. Thus Wacquant expresses the relation in the following terms:

> The grotesque overdevelopment of the penal sector over the past three decades is indeed the necessary counterpart to the shrivelling of the welfare sector, and the joining of remnants of the dark ghetto with the penitentiary is the logical compliment of the policy of the criminalisation of poverty pursued by the countries' authorities. Just as in other societies, the discourses that seek to connect crime and punishment in America have no value other than ideological. (Wacquant, 2005: 21)

In fact, there are two dimensions to Wacquant's functionalism. On one side, the decline in welfare is mechanically linked to the growth of imprisonment; on the other, he claims the prison has become the new surrogate ghetto (Wacquant, 2000). Wacquant suggests that the segregation of African Americans was a product of state regulation but that with the expansion of a neo-liberal market economy that African Americans are systematically being criminalised and imprisoned. But why would a more market-orientated economy want to take on the huge cost of incarcerating and taking responsibility for poor African Americans – not to mention Hispanics who are less ghettoised – when they could have been left in the ghettos to support and protect themselves. This type of analysis explains neither why the dominant mode of control of these groups is imprisonment nor why ethnic minority groups in Europe who have not been ghettoised make up a disproportionate number of prisoners in most countries.

In general, however, there are a number of issues that arise when examining the claim that changing welfare expenditure leads to the expansion of the 'penal state'. First, the nature, effectiveness and impact of the welfare sanction is not simply a function of the degree of expenditure that different states commit to in any period. In fact, the evidence from the US and the UK suggests a more complex change in the form of welfare expenditure, and indeed in the nature of the welfare state itself. One of the problems in comparing expenditures is that demographic shifts, employment levels, changing age structures and health of the population can all impact upon welfare budgets. Moreover, as David Greenberg (2001) has pointed out, in states like California, welfare expenditure increased rather than decreased between 1981 and 1997, as the prison population rose by a factor of four. While there has been a considerable increase in the amount spent on prisons in the US over the past two decades, there has also been an overall growth of welfare expenditure in the US and the UK. In fact, the degree of welfare state retrenchment in America over the last two or three decades has been frequently overstated (de Koster *et al.*, 2008). There have no doubt been cuts in certain forms of expenditure and recurring fiscal crises, but where retrenchment has occurred it has been pursued cautiously, mainly because there is considerable public support for the continuation of welfare programmes (Pierson, 1994). Although there has been a continuation in the growth of welfare spending in both the UK and the US, there has been a significant reconfiguration in the terrain of welfare state politics. Increasingly, welfare expenditure has become more targeted in response to claims concerning wastefulness of welfare funding, while the criteria for eligibility has also been modified in most countries. Rather than dismantling the welfare state, however, these changes have tended to involve both the extension and the decentralisation of state power (Harris and McDonald, 2000). It is the distribution of welfare that has changed, with health and medical budgets growing enormously in the US in recent years, as well as the benefits given to the increasing number of older people. At the same time, expenditures on family assistance have declined, while housing and education budgets have increased slowly in the US during the 1980s and 1990s.

Second, there has been a great deal of recent literature which has addressed the changing nature of the welfare state. However, rather than simply decline or disappear, much of this literature suggests that the old-style Keynesian welfare state has been replaced by a mixed economy and the emergence of a 'workfare' state in which the state is less concerned with meeting needs and tackling hardships and more preoccupied with creating conditions which will ensure international competitiveness in the global economy (Jessop, 1994). Although the official rhetoric in recent years claims that governments are 'rolling back the state', the fact is that new forms of mixed economy actually *extend* state power through new forms of contracting. Such developments represent a reconfiguration and dispersal of state power rather than a reduction (Crawford, 2006; Harris and McDonald, 2000).

A third and related point is that while a central feature of imprisonment was the discipline of labour, the welfare sanction has historically been focused on the process of socialisation, improving the health of the poor and the *quality* of labour power. Thus welfarist and penal strategies are not simply two sides of the same 'policy regime', but have different objectives and employ different strategies and techniques (Garland, 1985).

Fourth, probably the most significant shift over the last 20 years has not been the replacement of the welfare state by the penal state but the expansion of the punishment–welfare continuum and the blurring of the boundaries at certain points between the two (Cohen, 1985). Thus, rather than see a transition from inclusive to exclusive forms of social control, as some have suggested, what we have seen over the past two decades in both the US and the UK has been the simultaneous expansion of community-based sanctions and forms of custody. Just as the prison population in the US has quadrupled, so has the number of offenders subject to probation and parole. That is, between 1980 and 2000, the total number of people on probation in the US increased from 1.1 million to 3.8 million, while those on parole increased from 220,000 to nearly 726,000. Thus, in the US in 2000, twice as many individuals were under some form of non-custodial community-based supervision rather than in prison (Bureau of Justice, 2008). A similar development has occurred in the UK, with the prison population increasing from just over 61,000 in 1997 to just under 80,000 in 2007, while the numbers under a probation supervision order increased from 184,627 to 242,742 over the same period, representing a similar percentage increase (Ministry of Justice, 2008a).

In sum, although there may be links between the changing levels and forms of welfare provision and the growth of incarceration, the causal mechanisms remain to be identified. Indicatively, Beckett and Western (2001) resort to regression analysis in an attempt to inject some rigour into their investigation, but no amount of statistical manipulation can overcome weak conceptualisation.

The politics of crime and punishment

In conjunction with his claims that the welfare state is being replaced by a penal state, Wacquant (2001a, 2001b) also claims that welfare state retrenchment is a function of the growth of neo-liberal policies involving forms of deregulation. In this neo-liberal market-orientated world, Wacquant argues that prisons have become a major institution for maintaining social order. He sees neo-liberalism as being developed in the US and subsequently disseminated throughout Europe and elsewhere, albeit involving different forms of adaptation.

The development of neo-liberalism is closely associated in the US and the UK with the Thatcher–Reagan era of the 1980s. During this period, both leaders advocated free market principles, and forms of privatisation and deregulation. They both oversaw large prison-building programmes, with the Thatcher government overseeing the largest prison-building programme in the UK since Victorian times. Paradoxically, however, the Thatcher government sent fewer people to prison towards the end of the 1980s than had been sent at the beginning of the decade. This was partly a function of the decarceration of juveniles, on one hand, and the desire to reduce costs, on the other. Consequently, the Thatcher era was described by one penal reformer as 'one of the most remarkably progressive periods of juvenile policy' (Rutherford, 1995). The Thatcher government also oversaw the deployment of the amnesties that allowed the early release of thousands of prisoners. Significantly, in the UK, the replacement of the Conservative government with New Labour in 1997, with its 'mixed economy' and 'third way' strategies, did not halt the growth of imprisonment or stop the development of private prisons, as had been promised prior to their election. In fact, although New Labour have been largely apologetic in relation to the continued growth in the prison population, the political shift seems to have had little impact on the trajectory of imprisonment in England and Wales.

Theodore Caplow and Jonathan Simon (1999) have suggested that the increased use of imprisonment in the US transcends party politics and even different political configurations and argue that crime control is an issue which has become an essential part of modern governmental policies with the consequence that politicians and policy-makers increasingly 'govern through crime'. The growing disillusionment with welfare programmes, they argue, coupled with a shift away from traditional forms of class conflict has created a new political focus centred around values, morality, identity and risk. While suggesting that a major factor in the politicisation of crime control in the US was the 'war on drugs' in the 1980s, they argue that the tendency to use crime control as a vehicle of social control has increasingly become part of the repertoire of politicians and the media alike.

Jonathan Simon has elaborated this thesis more extensively in his book *Governing Through Crime* (2007), and argues that in a period of globalisation, 'law and order' is one area in which the state can exercise its authority and galvanise public opinion and support. Simon argues that the greater focus on the issue of crime, coupled with a growing fear of crime, has refashioned the normative structures of democratic society, incorporating not just the public realm, but also schools, the family and the workplace. Mass imprisonment, he argues, is the outcome of the increasing political preoccupation with crime, while also serving as a visible mechanism for responding to crime. In this context, prisons become warehouses or 'penal dustbins' and policy-makers and politicians are no longer interested in reforming or disciplining individuals, but simply want to incapacitate them. At this point, Simon's 'governing through crime' thesis dovetails with the influential thesis presented in his seminal article on the 'New Penology' written with Malcolm Feeley (1992). In that article, Feeley and Simon claim that prisons are moving away from the goal of reforming individual offenders and towards the management of the 'underclass', and that this involves a shift from rehabilitation to incapacitation.

Like the 'New Penology' thesis, the 'governing through crime' thesis provides a powerful and provocative analysis which undoubtedly captures some of the critical changes in the nature of social regulation in contemporary society. The policing of schools and families and the prominent role that the issue of crime has played during the 1980s and early 1990s are no doubt significant developments. However, there are some serious limitations to the 'governing through crime' thesis, both in relation to its general explanation of changes in crime control, and in particular in relation to the growth of imprisonment. Three major limitations may be noted. First, although crime represented a major point of reference in the 1980s and the first half of the 1990s, it has gradually slipped down the political and public agenda. In the 2004 and 2008 US presidential elections, reference to crime was muted and the focus shifted towards 'moral issues' such as abortion. Similarly, in the UK, crime received less attention as a campaigning issue in the last general election as well as featuring less prominently in public opinion polls.

Second, and relatedly, there is a suggestion that we are moving toward a 'pre-crime' society which is less interested in responding to crime after the event, but is more concerned with preventing and deflecting crime, while becoming more preoccupied with the broader issue of security (O'Malley, 2004). Indeed, Lucia Zedner (2007) has argued that we are moving away from a form of social control centred around crime and punishment to the anticipation and prevention of 'hazards' in the pursuit of 'security' in its various forms. This involves the generation of a wider and more varied range of concerns that have preoccupied criminology for the last 150 years. Interestingly, Zedner's 'pre-crime' thesis has some affinity with the 'New Penology' presented by Feeley and Simon which suggests that we are moving towards the management of risk rather than the control of crime and the orchestration of punishment.

Third, over the past two decades or so there has been a growing political and public preoccupation with what are often referred to as 'lifestyle' issues such as obesity, health, nutrition and clothing. In recent years there has been a significant increase in attention paid to these issues by the media, exemplified by an increasing preoccupation with the selection, preparation and consumption of food; this, in turn, is often associated with environmental issues. Similarly, styles of consumption and self-presentation are becoming central points of reference for both self-identity and the identification of social cleavages and divisions (Hayward and Yar, 2006).

While the political remains an important element of the debate on crime and punishment, we should be cautious about reading off policies from general political programmes. Politics is full of tensions and contradictions. However, what is interesting is that not only does 'law and order' seem to have slipped down the political agenda over the past few years, but there are very few politicians of any political persuasion in the UK, at least, who are claiming that 'prison works' or who are advocating prison expansion. Although we hear a great deal about security and terrorism, we hear less and less about crime, and the voices of the early 1990s that called for more prisons are now conspicuously silent. For the most part, politicians announce the building of new prisons apologetically and increasingly feel obliged to justify the expenditure. In the US there is an increasingly heated debate about the building of new prisons, particularly when it is seen to be taking funds away from the building of schools and other public services (Currie, 1998; Pew Center on the States, 2008).

Populist punitiveness

One of the most significant developments in recent years is what Anthony Bottoms (1995) describes as 'populist punitiveness', and what John Pratt (2007) refers to as 'penal populism'. In essence, these terms refer to a process in which politicians and the general public are seen to have moved towards the formation of increasingly punitive responses to crime, either to win votes or as a response to the increasing uncertainties and insecurities of modern life. This type of explanation involves a form of voluntarism in which social change is seen to be driven by individual or collective wills, decisions, attitudes or choices. These 'punitive' attitudes, Pratt argues, play a major part in pushing up prison populations by creating a demand for longer and harsher sentences of imprisonment in various countries, including the US, the UK and New Zealand (Garland, 2001; Simon, 2001; Wacquant, 2001a, 2001b).

The drift towards what is described as populist punitiveness or penal populism is seen to involve a qualitative change in policy. According to Pratt:

> [Overall, then,] penal populism involves a dramatic reconfiguration of the axis of penal power, with the strategic effect of reversing many of the previous assumptions that had hitherto informed post war policy. There should thus be more prisons rather than fewer; punishment should be turned into a public spectacle rather than take the form of a bureaucratic accomplishment hidden from public view; popular commonsense should be prioritized over the expert knowledge of criminal justice officials. By the same token, because of the much closer linkages between governments and those individuals and organizations who claim to speak on behalf of the public at large, and the much weaker linkages between governments and their own bureaucratic advisors, there is now a much greater likelihood of this collection of ideas being translated into policy. (Pratt, 2007: 35)

Thus, according to Pratt, penal populism represents a major transformation in the power to punish in which the general public and their representatives have a greater involvement in policy-making, as the old professional elites fall into disfavour. The public, it is suggested, have more say in issues of crime control, and this is reflected in the greater emphasis on crime victims and the loss of rights by defendants, as well as the public becoming increasingly viewed as an important point of reference by policy-makers. It is also claimed that it is not only the poor and the powerless who have become more punitive, but also the professional middle classes (Brown, 2006; Garland, 2001). In an increasingly globalised but fragmented world, the mass media is seen to play a prominent role in both shaping and expressing public opinion. The mass media conveniently divides the population into victims and offenders, the moral and the pathological, the respectable and the deviant. Through this form of categorisation, the media, it is suggested, encourages the process of 'othering', whereby social and personal distance is put between respectable people ('us') and the deviants ('them'), which allows the proliferation of more punitive policies. The mass media together with new forms of media technology opens the way for new modes of communication and the more extensive dissemination of knowledge. The process of democratisation is held to provide the opportunity for ordinary people to express their opinions more readily, through phone-ins, internet exchanges and emails. The once 'silent majority' are no longer silent, but are able, through the ready availability of the new media, to actively express their views on crime, punishment and other social issues. A consequence of the rise of penal populism, it is argued, is that the once relatively benign and liberal attitudes towards minor criminals, young people and women are increasingly being eclipsed by policies that are more punitive, more intrusive and more repressive, such that they include not just crime but also antisocial behaviour and disorder.

The difficulty that arises in relation to the populist punitiveness thesis is that, while it is no doubt the case that the public have become more involved in commenting on issues such as crime – although less involved regarding prisons and punishment – there remains a question of the extent to which the general public are actually influential in shaping policy. In most cases the public are 'consulted' at best, which means that either their views can be ignored or that they can be used to provide legitimation for policies that are already decided. At the same time, the notion that there has been a decrease in the number or influence of professional elites is mistaken. What we have seen in recent years has been the proliferation of teams of 'experts' as the crime control industry expands in the public sector not only at the national level, but also increasingly at the local level, as well as in the private sector. Some may wear T-shirts and trainers, but they still operate as professional experts in their field.

We also have to question the notion that popular opinion is necessarily punitive. Understanding and making sense of public attitudes is methodologically and conceptually very difficult, but the more rigorous and competent research on public attitudes towards crime and punishment indicates that they tend to be ambivalent (Durham, 1993; Hancock, 2004; Hutton, 2005). A study carried out for the Home Office Sentencing Review found that:

> The most common response by members of the public to the open-ended question: 'What should sentencing achieve?' do not include the words 'punish', 'deterrence' or 'rehabilitation' terms generally taken to summarise the objectives of punishment. The most common responses are 'stop offending', 'reduce crime' or 'create a safer community' without any explanation as to how sentencing might achieve this outcome. People are not generally wedded to a particular philosophy of punishment: they just want something done that changes offenders' behaviour. (Morgan, 2002: 221)

This finding not only expresses the incongruity of meaning between members of the general public and criminologists, but also captures the variability and diversity of public attitudes. It suggests that both policy-makers and criminologists persistently misperceive public views on crime control. There is also a related issue about the formation of these diverse responses and the role of the mass media. While it is no doubt the case that the media is preoccupied with 'law and order' issues, its message is not uniform; rather, it involves the expression of a range of viewpoints (Mason, 2003). A review of the national newspaper coverage of prisons in the UK would reveal that while tabloids express scepticism about the value of imprisonment and complain about the expense of prisons, the broadsheets consistently criticise government policy on prisons and sentencing and are critical of both overcrowding and prison-building programmes; they are generally sceptical of the contribution of private prisons and subscribe to a reductionist agenda. In fact, neither the tabloids nor the broadsheets have much to say that is positive about imprisonment, except when it comes to locking up high-profile killers and sex offenders.

The claim that the general public and politicians are becoming more punitive seems to be at the least overstated. The concept of 'punitiveness' is not clearly defined, and within the debate there is a tendency to describe virtually all forms of crime control as being in some way 'punitive' (Matthews, 2005). While it is not hard to find specific examples of punitiveness, it is hard to see it as a guiding or dominant policy. Indeed, it is the case that there is little public or political support for the expansion of imprisonment. It is difficult to find anyone these days, of whatever political persuasion, who is arguing for prison expansion or claiming that prisons work. There are a number of penal strategies in play besides punitiveness that shape the use of imprisonment, and one of these involves new forms of managerialism.

New managerialism

Closely associated with the drift towards neo-liberalism and the sustained critique of the welfare state has been the development of what is referred to as the new managerialism or the New Public Management (NPM). This involves the introduction of market principles into state agencies, which centre around the construction of measurable targets and outputs, often in association with the use of performance indicators. NPM involves the cultivation of new forms of expertise and has spawned not only a new set of priorities, but also a new vocabulary amongst criminal justice practitioners and policy-makers, with a focus on 'what works', 'best practice', 'mainstreaming', 'performance management', and the like. It also involves a form of depoliticisation through the deployment of evidence-based approaches that are presented as morally neutral and which frequently draw on risk analysis and actuarial techniques (Feeley and Simon, 1992).

NPM techniques and the associated language have increasingly permeated the criminal justice system and are seen as a strategy for breaking down the bureaucratic inefficiency of the public sector while at the same time introducing greater flexibility and competitiveness (McLaughlin and Murji, 2001). It is seen as a modernising discourse and a way of making criminal justice agencies more 'businesslike', flexible and accountable. In relation to the penal sphere, NPM has deeply affected not only how prisons are run, but also how decision making is carried out. NPM is widely practised in privately run prisons, and this style of management has gradually influenced the running of state prisons (Greene, 2002). The increased influence of NPM within the penal system is also evident in parole decisions. It has been suggested that parole boards under the influence of NPM have become more risk-averse, with the consequence that a lower proportion of parole applicants were given parole in the 1990s than was expected. In addition, it has been suggested that the new system of decision making and assessment in relation to parole is even less transparent than the old system (Hood and Shute, 2000).

In some of the literature these new managerialist practices have been seen as an example of the 'new punitiveness'. However, this proposition confuses outcomes with motivation. Although the pursuit of 'targets' necessarily involves an element of enforcement, the motivation in the new managerialism is a function of the desire to realise 'outputs' rather than the desire to inflict pain or suffering on 'clients'. NPM presents itself as morally neutral in this respect and is driven by different imperatives from the desire to be vindictive or cruel. It is more likely that motivation is linked to the realisation of performance indicators, as job security may well depend on achieving set targets (Brownlee, 1998).

Probably the most significant example of the effects of NPM on imprisonment has been through the more rigorous enforcement of the conditions of community-based punishments, particularly parole. It is estimated that approximately one in three admissions to US prisons is a result of parole violation. Joan Petersilia (2003) suggests that this significant development is in part due to the increased workloads of parole officers, as well as the changing nature of those given parole. However, the change in the level of parole revocations is also a consequence of significant change in the practice of parole officers:

> Historically, parole officers were viewed as paternalistic figures, who mixed authority with help. Officers provided direct services (for example, counselling) and also knew the community and brokered services (for example, job training) for needy offenders. As noted earlier, parole was originally designed to make the transition from prison to the community more gradual, and during this time, parole officers were to assist the offender in addressing personal problems and searching for employment and places to live. Many parole agencies still do assist in these service activities. Increasingly, however, parole supervision has shifted away from providing services to parolees and more towards providing surveillance activities, such as drug testing, monitoring curfews and collecting restitution. (Petersilia, 2003: 88)

A greater number of conditions are being imposed upon parolees, and parole officers are coming under increased pressure to monitor and enforce these conditions. There is also a reduction in housing and social support in many areas, and it is not surprising that, in the US, two-thirds of all prisoners are re-arrested and nearly a quarter are returned to prison for a new crime within three years of release (Langan and Levin, 2002).

According to Petersilia (2003), parolees may be returned to prison for either committing new crimes or failing to comply with the conditions of their parole. The number of offenders reincarcerated for violating parole or other release conditions has doubled in the US, from 17 per cent in 1980 to 35 per cent in 1999. In some states, such as California, the figures are even more dramatic, with 66 per cent of all persons admitted to state prisons being parole violators in 1999, while 70 per cent of inmates reported that their parole was revoked because of an arrest or conviction for a new offence, 22 per cent said that they had absconded or otherwise failed to report to a parole officer; 16 per cent said that they had a drug-related violation; and 18 per cent reported other reasons, such as the failure to maintain employment or to meet financial obligations. Indeed, the impact of prisoner re-entry in the US as a result of parole violation has become widely recognised as making a major contribution to the number of prison admissions in the US, and without this input, the level of admissions in some states, at least, would be in decline (Blumstein and Beck, 1999).

In a similar vein, but on a much smaller scale, the more active enforcement of criminally based sanctions has become a feature of the criminal justice system in England and Wales. Speaking in the language of the new managerialism, a thematic inspection report on the enforcement of community penalties published in 2007 reflects the changing concerns of those who manage the UK's probation service, the courts and the police (Home Office, 2007). The report calls for more rigorous enforcement of those who break the conditions of their community penalties and expresses alarm at the fact that 'some staff took no action against some offenders even though there was clear evidence of unacceptable absences'. In another Home Office report, *Rebalancing the Criminal Justice System in Favour of the Law Abiding Majority* (2006b), it is made clear that breaches of community penalties will be more strenuously enforced and will attract additional sanctions including imprisonment.

Although the main emphasis of managerialism is on increasing efficiency, it is often overlooked that this mode of regulation can create a mountain of paperwork, and endless forms of monitoring and assessment which can detract from the front-line work of many criminal justice agencies. It tends to create a work culture in which only that which can be measured counts, and tends to be more concerned with 'outputs' rather than 'outcomes'. That is, to fulfil set objectives, certain administrative targets need to be met, but this does not necessarily involve any change of conditions or practices. For example, the use of performance indicators can direct the police to focus on those crimes that are amongst their designated targets and to ignore those that are not. Moreover, working in relation to performance indicators can lead criminal justice agencies to focus on those activities that are accessible and manageable, while decreasing attention paid to other forms of crimes that may be more difficult to identify or to clear up (Cheliotis, 2006). However, the use of targets and performance indicators does not invariably have negative or undesirable effects. Targets can be established to reduce reconviction rates and prison populations, to increase detections, and to reduce court delays, and the like. Thus it is not so much the pursuit of specific targets which in themselves may be quite commendable, but the work culture and style of management and associated practices that the new managerialism creates that causes difficulties and often produces unexpected and undesirable consequences (Prime *et al.*, 2002).

Cultural variations

One of the most perplexing problems for those who believe that the growth of the prison population is due to the demise of the welfare state, the rise of neo-liberalism, the surge of populist punitiveness or the emergence of new forms of managerialism in advanced Western countries, is that there are a number of countries that have experienced some or all of these changes but whose prison population has remained stable or even decreased. These countries include Canada, Ireland, Finland, Sweden, Germany and Japan (Garland, 2006; Hinds, 2005; Pratt, 2008a; Tonry, 2001).

The observation that the use of imprisonment seems to operate with a degree of independence from the prevailing changes in economic conditions and political directives has encouraged some criminologists to examine the role of cultural processes in shaping attitudes towards punishment in general and the use of imprisonment in particular. In relation to the changing use of imprisonment in Italy, for example, David Nelken (2005) has argued that Italy can be considered to be a 'non-punitive society', particularly in relation to juveniles. Differences in religious makeup, family structure and attitudes towards youth in general produce a very different response to young people. There is, Nelken reports, an absence of 'moral panics' around youth, while juvenile incarceration has decreased significantly in recent years, except for foreigners. Judges and prosecutors have a larger role in defining the crime problem, whereas the police are given little chance to act as spokespeople. Victims are rarely the focus of concern, and it remains the 'state' rather than the 'community' that vindicates itself through the criminal law. Nelken points out that penal policies are often complex and contradictory, with harsh policies directed towards certain types of offenders but more tolerant attitudes towards other groups. Moreover, there is an important distinction, he notes, between formal and informal sanctions, and that, even in countries where the former appear to be 'punitive', this may occur against a background of a relatively benign and tolerant system of informal sanctions. It may also be the case that changes in the 'culture of control' in relation to 'normal' crime may take a very different form from changes taking place in relation to corporate crime (Braithwaite, 2003). Moreover, Dario Melossi (2001), in his examination of the differential use of imprisonment in the US and Italy, has suggested that the different levels of incarceration in these countries is a function of the way in which 'cultural embeddedness' fashions conceptual and rhetorical toolkits that allow for the shaping of specific policy orientations.

It is also apparent that Canada has missed the 'punitive term', adopting a more liberal and 'balanced' set of values emphasising opportunity, diversity and inclusion, combined with a continuing belief in the benefits of therapeutic intervention (Doob and Webster, 2006; Moore and Hannah-Moffat, 2005). There is a focus on the 'special needs' of aboriginals, women and offenders serving long sentences that has spawned an array of specialist support services. There remains a commitment to rehabilitation and the targeting of needs. There is less use of mandatory sentences, which are reserved for the most serious crimes such as first- and second-degree murder, high treason, firearms offences and living off the avails of child prostitution. The prison population in Canada has decreased by about 10 per cent since the mid 1990s. In addition, capital punishment was abolished in 1976 and there is little evidence of 'penal populism'. From the Canadian perspective, the US response to crime is officially regarded as having failed. In particular, the use of mass incarceration has been seen as counterproductive. There is a valorised cultural image of Canada as a civilised and 'peaceable kingdom', often specifically contrasted with the US (Meyer and O'Malley, 2005; Doob and Webster, 2006).

In many respects, there is an element of *orientalism* in much of this literature in which we describe other societies in terms of their relevance to ourselves. As much of the literature on punitiveness has emanated from the US, it tends to reflect the experiences and concerns of American commentators. However, as Michael Tonry (2001) notes, much of the prevailing debate reflects aspects of American exceptionalism, which, he argues, has a number of elements. The first is that despite the 'crime drop', the US has significantly higher crime rates than most Western countries. Second, public opinion surveys indicate that there is public support for tougher penalties for certain offences. Third, the 'experiment' of mass incarceration reflects a widespread acceptance in the US of the use of incarceration as a way of dealing with social problems.

In many respects, the US stands apart from penal developments in Europe and Scandinavia, where cultural and political attitudes are significantly different and where the issue of 'law and order' is conceived of in very different terms (Pratt, 2008b). Thus seeing the US as the norm from which other Western countries 'deviate' is a serious mistake. While there may be similar processes at work in different countries that affect the scale of imprisonment, it is clear that different countries have different cultural orientations that affect their attitudes towards crime and punishment. To some extent, these cultural differences appear to be more influential than political differences in shaping penal policy.

Conclusion

There is widespread agreement amongst criminologists and sociologists that the nature of the welfare state is changing alongside political con-figurations. At the same time, it is evident that prison populations are increasing in a number of English-speaking countries. Consequently, there has been a tendency simply to claim that the growth of imprisonment is a function of these political shifts. Thus, rather than try to identify the causal processes involved, many of the recent accounts of the changing scale of imprisonment gravitate towards empiricism, functionalism or voluntarism. In many cases they try to read off developments in the use of imprisonment directly from changes in the political sphere. From this perspective a move towards conservative or neo-liberal politics is seen necessarily to involve the development of a 'get tough' approach, since forms of privatisation and deregulation are seen to 'require' more punitive forms of crime control. However, a detailed empirical examination of the effects of political shifts on crime and punishment produces a more uneven and contradictory picture. We have seen how the emergence of New Labour in the UK has done little to slow down the growth of imprisonment, as was expected. Rhetoric and reality become blurred, just as the distinctions between 'left' and 'right' become harder to identify. As politicians in many advanced Western countries seek the middle ground of politics and cross-party alliances become more pronounced, clear lines of demarcation become less visible. At the same time, it is clear that cultural attributes can play a significant role in shaping attitudes towards crime and punishment, and appear to serve, in some countries at least, to keep down imprisonment rates even when significant changes are taking place in the social, economic and political spheres.

6
Crime, Sentencing and Imprisonment

Introduction

The main aim of this chapter is to examine the 'interior' processes that operate within the criminal justice system that are seen to affect the use and scale of imprisonment. This will include a review of the relationship between crime and imprisonment, the operation of the sentencing process and the use of alternatives to custody. In doing so the initial aim is to dispel the current criminological contentions that there is no meaningful or causal relationship between the nature and level of crime and the scale of imprisonment. Given the widespread scepticism about the role of crime in influencing imprisonment rates, a significant number of criminologists have instead identified the sentencing process as having a major role in determining the scale of imprisonment (Jacobson *et al.*, 2008; Mauer, 2001). This contention, however, will also be subject to critical scrutiny and it will be suggested that sentencing policies may be less influential in relation to prison use than is often suggested. In this light, a review will be undertaken of recent attempts to limit the scale of imprisonment through the deployment of alternatives to custody and the use of different diversionary and early release mechanisms that have been designed to take the pressure off the prison system. Lastly, this chapter will present an alternative model which attempts to capture the dynamics of prison expansion and which provides a form of explanation that involves a combination of 'exterior' and 'interior' processes that work together to bring about changes in the scale of imprisonment.

The relation between crime and imprisonment

It seems glaringly obvious that if no one were convicted of crime there would be no one in prison. Therefore, it would seem to follow that if crime increases, prison rates would also increase. However, criminologists repeatedly point out that there is no one-to-one relationship between the size of the prison population and the crime rate and that the relationship is complex and uncertain. At this point graphs are often presented showing that in some countries prison populations tend to decrease while crime rates soar, while in other countries prison populations increase while crime rates drop (Blumstein and Wallman, 2000). The recent substantial decrease in the recorded number of offences and victimisation in the UK and the US, which has taken place alongside the simultaneous increase in prison populations in both countries, has persuaded many criminologists that the impact of crime rates on imprisonment is negligible, and as a consequence they have turned their attention increasingly to explanations based on changing sentencing policies and political shifts (King *et al.*, 2005). In this way criminologists have maintained, and indeed extended, the division of labour in criminology between those who focus on crime and those who focus on punishment, with the result that these areas of investigation remain relatively distinct. The corollary of the claim that there is no meaningful or discernable relationship between crime rates and the scale of imprisonment is that changes in the use of imprisonment will have no significant effect upon the crime rate. Although some criminologists are prepared to admit that the increased use of imprisonment can have a negative effect on the crime rate by decanting severely marginalised people back into the community, far fewer endorse the view that the increased use of imprisonment may reduce or prevent crime (Karmen, 2000; Spelman, 2000).

In order to unpack the relation between crime and imprisonment it is useful to begin by clarifying the relative contributions of Michel Foucault (1977) and Rusche and Kirchheimer (1939 [2003]) on this issue. The general thesis that emerges from these writers is that the *form* of punishment in general, and imprisonment in particular, is not given by the nature of offending but is the product of changing socio-economic conditions and changes in the nature of power. For Foucault it is not so much that crime gave birth to the prison, but rather that the prison provided the institutional and material basis for the creation of a new criminological subject – the delinquent. In the same way, Rusche and Kirchheimer demonstrated that changes in the scale of imprisonment is a function of the changing nature of productive relations rather than fluctuations in the crime rate. This does not mean, however, that the scale of imprisonment, in the short term, at least, is not affected by the level of offending, or the way in which cases are processed through the criminal justice system. Thus while changes in the dominant form of punishment may be a function of changing socio-economic conditions, changes in the level of what is considered to be 'serious' crime will have a more or less direct effect on a day-to-day basis on the size and composition of the prison population.

In moving between these levels of analysis it is important to avoid falling into the trap of empiricism that claims that because there is no significant correlation between crime rates and incarceration rates that there is no significant relation at all (Tonry, 1999). Moreover, even if crime rates and imprisonment rates could be shown to co-vary, it does not mean that changes in imprisonment are wholly caused by changes in crime. What is needed is a detailed empirical investigation that can identify the complexities of this relation and demonstrate the causal mechanisms in play (Sayer, 1992).

An examination of the relationship between crime and imprisonment must begin by a critical review of the definitions of 'crime' that are being used and the related measures that are employed. That is, whether to use police data on recorded crimes, or alternatively to use victimisation surveys (sometimes mistakenly referred to as 'crime surveys') because they include unreported incidents and are held therefore to give a more accurate picture of 'the dark figure of crime'. The reality is, of course, that victimisation surveys are no more accurate or reliable than police generated figures but are based on different information and consequently produce a different picture of 'crime'. In a similar way, prison data, although appearing at first sight to be a robust form of data is beset with a number of limitations, not least of which involves a general confusion between offenders and offences.

In relation to imprisonment it is also important to decide whether it is the number of receptions into custody or the average daily population that will be taken as the point of reference. Needless to say, official statistics on crime and imprisonment come with a health warning and have to be treated with extreme caution. However, if we want to carry out large-scale quantitative analysis we have little choice but to draw on official statistics.

If we are going to unpack the relation between crime and imprisonment it is necessary to begin by disaggregating the data and breaking the figures down into different offences involving different levels of seriousness. Clearly, there are a large number of relatively minor offences that may be dismissed or cases in which guilt cannot be determined. These incidents remain 'offences' and are not processed by the criminal justice process. On the other hand, there are those cases in which offenders are prosecuted and sent to the criminal court. In these cases where the offender is found guilty or admits the charge, the 'offence' can be counted as a 'crime'. If such crimes are considered serious – involving, for example, violence, sexual offences or murder – there is a reasonably high likelihood of a prison sentence being given. Therefore, if there is a significant rise in the number of recorded offences of serious violence it is reasonable to expect *ceteris paribus* that this will lead to a greater number of prosecutions and this in turn will lead to a greater use of imprisonment. As realist criminologists have argued, 'crime' is the outcome of both an action and a reaction. Offences do not become 'crimes' until they have been processed by the criminal justice system, or in cases where guilt is established or admitted (Lea, 1992; Matthews and Young, 1992). Thus while the relation between 'offences' and imprisonment is relatively distant and highly mediated, the relation between 'crime' and imprisonment is more direct – although only a percentage, of course, of those found guilty by criminal justice agencies are sent to prison. Thus there is a need to distinguish between offending, crime and victimisation. Although these processes are related, they are distinct, and treating them as synonymous, as many criminologists tend to do, leads to confusion about the nature of the relations involved.

Thus to examine this process in more detail we need to look at the attrition rates between different types of offences and the likelihood of these cases being processed through the various stages of the criminal justice process. In contrast to the claim that only a very small percentage of offenders ever end up in prison, it is apparent that when it comes to the processing of the more serious cases, a significant percentage of those convicted receive a prison sentence. Thus, if we examine Table 6.1 presented by David Farrington and Darrick Jolliffe (2005), we see that the proportion of those who have been convicted of offences such as assault, rape or murder who receive a prison sentence tends to be considerably higher than that given to those convicted of burglary and theft, while the average length of sentence will also tend to be considerably longer. Thus it is reasonable to assume that a significant increase in the number of arrests and prosecutions for offences like rape and murder will serve to increase the prison population. In particular it will tend to push up the average daily population since these offenders are likely to be given long sentences, although it may only have a marginal impact on the number of receptions into custody.

The criminal justice process has been described as a 'funnel' or a 'sieve' in which the number and type of outlets in the system will determine what percentage of offenders will end up in prison. There are a number of key elements of this 'funnel', starting with reported and recorded offences, the decision to arrest or to caution, the decision to prosecute and the number of convictions. Sentencing decisions form an important stage and the decision of whether to give a custodial or non-custodial sentence will obviously affect the scale of imprisonment. What is important therefore when examining these attrition rates is not just to compare the input (offences/offenders) and the output (prison) but also to examine over time how decision-making at each of these stages changes (see Blumstein and Beck, 1999; Fagan, 2004, for US data).

Just as it would be very surprising if changes in the level and seriousness of offending did not have some impact on incarceration rates, so it would be equally surprising if the greater use of imprisonment did not have an impact on the level of offending, both positive and negative. Through a combination of incapacitation, deterrence and rehabilitation there are likely to be changes in the capacity and motivation of offenders to commit further crimes, although the specific and cumulative effect of these penal strategies is notoriously difficult to measure (Zimring and Hawkins, 1995). Some American researchers have tried to estimate the impact of imprisonment on crime rates, and Marvell and Moody (1994), for example, have claimed that 'each additional state prisoner averted at least 17 index crimes on average, mostly larcenies', while Steven Levitt (1996) claimed that a 10 per cent increase in the prison population led to a 4 per cent decrease in index crimes. William Spelman (2000), in contrast, claims that the strategy of mass incarceration has been responsible for about a quarter of the decrease in recorded number of offences during the 1990s. From a British perspective, Roger Tarling (1993) has suggested that an increase of 25 per cent in the country's prison population would be needed to reduce the rate of crime by 1 per cent.

Drawing on these estimates and the presumed deterrent and inacapacitative effects of imprisonment led some criminologists during the 1990s to claim that 'prison works'. This phrase, which was coined by Charles Murray (1997), is based on the assertion that the use of imprisonment is an effective way to reduce crime. But as Elliott Currie has argued, it is not clear what the phrase 'prison works' actually means:

If the question is whether there are people in our society who must be put in prison to protect the public, it would be hard to find anyone who disagrees. Likewise, if the question is whether we can incapacitate *individual* offenders by locking them up for life, then there is also no controversy: of course we can. But when it comes to tougher questions – the kind we need to develop if we want to develop sensible policies against crime – the slogan turns out to be remarkably unhelpful. If, for

Table 6.1 Changes in crime and punishment in England and Wales, 1991–99 (adults)

	Burglary		Vehicle theft		Robbery		Assault		Rape		Homicide	
	1991	1999	1991	1999	1991	1999	1991	1999	1991	1999	1991	1999
Total offences recorded (000s)	1,372,036	1,241,581	520,117	326,973	183,582	345,994	628,258	585,949	–	–	–	–
Reported offences	1,001,659	772,782	512,835	309,348	86,651	105,198	299,679	346,379	–	–	–	–
Recorded offences	624,946	462,333	581,901	381,449	45,323	78,884	183,653	218,433	4,045	7,705	725	746
No. of persons convicted	18,851	16,387	22,837	15,430	4,841	5,626	45,513	33,861	537	601	448	516
No. sent to custody	7,169	3,228	4,440	3,381	4,085	6,962	6,962	9,985	511	582	338	474
Custody per 1,000 offenders	2.9	4.53	2.47	4.75	7.22	4.2	4.74	7.27	114.84	68.65	499.06	577.60
Average sentence length	17.2	19.3	6.6	8.3	40.90	40.00	17.8	14.0	58.0	76.5	216.6	179.9
Time served	8.0	10.2	2.8	4.2	20.4	23.0	8.2	7.3	29.5	48.8	95.2	104.7

Source: Adapted from Farrington *et al.*, (2004)

example, the question is whether a five year prison sentence 'works' better than a two year sentence, the answer is suddenly quite unclear. If the question is whether a two year mandatory prison sentence 'works' better for an addicted burglar than a course of drug treatment outside of the prison walls it is even less clear. If the question is whether marginal increases in incarceration of repeat non-violent offenders 'work' better than high quality prevention programs for at risk adolescents, it is increasingly clear that the answer is 'no'. (Currie, 1998: 55)

The real limitation of Murray's claim that 'prison works', as Currie points out, is that it is based on the assumption that the alternative to imprisonment is doing nothing. The more challenging questions about crime control are what the most effective forms of intervention are and how the use of imprisonment compares to the deployment of prevention strategies, the use of community-based sanctions or engaging in substantial forms of social investment.

Although it is the case that incarceration in general and mass incarceration in particular have some effect in preventing and deterring potential offenders, these claims should be treated with caution as critics have suggested that there are at least three important qualifications that should be attached to these figures. First, that any reductions in offending are likely to be short term and specific. Second, that any impact is more likely to be on more minor offences; and third, that the crime control effects of incarceration are likely to become smaller as the prison population increases in size (O'Sullivan and O'Donnell, 2003).

The problem is that imprisonment has little direct influence over the basic social conditions that are associated with offending. In fact, it is increasingly argued that through the tendency to create recidivists, the prison creates a 'revolving door' syndrome whereby offenders continually circulate between the prison and the community. Because certain poor and disadvantaged urban areas supply a disproportionate number of prisoners it means that some neighbourhoods experience particularly high rates of incarceration. The absence of breadwinners and parents, it is argued, can destabilise neighbourhoods because they lack the infrastrucure to sustain effective informal controls. Drawing on social disorganisation theory, Todd Clear (2002) argues that when incarceration reaches a certain level in an area that is already impoverished the effects of imprisonment can undermine the stability of the social order. In this way imprisonment can fuel local offending rates and contribute to the increased disparity between high- and low-crime areas, particularly in periods in which the number of recorded offences is decreasing.

Sentencing policy

The sentencing process is widely seen as the key to the control of the scale of imprisonment, since it is apparent that the size and composition of the prison population will be a function of the numbers of people sent to prison and the length of sentence imposed. This simple calculation will, of course, be moderated by the possible reductions in the period of time actually served, which will be influenced by the availability of parole and other early release mechanisms.

Recent research has examined the contribution of sentencing to the growth of imprisonment in England and Wales. Millie *et al.* (2003) claim, like many other criminologists, that 'it has nothing to do with crime trends or with court workloads' and suggest that the rise in the prison population is a consequence of an increase in the proportion of offenders sentenced to imprisonment and the length of time that they actually serve. They note that the custody rates for Magistrates Courts increased from 5 per cent to 28 per cent between 1991 and 2001; while, over the same period, the use of custody by Crown Courts rose from 46 per cent to 64 per cent. More recent sentencing statistics report a 25 per cent increase in the average sentence length for indictable offences in the Crown Court between 1995 and 2005 (Home Office, 2006a). These changes have been widely interpreted to suggest that sentencers are becoming more punitive.

In addition to changes in the average length of sentences, there are three general trends in sentencing practice in England and Wales that have become evident over the last decade. First, there has been a significant increase in the use of longer sentences, particularly those over four years and this is seen to have driven up the average daily population of people in prison in England and Wales. In particular, there has been an increasing commitment to imposing long sentences on violent and sexual offences (Easton and Piper, 2005). Second, there is tendency to hand out longer sentences to persistent offenders. Third, breaches of any order, civil or criminal, are being more rigorously enforced. Between 2000/01 and 2004/05 the number of prisoners recalled to custody increased from 3,182 to 11,081. This is an increase of over 350 per cent (HM Inspectorate of Prisons, 2005). In particular, the number of people given the new indeterminate sentences for 'serious' offences has risen sharply. Following the passing of the Criminal Justice Act 2003 a new sentence of 'imprisonment for public protection' was introduced in April 2005 for what are deemed to be serious offences, and it is estimated that approximately 145 people per month are subject to this sentence (Ministry of Justice, 2008a).

The question arises, however, as Millie *et al.* (2003) point out, as to whether the sentencers' greater use of custody is a consequence of defendants having longer criminal records or having committed more serious offences, on one hand, or whether sentencers have become more severe in their sentencing decisions, on the other. Having dismissed the possibility that the growth of imprisonment has anything to do with levels of offences recorded, the authors allow for only one possible conclusion. The real possibility within certain offence categories, particularly violence, that the nature of the offences has become more serious and extreme, is what the sentencers claim has been their experience. The authors, however, dismiss this out of hand in favour of an explanation that lays the blame on the sentencers themselves, who are accused of becoming more punitive. The authors claim that because the evidence is 'patchy and inconsistent', they must conclude through a 'process of elimination' that the growth of imprisonment in England and Wales is a result of tougher sentencing. The development of tougher sentencing is in turn a function, the authors maintain, of a more punitive climate of public opinion in relation to crime and punishment, together with changes in the legislative framework. Consequently their proposed policy of reform is to liberalise sentencing policy and educate the public in order to change the climate of public opinion on crime and punishment, while improving the understanding of the range of non-custodial penalties, among both sentencers and the wider public. This conclusion, however, seems to be based on a leap of faith rather than a balanced and detailed consideration of the evidence.

There are three points that arise from the analysis carried out by Andrew Millie and his colleagues. The first is that the increase in the use of custody may well be due to changes in the nature of the cases coming before the courts, particularly cases of violence fuelled by alcohol and drugs *as well as* changes in sentencing practice. This is not likely to be an either/or situation. Second, in the interviews with sentencers it was reported by the majority of respondents that the change in sentencing was a function of the more disturbing and extreme forms of offending coming before the courts. While not wanting to take the sentencers' opinion uncritically, it is a little strange that the views of the respondents who themselves are normally considered to be sensible and intelligent people are rejected out of hand, and one wonders why the researchers bothered to do the research in the first place. It seems a case of judgement first, evidence later. Third, there is considerable evidence that the authors do not fully explore the fact that the number of persistent offenders coming before the courts has been growing significantly in recent years. Most significantly, of all sentences given for indictable offences, the proportion given to offenders with 15 or more previous convictions or cautions has risen steadily from 17 per cent in 2000 to 25 per cent in 2007. In fact, for nearly every offence category the numbers of offenders with 15 or more previous convictions or cautions increased significantly between 1997 and 2007. For violence, the number with 15 or more convictions increased from 9 per cent to 19 per cent; for drug offences, from 12 per cent to 19 per cent; for burglary, from 22 per cent to 36 per cent; for robbery, from 12 per cent to 15 per cent; for theft and handling of stolen goods, from 22 per cent to 36 per cent; while for fraud and forgery and criminal damage, the percentage remained fairly stable (Ministry of Justice, 2008a). As it is the case that the 'cumulative principle' suggests that sentencers should get tougher on persistent offenders, an increase in the number of persistent offenders would in itself make a significant contribution to sentence lengths and probably to time served for this group (Ashworth, 1983; Wasik, 2004). This is an important point and needs further examination since, if the number of persistent offenders is increasing significantly, this in itself would suggest that the growth of imprisonment may have less to do with changes in the nature of offending or sentencers becoming more punitive, but rather be more a function of the routine application of the long-established principle that repeat offenders are to be punished more severely (Roberts, 2003).

An examination of the recent data on sentencing in England and Wales suggests another significant trend in sentencing (Ministry of Justice, 2008a). The available evidence indicates that over the period 1997–2007 a *bifurcated* process has been in operation in England and Wales, with the highest proportionate increases in numbers sentenced being for robbery, up by 58.3 per cent, and violence against the person, up by 21.8 per cent. The largest proportionate decreases have been for burglary, down by 25.6 per cent, and handling of stolen goods, down by 10.8 per cent. This has led to changes in the mix of offence types dealt with in the Crown Court. Between 1997 and 2007 the proportion of violence against the person offences increased from 16.5 per cent of Crown Court sentences to 21.4 per cent. Over the same period there were significant reductions in the proportion of sentences given for theft and burglary. At the same time there has been a steady increase in the use of community-based sentences, while the use of fines has decreased over the same period. These developments suggest that sentencing policy in England and Wales has become more differentiated and therefore it would be inappropriate to characterise it simply as 'getting tough' or as an expression of an undifferentiated 'punitiveness'.

As in the UK, there are considerable number of American criminologists who claim that tougher sentencing policies have been the main reason for the growth of imprisonment in the US (Mauer, 2001). In particular, the use of determinate and mandatory minimum sentences is seen as an important factor in this process. These sentencing policies were designed to make sentencing decisions more consistent and more certain by minimising the role of mitigating and situational factors when making sentencing decisions. In general, they were a response to what was seen as the inconsistencies of highly individualised sentencing practices and the use of indeterminate sentences. Whereas the aim of these sentencing policies was to introduce more rigour into the sentencing process, critics have argued that they have served to drive up the prison population. The concerns about the perceived effects of these sentencing options has been highlighted in relation to the highly publicised 'Three Strikes and You're Out' legislation that promised to 'get tough' on those repeatedly convicted of three serious felony offences (Zimring *et al.*, 2001; Shichor and Sechrest, 1996).

The general change of emphasis from consideration of mitigation and rehabilitation towards a more rigid 'just deserts' model of sentencing is seen to have affected the propensity to imprison, to have increased average sentence lengths and, in combination with so-called 'truth in sentencing' policies, to have increased the average period of incarceration (Ditton and Wilson, 1999). The 'war on drugs' during the 1980s combined with the increased use of determinate sentencing has been identified as the main reason for the rapid growth of imprisonment, which is often held to far outweigh offending rates as a contributing factor (Blumstein and Beck, 1999; Mauer, 2001; Tonry, 1995). Research evidence indicates that in America there has been an increase over the last two decades in the propensity to imprison, in the average lengths of sentences given out by the courts and in the length of time served. The cumulative impact of these developments is seen as the basis for the rapid expansion of the prison during the 1980s and 1990s (Blumstein *et al.*, 2005). However, these developments do not necessarily lead to the conclusion that sentencers in America are becoming more punitive.

In relation to recidivism, 67.6 per cent of those released from state and federal prisons in 1994 were rearrested within three years. This is an increase of 5 per cent on those released in 1983 (Beck and Shipley, 1989; Langan and Levin, 2002). The reconviction rate, however, has remained roughly stable over this period. Drawing on Langan and Levin's

Indeterminate sentencing involves a form of variable or open-ended sentencing, rather than for a fixed period. Often sentences are given for a minimum and maximum period and the actual time served will be dependent on good behaviour or individual reform.

Suspended sentencing refers to those sentences given by the court which are suspended or deferred for a set period of time during which if the person reoffends the original sentence can be reactivated. In 2005 the suspended sentence order was introduced in England and Wales and it replaced the fully suspended sentence.

Exemplary sentencing usually involves passing an unusually long sentence for a particular type of offence, either because it is seen to cause heightened social concern or because it is increasing. The aim is to send out a clear message and to deter prospective offenders.

Cumulative sentencing refers to the sentencing of persistent offenders making the sentence more severe on each conviction. This may involve a loss of mitigation or simply moving offenders up the 'tariff'. Either way, the result will be a more severe sentence, even if the offence committed on each occasion is considered to be of the same level of seriousness.

Determinate sentencing involved passing a sentence for a specified period, particularly for repeat offenders. Probably the best known example of this form of sentencing is the 'Three Strikes and You're Out' policy that requires the passing of a long sentence for a third felony offence.

Mandatory minimum sentencing sets a minimum period to be served for anyone convicted of a specified offence, despite individual circumstances.

Truth in sentencing, sometimes referred to as 'honest' or 'no frills' sentencing, requires that offenders serve a substantial portion of their prison sentence. Parole eligibility and other forms of early release are restricted or eliminated.

Sentencing guidelines create a range of sentences for a given offence and offender characteristics which judges can use when passing sentences in order to increase the consistency of sentences.

Figure 6.1   Sentencing options

(2002) data, other researchers have estimated the contribution of released offenders to re-arrests and have found that while the share of re-arrests among property offenders and drug offenders has increased significantly, the increase in relation to violence has been even higher (Hughes and Wilson, 2003). These data suggest that recidivism has almost certainly played a critical role in relation to re-arrests, reconviction and re-entry into prison and, as in the UK, that the increase in recidivism may itself account to some extent for the growth of imprisonment.

Despite the concerns that have been expressed about the use of determinate, mandatory minimum and truth in sentencing reforms recent reviews of the impact of these changes to sentencing policy suggest that their impact may have been more symbolic than practical, and that 'three strikes' legislation, for example, was only implemented in certain states and in most of the others already operated with sentencing policies that heavily punished serious repeat offenders. As James Austin and his colleagues have pointed out:

> The national movement towards three strikes and you're out legislation has been a symbolic campaign that has had little if any effect on the criminal justice system or public safety. With the noted exception of California, all of the States followed the initial lead of the State of Washington by carefully wording their legislative reforms to ensure that few offenders would be impacted by the law. Contrary to the perceptions of the public and policy makers, there are very few offenders who have a prior conviction for very serious crimes and then repeat the crime. In those rare instances that fit this profile, states already had the capacity to and were sentencing such offenders to very lengthy prison terms. (Austin *et al.*, 1999: 158)

It has become evident that sentencers maintained a considerable amount of discretion when passing sentence, and in fact these laws may well have served to extend rather than restrict the sentencing powers of the judiciary. It would appear that while 'three strikes' laws had some impact in relation to drug offenders, it seems to have had little impact on violent offences. It has also been claimed that 'truth in sentencing' has had little or no effect on incarceration (Sorensen and Steman, 2002). These findings suggest that the impact of sentencing policy on imprisonment may have been much less than is generally assumed. This conclusion reminds us of the need to distinguish policy from practice and rhetoric from reality when examining penal reform.

It is also interesting to note that while a great deal of emphasis has been placed on the role of the 'war on drugs' in relation to the growth of imprisonment, a closer examination reveals that, like the UK, while there has been an increase in the number of offenders incarcerated for drug-related offences, it is the increased proportion of offenders who have been imprisoned for violence that is the most significant change over the last decade. As James Jacobs (2001) has argued, the focus on the incarceration of drug offenders makes the process appear arbitrary, since many see drugs as a non-victim crime and the disproportionate focus on poor inner-city African American drug-users makes the use of imprisonment for this group appear discriminatory and overly punitive. However, when we discover that many of those behind bars in America have been imprisoned for violence we may take a different view. As Figure 6.2 indicates, prisoners convicted of violent offences make up over half of the prison population.

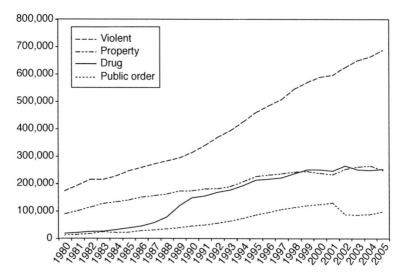

Figure 6.2   Prisoners in state prisons by offence type, 1980–2005

Source: Bureau of Justice (2007).

At the same time we should note that America has approximately 1 million non-violent offenders in prison (Irwin *et al.*, 1999). However, it has been pointed out that among these 'non-violent' offenders, about a third had a history of arrests for violent crime (Durose and Murnola, 2004). Moreover, as in the UK, a significant proportion of these offenders will have been imprisoned not so much as a result of the seriousness of their offence but because they are persistent offenders. Indeed, it is not enough to point out that a significant proportion of people are in prison for non-violent offences without considering the issue of persistence, since deflecting these minor offenders from prison will involve challenging the cumulative principle and the belief that those who repeatedly offend should be punished more severely.

Another way of looking at the relative 'punitiveness' of different countries is to examine cross-national sentencing practices. Significantly, there appears to be considerable agreement regarding the perceived seriousness of different types of offences and a degree of consistency in the responses to different types of crimes in most western countries.

Although the time served per conviction in America tends to be longer for most crimes than other Western countries, the time served for assault is roughly the same as in Australia and less than in Canada, and while for homicide the average time served in the US is significantly more than in other countries, it is less than in Australia. However, James Lynch (1983) has criticised the contention that time served in the US is longer than other nations and argues that when the type of crime is held constant, and the US jail population is included, time served for violent crime is similar to that in other Western countries, although differences persist for property crime. Interestingly, the comparative data on burglary and robbery in all eight countries found that the average sentence length hovered at around 40 months between 1980 and 1994, while for other offences there is considerable variation in sentence lengths and time served.

An interesting feature of this cross-national research is that some countries are more punitive in relation to certain types of offences and less punitive in relation to others. This observation suggests that public and official attitudes in different countries are varied and often ambivalent (Brown, 2006; Hutton, 2005; O'Malley, 1999). A cross-national survey conducted by Alfred Blumstein and his colleagues (2005) has produced some interesting results. They found, for example, that the average time served for a range of offences is generally longer in America than other countries. However, for homicide, the time served is greater in Australia than in America; while for assault, the time served in Australia and Canada is longer than in the US (see Table 6.2). In Canada, however, which has had a relatively stable prison population in recent years and is seen to have missed the 'punitive turn', the time served for homicide, robbery, residential burglary and assault is consistently longer on average than is the case in England and Wales which are widely seen as relatively punitive countries with a steadily growing prison population.

Despite the substantial growth of imprisonment in England and Wales over the last decade, the proportion of offenders given a custodial sentence has been decreasing. The preoccupation with overcrowding and its associated problems, together with the ongoing debates about the possible effects of the prison-building programme fuelling an expansionist programme, has deflected attention away from the growing number of offenders who receive a non-custodial sanction. As Andrew Ashworth (1983) has pointed out, one of the dominant themes in penal policy since the 1970s has been how to stabilise and reduce the prison population, and this has meant providing the courts with a number of new alternatives to custody. Thus, during the 1980s, as the numbers incarcerated increased,

the proportionate use of custody for convicted offenders has been systematically falling (Bottoms, 1983).

Table 6.2   Average time served (in months) by country and crime type

	Homicide	Rape	Robbery	Residential burglary	Assault	MVT
England and Wales	88.33	34.05	18.00	7.28	6.66	3.83
United States	113.63	59.78	41.60	18.65	23.40	11.94
Sweden	86.95	15.41	15.20	5.23	3.07	2.47
Australia	120.33	50.91	36.20	15.18	23.08	8.71
Scotland	94.70	36.40	17.60	3.56	7.00	2.66
Canada	72.39	ND	25.90	15.40	27.95	3.00
Switzerland	46.16	25.14	20.50	14.30	10.13	9.46
Netherlands	69.20	15.80	12.14	11.40	4.91	8.10
Mean of all eight	86.42	33.93	23.39	11.38	13.28	6.27

Source: Blumstein *et al.* (2005).

Limiting prison use

If the aim is to limit prison use, one option is to reduce the number of
offenders given custodial sentences by diverting them into community-
based alternatives. This involves what is frequently referred to as the
adoption of 'front door' strategies. Alternatively measures can be
developed which shorten the length of time actually served – 'back door'
strategies – through the use of parole of other forms of early release
(Bottoms *et al.*, 2004).

Front door strategies involve the development of non-custodial
sanctions such as fines, probation, community service orders, electronic
monitoring and reparation, which are designed as alternatives to custody.
Over the past two decades we have seen a significant expansion in the
use of non-custodial sanctions. The main types of community sentences
currently in use in England and Wales are the community order for
adults and the referral order and supervision order for juveniles. The
community order was introduced by the Criminal Justice Act 2003 and
came into force in 2005. The total number of community sentences in
all courts in 2007 was just under 200,000; that is, 40 per cent higher than
in 1997, although slightly lower than in 2004 and 2005. Significantly,
the percentage of offenders given community sentences for all offences
has increased from 10.2 per cent in 1997 to 14.0 per cent in 2007, while
for indictable offences it has increased from 28.5 per cent to 33.8 per
cent over the same period (Ministry of Justice, 2008a). In relation to

probation, the number of people starting probation increased by 21 per cent between 1997 and 2007, with just under 200,000 people under the supervision of the probation service (Ministry of Justice, 2008b).

Despite the increased use of community-based sentences and other diversionary measures during the 1970s and 1980s, the impact of 'front door' strategies on the prison population has been less than anticipated and instead there has been a simultaneous increase in both community-based sanctions and the prison population in England and Wales. A similar development has taken place in the US where the number of people on probation has increased almost fourfold between 1980 and 2006, rising from 1,118,000 to 4,215,000. The numbers on parole have also increased dramatically by roughly the same factor, rising from 220,000 in 1980 to just under 800,000 in 2006 (Glaze and Bonczar, 2007). Consequently, in America the number of people under some form of correctional supervision in 2005 was in excess of 7 million.

Although there has been a systematic increase in the use of community-based sanctions on both sides of the Atlantic over the past two decades, their use has attracted growing criticism. Rather than reduce the size of the prison population and solve the problems of overcrowding, community-based sanctions appear to have grown alongside the prison and, instead of undermining the use of custody, seem to have performed a complementary and reinforcing role. As Figures 6.3 and 6.4 indicate, the growth of probation has increased exponentially on both sides of the Atlantic alongside the growth in imprisonment. The use of parole has increased significantly in America, while in England and Wales the number given parole has fluctuated between 2,000 and 4,000 per annum over the last decade (Parole Board, 2008). In 1997, just over 2,000 people were given parole, and the number rose steadily over the next five years, peaking at just under 4,000 in 2004/05, thereafter decreasing to approximately 2,100 in 2007/08.

The question which a growing number of criminologists asked in the 1980s was, how could the development of community-based alternatives to custody fail to reduce the number of people in prison? Some have also asked why both community-based sanctions and the prison population should grow simultaneously (Matthews, 1987). In essence, there were four types of answer that were given to these related questions. The first was that development of alternatives to custody had instigated a process of 'net widening' (McMahon, 1990). The proliferation of non-custodial sanctions, it was argued, had inadvertently drawn more offenders into the criminal justice system, thus expanding the system as a whole. Paradoxically, the consequence of the introduction of a range of what

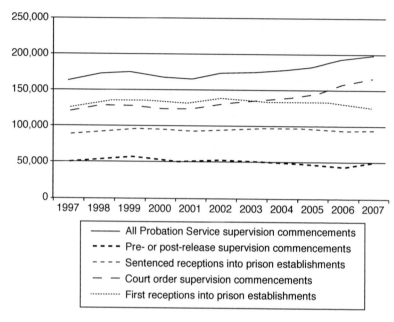

Figure 6.3 Flows into Probation Service supervision and prison establishments
Source: Ministry of Justice (2008b).

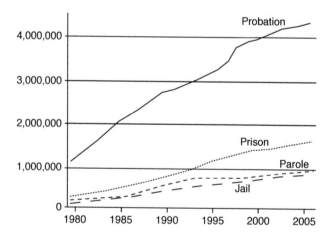

Figure 6.4 Adult correctional populations, 1980–2006
Source: Bureau of Justice Statistics Correctional Surveys (2007).

appeared as more benign and humane sanctions was that more and more people were drawn into the net of social control, with the result that through the processes of stigmatisation and marginalisation, many minor offenders became labelled as 'criminal' and were thereby confirmed in their deviancy (Cohen, 1985).

The second and related critique of the deployment of community-based sanctions was that they catered predominantly for minor offenders rather than for those who were realistically at risk of receiving a prison sentence. Thus some alternatives were seen as largely irrelevant to the growing problem of overcrowding within prisons. For others, the use of alternatives for mainly minor offenders was seen as fuelling the prison crisis by increasing the number of recidivists who had initially been convicted of a relatively minor offence within the criminal justice system, since it was predicted that a percentage would make their way up the tariff and would eventually receive a prison sentence.

The third concern which became associated with the use of alternatives to custody was that as each new 'alternative' came into operation, it drew a significant proportion of its clientele not from the potential prison population but from existing alternatives. Thus it was estimated, for example, that the community service orders drew half their clients from those who might reasonably have been expected to receive a prison sentence, while the other half were drawn from the other non-custodial systems (Pease, 1985). The movement of offenders between different alternatives created a situation in which many offenders were being diverted 'within' the system rather than out of it. The consequence thus was to create a self-reinforcing system which involved not so much a policy of 'decarceration' but of 'transcarceration', through which offenders became continuously recycled through a range of different agencies (Lowman *et al.*, 1987).

The fourth problem which became associated with the use of non-custodial sanctions in the 1970s and 1980s was to do with their appropriateness and availability. Fines, for example, which had been widely seen in the postwar period as an appropriate sanction for a wide range of offences, became seen as less appropriate during the 1980s as levels of poverty and inequality increased (O'Malley, 2009). Similar difficulties have occurred in relation to the use of community service orders in that suitable activities are not readily available in certain areas, and therefore the deployment of this sanction is limited (Carlen, 1990; Robinson and McNeill, 2008).

In a review of the impact of non-custodial sentences, Tony Bottoms, summarising the views of many criminologists, stated that:

The recent English experience offers no support at all to the optimistic suggestion made in the past, namely that the progressive adoption of various measures to limit prison use would, in a gradual way, erode the central importance of the prison in modern penality. (Bottoms, 1987: 177)

Thus by the late 1980s the suggested introduction of other non-custodial penalties was met with increasing scepticism and it was widely felt that if measures were to be introduced to limit prison use then they would need to be directed at those offenders who were actually 'at risk' of receiving a prison sentence, and at the same time would need to provide an option which the judiciary would see as a viable alternative to custody. In response it has been suggested that there is a need to introduce 'intermediate sanctions' which can act as effective alternatives and not just 'soft' options (Morris and Tonry, 1990). However, the introduction of intermediate sanctions in the form of house arrest, electronic monitoring or forms of intensive probation will have to face the problem of ensuring that these sanctions are used for the types of offenders for whom they were designed and that they avoid the likelihood that they will, to some extent at least, be used as alternatives to existing alternatives (Byrne *et al.*, 1992).

In relation to 'back door' strategies the results are equally uncertain. The introduction of parole in England in 1968 was designed to shorten the length of time actually served. As with the expression of 'front door' strategies in the 1970s, the introduction of parole was seen as having an obvious and direct effect in reducing the average daily population in prison. But the introduction of parole has been seen as providing only a limited reduction in prison populations and creating new tensions and anxieties within the prison system. This was because it was seen by some as undermining the 'honesty' of sentencing policy, introducing increased uncertainty into the lives of prisoners and their families, and ultimately being self-defeating by encouraging the judiciary to pass longer sentences which anticipated the possibility of early release (Bottomley, 1984; Hood and Shute, 2000). Despite these shortcomings, however, it has with some justification been claimed that without the availability of parole in the 1980s, the prison population would have been considerably higher. The use of parole, according to Worrall and Pease (1986), stabilised the prison population between 1975 and 1984 and balanced off the increase in the prison population which would have resulted from changes in sentencing decisions. In 2007, 18,600 prisoners were released early in England and Wales under emergency measures to tackle overcrowding.

In sum, the expectations and optimism which were widely associated with the development of alternatives to custody and parole have not been met. The haphazard and often pragmatic way in which these measures have been implemented has produced various anomalies and uncertainties. One consequence is that rather than simply reduce the size of the prison population or remove the problem of overcrowding, they have resulted in the construction of a much more elaborate system of penality in which the processes are more complex and the outcomes more uncertain. Given these limitations, the challenge is to develop community-based sanctions that do not result in 'net widening' or generate 'alternatives' to the existing alternatives, and which are designed and implemented in a way that reduces the pressure on the prison system in both the short and the long run.

Thus, if prison use is to be more effectively controlled through the use of these options, it will be necessary in the longer term to develop non-custodial sanctions in a more systematic and integrated form. The way forward is not simply to create more 'alternatives' to custody or more effective forms of early release, but to develop appropriate sanctions for different types of offences which are commensurate with current notions of justice, fairness and culpability. In short, such sanctions need to be realistic, effective and appropriate (Matthews, 1989b). Simply adding new, well-meaning alternatives to the existing array of sanctions is unlikely to have the desired effect.

What is clear from this review of sentencing policy and the development of community-based sanctions is that there are no easy answers or quick fixes. The history of policy development in this area is replete with disappointment and disillusionment and it seems at times that the dynamics of the criminal justice system operate behind the backs of the agents and decision-makers. Part of the difficulty is in bringing together the micro and macro aspects of these developments and incorporating considerations of agency and structure (Young, 2003). While not resolving all of the problems outlined above, there have been some promising explanations of the growth of imprisonment that do not rely on voluntaristic notions of 'punitiveness' or fall into the trap of empiricism, but instead attempt to identify the situational and structural causal dynamics that can affect prison use.

Explaining the dynamics of prison expansion

A recent study by Jeffrey Fagan (2004) that draws on the work of a number of other New York-based criminologists provides a plausible and coherent account of the rise of the prison population in New York in a period in which recorded crime, including violence and homicide, has decreased significantly (Clear, 2002; Lawrence and Travis, 2004). The explanation that Fagan presents is based on the 'revolving door' hypothesis that traces the circulation of offenders from the community to the prison and back into the community. Previous research has shown that the prison population in New York is drawn from a limited number of neighbourhoods, and that the majority of these offenders are at a later date decanted back into the same neighbourhoods. This leads to a concentration of an increasingly marginalised population who become the objects of increased surveillance and police attention. This in turn results in a growing number of re-arrest and reconvictions even in a period where recorded crime rates are falling. In line with the arguments presented by Todd Clear (2002) which have been discussed above, the substantial number of males incarcerated at any one time fosters a culture of welfare dependency by the families of inmates and creates cycles of disadvantage. The destabilising effect on the community of such a large number of local residents spending time in prison leads to a breakdown of informal controls, uneven patterns of socialisation and a growing pressure to engage in illegitimate activities.

On the basis of this dynamic process, Fagan suggests that this spatial concentration has transformed the spike in incarceration which was associated with the 'war on drugs' that occurred at the end of the 1980s into an enduring feature of particular neighbourhoods, and he argues that this process persists regardless of law and policy. Thus what Fagan argues is that this dynamic has set in motion a self-generating or autopoietic system which constantly recycles and regenerates 'the usual suspects' back into the prison system. He notes that the percentage of those admitted to prison between 1985 and 1996 with prior arrests and prior convictions rose over the period, and concludes that the recycling of prisoners was a driving force in maintaining high prison populations even in an era of sharply declining crime rates. This form of analysis leads to an appreciation of the combination of both external and internal process in affecting the scale of imprisonment. Alongside this form of explanation we might add that for many of these offenders, their experience often goes beyond that presented in the standard 'revolving door' hypothesis, and that many of these offenders will not simply move between the prison and community but will move between an increasingly elaborate network of regulatory agencies – both custodial and non-custodial. The proliferation of community justice and ancillary agencies, which offenders may pass through in the course of their lives, means that the period of time under which they are under state control and supervision is also in many cases becoming more extensive. It is increasingly a process of transcarceration rather than decarceration that many of those who become caught up in the expanding criminal justice system experience. Consequently, a form of systems analysis is required that can capture the dynamics involved and which can both trace the processes within the criminal justice system and link them to an appreciation of related social, economic and political processes (Matthews, 2003).

The analysis presented by Fagan goes some way to explaining the dynamics of prison growth in New York and possibly in some other cities in America but, as we have seen, there are considerable cultural differences that are evident in different countries as well as significant social and economic variations, Thus, applying this form of analysis to the UK would need to be adapted and placed in context. However, there is evidence that prisoners are drawn disproportionately from particular neighbourhoods and return to these areas when they leave prison. There is also, as we have seen above, evidence of a growing number of repeat offenders being processed by criminal justice agencies. This will tend to increase the average sentence length and time served even if the repeat offences are not particularly serious. There is also some evidence that sentencers on both sides of the Atlantic are handing out longer prison sentences to those convicted of violence and sexual offences, and we cannot rule out the possibility that the cases of violence coming before the courts are more serious and disturbing. Alongside these developments we have seen the expansion of the punishment–welfare continuum involving a more elaborate combination of 'inclusive' and 'exclusive' sanctions. In this process the boundaries between therapy and punishment are becoming increasingly blurred (Moore, 2007). Increasingly, offenders are likely to pass through a more complex array of agencies during their lives and, rather than seeing those in prison and those on some form of community sanction as two distinct groups, we need to examine in more detail the *flow* of offenders through the growing network of agencies and institutions – both public and private – associated with the expanding criminal justice system.

Conclusion

The two most significant developments in criminology over the last decade or so have been the decrease in crime, on one hand, and the significant growth of the prison populations on both sides of the Atlantic, on the other. Indicatively, criminology has not been very good at explaining either of these developments, and when it has come to explaining the connections between the two it has been even less convincing. There is a fault line that runs through the middle of academic criminology that divides the study of crime from that of imprisonment and which loses sight of the fact that crime is a product of action and reaction. The result is a tendency towards one-sided and partial explanations of change. At the same time, explanations of the changing use and scale of imprisonment tend to focus on either 'external' processes, seeing it as a product of the economy, politics or cultural shifts, on one hand, or of internal processes such as sentencing and the use of alternatives to custody, on the other. Very few explanations link macro and micro processes and attempt to identify the causal dynamics in play. There are, however, a few promising explanations that move beyond voluntarism and empiricism and which attempt to link agency and structure in a way that connects crime and imprisonment and simultaneously locates the operation of the prison within the changing dynamics of the family and the community, as well as wider socio-economic processes.

7
Youth Justice and Youth Custody

Introduction

During the nineteenth century two new characters appeared on the social landscape – the adolescent and the juvenile delinquent. Adolescence came to denote a new phase in personal development that stood between childhood and adulthood. Young people were no longer seen as 'little adults', but rather as persons still in the process of personal development who were not, as yet, fully responsible for their actions. Closely associated with these new conceptions of childhood and adolescence was the formation of the modern family and the introduction of compulsory education. These two agencies took on an increasing responsibility for both extending and deepening the processes of socialisation (May, 1973).

Alongside the adolescent the related figure of the juvenile delinquent was formed. The juvenile delinquent stood in contrast to the healthy adolescent and was seen as a product of faulty socialisation, inadequate parental supervision, or a lack of proper education. He or she was someone who was predisposed towards crime as a result of under-socialisation or a product of environmental conditions and was therefore in need of guidance and reform. Fortunately for the delinquent there was a growing body of experts who had already developed their expertise through their involvement in prisons – lawyers, doctors, psychiatrists and criminologists – and who were on hand with an extensive repertoire of explanations which they claimed could account for delinquency amongst young people.

The juvenile delinquent provided a convenient object for the growing debates on the causes of crime and the relative contribution of environmental, domestic, hereditary and other factors, which were held by criminologists and psychologists to lead to criminality. Although there were differences of opinion over the primary determinants of criminality, most commentators agreed that if the problem was to be addressed it was necessary to catch delinquents while they were young and reformable. The growing concerns of juvenile delinquency and the thousands of 'lost' children and hooligans who were becoming a more visible feature of inner-city life were expressed at the end of the nineteenth century by General Booth:

> The lawlessness of our lads, the increased licence of our girls, the general shiftlessness from the home-making point of view of the product of our factories and schools are far from reassuring. Our young people have never learned to obey. The fighting gangs of half-grown lads in Lisson Grove and the Scuttlers of Manchester are ugly symptoms of a social condition that will not grow better by being left alone. (Booth, 1890: 66)

In this statement General Booth identified the three key points of reference by which the processes of juvenile socialisation were to be measured in future decades: the family, education and the labour market. One of the defining features, however, of the young delinquent was precisely his or her marginality from all three processes. What was also evident in the pronouncements of General Booth and many of his contemporaries was that it was clearly no longer possible to rely on the established forms of philanthropy to deal with the problems affecting the poor living in the inner cities. Instead, the situation required a more formal and impersonal approach.

Establishing a separate system of juvenile justice

At the beginning of the twentieth century attitudes towards juvenile offenders changed significantly. Against a backdrop of a shift to post-Fordism and the introduction of the welfare state in Britain, the emphasis changed from simply punishing delinquents in segregative institutions towards attempts to deal with them in the community and, wherever possible, to resocialise and rehabilitate them. This period involved what has been described as the birth of 'the social', by which it is meant that an array of social strategies emerged to train, reorient and properly socialise the poor. It was in this period that a separate system of juvenile justice was established (1908) in England and Wales, together with a range of welfare institutions such as Barnardos and the Boy Scouts, as well as restrictions on incest and other sexual activities that were seen to undermine the physical and mental qualities of the young.

It was this period, according to Jacques Donzelot (1979), that saw the formation of the modern family, the development of social work and the dissemination of psychoanalysis. The significance of social work, Donzelot suggests, is that it acts as a link agency able to connect a range of agencies and institutions that had previously operated relatively independently – the family, the court and the school. As a result of this development the young delinquent became encircled by a range of experts working in collaboration – the social worker, the doctor, the psychiatrist, the educator and the judge. The family became a central fulcrum through which the child could be approached and evaluated. Failing or dysfunctional families could be identified and corrected, while stable families were to be encouraged to participate in the task of resocialising and disciplining wayward youth. Psychoanalysis was to provide the initial discourse, rationale and procedure through which the morals and mentalities of the young delinquent could be identified and treated. Psychoanalysis provided the professional ideology for social work, and psychologists were seen to be able through examinations and 'confessions' to both understand and correct deviations – ideally without resorting to law and punishment.

But the emphasis on law and punishment did not decrease; it was rather placed on a new footing. Consequently, the establishment of the juvenile court in 1908 in England and Wales marked the creation of a new mode of adjudication. These courts were designed to be more informal and excluded the general public. Those attending the court included social workers, psychiatrists, doctors, educators and members of the family – usually the mother. Donzelot explains how the operation of the court was transformed:

> There are no longer two authorities facing one another: the family and the apparatus but a series of concentric circles around the child: the family circle, the circle of technicians, and the circle of social guardians. A paradoxical result of the liberalization of the family, of the emergence of children's rights, of the rebalancing of the man–woman relationship: the more these rights are proclaimed, the more the strangle hold of a tutelary authority tightens around the poor family. In this system, family patriachalism is destroyed only at the cost of the patriarchy of the state. The very frequent absence of the father testifies to this (Donzelot, 1979: 103)

The juvenile court diminishes the old antagonisms of the adversarial system and the preoccupation with finding of guilt or innocence and replaces it with a more subtle and engaging system of regulation aimed at protecting and controlling the child. In this way the juvenile court is not so much concerned with the passing judgment on crimes, but is more preoccupied, Donzelot argues, with the examination of individuals. The offence becomes the springboard of investigation and perpetual judgment. The result was a metamorphosis of the two systems, although the power of the court continued to rest on the threat of imprisonment. When administering punishment there is a preference for probation or some form of conditional sentence, but by blurring the distinction between the penal and welfare spheres the juvenile court is able to extend the range of measures that can be deployed. In this way the normalising process of welfare acts as filter into the penal sphere, as those who fail to respond to treatment and are impervious to the normalising process move towards a career as delinquents. The emergence of a number of experts shifts attention to the prediction or prevention of delinquency and the focus on 'pre-delinquency' or those 'at risk'. The family and the school also become sites for the observation and identification of 'anti-social' tendencies.

Alongside the development of these inclusive community-based regulatory strategies new forms of custody were also being introduced for juveniles. In 1905 borstals were introduced for persistent young offenders aged between 16 and 21 who had been given sentences of between one and three years with the possibility of early release after six months. Borstals, which offered training and education, were located on the custodial continuum somewhere between prisons and reformatories. By 1921 there were 900 males and 250 females undergoing borstal training in England and Wales. By the 1930s just over half of those sentenced to a custodial institution were sent to borstals, and the number continued to grow in the immediate postwar period (Hood, 1965). However, during the 1950s borstals came into disfavour. Not only were they seen increasingly to resemble the prisons they were designed to replace, but they were also seen as offering little prospect of rehabilitation.

In 1948 the Criminal Justice Act introduced detention centres for young people seen to be less in need of lengthy training. Detention centres were explicitly punitive and were devoid of any educational or training component and were designed for young people between 17 and 21 who were seen as unsuitable for probation. They provided a tough regime designed to take the pressure off borstals and the prison system.

Approved schools were established in the 1930s for those described as being in need of 'care and protection' or being 'beyond control'. Despite their custodial functions they were not highly controlled institutions.

As Millham *et al.* (1975) have pointed out, 'they are open to the outside world, and in many ways boys are less constrained in them than in ordinary boarding schools'. Comparisons between approved schools and boarding schools have been common in the literature, with many commentators arguing that approved schools were in fact better in many respects than some boarding schools since, unlike the latter, at least they were 'approved' (Dunlop, 1974; Hood and Sparks, 1969).

Thus, by the 1950s an array of custodial institutions was available in England and Wales for young people. Alongside the borstal, the detention centre and the approved school, remand centres were introduced for those aged between 17 and 21 years who would otherwise be sent to a local prison. Other forms of detention were also available for young people, including community homes, attendance centres and secure units. 'Community homes' became the generic term used to cover all those institutions, which formed part of a growing system of residential care. The aim had been to introduce greater flexibility into the system in order to accommodate both offenders and non-offenders who were seen to exhibit similar personal and social problems. The flexibility of this process resulted in a more elaborate system of classification and assessment and the provision of a range of open and closed institutions (Hood and Sparks, 1969). Among these institutions were 'secure units' for those deemed to require control rather than care, although the actual differences in behaviour between those sent to secure units and those placed in care were not great (Millham *et al.*, 1978). Attendance centres were established in 1948 and were designed to deprive young offenders of their leisure time. Remand centres were set up at the same time for young people awaiting trial or sentence.

Increasingly in the postwar period the juvenile justice and child care systems became intertwined. The Children Act (1948) created local authority children's departments. This expanded the role of social work and consequently increased forms of welfare intervention aimed at promoting inclusive strategies. The blurring of the distinction between the deprived and depraved child was a feature of the 1933 Children and Young Persons Act, which stated that:

There is little or no difference in character and needs between the neglected and the delinquent child. It is often a mere accident whether he is brought before the court because he is wandering or beyond control or because he has committed some offence. Neglect leads to delinquency. (Home Office, 1933: 6)

The tension between care and control, welfare and punishment, inclusionary and exclusionary forms of intervention took a number of distinct turns in the 1960s, 1970s and 1980s, which had profound effects on the number of young people locked up in custodial institutions and the kinds of regimes they experienced (Morris and Giller, 1987).

The incarceration of juveniles in the postwar period

In the postwar period the term 'youth' became widely identified as a metaphor for social change. The development of youth subcultures, particularly during the 1950s and 1960s, the growing autonomy and affluence of certain sections of the teenage population generated different images and attitudes towards young people (Clarke *et al.*, 1975). It was against this background that the incarceration of young people was organised in the postwar period. By the 1950s a complex system of care and control, involving different forms of custody and detention, had been established. The 1948 Criminal Justice Act was something of a landmark in the juvenile justice reform. Although it had introduced remand centres, attendance centres and detention centres, it simultaneously gave financial backing to the provision of probation hostels, while abolishing corporal punishment and attempting to place further restrictions on the use of imprisonment for young people (Bailey, 1987). The attempt to place restrictions on the use of imprisonment and the encouragement of community-based sanctions can be seen as a precursor to the more general strategy of juvenile decarceration which developed during the 1960s.

In the pre-war period there had been a number of penal reformers who had argued that incarceration should be used for young people as sparingly as possible. But it was not until the 1960s that these arguments found a wide audience both in official and professional circles. Thus, from the mid 1960s onwards, there was a continuous, but not always consistent, movement towards the decarceration of young people. The term 'decarceration' is meant to embrace a range of strategies that include decriminalisation, diversion and deinstitutionalisation, with the aim of each strategy or a combination of strategies being to reduce the number of people in custody (Matthews, 1979; Scull, 1977). Although these strategies became particularly pronounced in the 1960s, it should be noted that there were oppositional voices which expressed deep scepticism about the possible benefits of any form of decarceration and called for the increased use of penal custody for young people in order to deter juvenile offenders during those periods in which they are most actively involved in crime (Boland, 1980; Boland and Wilson, 1978).

Despite continuous and at times vigorous objections, the period between 1960 and 1990 can be seen as an era in which decarceration in its various forms was pursued through a number of different channels. Within the juvenile justice literature it has become a convention to identify three general approaches – welfarism, the justice model and corporatism – as the three dominant approaches through which the reduction in the number of juveniles in custody was attempted. An examination of the application of these three approaches allows an assessment to be made about the most appropriate and effective decarceration strategy, and a review of the developments between 1960 and 1990 provides some salutary lessons about the difficulties in attempting to influence the scale of imprisonment and the problems associated with reorganising the distribution of sanctions between custodial and non-custodial options.

1. The welfare approach (1965–72)

During the 1960s a number of critiques of the use of incarceration were forcibly expressed, particularly where it was used for young people. These critiques in many cases were far from new, but during the 1960s they gathered momentum and crystallised around three main themes. These critiques were for the most part premised on the assumption that welfare-orientated, inclusive and community-based sanctions are in general preferable, and that penal custody, whether it be in the form of prison, borstal, remand centre or detention centre, was either inappropriate or counterproductive. The three major themes can be summarised as (a) debilitation; (b) decriminalisation and (c) discrimination.

(a) Debilitation

A significant impetus to the decarceration movement was given by Erving Goffman's (1968) critique of 'total institutions', which argued that rather than reform or rehabilitate offenders, the experience of institutionalisation was more likely to have a negative impact upon prisoners, resulting in a process of 'debilitation' through the combined effects of alienation, institutionalisation and marginalisation. A few years later Norval Morris's (1974) critique of enforced forms of rehabilitation within prisons pointed out the ethical and practical issues associated with 'enforced cures'. These combined critiques placed considerable doubt upon the extent of reform and rehabilitation which could be achieved within the prison setting since they suggested that short periods of incarceration did not allow for the possibility of rehabilitation while longer periods of confinement

always carried the danger of institutionalisation and further marginalisation. For a number of critics, arguments relating to the damaging
effects of incarceration were combined with the long-standing assertion
that rather than reform offenders, penal institutions serve as 'schools of
crime', turning young and inexperienced offenders into hardened and
committed criminals.

(b) Decriminalisation

A second theme that gained prominence during the 1960s was a
questioning of both the degree of criminal responsibility of young
people as well as the significance of juvenile offending. For a number
of commentators, juvenile offending was seen as a symptom of an
underlying personal or social problem, which needed to be addressed.
For this reason it was not enough simply to respond to a specific act or an
offence; the aim should be to uncover the underlying processes which had
led to the offending. In the more radical version of this argument it was
suggested that juvenile misbehaviour was a normal part of growing up,
and therefore juvenile offending should be tolerated as much as possible
without implementing formal sanctions (Schur, 1973). Young people, it
was suggested, would grow out of crime and there are very real dangers
of entangling them unnecessarily in the criminal justice system since
this might serve to reinforce their delinquency through the process of
stigmatisation and labelling (Lemert, 1970; Rutherford, 1986).

Closely related to the drive towards the decriminalisation of juvenile
misbehaviour was the apparent inappropriateness of the juvenile court to
identify the underlying problems and needs of the child. The emphasis
within the adversarial system on the determination of guilt or innocence
was seen by many as largely irrelevant to the situation of the young
person. As the authors of the Kilbrandon Committee of Inquiry Report
(1964) pointed out, the vast majority of cases in the juvenile court are
not contested. The aim of any court or panel, Kilbrandon argued, was
to identify the needs of the young person within a context that allowed
for the proper formulation of a suitable disposal.

(c) Discrimination

A third theme which ran through much of the literature in the 1960s
was that penal sanctions are largely reserved for working class and poor
people, while middle-class young people who may be troublesome tend
to be dealt with in more informal and less stigmatising ways. Echoing
the sentiments that had been expressed by the young Winston Churchill

some 50 years earlier, the authors of the influential 1964 Longford Report, *Crime – A Challenge To Us All*, wrote:

> Chronic or serious delinquency in a child is, in the main we believe, evidence of the lack of the care, guidance and the opportunities to which every child is entitled. There are few children who do not behave badly at times, but the children of parents with ample means rarely appear before the juvenile courts. The machinery of law is reserved mainly for working class children, who, more often than not, are also handicapped by being taught in too big classes in unsatisfactory school buildings with few amenities or opportunities for out of school activities. (Longford Report, 1964: 21)

The fact that troublesome young people from middle- and upper-class backgrounds were in practice excluded from the juvenile justice system and from penal institutions and dealt with in more informal and less stigmatising ways persuaded Longford that a similar approach could and ought to be employed in relation to working-class youth. Thus it was suggested that the age of criminal responsibility should be increased to the current school leaving age and that 'children should receive the kind of treatment they need without any stigma or association with the penal system'. The accusation that the juvenile courts and penal institutions were highly selective in terms of class was extended during the 1970s and 1980s to include what was seen as the discriminatory treatment of young African Caribbeans and young disadvantaged females.

In many respects these objections to the use of penal custody for young people are generally seen as applicable to other groups of offenders. The growing scepticism about the benefits of imprisonment, which was expressed throughout the 1960s, led to the development of a number of alternatives to custody, which were designed to reduce the reliance on the prison, the borstal and the detention centre. Much of this anti-custodial thinking was encapsulated in the *Children in Trouble* (1968) White Paper that set out to both decriminalise and deinstitutionalise juveniles. The White Paper included proposals to abandon the juvenile court and to replace it with informal and voluntary agreements between the parties involved wherever possible in order to minimise the effects of stigmatisation. Exhibiting a deep social work influence, the *Children in Trouble* White Paper reinforced the view that delinquency was presenting a symptom of deeper maladjustment.

The proposals included in the 1968 White Paper formed the basis of the 1969 Children and Young Persons Act (CYPA), which is widely seen as a watershed in juvenile justice. This Act raised the age of criminal responsibility to 14 and proposed that young offenders should not have to go to court, but should be allowed to negotiate a suitable form of treatment in conjunction with their parents and social workers. At the same time the 1969 CYPA directed that considerable power was to be placed in the hands of local authorities through the provision of care orders which were to replace the use of approved schools. Attendance centres and detention centres were also to be replaced by a new form of intermediate treatment which was to be run by local authorities, with the consequence that decisions over the implementation of sanctions shifted away from magistrates and towards juvenile justice practitioners (Pitts, 1996).

It is interesting to note that the movement towards decriminalisation and deinstitutionalisation of juveniles took place against a background of rising juvenile crime (Bottoms, 1974). In 1961 the delinquency rate for males aged between 10 and 16 was around 28 per 1,000 population. By 1966 it had increased to 30.5 per 1,000, and by 1971 it was just over 42 per 1,000. Thus there had been a 50 per cent increase in the number of young people aged 10–16 who had been cautioned or convicted for an indictable offence (Farrington, 1992). During the same period it should also be noted that despite the growing emphasis upon the need to deal with young people in less stigmatising and more informal ways, the number of young people in borstals, detention centres and prisons continued to increase.

The aspirations of the 1969 CYPA were, however, never fully realised. This was mainly because the Act was not implemented in its entirety since there were considerable objections to parts of the Act by the Magistrates' Association and by members of the Conservative government which was elected in 1972. Some commentators have, however, argued that even if the Act had been fully implemented it would never have achieved its objectives as it lacked consistency, and because of its conceptual inadequacies. Andrew Rutherford (1983), for example, has argued that the 1969 CYPA failed to face up squarely to the issue of the role of penal custody in relation to young offenders and it did not provide a clear indication of the allocation of responsibilities between central and local government.

The outcome of the 1969 CYPA was that elements of the new system such as intermediate treatment were brought in, but the existing system centred around the juvenile court, and the use of penal custody for juveniles was not phased out. The result was an expansion of the welfare–justice continuum and the creation of a more complex and diverse system of juvenile justice, involving a mix of care and control, punishment and welfare, organised through a combination of local and central government systems of control. Detention centres, borstals and remand centres remained in place and the numbers incarcerated continued to increase (Pitts, 1988).

Within this expanded juvenile justice system there was a steady growth throughout the 1970s in the number of young people detained both in penal custody and in institutions providing care and protection. Writing in the mid 1970s, Spenser Millham (Millham *et al.*, 1978) found that there were some 6,000 boys aged between 14 and 16 who had experienced the detention centre and 1,200 boys aged 15 and 16 who were sent to borstal in 1975. In the same year there were also 5,400 juveniles remanded in adult prisons or remand centres. On the basis of these figures he concluded that during this period more juveniles experienced a spell of penal custody than at any time since 1908.

2. The justice model (1973–82)

The realisation that the numbers of juveniles in penal custody was steadily increasing led a number of critics to blame the 'welfarism' of the 1960s for producing a system that was both more pervasive and more punitive. The road to the expansion of penal custody, it was argued, was littered with well meaning liberals with good intentions. The treatment orientation of 1960s 'welfarism' had over-pathologised the delinquent and encouraged the development of an extensive range of intrusive and ultimately counterproductive interventions. Rather than decarceration, what had occurred, critics claimed, was a process of 'net widening' and a 'blurring of the boundaries' between care and control (Cohen, 1979).

By the term 'net widening', critics referred to the process by which more people are drawn into the control system and the simultaneous development of new agencies which create a complex network of interventions, many of which are ostensibly benign, into which a growing number of young people become entangled. As a consequence they are recycled through the system of welfare and justice, care and control agencies; some of them public, and some private (Lerman, 1982). Within the system the continual movement of individuals between agencies and the shifting remits of the agencies themselves resulted in a blurring of the boundaries between those agencies which are formally charged with providing care and treatment and those which are involved in the administration of punishment. Consequently the demarcations between care and control, inclusion and exclusion, community-based and custodial forms of intervention begin to blur and eventually become less clearly defined (Cohen, 1985).

The culmination of these explanations turned the optimism that was prevalent in the 1960s about the possibility of reducing the custodial population through the development of community-based sanctions into pessimism. It became widely believed that the proliferation of apparently benign agencies can, and often does, contribute to the expansion of a more punitive juvenile justice system (Giller and Morris, 1983). Consequently it became widely suggested that the aim of intervention should be to do 'less harm' rather than 'more good'. In the words of Edwin Schur (1973), the aim should be 'to leave the kids alone whenever possible'.

Thus the 'back to justice' movement was premised on a reduction in the level of intervention. Welfarism, it was argued, had overextended the range and depth of state intervention, and the aim of penal policy should be to reduce the degree of intervention by focusing more on the act than on the actor. The failure of welfarism was that it subjected juveniles to forms of intervention, which were overly intrusive while negating individual rights. In a reformulation of the tenets of classicism, the emphasis shifted from the welfare of the child to the protection of the offenders by the strict observation of due process and through the extension of formal legal representation. By moving the focus away from the care and welfare of the young person, the justice model shifted the locus of decision-making back to the magistrates and to the juvenile court.

The growing revelations about the abuses inflicted on young people in local authority care provided the necessary ammunition to close down a number of these institutions and to reduce the number of young people in residential care (Thorpe *et al.*, 1980). Between 1977 and 1986 the use of the care order fell from 14 per cent of court disposals for all juveniles aged 14–17, to 4 per cent. Seeing the delinquent as a rational and largely responsible actor, the 'back to justice' lobby sought to impose the same 'safeguards' as the adult court, thereby reducing the distinction between the two (Morris *et al.*, 1980).

The 'back to justice' lobby had a strong punitive edge. It lent itself readily to the calls of the incoming Thatcher government to introduce a system of 'short, sharp shocks' through the implementation of tough military-style custodial regimes for juveniles. The rapid realisation that many of the young men subject to these regimes saw the military training as a perk rather than a punishment and were attracted to rather than deterred by these institutions, led to the 'experiment' being abandoned, and custodial institutions for juveniles reverted to their previous form (Shaw, 1985).

Although it was the aim of the justice model to ensure that juveniles were given the least restrictive sentence in each case and that sentences should be determinate rather than indeterminate, the numbers given penal custody between 1973 and 1982 continued to increase. The number of males aged 14–16 who were sent to a detention centre increased from 4,890 in 1976 to 5,958 in 1981. Over the same period the number of males aged 14–16 held in detention centres remained relatively stable at around 1,500 a year.

Much of the thinking which was associated with the 'back to justice' lobby was incorporated into the 1982 Criminal Justice Act that made provision for legal representation, which was taken up in a significant number of cases (Burney, 1985). But probably the most important aspect of the 1982 Act was that it set limitations on judicial discretion to make custodial orders. Before passing a custodial sentence the magistrate was required publicly to justify his or her decision in court. In order to pass a custodial sentence, three criteria had to be considered: that the offender is unable and unwilling to respond to non-custodial penalties; that a custodial sentence is necessary for the protection of the public, or that the offence is so serious that a non-custodial sentence cannot be justified. Although there was an increase in the number of custodial sentences given to juveniles in the period immediately after the passing of the Act, the number of juveniles in custody began to decrease in 1985–86, and the supporters of the Act and the advocates of the justice model claimed that the control of judicial discretion played a major role in achieving this decrease.

Critics of the justice model did not agree. On the contrary, they claimed that the emphasis on legal processes and safeguards had undermined the juvenile justice system by increasingly treating juveniles like adults. The emphasis upon legality and formal equality masked, critics claimed, the underlying inequalities, social disadvantages and social problems experienced by many of the young people who appeared in the juvenile court (Hudson, 1987).

While academics were debating the advantages and disadvantages of 'welfare' and 'justice' or trying to find ways of reconciling these apparently oppositional approaches, practitioners and policy-makers were developing other strategies to reduce the numbers of juveniles in custody and to reorientate the juvenile justice system. Juvenile justice workers around the country were publicly claiming to establish 'custody-free' zones, and different areas were being increasingly assessed by the numbers of juveniles given custody, with those areas with the highest juvenile custody rates being seen to be failing.

In the mid 1980s the emphasis shifted away from the concerns about welfare and justice and towards the management and administration of delinquency. Through strategies of diversion and the introduction of effective 'gatekeepers', the aim was to prevent juveniles becoming entangled in the formal system of juvenile justice and to overcome blockages and bottlenecks within the system. During the latter half of the 1980s as this 'delinquency management' or 'corporatist' approach became more widespread, the numbers of juveniles in custody decreased dramatically and the nature of juvenile penal institutions also changed significantly. The question that arises is the extent to which these emerging forms of managerialism were responsible for reducing the reliance on juvenile penal institutions and for fostering the eventual demise of the detention centre and the borstal in the late 1980s.

3. Corporatism (1984–95)

The term 'corporatism' is used as a generic term to cover a range of strategies that emerged in England and Wales during the 1980s. John Pratt (1989) has identified the key components of a 'corporatist' strategy as the increased use of administrative discretion, the extension of pre-court tribunals, and the increased use of cautioning and other forms of diversion. Corporatism in the 1980s also involved the increase of interagency co-operation, which served to blur the boundaries between public and private realms and between statutory and voluntary agencies. In many respects corporatism aims to side-step the controversies between welfare and justice and focuses instead on the management and the cost-effectiveness of the system.

Between 1981 and 1987 the number of males aged 14–16 sent to detention centres and borstals almost halved, falling from 7,473 to 3,689. The decrease in the average daily population was even more dramatic, with the number of males aged 14–16 in custody falling from 1637 in 1981 to 547 in 1988. Apart from the possibly delayed impact of the 1982 Criminal Justice Act, there were significant demographic shifts in the 1980s that reduced the numbers of young people in the population. During this period delinquency became something of a 'scarce resource' and a number of agencies expressed difficulties in recruiting a suitable number of 'clients' (Pratt, 1985). These demographic changes have been identified as being responsible for up to 30 per cent of the decrease in the numbers of juveniles in custody over this period (Allen, 1991).

There was a significant increase in the use of cautioning. Between 1969 and 1986 the total number of juveniles given a police caution increased from 33,702 to 69,900. Changes in the use of cautioning have also been credited with reducing the numbers of juveniles appearing in court and being given a custodial sentence. Whereas in previous decades cautioning had been merely associated with 'net widening', during the 1980s it became widely viewed as an effective form of diversion. Although the number of juveniles cautioned increased significantly, it should be noted that the offences for which the majority of juveniles received a caution were not normally those which would have resulted in a custodial sentence.

Probably a more significant development in relation to the decreased number of juveniles appearing in court and receiving a custodial sentence was the introduction of multi-agency pre-court diversion panels. These panels were designed to keep young people out of the juvenile court and in particular to find a suitable disposal for those petty persistent offenders who had 'used up' their cautions. These Juvenile Liaison Bureaux (JLBs), as they became known, could make recommendations ranging from no further action to a caution or reparation, as well as other informal sanctions.

It is difficult to assess how effective these multi-agency panels were in reducing the custodial population since the majority of serious offences were not referred to them. However, what was interesting was the ways in which these panels, which had no statutory role or formal constitution, could make critical decisions about juvenile disposals. These panels which expressed a preference for administrative as opposed to judicial decision-making raised questions about the operation of the juvenile justice system, since:

> Some might think it paradoxical that a whole new agency (the JLB) has been created in order to divert young offenders from a system of justice and welfare created (very expensively) for their reception. It is certainly intriguing that the state, having organised a network of statutory services intended to cater for the needs of children, should support this new hybrid organisation which defines its brief in terms of keeping young offenders out of the clutches of those same agencies. (Davis *et al.*, 1989: 232)

A related corporatist strategy, which was designed to focus on those young offenders who were seen as being at risk of receiving a custodial sentence, was the development of 'intensive' intermediate treatment.

This initiative, known as LAC 83(3) was funded by the Department for Health and Social Security and was designed to develop specialist projects over a two- or three-year period specifically aimed at serious offenders. It involved the creation of more realistic non-custodial alternatives to custody for 'hardened' offenders that would involve interagency co-operation. This form of delinquency management was less concerned with the causes of crime or with the questions of 'just deserts'. Instead, it embraced elements of labelling theory and propounded a minimalist and anti-custodial approach.

Thus the combined effect of demographic changes and corporatist strategies do appear to have had a significant impact upon the custodial population. But what was equally if not more significant in this period was the changes in the types of alternatives to custody which were being developed, as well as changes in the nature of juvenile incarceration itself. There were three important developments which took place during the 1980s in relation to the use of custodial and non-custodial options. These involved, first, a growing emphasis upon the use of time-based sanctions; second, a growing preoccupation with the monitoring of offenders; and third, the demise of the borstal and the detention centre and their replacement by a new form of 'youth custody'.

Time in different forms has become increasingly the focus of sanctions in this period. In relation to community-based sanctions, greater emphasis is placed upon using up the spare time of offenders through the increased use of sanctions such a community service orders. Although this sanction involves the use of a time-based punishment, it is not work time which is the focus but the offender's spare time, and involves placing a limit on the availability of leisure time. At the other end of the spectrum the use of custody for juveniles has become more time-orientated. The concerns about the cost-effectiveness of custody have given impetus to the claims that the period of incarceration should be as short as possible. Sentences have become determinate with an emphasis on the offender serving the full length of sentence (Pratt, 1989).

The growing emphasis upon surveillance and the monitoring of offenders was evident in the development of 'intensive' intermediate treatment. Whereas intermediate treatment in the 1970s had been mainly concerned with counselling, face-to-face work and group work, in the 1980s it became increasingly directed towards the monitoring of young people 'at risk'. The aim of the strategy was to closely monitor the daily activities of juveniles and provide forms of 'enhanced' supervision. The growing emphasis upon monitoring and supervision has been characterised by Stanley Cohen (1985) as the 'new behaviourism'.

This strategy, he suggests, has developed out of the belief that 'solving problems by changing people is simply unproductive' and that rather than engage in forms of treatment, counselling or supervision, 'we have to accept them as they are, modify their circumstances or deal with the consequences of their intractability'. The recent movement towards the imposition of curfews and night restriction orders can be seen as an extension of a strategy which is concerned with regulating behaviour rather than changing minds (Audit Commission, 1996).

The demise of the borstal in 1982 was met with little comment or apparent regret. Its replacement by the new forms of youth custody, however, involved more than just a change of name. The new institutions were to be largely devoid of rehabilitative goals and were designed to be primarily punitive. They signalled a retreat from the notion of a therapeutic institution into something more restrictive. Corresponding changes in the internal nature of these regimes were reflected in the fact that the staff began to wear uniforms and there was a decreased emphasis upon the provision of training facilities and education in these establishments. The recent interest in American-style 'boot camps', with their emphasis upon strict discipline and military-style training, indicates how far removed contemporary custodial thinking is from the pioneering ambitions which were associated with the introduction of the borstal as an alternative to the prison at the beginning of the twentieth century (Farrington, *et al.*, 2002; Simon, 1999).

Thus, with a general shift from judicial to administrative forms of decision-making within the juvenile justice system, important changes have taken place in the nature of the penal institutions as well as in community-based sanctions. These do not appear to involve the process of 'net widening' and the 'blurring of boundaries'. Instead, as John Pratt (1989) has argued, it has produced a more rationalised and differentiated system of juvenile justice in which the gulf between custodial and non-custodial sanctions has widened, while the gap between different forms of custody has narrowed.

In assessing these developments in England and Wales it is interesting to compare changes that have taken place in relation to the regulation of juveniles in other European countries, since it is evident that other European countries experienced substantial reductions in the number of juveniles incarcerated during the 1980s.

Decarceration in Europe

Some brief comments on the use of custody for juveniles in Europe are necessary because there appear to be some parallel developments that occurred during the 1980s in a number of different countries. In Germany, for example, which also experienced a reduction in the number of 14–16-year-olds in the population during this period, there was a considerable reduction in the number of young people who were subject to formal prosecution. Between 1982 and 1987 the number of 14–20-year-olds sentenced to imprisonment in West Germany fell by just under 40 per cent. It has been argued that it was a reduction of the number of young people appearing in court as well as limiting the number held on remand, rather than a reduction in sentence lengths, which caused the reduction of the juvenile custodial population (Feest, 1991; Graham, 1990). What is interesting about these developments, particularly in relation to England and Wales and West Germany, is that the policies of decarceration appear to have been mobilised primarily by practitioners rather than policy-makers and academics. These changing practices reflected a changing climate of opinion about how best to respond to juvenile crime and on the appropriateness of custodial sentences for certain juvenile offenders.

In France, where the number of juveniles in custody also decreased during the 1980s, the juvenile justice system veers much more towards forms of social crime prevention which aim to reduce the level of crime engaged in by young people and limit the number of cases which come to the attention of the authorities. Within the French system there is a specialist children's judiciary in the form of the *juge des enfants* who handle all child protection and juvenile delinquency cases that reach the courts. These judges can exercise a large degree of discretion and work closely with social workers and child care experts (Pitts, 1997).

What is interesting, although a little perplexing, is that the decarceration of juveniles occurred in the 1980s in a number of different European countries through a different combination of strategies. Underpinning these different approaches appears to be a significant change in how juveniles were conceived in this period and in particular how responses to much juvenile misbehaviour appeared to take more tolerant forms. These shifts in social attitudes are even more remarkable when the extensive restructuring of Europe which occurred at this time is taken into consideration.

New Labour – New Penology?

Controlling juvenile crime was established as a priority for the incoming Labour government in 1997. In an attempt to 'get tough on crime' (and the causes of crime), New Labour focused on juvenile crime and juvenile justice, and its approach to these issues was articulated in the Crime and Disorder Act (1998). This Act brought into being multi-agency Youth Offending Teams in each local authority and created the Youth Justice Board in England and Wales to oversee their development and to assume control of secure and penal provision for juveniles, which became known as the 'secure estate'. The Act also sought to introduce new penalties such as anti-social behaviour orders (ASBOs) and parenting orders, while expanding the range of community penalties. These new penalties could be imposed on a maximum of two occasions, after which a detention training order (DTO) was to be imposed. The new order replaced all existing custodial penalties available in the youth court with a single uniform sentence that was to be served half in custody and half in the community, with potential for early or late release. The transition from custody to community was intended to be 'seamless', with sentence planning ensuring that the custodial phase was characterised by purposeful activity, appropriate to the child's needs, which could be built upon through supervision under licence when offenders return to the community (Blyth and Newman, 2008)

During the 1990s there had been a growth in the secure estate and a growing sense of crisis in Young Offenders' Institutions. A series of damning reports from the Prisons Inspectorate identified disturbing levels of violence, intimidation, extortion, sexual assault and drug taking in a number of establishments (Goldson, 2002a). These institutions contained a mixture in terms of age, gender, length of stay, distance from home and levels of vulnerability. In a Thematic Review conducted by the Chief Inspector of Prisons in 1997 it was stated that the part of the Prison Service that gave greatest cause for concern was the Young Prisoners estate. In a subsequent report, concern is expressed in relation to bullying and harassment:

Children are made worse by the experience of imprisonment (and) the bullying and harassment that they inflict on each other ... The emphasis on Child Protection procedures should be not so much on children being molested by staff, although this must, of course, be guarded against, but on protecting them from bullying and intimidation by their peers when staff are not present. The worst examples of this are reflected in establishments where verbal intimidation is practiced by shouting from cells and physical bullying takes place in unsupervised places such as showers and recesses on landings. It is essential that all parts of establishments holding children and young adults are made safe, so that the ravages of bullying and intimidation cannot be wrought. (HM Chief Inspector of Prisons, 2001: 9)

A further report by HM Inspectorate of Prisons (2008b) on a newly opened secure training centre at Oakhill found serious problems in maintaining order and expressed deep concern in relation to the safety of children placed there. The Inspectorate reported 'staggering levels of the use of force by staff', noting that in the previous nine-month period, force had been used 757 times and that more than 70 per cent of these episodes involved the highest level of restrain, requiring at least three members of staff, one of whom would hold the young person's head.

Alongside high levels of violence, bullying and intimidation are high levels of suicide and self-harming in these institutions. Between 2000 and 2005 the number of recorded incidents of self-harming within the juvenile secure estate increased from 215 to 622 (Bateman, 2006). The Chief Inspector of Prisons frequently refers to the young people in these establishments as 'lost'. There has, however, been an increase in the number of short custodial sentences being imposed on young people and secure accommodation is increasingly 'silting up' with younger children serving short sentences, while their older counterparts are left to the vagaries of the prison system.

Within youth justice the attempt to explain the causes of crime has given way to a growing emphasis on risk analysis. Risk-based forms of analysis are attractive to policy makers since they promise the prospect of developing effective preventative measures, while they are also attractive to prison administrators since they offer the possibility of developing what are seen as more objective and rigorous forms of assessment. In terms of crime prevention, a series of factors tend to be presented as indicators of risk. These include poor parenting, truancy, homelessness, unemployment, drug abuse and the like (Audit Commission, 1996). Over time, however, because of the problems of attributing the appropriate weight to this array of factors and developing appropriate interventions, this list of risk factors tends to be divided into 'foreground' and 'background' factors. The foreground factors are those that are seen to be more amenable to manipulation and normally involve poor parenting and lack of educational achievement, while unemployment, homelessness, poverty and the like are relegated to 'background' factors, since they are seen as being less amenable to change.

It is claimed that there has been something of a paradigm shift in juvenile justice towards risk-based or actuarial techniques involving a shift from rehabilitative strategies to the management of offenders based on risk assessments (Kempf-Leonard and Peterson, 2000). This 'New Penology' is seen to provide a response to the perceived failures and inefficiency in the system and to provide beleaguered personnel with a less burdensome 'evidence-based' framework for conducting their work (Brownlee, 1998; Pitts, 2003). The growing emphasis on cost-effectiveness, performance management, privatisation and 'outputs' rather than 'outcomes' is seen as indicative of a significant policy change. The attempt to identify the risk of offending and reoffending and linking this to the 'crimogenic needs' of offenders has provided a powerful rationale for responding to young offenders (Bonta, 1996). New forms of classification and screening have been developed in order to improve the management of offenders, and these techniques have been linked to new modes of enforcement. Risk assessments are also used in relation to sentencing decisions, and the offender's age, offence severity and prior record can all be considered when deciding on sentence.

There is no doubt that risk-based forms of assessment have permeated the juvenile justice system in Britain and other countries. However, there are at least three major limitations to the use of actuarial techniques. First, the quality of information and the risk-assessment tools leave a great deal to be desired. Barry Goldson (2002a, 2002b), for example, has pointed out that there are serious limitations to the forms of assessment that have been undertaken in many establishments, and that many young prisoners arrive at Young Offenders' Institutions with inadequate documentation. Goldson reports that in a survey that he carried out with prison staff, in only one-third of cases did they receive the appropriate information on remand prisoners. Second, that although there has been a growing emphasis on risk assessment, there has also been a significant expansion of rehabilitative programmes in different establishments, particularly in relation to training and education. Third, it has been suggested that the forms of risk assessment that are used are much less objective than is assumed, and that rather than providing a rigorous mode of assessment, they provide a rationale for justifying subjective decision-making (Silver and Miller, 2002).

One feature of the changing emphasis on the rehabilitation of offenders is the development of cognitive behavioural therapy (CBT) programmes (Pitts, 2001). Between 1999 and 2002 the Youth Justice Board established a development fund of £3.9 million, which was allocated to 23 cognitive behavioural projects. These programmes, which were first developed in Canada, aim to help offenders 'think straight' and develop the capacity to deal with problems and conflicts more effectively. The assumption underpinning the development of CBT is that people engage in crime because they fail to develop the requisite cognitive skills for conformity. The assumption or claim that people become involved in crime because they do not have the capacity to reason effectively is, however, very questionable and does not go far in explaining the widespread incidence of white-collar and corporate crime. Nor does it sit well with the growing body of cultural criminology that emphasises excitement as a significant factor in the motivation to engage in crime (Hayward *et al.*, 2008). A lack of cognitive skills may explain why people get caught and convicted, rather than explain why they become involved in crime. Although some evaluations claimed that those undergoing CBT show significantly lower reconviction rates (Friendship *et al.*, 2002), other evaluations have been highly critical of these claims (Pitts, 2001; Pawson and Tilley, 1997; Kendall, 2002). If it is effective, its benefits seem to be limited to less serious offenders, amongst whom reoffending rates tend to be relatively low anyway. Completion rates of these programmes have been found to be relatively low at 47 per cent, while reoffending, by contrast, has been found to be high, with over 70 per cent of completers reoffending within twelve months (Feilzer *et al.*, 2004). Despite these negative findings, which have persuaded some that CBT has been an expensive failure, it continues to command a central role in penal policy.

Alongside the emphasis on rehabilitative and risk-based assessments, New Labour has also developed a number of other measures either to deal with young offenders in the community, to divert them from custody or to rehabilitate them. These strategies include a growing emphasis on restorative justice, forms of contractual governance, mentoring, and the development of surveillance and monitoring techniques.

Restorative justice in its various forms has come to prominence in Western societies during the 1990s. For many commentators the principles of restorative justice seem particularly appropriate to young people. The aim is to resolve 'conflicts' while avoiding the formality of a formal court hearing. Offenders are given the opportunity to make amends for what they have done and are given the opportunity to take responsibility for their actions. In some cases they are invited to express remorse and apologise to the victim. In essence, restorative justice aims to 'make good' by bringing the victim and offender together (Gelsthorpe and Morris, 2002b). There are different models of restorative justice deployed in different countries, and most are based on the notion of 'reintegrative shaming', as outlined by John Braithwaite (1989). The Crime and Disorder Act (1998) and the Youth Justice and Criminal Evidence Act (1999) introduced elements of restorative justice either as a diversionary measure normally involving some form of reparation, or as a court referral to youth offender panels.

Despite the widespread appeal of restorative justice, a number of issues have arisen in relation to its design and implementation. There are concerns about the authenticity of apologies and the willingness of offenders to engage in the process in the absence of the threat of a more formal response (Dignan, 1999). There are also concerns that restorative justice is reserved for minor offenders and that it can involve a form of 'net widening' (Young and Hoyle, 2003). For example, one study, conducted in Northern Ireland found that some 80 per cent of cases were for offences involving property worth less than £15 (O'Mahoney and Doak, 2004). Concerns have also been expressed about the lack of legal representation and the erosion of rights, as well as in relation to procedural fairness and accountability (Roche, 2003). Moreover, doubts have been expressed about the appropriateness of shaming rituals in this process and their capacity to detract from the restorative ideal (Matthews, 2006). However, despite these limitations restorative justice continues to flourish in England and Wales and elsewhere, and is now been incorporated into schools and prisons as a way of dealing with conflict.

Mentoring is another measure that has found favour amongst practitioners and policy-makers. Between 1999 and 2001 the Youth Justice Board committed £45 million to funding 43 mentoring projects involving some 3,596 young people. Mentoring is seen as a way of providing guidance and advice to young people to help them overcome difficulties and to counter the influence of inappropriate peer pressure. An evaluation of these projects found that while there were some examples of beneficial outcomes, the rate of reoffending, which was one of the principal points of reference in evaluating this initiative, was high (Tarling *et al.*, 2004). This finding was repeated in a rapid evidence assessment of the impact of mentoring on reoffending conducted by the Home Office. This assessment concluded that mentoring is 'a promising but not proven intervention' (Jolliffe and Farrington, 2007). Both evaluations noted the difficulties in recruiting and retaining appropriate mentors, matching mentors and clients, establishing trust and sustaining relationships over time (Easton, 2009; Porteous, 1998). The national evaluation sponsored by the Youth Justice Board found that 42 per cent of the relationships were terminated prematurely, normally by the young person (Tarling *et al.*, 2004). Similar findings have been reported from the US. One study carried out by the Department of Justice in the early 1990s involving a review of the ten 'best evaluated' mentoring programmes showed that they failed to achieve their goals in terms of academic achievement, behavioural change or employment (Brewer *et al.*, 1995).

An important development in recent years that has received limited attention has been the steady growth of forms of what Adam Crawford (2003) refers to as 'contractual governance'. This is a form of regulation centred around the use of different kinds of contracts that aim to encourage offenders to take responsibility for their actions and in some cases take on certain obligations. Crawford argues that the emerging forms of 'self-regulation' and 'self-policing' have arisen as a response to the failure of penal modernism, on one hand, and the limitations of crime prevention strategies, on the other. In relation to young people, the three most common forms of contractual governance are school–home agreements, acceptable behaviour contracts (ABCs) and referral orders. School–home agreements aim to regulate anti-social behaviour of pupils in schools as well as setting out the responsibilities of parents in relation to the supervision of their children. ABCs, which have become widely used in relation to the anti-social behaviour of young people, are designed for youngsters aged 10–18. These contracts are implemented by the police and normally involve an agreement on the part of the young person to desist from certain acts over a certain period (Bullock and Jones, 2004). Referral orders, which have been implemented nationally since 2002, are aimed at young people aged 10–17 who plead guilty and are convicted for the first time. These orders incorporate a restorative justice component and involve drawing up an agreed contract which, when signed, activates the order made by the court. Thus contracts are increasingly seen as being an appropriate way of responding to juvenile misbehaviour. They aim to 'responsibilise' young people, providing a form of regulation that emphasises security rather than justice.

There has also been a growing emphasis on the development of surveillance and monitoring programmes for young people. The Intensive Supervision and Surveillance Programme (ISSP), for example, was developed specifically as an alternative to custody and became available in 2003. It is by far the most restrictive available community-based disposal and was designed to be 'sufficiently tough' to be credible to the courts. The programme provides 25 hours of purposeful activity a week for the first three months of the order with additional surveillance outside of office hours, most frequently in the form of an electronically monitored curfew (Moore *et al.*, 2004).

It has been suggested that New Labour's approach to youth justice involves a combination of populism and punitivism. Barry Goldson (2002b), for example, claims that 'punitive imperatives have shaped contemporary policy responses to child offenders in England and Wales', and that this punitiveness is frequently expressed through the practices of 'institutionalised containment'. In a similar vein, John Muncie (1999) has accused New Labour of 'institutional intolerance'. While there can be little doubt that New Labour's policies on crime control incorporate elements of populism and punitiveness, the claim that this characterises the essence of their approach over the last decade is a gross overstatement.

One popular strand of argument for those who see recent government policy as an expression of populist punitiveness is that the proportion of young people in custody in England and Wales is significantly higher than in other European countries. However, as Ken Pease (1994) has pointed out, if the number of arrests and convictions for serious crime is taken into account, then the scale of imprisonment appears more moderate. Moreover, there has been a decline in the number of custodial sentences imposed on children since 2001 (Ministry of Justice, 2008a). There was a substantial drop in 2003 followed by three years of relative stability, while there has been a simultaneous levelling-out of the number of juveniles in the secure estate (see Figure 7.1).

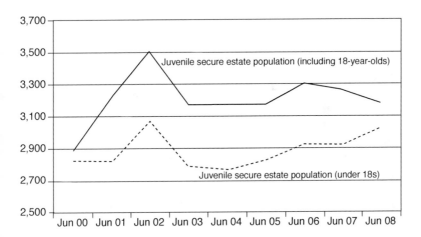

Figure 7.1   Secure estate population trends, 2000–08

Source: Youth Justice Board (2001).

Overall, however, it seems that much of the 'get tough' rhetoric that characterised the early period of New Labour has gradually waned. In its place, a multifaceted system of juvenile justice has been created that involves a number of different components. These include attempts to reduce reoffending and reconviction rates, to reduce the use of the secure estate, to increase the use of restorative justice processes, to make the juvenile justice more efficient and minimise delays, to develop more effective systems of assessment, to provide more 'joined up' services, to encourage offenders to consider the consequences of their actions, to develop more education and training programmes for young offenders, to reinforce parental responsibility and to tackle some of the problems underlying offending (Youth Justice Board, 2001; Burnett and Appleton, 2004). It may be the case that the way in which New Labour has attempted to meet these objectives has been inconsistent, but this does not detract from the viability of the objectives themselves. It may also be the case that there are tensions and contradictions in the policy objectives and that implementation may have been patchy, but the aims embody a number of positive components (Crawford, 2001). As John Pitts (2001) has argued, rather than a more intrusive, controlling and punitive form of youth justice, we are witnessing a more ambiguous process in which some elements of recent governmental interventions can be read as involving progressive gains for young people.

Conclusion

The history of juvenile justice in England and Wales can be seen as a series of oscillations between different 'inclusive' and 'exclusive' policy options, particularly in the postwar period. The 1960s saw the development of a strategy of welfarist intervention culminating in the Children and Young Persons Act (1969). However, in the 1970s there was a backlash against welfarism, resulting in a significant increase in the use of custody for juveniles, linked to the rise of the 'back to justice' lobby. This decidedly punitive approach culminated in the Criminal Justice Act (1982). Surprisingly, the 1980s saw an unprecedented shift towards decarceration and forms of minimalism which resulted in a reduction in the number of young people being formally processed and imprisoned.

The early 1990s saw another surge of punitivism, with Michael Howard, who was the Home Secretary at the time, claiming that 'prison works', which was seen as providing encouragement for the increased use of custodial sanctions. The election of New Labour in 1997 was widely expected to reverse the conservatives 'get tough' policy agenda, but instead Labour leaders, not wanting to be seen as 'soft on crime', continued the tough rhetoric and identified youth crime as a central object of intervention. However, by the end of the 1990s the rhetoric softened and a new set of discourses and practices began to take shape. Indeed, a whole raft of measures has been developed over the last few years – supportive, welfarist and punitive and preventative – in an attempt to address juvenile misbehaviour. These include new forms of monitoring and surveillance, the greater use of 'contracts', mentoring, reparation and growing emphasis on restorative justice, the widespread deployment of ABCs and ASBOs, a growing emphasis on risk-based assessments, and a growing emphasis on education and rehabilitation within the secure estate. These policies may involve tensions and problems, but they cannot be simply seen as an example of 'populist punitiveness', or, for that matter, a shift towards the 'New Penology' with its emphasis on the management and incapacitation of problem populations. As we have seen, the number of children sentenced to custody has decreased over the past few years. The number of juveniles held in the secure estate decreased in 2003–04 but has remained relatively high, although this may be less to do with a surge of punitiveness than with an increasing number of disaffected, disadvantaged and damaged young people in need of care and containment.

8
Women's Imprisonment

Introduction

An official report published in 1970 predicted that 'It may well be that as the end of the century draws nearer, penological progress will result in even fewer or no women at all being given prison sentences' (Home Office, 1970). However, despite various predictions of this type during this period the number of women incarcerated did not decrease during the 1970s and 1980s, and at the end of the 1990s the average daily population in England and Wales had risen to just under 3,000 (Home Office, 1998). By 2009 the number had reached just over 4,500. Consequently penologists have turned their attention away from explaining the reasons for the decrease in women's imprisonment and instead to addressing the question of why the anticipated reduction did not take place. In the course of doing so, they have examined the changing nature of female crime and sentencing as well as social and political changes. The significant increase in the number of women in prison during the 1990s has raised questions about the presumed 'leniency' given to women offenders as well as questions about equality before the law. The literature tends be divided between those who see changing patterns of offending by women as the main motor of change and those who see the growth in imprisonment as more or less a result of tougher sentencing policies and practices.

The growth of women's imprisonment, 1980–2007

The increase in the scale of women's imprisonment in recent years has been dramatic. In England and Wales the number of women imprisoned more than doubled between 1993 and 2001, increasing from 1,560 to 3,740 over this period. The number of women imprisoned increased by 140 per cent over this period compared to a 46 per cent increase in the number of men incarcerated. In 1992 women comprised 3.5 per cent of the prison population in England and Wales and by 2000 they represented 5.2 per cent (Home Office, 2002).

In America, the rate of increase has been even greater, with the number of women incarcerated increasing from 20,479 in 1980 to 104,848 in 2004. Thus over the 24-year period the number of women imprisoned in America increased almost fivefold and has increased at nearly double the rate of men (Greene *et al.*, 2006; Hill and Harrison, 2005). In Australia the number of female prisoners increased by 78 per cent between 1995 and 2002, while the number of male prisoners increased by 27 per cent. Over the same period the proportion of women in Australian prisons increased from 4.8 per cent in 1995 to 6.6 per cent in 2002 (Gelb, 2003). In Canada there has been a 30 per cent increase in the number of women in provincial/territorial custody between 1996 and 2007, which has been largely a result of a doubling of the remand population rather than an increase in sentenced prisoners. In 2007, women accounted for 6 per cent of offenders in provincial/territorial custody and 4 per cent of those in federal prisons (Kong and AuCoin, 2008).

The growth of female incarceration in these countries suggests that it is not a limited or idiosyncratic development and the international nature of these changes has raised important questions regarding the use of imprisonment and the reasons for the increased incarceration of women. Although the official statistics on female crime in these four countries reveal different and changing patterns, in all four jurisdictions the level of recorded violent crime by women has increased significantly.

Between 1987 and 1994 the arrest rate for girls in America more than doubled. In relation to violent crime the recorded crime figures show that between 1988 and 1997, violent offences were up for girls by over 100 per cent, arrests for aggravated assaults increased by 142 per cent and arrests for robberies increased by 95.3 per cent (Chesney-Lind and Paramore, 2001). By 2005, 35.4 per cent of women imprisoned in state prisons in America had been convicted of a violent offence. The next largest offence group was for drug offences, which made up 28.7 per cent of the female imprisoned population, which was fractionally higher than property offences, which stood at 28.6 per cent (Sabol *et al.*, 2007).

A review of the increased use of imprisonment for women in Australia between 1995 and 2002 indicates that there has been a significant increase in the proportion of female prisoners who have been convicted of violent crime, particularly robbery. At the same time there has been a decrease of approximately 40 per cent in deception offences, as well as 50 per cent decrease in drug use. Imprisonment for violence does not appear to be linked to prior offences, while sentence lengths for most offences have remained fairly stable over the period (Gelb, 2003). Significantly, between 2002 and 2006 the number of men in federal prisons in Australia decreased by 19 per cent while the number of females increased by 17 per cent. By 2007 a third of all sentenced female prisoners were imprisoned for violence related offences. (Australian Institute of Criminology, 2009).

In Canada, property crime accounted for nearly half (47 per cent) of arrests in 2005, while 28 per cent of offenders were accused of violence against the person. These offences of violence by women tended to involve friends, acquaintances or spouses. Significantly, the rate at which women (and men) have been charged for criminal code offences has fallen 28 per cent between 1992 and 2005. However, for female youth aged 12–17 the rate of serious violent crime more than doubled between 1986 and 2001, after which it has declined slightly. The number of violent crimes recorded for adult women also increased between 1986 and 2001. In 2006 just over half (55 per cent) of federally sentenced women in Canada were serving time for a violent offence and a quarter for drug offences. Within the provincial correctional system an estimated 30 per cent of women are under supervision for violent offences. A disproportionate number of these women are young, single and Aboriginal (Kong and AuCoin, 2008).

Although there are considerable similarities in the recorded crime and imprisonment patterns for women in these countries, criminologists are reluctant to accept these figures at face value and their interpretation is highly contested. In general, the majority of criminologists tend to focus on the sentencing process rather than offending data and tend to see the increase in the scale of imprisonment for women as resulting from a change in the reaction to female offenders rather than their involvement in crime. In the next section a more detailed examination of the flow of women through the criminal justice system in England and Wales is undertaken.

From arrest to imprisonment

In order to assess the impact of changing levels of arrest for different offences on the use of custody it is necessary to trace the progress of offenders through the criminal justice system. As symbolic interactionists have pointed out, each stage of the process involves different forms of decision-making which can affect the movement of women from one stage to the next. Thus the greater use of cautions, community-based sanctions or forms of diversion can have a significant impact on the flow of offenders through the criminal justice system and ultimately on the scale of imprisonment.

In Table 8.1 four types of offence have been selected – violence against the person, theft and handling, drug use and fraud and forgery – on the basis that these are the offences in which women are mainly involved or for which they tend to be imprisoned. Although this figure represents a series of snapshots rather than tracing specific cohorts of women through the criminal justice process, the aim is to try to identify the ways in which decision-making has changed and how this has affected the number of women sent to prison and how long they serve. The figures presented in Table 8.1 are incomplete and there is limited information on arrests in England and Wales prior to 1999. However, given these limitations the available data indicate that the number of women arrested for violence against the person more than doubled between 1999 and 2007, increasing from 37,100 to 87,200. There was a substantial increase in the use of cautions for this offence, while average sentence lengths have remained relatively constant. The increase in the use of custody for violence against the person has resulted in a significant increase in the number of women sentenced to immediate custody for this offence since 2001 (Home Office, 2007). The processing of theft and handling cases has taken a slightly different course over the past 15 years. The number of arrests has decreased since 2001, as have the use of cautions. The number found guilty and average sentence lengths have increased over the past six years. In line with other offences, there has been a significant increase in the use of immediate custody. Since 2001, however, the number sentenced to immediate custody for theft and handling has decreased by 7.5 per cent.

There has been an increased focus on drug-related offences in recent years as a factor influencing the use of custody for women. However, the arrest rate for drug related offences has been relatively stable between 2001 and 2007, although the number found guilty has increased slightly over this period. The use of community sentences for this offence has decreased by almost a quarter between 2001 and 2007. Sentence lengths have decreased since 2001 for this offence, while the number sentenced to immediate custody has more than doubled between 1996 and 2006. Figure 8.1 clearly shows how the use of immediate custody has increased between 1996 and 2006, particularly for drug-related offences, robbery and violence against the person.

The number of arrests from fraud and forgery in England and Wales decreased between 2001 and 2007, as did the percentage given a community sentence. The most significant change over the past decade has been the dramatic increase in the number of women sentenced to

Table 8.1 The number and proportion of women processed in the criminal justice system for selected offences, 1992–2007 (England and Wales)

	Violence against the person				Theft and handling				Drug use				Fraud and forgery			
	1992	1996	2001	2007	1992	1996	2001	2007	1992	1996	2001	2007	1992	1996	2001	2007
Arrests	–	–	37,100	87,200	–	–	94,500	80,250	–	–	13,950	12,100	–	–	10,900	7,800
Cautions	6,000	5,200	4,400	12,690	4,750	3,360	2,690	3,090	2,850	5,100	4,500	51,470	2,500	2,500	2,250	2,960
No. found guilty or cautioned in court (indictable offences)	9,700	7,900	7,800	17,300	7,150	5,450	5,270	5,210	4,900	8,700	8,900	9,600	7,000	6,200	7,300	9,500
Percentage given community sentence	–	35.6	41.1	41.1	–	33.8	33.4	29.3	–	25.7	20.5	16.6	–	33.6	32.89	20.8
Average sentence lengths (months) Crown Court	21.2	24.6	23.1	23.5	8.7	9.9	9.5	14.8	37.8	32.1	40.5	36.5	11.3	11.1	11.2	10.6
All courts	–	17.0	15.2	15.5	–	4.6	3.3	3.4	–	28.9	35.2	31.5	–	8.0	6.5	8.7
Sentenced to immediate custody	–	440	754	707	–	1710	3032	2783	–	580	992	784	–	210	279	951
Percentage sentenced to immediate custody for indictable offences	–	14.9	18.5	15.7	–	9.4	13.2	13.2	–	18.3	23.9	18.7	–	12.1	12.3	14.6
Proportionate use of immediate custody for women 21 and over Crown Court	22	32	34	?	21	33	40	?	39	43	60	–	22	34	34	–
Magistrates Court	2	7	10	–	2	7	14	–	1	2	4	–	2	5	9	–

Sources: Ministry of Justice, Statistics on Women and the Criminal Justice System, 1999, 2003, 2007, 2009, Criminal Statistics, 2007.

178

immediate custody for this offence, while average sentence lengths have increased between 2001 and 2007. Arrest rates for drug-related offences more than doubled during the 1990s, but have levelled out over the past six or seven years.

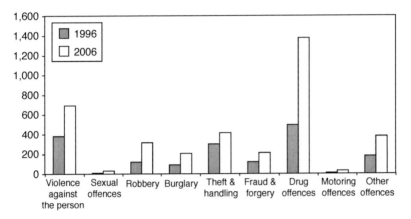

Figure 8.1 Female immediate custodial sentenced prison population by offence group and year

Source: Ministry of Justice, *Offender Management Caseload Statistics 2006.*

In sum, there would appear to have been increases in arrest rates as well as in sentencing practices over the last 15 years. Although the figures are incomplete, there has obviously been a considerable increase in the number of women arrested for violence, and there has been a substantial increase in the number of women given an immediate custodial sentence for a range of offences. The changes in sentence lengths have been much less than might have been expected, and the use of community sentences has decreased for theft, fraud and drug related offences but has increased for violence over the past 15 years. In the next sections the aim is to examine these processes in more detail and to 'get behind' the data and to look in particular at the changing nature of female crime and the use of community sentences and sentencing policy.

Explaining the increase in crime

In the mid 1970s, Freda Adler (1975) claimed that the increase in female criminality and, by implication, women's imprisonment was a function of the development of the Women's Liberation Movement.

The changing aspirations associated with the rise of the first phase of women's liberation, Adler argued, spawned a new generation of female offenders who were turning to more masculine forms of crime. This claim was strongly rebutted by Carol Smart (1979), who pointed out that the vast majority of poor and working-class women who came into contact with the criminal justice system had little contact with the Women's Liberation Movement, which at the time involved predominantly middle-class women. In response, Roy Austin (1981) pointed out that there was not only a significant increase in the level of recorded female crime, but also that there were signs of a 'convergence' between patterns of male and female offending. In a further contribution to this debate, Steven Box and Chris Hale (1983) argued that the various commentators on this issue had failed to identify any clear causal links between women's liberation and changing levels of crime and punishment.

In a further rejoinder to the debate, Carol Smart (1990) rejected not only the general thesis that women are becoming more heavily involved in crime, but also questioned the preoccupation with causality, which she identified as being a function of an outdated modernist approach and a realist problematic. Under the influence of the rise in postmodernism, she argues that there is a need to move away from the category of 'crime', and she is critical of female academics who engage in empirical investigation of crime. These academics she sees as adopting the tenets of 'malestream' criminology, and do little more than fill in the gaps of a fundamentally masculinist criminology. In opposition, Smart wants to deconstruct 'crime' and develop an alternative approach based on a feminist epistemology that can 'analyse the power effects of resistance' and wants to discover and promote 'those voices that have been forced into silence by mainstream criminology'.

Smart's arguments have become very influential amongst a growing body of anti-criminologists who want to move away from the concept of 'crime' and are not particularly interested in developing causal explanations and engaging in policy formation. However, as Pat Carlen (1992) has argued, Smart contents herself with elaborating different theoretical positions which have little analytic usefulness. Carlen argues that the purpose of deconstruction should be to find out how and why things work in order to generate new knowledge and new practices. Smart, Carlen argues, by denying the reality of crime, in effect denies the effects of crime on its victims. Moreover, as realist criminologists have suggested, crime is not simply a social 'construction' but involves tangible events with real effects (Matthews, 2009). Also, John Lea (1998) asks the question, what is feminist about letting people 'speak for themselves?'

Without a notion of causality and an understanding of how 'crime' is constructed, Lea argues, we have no basis for developing a critical criminology.

In a slightly different vein, Laureen Snider (2003) claims that critical and feminist criminologies have inadvertently contributed to the increase in female incarceration by creating the 'punishable woman'. Criminology, she argues, has added to the recent surge of punitiveness and has been complicit in developing the female criminal subject and associated images, to which women themselves may aspire. She claims that when we categorise women as victims in need of treatment and the like, we may be complicit in legitimising certain forms of regulation. In general, she explores these long-standing liberal arguments that good intentions can often have unanticipated consequences (see Cohen, 1985). However, like Smart, her critiques and concerns are misplaced and ultimately disarming. While there is always the possibility, as Thomas Mathieson (1974) pointed out many years ago, of positive reforms being co-opted, it is the case that critical (and feminist criminologists) have consistently argued against more repression or increased punitiveness and have criticised dominant stereotypes of 'the female offender' and generally argued for greater tolerance towards female transgressions as well as a reduction of women's imprisonment (Silvestri and Crowther-Dowey, 2008; Walklate, 2004).

A more grounded and arguably more constructive response to the issue of the changing nature of female crime, particularly violent crime, has been presented by Meda Chesney-Lind (2004). In response to the claims that women are becoming increasingly involved in serious crime and particularly violent crime, Chesney-Lind (2004) has argued that it is necessary to critically investigate how these data are constructed. She suggests that rather than accepting the data at face value, there is a need to identify changes in the way that different activities are interpreted and recorded. She claims that we need to be sceptical of the official figures, and that their construction may have been conditioned by three related processes: 'relabelling', 'rediscovery' and 'upcriming' (Chesney-Lind and Paramore, 2001).

Relabelling involves the process by which offences that were previously considered to be minor or status offences become relabelled as violent offences. Therefore minor infractions that would have been dismissed by the police or involved a warning are now being recorded as offences.

Rediscovery refers to the realisation that women have probably always been more aggressive than the standard stereotype of them as passive and submissive subjects suggests. Thus, it is suggested, women are not so much undergoing a change of behaviour, but actions which previously have been ignored or trivialised are now becoming recognised.

Upcriming involves a changing response to certain types of behaviour such as treating playground scuffles or parent–daughter altercations as forms of violence. This may reflect changing public attitudes and growing intolerance of low level interpersonal violence. In addition, women who carry weapons for self-defence are thereby committing an offence.

There is no doubt an element of truth in the argument put forward by Chesney-Lind, and we know that social and legal definitions and responses to different types of activities change in different periods. It is also the case that social attitudes and tolerance towards most forms of interpersonal violence, including domestic violence, bullying, racial harassment and child abuse, have changed considerably over the last two or three decades.

Alternative approaches to the issue of female offending involve the use of self-report studies, victimisation surveys and arrestee surveys. One self-report study conducted in the UK is the Youth Lifestyles Survey which found that, in 1998/99, 11 per cent of females admitted engaging in a core offence, while a subsequent self-report survey carried out by the Offending Crime and Justice Survey (OCJS) in 2006 found that the proportion had increased to 17 per cent (Flood-Page *et al.*, 2000). Significantly, the proportion of men admitting a core offence remained the same in both surveys, at 26 per cent. The OCJS survey, however, notes that males were more likely to be classed as frequent offenders, while women's involvement in crime tends to be more short-lived, lasting less than a year in over 80 per cent of cases. Other information on female offending in England and Wales is available through the arrestee survey which found that while women were more likely to report Class A drug use than men, 35 per cent admitted taking cannabis over the last year compared to 49 per cent of males (Hunter *et al.*, 2009). The British Crime Survey 2007/08 found that 30 per cent of females aged 16–24 admitted taking an illicit drug in the last month.

Thus the picture of the changing nature of female offending over the past decade or so is dependent to some extent on the types of data sources used and the way in which they are interpreted. Probably the best way to approach this issue is to try to build up a composite picture which, while having certain gaps and limitations, allows us to say something meaningful about changing attitudes and behaviour.

It would appear that there are four general points that emerge from these data. The first is that women's involvement in violence and illicit drug use has almost certainly increased over the last decade. Second, that women's involvement in offending in general is significantly higher than is often suggested. Third, that the range of women's offending is much wider than is generally assumed, although there is a disproportionate involvement in certain offences such as theft and shoplifting. Fourth, that attitudes are changing towards female offenders, who are seen as more culpable and responsible and therefore more deserving of punishment.

Unpacking these processes and understanding the changing nature of action and reaction will require more detailed investigation, but in the meantime it is evident that as the number of women being arrested and processed for a range of imprisonable offences increases, there is a probability that a percentage will end up in prison. There are, however, a number of stages between arrest and imprisonment that need to be examined in order to gauge the impact of the increasing arrest rate for women on the scale of imprisonment. In recent years it has been widely argued by penal reformers that greater use should be made of community sentences but, as we have seen, the use of community sentences has decreased for three of the four selected offences over the past 15 years.

The use of community-based sanctions

What impact has the use of community sanctions had on the use of custody between 1992 and 2007? The number of women given probation increased throughout the 1990s, such that in 1991 there were 8,399 on what is now called community rehabilitation orders, and by 2001 the number had increased to 11,376. The number of women on what are now called community punishment orders increased from 2,330 to 6,287, while those given community punishment and rehabilitation orders increased from 125 to 1,624 over this period (Home Office, 2001b). Community punishment orders are considered to be the most punitive of the three orders.

In her book *Alternatives to Women's Imprisonment* (1990), Pat Carlen points out that the provision of community-based sanctions for women is patchy and limited. She found significant geographical variations in the provision of community-based alternatives, while noting that such provision was in some cases not particularly appropriate for women with child-minding responsibilities. She also expressed concern about the possible 'net widening' effects of these alternatives and the possibility of ostensibly benign non-custodial sanctions drawing minor offenders into the mainstream criminal justice process. She did recognise, however, that some alternatives were positive and allowed women space to discuss issues of concern and in some cases provide support, particularly through women only groups.

There are, however, issues about the appropriate forms of activity to be undertaken by women sentenced to community-based alternatives (Worrall, 1997). Recent research has found that sentencers are in some cases reticent about giving community-based alternatives because they claim that they are 'too tough' and that prisons are better able to meet the needs of women offenders. Sentencers also tend to justify the use of imprisonment rather than community-based sanctions because they feel that women are not able to meet the demands of a community sentence as a result of their 'chaotic lifestyles', and that offering women this option would be 'setting them up to fail' (Carlen and Tombs, 2006).

Apart from the use of these community-based sanctions, another significant non-custodial option is the fine. Although the use of fines for women offenders has decreased in recent years, it was still the most widely used sanction for women in 2007, accounting for approximately 75 per cent of all sentences. Between 1997 and 2007 the use of fines decreased for both male and female offenders from 77,594 to 42,971. For women the number decreased from 9,175 to 5,481 over this period. Paradoxically, the use of fines for indictable offences for women has decreased significantly over the past decade or so, while its use has increased for summary offences. The decrease of the fine for women appears to be a consequence of the problems of enforcement, with many poor people ending up in prison in default of payment of fines. Consequently there has been a shift away from the use of fines since the mid 1990s for criminal offences and it has become more of an administrative sanction for offences such as motoring. Consequently fines are less in evidence in Crown Courts but have increased in Magistrates Courts over the past decade (O'Malley, 2009).

Other community-based sanctions that are available include drug treatment and testing orders (DTTOs), electronic monitoring, restorative justice and forms of intensive supervision. The Criminal Justice Act (2003) also introduced the suspended sentence order (SSO) by which a custodial sentence can be suspended for between six months and two years. Since its introduction the use of the suspended sentence order has grown while the number of community sentences given to women has decreased.

Overall, the use of community sentences has remained fairly stable for women between 1992 and 2007, with a slight increase in their use for violent offenders between 1996 and 2007 and a corresponding decrease for drug-related offences and fraud and forgery. Given these variations, the changing use of community sentences over the last 15 years has probably made only a limited impact on the number of women in prison in England and Wales (Carlen and Worrall, 2004).

Sentencing, leniency and equality

It has been frequently claimed that women are treated more leniently by courts than their male counterparts. Framing this issue in terms of 'leniency', however, has two potentially negative effects. First, it assumes that the sentences handed out to men are the norm. Second, and correspondingly, when demands are made for greater equality in sentencing there is a tendency to increase the severity of women's sentencing towards the presumed 'norm'. It is also the case historically that women have been incarcerated for lesser crimes and for longer periods than men. The introduction of reformatories at the beginning of the twentieth century, for example, which were designed to be more benign and more responsive to women's needs, resulted in more minor offenders being locked up for longer periods of time 'for their own good' in order to allow them time to 'reform'. This strategy has been described as involving a form of 'benevolent repression' (Heidensohn, 1986).

The point of reference for the 'leniency' argument is that women are more likely to be given a non-custodial sentence than men for similar offences, and when women are imprisoned they tend to receive shorter sentences (Genders and Player, 1986). However, direct comparisons are difficult to make in an individualised criminal justice system, and even in relation to offences that appear gender-neutral, such as theft or burglary, there may be different motivations, contexts and impacts associated with these offences. It is also difficult to untangle the gender and class dimensions of sentencing. When women transgress in ways that deviate from conventional female roles they may be treated particularly harshly. As Pat Carlen (1983), has argued, this is because women make not only a 'class deal' but also a 'gender deal'. The 'class deal', she argues, which operates in relation to work, affords fewer rewards for women than for men. The implications of the 'gender deal', on the other hand, relate to dominant conceptions of 'femininity' and can play a significant part in shaping the meaning and by implication the response to women's transgressions. Carlen has added that considerations of gender justice should take into account the 'dangerousness of women, their experience of prior victimisation, and the degree of informal control that women are subject to' (Carlen, 2002c). These considerations raise, in turn, issues of culpability and responsibility (Hudson, 2002).

The claims that women are treated more 'leniently' than men tend to be based on the observation that female first-time offenders are half as likely to be given a sentence of immediate imprisonment as male first-time offenders (4 per cent compared to 8 per cent), while women with one, two, three or more convictions are less likely to receive custodial sentences than the equivalent men, and these claims should be treated with caution. Carol Hedderman and Mike Hough (1994), for example, argue that:

> Although the statistical data presents a strong indication that female offenders on average are less likely to receive a custodial sentence than their male counterparts for most offence categories, some of the limitations of these statistical comparisons become apparent when we compare specific crimes and specific cases. If we take domestic homicide, for example, we find that an analysis of cases dealt with between 1984 and 1992 shows that 23% of females compared with only 4% of males indicted for homicide were acquitted on all charges. Of those found guilty 80% of the women compared with 61% of the men were found guilty of the lesser charge of manslaughter and more than two-thirds of men convicted of manslaughter received a prison sentence compared with less than half of the women. (Hedderman and Hough, 1994: 3–4)

This type of statistical comparison is weak, in as much as the cases are not clearly matched, and the greater acquittal rates of women can be read as evidence that they are more readily prosecuted on flimsier evidence than men; whereas the greater percentage of cases in which the charge is reduced to manslaughter may well be a consequence of greater provocation and systematic abuse suffered by women, which is often reported to be associated with these cases. It is also likely that there are significant differences in the circumstances in which these cases of domestic homicide have taken place, given the differences in physical and social resources of the two parties (Walklate, 1995). It is not an unreasonable assumption that those women who engage in domestic homicide do so for different reasons and employ different methods from those routinely employed by men in the commission of this offence, with the consequence that substantial differences of culpability are likely to be apportioned to males and females who commit domestic homicide. In short, reducing the charge or comparing the percentage of males and females given custodial sentences in these circumstances cannot be directly interpreted as evidence of 'leniency'.

A major issue which arises is the substantive inequalities and power differentials that operate in relation to men and women (Connell, 1987). Correspondingly the question is whether the aim should be the pursuit of formal equality, so that men and women are treated in the same way, or whether, given the substantive differences in power and resources, the aim should be to treat men and women differently. Thus the choice appears to be whether to aim for 'parity' or 'equality'. If the latter is the aim, then statistical comparisons of sentencing outcomes are of limited relevance. The focus on 'equality' is likely to require more detailed qualitative information that can incorporate details of the background and the circumstances in which the offences to be compared were carried out.

As Kathleen Daly (1994) has argued, most disparity studies do not readily address issues of domination and subordination between the sexes, and do not take account of how 'constructs of masculinity and femininity shape what people think about themselves, how they act and how they make sense of the behaviour of others'. In many of these studies, men are taken as the point of reference. The danger of taking men as *the* point of reference is clearly exemplified in those American states that have introduced greater parity in sentencing outcomes or mandatory sentencing policies, and as a consequence have increased the severity of the sentences imposed on women in order to bring them into line with men. It apparently never occurred to anyone to take women as *the* standard and thereby reduce average sentence lengths for certain offences (Pollock-Byrne, 1992). Daly (1994) suggests that an analysis of the gendered dimensions of sentencing should aim to identify causal relations through the analysis of 'pathways' by which researchers can trace through the backgrounds and life histories of the men and women concerned. Employing this form of detailed qualitative analysis, involving paired cases and incorporating detailed narrative material, Daly found that, in contrast to the statistical studies which claim considerable disparities in sentencing, gender differences in sentencing were often negligible.

A study carried out by Carol Hedderman and Loraine Gelsthorpe (1997) on magistrates' attitudes towards female defendants provides a useful vantage point from which to examine this process. This study suggests that female offenders are more likely to be perceived by magistrates as 'troubled' rather than 'troublesome', and as being subject to different pressures from male defendants. The nature of the offender's motivation, her demeanour and the level of deference displayed in court are all likely to influence decision-making. 'Troubled' defendants are seen as more in need of help than punishment, and probation is widely seen as the most appropriate response for a large percentage of female offenders. At the same time magistrates were found to be more reluctant to impose fines on women if they thought it would adversely affect their children. Family circumstances were found to be an important consideration in passing sentence, particularly if the women had dependant children, while an effort was normally made to help those in employment.

Thus issues of parity, equality and leniency remain contested and unresolved. It has been suggested that there is a need to develop a feminist jurisprudence, which can move beyond the 'masculinist' preoccupation with abstract universal principles and the 'rule of law' and replace it by a feminist perspective on justice, which emphasises personal and informal processes grounded in relationships (Heidensohn, 1975; Worrall, 1990). It may well be, as Catherine MacKinnon (1987) put it, that real 'equality means the aspirations to eradicate not gender differentiation but gender hierarchy'. Other writers have claimed that the aim should be to argue for both equality *and* difference by demanding, for example, equality in terms of resources and expenditure, while recognising the differences in need between male and female prisoners and consequently the different ways in which available resources should be distributed (Naffine, 1997; Young, 1997).

It has been argued that the increased use of custody for women in England and Wales has been influenced by the increasing focus on 'risk management' and the reformulation of the notion of proportionality, particularly in relation to the sentencing of 'persistent' offenders. The implication is that those women who do not fit the stereotypes of dependency and lacking agency will be harder hit (Player, 2005).

In a slightly different vein, Lorraine Gelsthorpe and Alison Morris (2002a) argue that the increase in the rate of imprisonment for women between 1992 and 2002 is not a result of changes in the nature and seriousness of women's crime, changes in sentencing patterns or changes in the lengths of women's sentences. Gelsthorpe and Morris point out in contrast to Player that women in general have fewer prison convictions than men and that therefore, in terms of risk assessment, they should on average receive a lesser sentence. By the same token the lower levels of recidivism for women should increase the likelihood of early release under an actuarial system.

It is difficult to draw any clear conclusions from the available data. However, it is evident that the processing of women through the criminal justice system over the past 15 years cannot be seen as simply a unilateral 'get tough' policy. In addition, there is evidence of a discernable policy of diversion and the increased use of cautions for violence and drug related offences since 2001 as well as a general increase in the use of immediate custody, while the average custodial sentence length for women decreased from 10.7 months in 2002 to 9.4 months in 2007. However, it should be noted that these figures exclude indeterminate sentences, which were introduced in 2005 (Hunter et al., 2009).

There are four features of the sentencing of women that have had an impact on the level and composition of the prison population. The first is the increased number of women on remand, which has increased by approximately 50 per cent between 1997 and 2007, while the rate of increase of adult female prisoners has been greater than female young offenders (Ministry of Justice, 2007).

The second important development that has taken place in relation to sentencing for women is the growth over the past few years of the number of women serving longer sentences. A considerable amount of attention has been paid to the growth of short prison sentences for women, but between 2003 and 2007 there has been a reduction in the number of women receiving very short sentences (less than three months) while the number receiving sentences over twelve months has almost doubled over the period (see Figure 8.2).

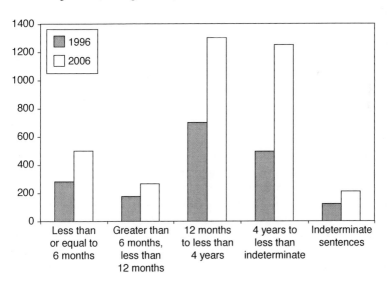

Figure 8.2 Female immediate custodial sentenced prison population by length of sentence and year

Source: Ministry of Justice, *Offender Management Caseload Statistics 2006*.

The third significant development which will have an impact on the average daily population in prison is the number of women with numerous previous convictions. Significantly, between 2002 and 2007 the number of women in prison with 15 or more previous convictions increased from 14 per cent to 21 per cent.

The fourth consideration has been an ageing of the female custodial population in recent years which reflects an ageing of women going through the criminal justice system. This has implications for the treatment needs and rehabilitative programmes in prison as well as the development of community-based alternatives to custody (Newman, 2003). The predictions are that the number of prisoners aged over 50 will continue to increase in the future (HM Inspectorate of Prisons, 2004).

In sum, the combination of an increase in the remand population, more women receiving longer sentences, an increasing number of persistent offenders and the ageing of the women going through the criminal justice process, is changing the composition of the female custodial population and creating new problems for the management of women's prisons.

Characteristics of the female prison population

The profile of women prisoners presented by the *National Prison Survey* (Walmsley *et al.*, 1992) indicates that in broad terms it is generally similar to the male prison population, in that the majority of prisoners are drawn from disadvantaged sections of society and inner-city areas, and have poor education and employment records. The *Thematic Review: Women in Prison* (HM Inspectorate of Prisons, 1997b), which was carried out by the Prisons Inspectorate and based on a survey of 234 women, found that 70 per cent of the women claimed to have had no previous employment, one in ten had 'no fixed abode', and the majority had problems of accommodation prior to imprisonment. Nearly half of the women reported that they had been abused, almost one-third sexually. About 40 per cent had misused at least one controlled drug. Among those who reported heavy abuse or addiction, over half had used heroin, and about a quarter had used cocaine or crack. Approximately 40 per cent of the women interviewed reported that they had harmed themselves intentionally or had attempted suicide. Just over half had children aged under 16, and over a third had one child or more under five years old (HM Inspectorate of Prisons, 1997b). Other research has confirmed this picture. Alison Morris and Christine Wilkinson (1995) found that over 60 per cent of women in their survey had been living solely on benefits prior to their imprisonment, while one-third said they had been in debt.

However, given this profile, it is surprising that about half of the women in prison had no previous convictions and just over 70 per cent had not been in prison before (Prison Reform Trust, 1993).

The conclusion that arises from these surveys of women prisoners is that, while they are similar in terms of a number of basic socio-economic characteristics to male prisoners, they have a different range of physical and psychological needs. Moreover, as the Prison Inspectorate (1997b) reported, 55 per cent of the women interviewed said that they had received little or no help in prison, while nearly 40 per cent thought that the prison had not improved them in any way at all, and only about one in ten had received any type of counselling. Significantly, when asked what they would need to help them not to reoffend, their replies were: a job and money, a home, counselling, help with drug and alcohol problems, and moving to a new area. It is indicative that 150 years after the establishment of women's prisons, such a fundamental review of the needs of women prisoners is considered necessary as a basis for providing an appropriate set of policies for health care, education, employment, tackling drug and alcohol misuse and for providing proper child care and counselling services.

One of the most significant features of the female prison population is the disproportionate number drawn from ethnic minorities. Among the female prison population in England and Wales in 2007, some 30 per cent were described as being members of an ethnic minority group, of whom the majority were categorised as 'black' or 'black British'. Some 58 per cent of female foreign nationals had been convicted and imprisoned for a drug offence, compared to 32 of male foreign nationals. Those convicted of drug-related offences tend to receive relatively long sentences, often in excess of three years, while those women who have been convicted of importing illegal drugs – 'mules' – can receive even longer sentences, which may be accompanied by deportation on completion of the sentence (Green, 1991). Two direct implications follow from the particularly long sentences given to those convicted of the importation and distribution of illegal drugs. The first is that there is a pronounced imbalance in the profile of women sent to prison and the makeup of the female prison population on any one day. The second is that there are growing problems in managing the increased percentage of long-term prisoners in women's prisons, particularly non-nationals (Ministry of Justice, 2008b).

Women in prison

Women make up a relatively small proportion of the prison population. The most immediate consequence is that the number of units holding women are few in number. As a result, female prisoners tend to be held some distance from home, making visits more difficult to organise. The second implication is that the available prisons will necessarily have to accommodate a wider range of offenders in terms of age and offence category than men's prisons. The third implication is that the availability of work, training, education and various other specialist programmes in prison is likely to be limited.

Based on her pioneering work in Cornton Vale Prison in Scotland, Pat Carlen (1983) argues that female prisoners are defined as being without 'sociability, femininity and adulthood and as being beyond care or cure'. The impact of these ideological and stereotypical constructions is that female prisoners are seen as not being real women but as deviants who need to be disciplined, medicalised and feminised. Thus, typically, work and training programmes tend to be linked to traditional domestic roles and may have little relevance to the reality of the women's lives on the outside (Eaton, 1993). It may also be the case that the forms of domestic training which many female prisoners are given may paradoxically be designed to push them back into those domestic roles and situations from which they may be attempting to escape. By the same token, the ideals of femininity promoted by prison authorities are denied by the removal of the normal physical and psychological props through which the ideal of femininity is socially maintained. This fundamental contradiction, Carlen (1983) suggests, leads to both a celebration and a denial of the feminine myth and results in confusion and bitterness.

Historically, women's prisons have been characterised by intensive forms of discipline, which result in greater levels of intrusiveness and surveillance than is normally experienced in men's prisons (Devlin, 1998). What prisoners say, who they talk with, their movements and moods are all closely monitored. It is this detailed form of supervision which is seen to explain, in part, the relatively high number of disciplinary offences in women's prisons and the tendency for personal relations to oscillate between punitiveness and support (Dobash *et al.*, 1986).

In a number of ways women are held to experience the 'pains of imprisonment' more acutely than men. This is not because women prisoners are any less resilient than their male counterparts, but because the material, physical and social conditions of their confinement are significantly different. Differences in perceived domestic responsibilities, lesser experience of confinement, limited criminal careers, as well as histories of physical and sexual abuse, suggest that a considerable percentage of women are already socially and personally 'damaged' before entering this alien environment. Child care and the frequency and quality of visits are a major concern among women in prison.

The culture within women's prisons is influenced by women's identities as mothers. The mothering role provides women with a sense of identity and serves as a means of shared experience and information within the prison. However, the dynamics of imprisonment generate dependence and infantilisation among inmates. These twin processes have paradoxical consequences for the well-being of mothers and the development of children, since:

> Infantilization and the push toward conformity undermine women's efforts to take responsibility as adults, mothers and citizens. The deprivational and controlling character of prison gives rise to reactive, self-serving modes of adapting and reinforces punitive parenting models. The prison reproduces some of the same destructive relational dynamics that the mothers experienced within their own families. Treatment modalities, although diverse, operate within and draw authority from the coercive prison order. (Clark, 1995: 326)

The detrimental and negative effects of women's imprisonment have become widely recognised. In different countries there are signs that attitudes towards women's imprisonment are changing, and there has been an attempt to move away from the old-style prisons and to develop more appropriate and less damaging forms of confinement. In England and Wales, as we have seen, there has been something of a watershed in penal policy relating to women over the past five or six years, with a greater emphasis on the diversion of women from custody and prosecution and decreasing the number of minor offenders in the prison system.

The influential report by Baroness Corston (Ministry of Justice, 2007a), which focused on women with particular vulnerabilities in the criminal justice system, called for nothing less than 'a distinct, radically different, visibly-led, strategic, proportionate, holistic, woman-centered, integrated approach'. The report advocates the replacement of existing prisons with small, multifunctional custodial centres together with a greater use of community based sanctions. At the same time she wants to develop diversion strategies by using newly established women's centres and to limit the number of women entering prison as a result of breaches (Home

Office, 2007). The government's response to the recommendations of the report has been positive, and 40 of the 43 recommendations have been accepted (Ministry of Justice, 2007a) with the Criminal Justice Women's Unit being set up. There is a commitment to reducing the number of women entering the criminal justice system and of reserving custody for only the most serious offenders. There is also an intention to improve prison facilities for women and make them more appropriate to women's needs (Gelsthorpe *et al.*, 2007). The recommendations have been repeated in a recent report by the Fawcett Society (2007) on *Women and Justice* which addresses issues of discrimination against women at the various stages of the criminal justice system and calls for the greater use of non-custodial sanctions for women. The report is also critical of the money being spent on two newly-built, privately-run, purpose-built prisons for women, one of which was opened in Ashford, Middlesex, in 2004. Although it has a health care centre and a gym, a prayer facility for Muslim prisoners, and is reported to feature 'an attractive beige and fuchsia colour scheme' designed to give the prison a 'more domestic feel' than is found in many prisons, there are concerns about the impact of such prison-building programmes on the projected population of women in prison (Travis, 2004). Thus there is a clear intention in England and Wales to reduce the size of the female prison population and develop woman-centred prisons while diverting minor offenders from custody. In developing these strategies, reformers have drawn on recent experiences from other countries in order to consider the different available options.

Alternative models of women's imprisonment

Woman-centred prisons

The recurring problem with women's prisons, as we have seen, is that they are often too remote, too diverse and generally lacking in facilities. For the most part they have not been developed around principles which relate to the reality of women prisoners' lived experience and needs, but rather regimes are organised around ideologies of femininity and domesticity.

What is required, critics argue, are more local prisons with lower levels of security, and which are designed to cater specifically for women's needs (Hannah-Moffat, 1995; M. Shaw, 1992). This approach draws on the writings of Carol Gilligan (1982), who stresses the 'politics of difference' and argues that men and women hold different moral codes: women stress moral integrity and care for the self and others through a commitment to personal relationships, rather than employing 'objective' criteria in order to arrive at 'just' solutions. This, for Gilligan, means an emphasis on listening to the voice of otherness rather than the masculinist approach, which she claims involves masking different voices under an abstract cloud of universality.

Recent developments in Canada exemplify this growing interest in developing a 'woman-centred' approach. In the report *Creating Choices* (Correctional Services Canada, 1990), it was proposed that five new facilities, to be situated close to the major centres of population, would replace the existing prison for women at Kingston. The strategy was based on five 'feminist' principles: empowerment; the provision of meaningful choices; treating women with respect and dignity; providing a physically and emotionally supportive environment; and, finally, the sharing of the responsibility for women's welfare between institutional staff, community members, and the women themselves (Shaw, 1996). The aim was to construct new facilities in several acres of land with cottage-style houses accommodating six to ten women in each, as well as providing a 'healing lodge' for Aboriginal women. Programmes in these 'houses' were to be holistic, in that they were to deal with the interrelated nature of women's experience. The aim of the various programmes was to enable women to understand their situation better within a broader social context and to encourage them to take greater control over their lives.

Exactly how effective these new facilities have been in achieving their objectives and in providing a more constructive environment for female offenders has been subject to some debate. Problems of funding and developing appropriate rehabilitative programmes in a setting which remains, after all, coercive and segregative, has resulted in a number of ongoing difficulties. Restrictions of movement and limited work and training opportunities have been seen as the negative attributes of these small local units, despite the fact that the women prisoners appear to have gained more self-confidence and an improved understanding of their situation (M. Shaw, 1992).

The thinking behind the development of small, woman-centred prisons has also been criticised for treating women as a homogeneous group and for not paying enough attention to issues of race and class (Hannah-Moffat, 1995). It has been argued that the language of 'empowerment' can serve to encourage women prisoners to take responsibility for their actions within a context where the ultimate objectives are not of their own making. Although woman-centred regimes may emphasise treatment over punishment, self-determination over passivity, vertical collaboration and decision-making over hierarchical and authoritarian structures, there is a danger that the social and political context in which women's offending takes place is ignored and the oppressive nature of imprisonment is obscured. Thus, as one critic has argued:

> The woman-centred prison and its capacity for empowerment is constructed as a challenge to the hegemony of punitive carceral regimes and oppressive technologies of surveillance and discipline. Woman-centred prisons and the ethics of empowerment have not significantly challenged this hegemony; rather they have softened some of the rough edges of incarceration. Despite the influx of 'empowerment discourse', woman-centred corrections is about 'responsibilising' the prisoner and not empowerment as defined by some feminists. Corrections Canada's acknowledgement of the structural barriers facing women and their attempt to remove some of the 'pains of imprisonment' are compatible with the liberal notion of individual responsibility. The emphasis on responsibility decontextualises feminist constructions of women's resistance and it disregards feminist analysis of the social, economic, and political barriers experienced by women – and in particular, by marginalised women. (Hannah-Moffat, 1995: 159)

Hannah-Moffat concludes her critique by arguing that woman-centred prisons tend to reproduce normative standards of 'femininity', and although they appear to be a less intrusive and less punitive form of incarceration, the coercive qualities of incarceration 'are simply obscured by feminized social control talk that tends to deny the legal and material realities of imprisonment'. Recently, Pat Carlen has introduced the notion of 'carceral clawback', which refers to the process by which certain gains made through reforms are countered by other managerial or organisational imperatives. This, she argues, places a continuing limit on the scope of penal reform (Carlen, 2002b).

These critiques of the Canadian initiative, however, appear to be overly negative and pessimistic and the objective of progressive prison reform itself is denied. They dwell on what has not been achieved rather than what has. The reform process is invariably uncertain and there is always the likelihood that well-meaning ideals are not realised. This does not mean that reforms have 'failed', but that there is a need to remain realistic about what might be achieved and recognise that reform is an ongoing process. The critiques of penal reform by liberal pessimists tend to involve a predictable set of arguments. These include claims such as:

- However much you improve conditions, 'a prison is a prison' which deprives people of their liberty.

- There is always a mismatch between intentions and outcomes.
- You may change or improve certain aspects of incarceration but you have left the overarching structure intact.
- There may be some improvements, but you could have done something else that would have been better.
- Rather than try and improve prisons, your efforts would be better spent diverting offenders from custody.

The classic response from liberal pessimists is that, on one hand, if you improve conditions you just religitimse the prison and reinforce and even extend the use of custody. On the other hand, if you do not improve conditions you increase the pains of imprisonment such that offenders are more damaged and marginalised and therefore more prone to reoffending. In a similar vein, they are critical of efforts to 'empower' and 'responsibilise' prisoners and offer no response to the routine disempowerment and infantalisation of prisoners which is rife in women's prisons.

A more positive and constructive account of a woman-centred approach has been presented by Barbara Mason (2006). In 1999, a new centre was developed in Dublin known as the Dochas Centre. It was built around a number of small houses and was designed to offer a more constructive regime with more visits and more activities, and generally more open to outside agencies. The aim was to encourage women to take responsibility while addressing their needs. In 2003 the Irish Prisons Inspectorate reported that there had been a decrease in disciplinary measures in the Centre and an increase in mutual respect. Overall, the report was complimentary about the new Dochas Centre and noted the increased educational opportunities and increased well-being of the women prisoners, and concluded that the new regime had fostered the women's personal development. There are consequently plans to extend and develop the Centre (Irish Penal Reform Trust, 2008). Thus it is important to recognise that even small gains are gains and often provide the conditions for further gains. The woman-centred approach offers the possibility of tailoring prison regimes to the needs of the women and developing the conditions in which the women's quality of life is increased and their ability to make meaningful choices and decisions is enhanced.

Mixed prisons

There has been growing interest in a number of countries in mixing male and female prisoners, encouraged by both the desire to locate female prisoners closer to their homes and the desire to reduce the costs of imprisonment. Separate prisons for women are expensive, particularly if they have any pretensions to provide a comprehensive range of educational, training and recreational facilities. The degree and style of integration of males and females in prison varies considerably between different countries, but in England and Wales the debate has focused on the advantages and disadvantages of either creating more accommodation within men's prisons, so that women prisoners would be increasingly dispersed throughout the prison system but would be kept on separate wings or landings from men, or organising prisons so that male and female prisoners work together during the day and/or meet during association and recreational periods.

Apart from the arguments about the greater proximity to family and friends, the potential savings, and the possibility of providing women with a wider range of facilities in prison, there are two related arguments which have been mobilised in support of greater integration of the sexes. One set of arguments is associated with the concept of normalisation and the other with the notion of rehabilitation. The strategy of normalisation is based upon the premise that the aim of imprisonment is the deprivation of liberty and that apart from this sanction prisoners should be allowed to live as normally as possible within the constraints of confinement (King and Morgan, 1980). Thus all democratic and legal rights remain in place during the period of imprisonment, and prisoners should be able to engage in all those activities they would normally be involved in outside the prison. This would include mixing and engaging in relationships with people of the opposite sex. By segregating men and women in prisons, it is argued, an abnormal and distorted environment is created. Thus the strategy of normalisation is seen as being directly linked to that of rehabilitation, since one of the central rehabilitative aims of imprisonment is to prepare prisoners to manage in the outside world, and keeping men and women apart is seen as potentially undermining this objective (M. Shaw, 1992). While certain countries such as Spain, Sweden and the US have practised various degrees of integration between male and female prisoners in recent years, the interest in mixed prisons in Britain is less to do with the development of fully integrated regimes and more focused on placing males and females in the same institutions in order that they can share facilities while being kept physically apart (Hayman, 1996; Leander, 1995).

There have, however, been a number of objections to men and women either sharing the same site or actually mixing together in prison. The objection to shared-site detention is that it would result in women being subject to much higher levels of security than would otherwise be considered necessary, combined with a probable lack of appropriate facilities. The principal objection to the physical integration of male and female prisoners, on the other hand, is that a large percentage of female prisoners have been victims of violence and abuse at the hands of men, and that women's prisons provide, if nothing else, some respite from this abuse. For some of the more damaged women, confronting men, and particularly violent men, could be a traumatic experience. Thus it is claimed that mixed prisons are likely to be more stressful for women than for men, and that the advantages of 'normalisation' would be outweighed by the negative effects upon many women. The gendered nature of power, combined with the numerical domination of men, it is suggested, would ensure that the resources would go mainly to the majority group and that the needs of female prisoners would become marginalised (Tchaikovsky, 1991). There could also be problems associated with relationships that might develop between male and female inmates, which might cause additional stress and anxiety within the enclosed world of the prison, while potentially creating further difficulties for already strained relationships with those outside the prison.

Partial abolitionism and reductionism

The third option available is the adoption of a strategy of partial abolitionism or reductionism whereby the sanction of imprisonment is removed for all or some female offenders. These strategies stand in opposition to the previous two 'reformist' approaches, which aim to improve and reorganise women's imprisonment (Fitzgerald and Sim, 1979). From an abolitionist perspective the danger of reformist strategies is 'incorporation' (Mathieson, 1974; Sim, 1994). In line with critiques of woman-centred prisons, abolitionists claim that the danger of reforming these problematic institutions is that they become relegitimised and revitalised. The shared premise of partial abolitionism and reductionism is that prisons, for certain categories of prisoners at least, have lost their legitimacy, and rather than trying to reform them it is more constructive to find some other way of dealing with certain groups of female offenders. The difference between these two approaches as applied to female prisoners is that, whereas the abolitionists question the basic legitimacy of imprisonment for the vast majority of female offenders, the reductionists limit their focus to certain types of offenders and offences (Rutherford, 1984). Underlying these different penal reform strategies are different sets of assumptions and rationales, and therefore it is not necessarily the case that those who support one type of reform will support the other.

The partial abolitionists point out that the majority of women in prison are there because they have been denied work, housing and educational opportunities, but they believe that the reduction of poverty and inequality will not in itself resolve the problems of imprisonment (Carlen, 1990). They argue that attempts to reduce the prison population through the development of more community-based 'alternatives' to custody or by simply altering sentencing policies are going to have at best a marginal impact and, at worst, as the American experience demonstrates, it could result in women inadvertently serving longer sentences. Moreover, they claim that the level of imprisonment in general has little or no effect on the level of crime (Carlen, 1990; Mathieson, 1990). In developing this form of abolitionism, Pat Carlen (1990) argues that there is a need to abolish the 'tariff' system of punishments and to abandon the assumption that imprisonment is the inevitable backup to non-custodial penalties. The abolitionists believe that imprisonment for the vast majority of women is unjustified, inappropriate and in many cases counterproductive. On the basis that a relatively small number of women are incarcerated, it is argued that there is the possibility that 'an experimental period of five years' imprisonment should be abolished as a "normal" punishment for women and that a maximum of only a hundred places should be retained for female offenders convicted or accused or abnormally serious crimes' (Carlen and Tchaikovsky, 1996).

The immediate problem which arises in relation to this form of partial abolitionism is that, while it is recognised that the needs and experiences of female prisoners are in certain respects different from those of men, it is difficult to argue, particularly in the present political climate, that in cases in which men and women suffer similar levels of disadvantage and have committed similar crimes in similar circumstances, one should be imprisoned while the other is exempted. The strategy of abolitionism applied only to women's prisons would appear to be particularly divisive if it means that a woman convicted of a relatively serious crime is given a non-custodial sentence, while a man with a similar background who is convicted of a lesser crime receives a term of imprisonment. Even during the proposed 'experimental' period, these discrepancies would be extremely difficult to 'sell' to the general public and would undoubtedly undermine notions of fairness and justice. By the same token, it is not clear why some abolitionists believe that female drug-users should be dealt with outside the prison, while it is apparently acceptable that rehabilitation for male drug-users should continue to be carried out within the prison. Finally, the desire not to use prison as the backup institution to non-custodial penalties overlooks the fact that prison is distinguished from all other penalties (except of course in countries with capital punishment) in that it is the ultimately coercive sanction employed when offenders do not comply with non-custodial penalties (de Haan, 1990; Matthews, 1992).

Reductionism, on the other hand, adopts a more limited approach, which focuses on the removal of certain categories of offenders from prison. In a recent report by the Howard League (1997) on the use of custody for girls under 18 years of age, for example, it is argued that 'prison is a brutalising experience and it is ineffective in combating youth crime', while they point out that reoffending rates for young people following terms of imprisonment have been consistently between 80 and 90 per cent. On the basis of these observations it is argued that neither the offenders nor the community at large gains any real benefits from placing the 300 or so girls aged 18 and under in prison each year. Women's prisons have no specialist educational or rehabilitative programmes for teenagers, while many of these young girls, it is argued, are vulnerable and should not have to mix with adult female offenders. Despite the fact that some 50 per cent of girls under the age of 18 in prison were found to have been imprisoned for violent offences, the report concludes with the recommendation that prison for those under 18 should be prohibited by law. In line with the abolitionists, they suggest that the few girls who require secure conditions should be placed in secure units, while the others should be dealt with through the promotion of non-custodial sentences. This form of reductionism, however, raises similar questions of fairness and justice if girls are to be given non-custodial sentences in situations in which boys committing the same offence would receive a prison sentence. Moreover, the proliferation of alternatives to custody, as Carlen and others have pointed out, may produce a 'net widening' effect and ultimately serve to increase the prison population as the use of 'alternatives' for particular offenders is 'exhausted', or in cases in which community-based sanctions are breached (Carlen, 1990; Matthews, 1989b).

An alternative reductionist strategy aims to abolish the use of imprisonment for specific offences. Two recent examples of this strategy in England and Wales are the attempt in 1983 to remove the sanction of imprisonment for those women convicted of 'soliciting for the purposes of prostitution' and, more recently, the abolition of imprisonment for those convicted of not paying fines. The removal of imprisonment as the formal sanction for women convicted of 'soliciting for the purposes of prostitution' had the initial effect of reducing the number of women sent to prison for this offence, but the inability or unwillingness of those arrested for this offence to pay the often frequently imposed fines meant that many were eventually imprisoned by the back door, as it were, due to the non-payment of fines. As we have seen, the use of fines for indictable offences for women has decreased over the last decade.

The partial abolitionist strategy aimed at removing virtually all women from prison and the reductionist strategy of removing certain categories of female offenders from prison overlap at two critical points in that neither, in fact, really challenges the overall legitimacy of imprisonment as the dominant sanction, and as a result this raises issues about fairness and justice. Unless it can be demonstrated that the culpability of women is essentially different from that of men, both positions are left with the question of why imprisonment should remain appropriate for certain types of offenders rather than others. It would also seem that if abolitionism is to be consistent and to distance itself effectively from reductionism, it needs to confront imprisonment as a totality. Paradoxically, however, abolitionism is at its most theoretically coherent when it is at its most far-reaching, but it is precisely at this point that it is politically least viable. Reductionism, on the other hand, while effecting the decarceration of specific groups of offenders or certain types of offences, leaves the central issues of legitimacy untouched and offers a selective strategy of reform working mainly at the margins (Matthews, 1992; Rutherford, 1984).

Conclusion

The increase in recorded crime, particularly violence committed by women, as well as the dramatic increase in the use of imprisonment for women in England and Wales, America, Canada and Australia, suggests a change in patterns of offending and in the response by authorities. A relatively detailed investigation of the processing of women through the different stages of the criminal justice system in England and Wales produces a mixed picture which indicates an increase in some forms of recorded crime and a decrease in others over the last 15 years. The most significant increase has been in the level of violence against the person, which more than doubled in England and Wales between 2001 and 2007. There has been an increase in the use of cautioning for violence and drug-related offences, but a decrease for theft and handling. The use of community sentences has increased slightly, while average sentence lengths have remained fairly consistent for most offences over this period. One of the most significant changes has been an increase in the use of immediate custody, which has more than doubled for violence, robbery, burglary and drug offences between 1996 and 2006. In relation to sentencing, four recent trends have been identified which have impacted on the use of imprisonment and the composition of the custodial population. These changes include a substantial increase in the use of remand, a shift towards longer sentences, an increased number of persistent offenders with 15 or more convictions and a general ageing of the population of women passing through the criminal justice process and going to prison.

There are signs, however, of a watershed in penal policy relating to women in England and Wales. Over the past five or six years a number of influential reports have argued strongly for limiting the use of imprisonment for women and for diverting minor offenders from prosecution and custody. The Corston Report has signalled the intention to move towards a more woman-centred and holistic approach which is able to respond to the needs of women offenders and provide a more integrated approach that aims to replace existing prisons with small, multifunctional custodial centres, together with a greater use of community-based sanctions. The experience of previous reforms suggests that there are likely to be problems of implementation and there will be critics who will be sceptical of the ability of such reforms to make any significant difference in the nature of imprisonment for women. However, there are a number of examples of how reformers have developed more constructive and less damaging responses for women, and the challenge now is to build upon these achievements.

9
Race and Imprisonment

Introduction

When the system of ethnic monitoring was first adopted by the Prisons Department in England and Wales in 1985, it was revealed that those who were identified as black constituted 8 per cent of the prison population, although they only made up approximately 1 per cent of the general population. Since that time the proportion of both male and female black prisoners has grown steadily, such that by 1995, 11 per cent of the male prison population and 20 per cent of the female population were classified as black. By 2005, minority ethnic groups accounted for 24 per cent of the male prison population and 28 per cent of the female prison population, including foreign nations. The racial disproportionality among those incarcerated is particularly pronounced amongst the remand population (Ministry of Justice, 2007b).

A similar pattern of racial disproportionality is evident amongst the American prison population in which, according to the Bureau of Justice Statistics, there were 250,500 African American males and 10,200 females in state and federal prisons in 1985. A decade later, these numbers have more than doubled to 500,900 for black males, and has more than tripled for women classified as black. However, between 2000 and 2006 the percentage of African Americans in the prison population decreased from 43 per cent to 38 per cent. Similarly, the number of African American women in prison decreased from 175 per 100,000 in 2000 to 148 per 100,000 in 2006 (Sabol, *et al.*, 2007). Although the proportion of African American males and females has been decreasing in recent years, the numbers remain high in relation to those described as 'white'. The evidence of racial disproportionality in prisons has been taken by some observers as *prima facie* evidence of the discriminatory nature of the criminal justice system and has been used to counteract the suggestions which were put forward by official bodies and sections of the media that the differential rate of involvement in the criminal justice system by those classified as 'black' is a function of their greater involvement in crime, particularly street crime (Holdaway, 1996; Petersilia, 1985; Smith, 1997b).

The debate about whether racial disproportionality in prison is a consequence of the nature of offending by particular ethnic minority groups or the operation of a discriminatory criminal justice system remains the central point of reference. This ongoing debate has been underpinned by a somewhat less visible but no less acrimonious debate about whether or not ethnic monitoring should take place at all. On one side, it is argued that collecting data of the involvement of different ethnic groups in crime and the criminal justice system is likely to reinforce racial prejudice, on the other, there are those who argue that ethnic monitoring is a necessary step in gathering the information which is required to combat racial prejudice and discrimination. Over the years the argument has been gradually won by those who favour the collection of ethnic data, although a number of critics continue to maintain that systems of data collection are never neutral, and that close attention needs to be paid to the classification schemes which are used in collecting, organising and presenting the data.

The problem of categorisation

The categories that we use are to organise and interpret social reality are critical and some thought needs to be given to ensure that these categories are consistent and clear. However, when it comes to discussions of race it is evident that the categories used are far from consistent. For example, in the official criminal statistics in England and Wales and in much of the criminological literature, ethnic groups are divided into those that are deemed to be black, white and Asian. Significantly, the first two categories distinguish subjects by skin colour, whereas the third category identifies subjects in terms of country of origin. We find similar form of classification in America where ethnic groups are usually divided into white, black and Hispanic. Categorising different ethnic groups in relation to country of origin raises the issue of nationality. Of those imprisoned in England in 1995, 8 per cent were known to be foreign nationals, while approximately 24 per cent of black prisoners and 42 per cent of South Asians were foreign nationals. Interestingly, a new form of self-classification was introduced in England and Wales in 2003 based on 16 classifications of ethnicity which aim to distinguish between blacks and Asians born abroad and those born in Britain. However, the official criminal statistics present data on ethnicity in relation to five main categories – white, black, Asian or Chinese, mixed, and other.

It is only when we begin to consider these variations that we begin to realise that the categories which are used in the official statistics are largely a product of common-sense distinctions. The fact that the same forms of categorisation are widely used for general systems of ethnic and equal opportunities monitoring does not make them any more objective or consistent.

A major obstacle to the examination of race and racism in the criminal justice system is that each of the different agencies use different types of classification. The police, for example, normally use six ethnic categories – white, black, European, Asian, Chinese and Other – while the Prisons Department up to 1992 used four main categories – white, black, South Asian and Other – which have subsequently been subdivided into black (African, Caribbean and Other), South Asian (Indian, Bangladeshi, Pakistani) and Chinese (Other Asian and Other). Interestingly, white remains an undifferentiated category in this system of classification, although the category 'white' is no less problematic.

Probation statistics, in contrast, divide clients into four slightly different groups – white, black, South Asian, and a general category, 'all ethnic minority groups'. Although the annual probation statistics take the trouble in the footnotes to point out that the category 'South Asian' includes Indian, Pakistanis and Bangladeshis, separate figures for these sub-groups are not actually given. The Probation Service has, over the last few years, encountered what have been described as a series of 'technical problems' in recorded ethnic data. The Crown Prosecution Service (CPS), on the other hand, tends to rely on the forms of classification employed by the police; while Magistrates Courts currently record ethnicity in only 19 per cent of cases. The Crown Court has recently increased the level of ethnic monitoring from 65 per cent in 2004 to 78 per cent in 2006 (FitzGerald, 1995; Ministry of Justice, 2007b). These omissions, changes and inconsistencies make the task of examining the process of discrimination a difficult and uncertain business. There has been considerable criticism of criminal justice agencies imposing rigid categorical distinctions on suspects and offenders, and increasingly it has been seen to be preferable to allow individuals to identify their own ethnic group. However, this approach still leaves open the problem that the framework for identifying ethnic differences is pre-given, and therefore the range of choice is structured in advance. Moreover, significant differences may arise between the ways in which individuals classify themselves and those forms of classification that are imposed by criminal justice agencies.

To some extent the type of ethnic classification adopted in official circles and by researchers is conditioned by the desire to construct large enough sample sizes to carry out statistical analysis and to run significance tests. Since African Caribbeans' make up 2.8 per cent of those aged ten and over in the UK, while Asians account for 4.7 per cent and a further 1 per cent were classified as Chinese or 'other' in the 2001 census, it can be seen that dealing with sub-categories will produce relatively small datasets. Consequently, in much of the literature various ethnic groups whose geographical, linguistic or cultural interests may be entirely different are lumped together into one undifferentiated category in the course of analysis. The more regularly this is done, the more that specific ethnic differences are overlooked, and what may in reality be diverse and in some cases oppositional groupings are treated as if they were homogeneous.

Race and racism

In the various forms of classification, which are adopted in different countries, there is a tendency, as we have seen, to equate race with skin colour. It is small step from this point to associate race with certain essential biological characteristics or to generate differences which are held to define racial 'types'. The fact that there is no scientific basis on which the world's population can be legitimately categorised in this way does not prevent popular commentators talking as if there were. Notions of racial 'types' are often used to attribute (usually negative) characteristics to certain groups, and to establish claims of superiority and thereby legitimate forms of domination and exploitation (Jones, 1993; Miles, 1993; Webster, 2007).

Despite the lack of a real object, the idea of race remains a common-sense construct, or an ideology, which is sustained by the everyday reality of semantic and cultural differences between people. Ethnologists, however, rather than seeing race as a taken-for-granted category, have turned their attention to the social and historical conditions under which notions of 'race' have emerged, and in particular to the role of colonialism and imperialism in fostering the conditions for the creation of modern racist ideologies (Gilroy, 1987). The dilemma for ethnologists is that, although it has become the convention to place terms such as 'race' or 'black' (but not normally 'white') in parenthesis in order to draw attention to the problematic, and at times racist, ways in which these terms are used, it is necessary constantly to employ these key terms in order to engage in the debate on race.

Thus, the immediate problem is how to engage in academic, social and political debates about 'race and imprisonment' without uncritically adopting common-sense categories or alternatively assuming that certain groups have a natural propensity towards anti-social behaviour which is based on an assumed transhistorical essence. The claim, for example, by Richard Herrnstein and Charles Murray (1994) in *The Bell Curve* that blacks have a lower IQ than other races and that this accounts for their low socio-economic status and their subsequent involvement in illegitimate opportunity structures is spurious because it reduces social to biological processes. The fact that this assertion has been confounded by research which shows considerable variation in the IQ levels of blacks and which has pointed to the culturally and socially biased nature of IQ tests has largely discredited these assertions (Cullen *et al.*, 1997; Jones, 1993).

In an attempt to see race as a changing socially constructed concept, a number of writers have shifted their attention towards the analysis of racism and racialist discourses in order to de-reify and critically deconstruct the key terms. Such a strategy is seen as necessary in order to engage critically in the issue of race, and embodies a number of key elements. First, there is a focus on the historical evolution of racial ideologies in order to uncover the conditions of their emergence and to assess their effects. Second, critics have turned their attention to the examination of racist stereotypes in order to question their validity. Third, since race itself is a contested issue, attention has shifted to an examination of the process of cultural identification and identity formation among different ethnic groups (Back, 1996). Fourth, researchers have deconstructed race into its component parts, rather than treating blacks, for example, as a homogeneous group with fixed characteristics. Fifth, attempts have been made to counter those over-racialised conceptions which circulate widely in the sphere of criminal justice, which tend to see crime, victimisation and the operation of the criminal justice process primarily in terms of race rather than as a function of other variables (Miles, 1993; Solomos and Back, 1996).

These considerations will remain an ongoing point of reference in our examination of the relation between race, crime and imprisonment, and also in relation to the charges of racial discrimination which have been levelled against the operation of the criminal justice system. The charge of discrimination has been made in a number of different forms, including that of systematic and institutionalised racism. Institutionalised racism is normally seen to operate in both direct and indirect forms. In its direct form it is consciously aimed towards ethnic minorities, while indirect discrimination is seen to operate in those situations in which certain policies, although not specifically designed to disadvantage particular ethnic minority groups, operate in such a way that they work consistently to their disadvantage. A related concern is whether the operation of racism within the criminal justice system is largely attributable to one or two particular agencies, or whether discrimination works in a cumulative way with different degrees of discrimination operating at each stage of the criminal justice process (Smith, 1997a; Waters, 1990).

Race and crime

Do blacks commit more crime than whites? This is the question that dominates contemporary criminological thinking on both sides of the Atlantic. Putting the question in this stark form, however, is not only seriously misdirected but is also likely to produce racist conclusions and reinforce racist ideologies. This is principally because the question invites a false comparison (Lea and Young, 1984).

One of the major problems in engaging in the debate on 'race and crime' is comparing like with like. We know that crime is not evenly distributed across the social spectrum and that the best indicators of both offending and victimisation are socio-economic position, age, location and gender. Endless volumes of criminological research demonstrate that most forms of recorded crime and victimisation are concentrated among the poor and disadvantaged, the young, and those living in certain parts of the inner city (Bottoms and Wiles, 1997). The experience of crime and victimisation is, of course, also highly gendered. For a number of social and political reasons, the immigrants who came to Britain from the West Indies in the postwar period have been mainly involved in manual and unskilled work and have experienced high levels of unemployment, poor housing and education, and tend to be concentrated in those parts of the inner city which have historically been high-crime areas. Thus to compare the black population in Britain with the general population of whites is not only sociologically and criminologically meaningless, it is also politically disingenuous. Every apprentice criminologist could predict on the basis of socio-demographic data alone that an unqualified comparison between black and white populations will demonstrate that blacks are proportionately responsible for more crimes than whites.

The corollary of the claim that blacks commit more crime than whites is that Asians, although a minority group, tend to have a generally lower level of criminal involvement than whites (Smith, 1997a; Tonry, 1997). This is because, it is intimated, Asians are 'naturally' more law-abiding than either blacks or whites. This second assertion, although no less spurious than the first, has the added appeal to many criminologists that it demonstrates not only their own even-handedness in relation to this issue, but also that the relatively low proportion of Asians involved in the criminal justice system shows that, at worst, racial discrimination is selective or, at best minimal, since they argue that if racism were endemic in the system, all racial minorities would receive the same discriminatory treatment. This is an exercise in wishful thinking, not sociological analysis. It is not their natural predisposition towards law-abiding behaviour which distinguishes Asian involvement in crime and the criminal justice system. Instead, their limited involvement in these processes can be largely explained through an analysis involving the four key variables: class, age, gender and location.

In one of the few British studies which has attempted to incorporate some consideration of socio-economic grouping, age and location into a study of different ethnic groups, Stevens and Willis (1979) showed that there is good evidence of an association between deprivation, location and arrests. Although the kind of deprivation which is significant varies between the different ethnic groups. Moreover, they argue that when demographic differences are taken into account, the level of arrests between whites, blacks and Asians is roughly similar. Thus it is suggested that if we are to determine the 'race effect', some account of socio-economic status, age distribution, gender relations and location must be taken into account. The conspicuous lack of attention in the literature to the socio-economic characteristics of offenders has resulted in a disproportionate amount of crime being attributed to race. Whereas in the past, many criminologists were accused of 'colour-blindness', they now appear to suffer from 'class-blindness'.

Decontextualised comparisons between blacks and whites are not only sociologically bankrupt, but can lead to the over-racialisation of offending. It is therefore necessary, as Stuart Hall and his colleagues argued in *Policing the Crisis* (1978), to confront the stereotypical images of black youth presented by the mass media and the disproportionate amount of attention which they pay to certain forms of crime. In a similar vein, the riots of the 1980s which occurred in a number of urban centres were presented as overwhelmingly black riots, despite the fact that they involved different ethnic groups in different parts of the country (Campbell, 1993; Gilroy, 1987).

However, recognising that the media tend to racialise, dramatise and decontextualise crime, is not to deny or romanticise the significant involvement of young black people in certain forms of crime. Nor is this involvement adequately conceptualised as a process of labelling or criminalisation (Keith, 1993). The overwhelming evidence is that the victims of crimes committed by black offenders are also generally disadvantaged and live in the same area. This means that, given the nature of racial concentration in the inner city, a significant percentage of the victims are also going to be drawn from the same racial group (Burney, 1990). This should, however, not be read simply as 'black on black' crime, since it is not only intraracial but also intraclass. It is neighbour on neighbour, youth on youth, and poor on poor. It has also been suggested in relation to the involvement of African Americans in crime that it may be a function of continuing their involvement in crime until a later age. That is, rather than 'grow out of crime', which is the normal pattern for many young people as they take up employment and start a family, that a significant number of African Caribbeans do not enter the formal labour market and are less likely to settle down into a stable domestic relationship. The result of continuing in crime means that it is likely to become more serious over time, and that as African Caribbeans enter their twenties, they have a longer history of criminal involvement and in some cases an established criminal record. As adults, these offenders are more likely to receive a prison sentence if convicted (Bowling and Phillips, 2002; Mauer, 1999).

The lack of a distinctive black middle class in Britain means that it is difficult to make accurate class comparisons, but the probability is that the involvement of middle-class blacks in crime in Britain is roughly similar to middle-class whites. As John Pitts (1993) has suggested, the level of street crime among black middle-class accountants is probably the same as that of white middle-class accountants. Indicatively, in William Julius Wilson's (1987) study, delinquency rates among non-underclass African Americans were very similar to those of white youths living in similar areas.

In many respects the nature, level and intensity of black crime is much as might be expected given the socio-economic characteristics, age distribution and social location of black people living in Britain. Thus in terms of the different levels of recorded crime between blacks and Asians the real issue is not so much how do we explain the apparently high level of black crime but, conversely, how we explain the relatively low level of Asian criminality. Although this question remains, as yet, relatively under-researched, there are a number of factors that might help to account for the difference. The first involves the very different experience of colonisation experienced by Asians and African Caribbeans, and in particular the effects of slavery and other forms of degradation and dislocation suffered by Africans that did not form part of the Asian experience. As Edward Said (1993) has argued, the experience of colonisation and imperialism not only played a critical role in shaping forms of exploitation and subordination but also deeply influenced the ways in which different races are viewed by the imperialist powers.

Second, the sequence of immigration in the postwar period was important in that second-generation African Caribbeans fell victims of the fiscal crisis which developed in Britain in the 1970s and to the shift from full employment to structural unemployment. Third, the largest group of Asians were the more entrepreneurial and middle-class Indians, who were more easily assimilated into British society. Although the Pakistanis and Bangladeshis were less well-qualified and experienced greater levels of unemployment, the presence of a large group of Indians gave these other minority groups a lower political profile and lower 'specific weight'. Fourth, as a result of cultural and religious differences, the Asian community operated with different forms of informal control, greater privatisation and better opportunity structures within their own community. In a sense, it was the greater distance between Asian and British culture than that which existed between West Indian and British culture that facilitated assimilation. Although the assimilation of West Indian youth has been more rapid, opportunity structures for this group has been more restricted, and particularly since the late 1970s they have experienced a greater level of relative deprivation, which in turn has fostered a different form of subcultural adaption (Lea and Young, 1984).

Thus, if proper comparisons are to made between different ethnic minority groups, and if blacks, Asians and whites are to be compared, it is essential to compare like with like. This means that it is necessary to at least begin by allowing for socio-economic variations, demographic characteristics and geographical location. Different patterns of offending between different groups are not simply a function of absolute deprivation, however: they are also linked to forms of relative deprivation and styles of subcultural adaption. Once these processes are examined, the variations in offence levels and patterns become less surprising and it is possible to begin to identify the 'race effect' in terms of both crime and victimisation.

Arrests, cautioning and prosecution

A great deal has been written about racist attitudes among the police, but the question is to what extent these attitudes are translated into discriminatory practices (Holdaway, 1996). In the aftermath of the 1980s riots, the consensus was that these disturbances were caused by antagonistic and unmediated relationships between ethnic minorities and the police, which were a function of what was seen as heavy-handed and selective law enforcement practices adopted by the police (Scarman, 1982). One of the first major studies which examined the relationship between the police and ethnic minorities was carried out by the Policy Studies Institute in the mid 1980s. They found that 'racialist language and racial prejudice were prominent and pervasive and many individual officers and also whole groups were preoccupied with ethnic differences' (Smith, 1983). Thus the problem of racism in the police went far beyond a few 'bad apples' and appeared to be an endemic part of police culture at that time (Lea, 1986).

One indication of the translation of racist attitude into racist practices has been the use of stop-and-search strategies. Although the available evidence confirms the suspicion that African Caribbeans are more likely to be stopped and searched than other groups, there is some doubt about how many prosecutions of a serious nature result from stop and search, and therefore ultimately what impact this policy has on the prison population. David Smith (1997a), for example, claims that only 3 per cent of stop and searches result in a prosecution, while Roger Hood (1992) in his study found a significant number of African Caribbeans appearing in Crown Court on quite serious charges – particularly those involving drugs – who had come to police attention through stop and search.

It is certainly the case, however, that the primary definers of 'crime' are the victims who make the critical decision of whether or not to report incidents to the police. It is clear that this decision is not only a function of the nature and severity of the offence, but is also conditioned by the victim's belief that the police will take the report seriously and will be willing and able to do something about it. For this reason there is a symbiotic relationship between the police and the public, in which the police response will itself influence the decision to report. Therefore it is not possible to maintain a clear distinction between 'crime' and the response, since the construction of 'crime' itself is a product of a dynamic process of action and reaction (Matthews, 1994; Matthews and Young, 1992). The implication of this process is that the question of whether it is the involvement of certain ethnic minorities in crime or the discriminatory practices of the criminal justice system which results in racial disproportionately among the prison population is never a clear-cut issue.

There are two implications that follow from this analysis. The first is that the decision of the police to prosecute will also be influenced by their assessment of the likelihood of a case being acted upon by the Crown Prosecution Service and the possibility of conviction. This decision, again, is not taken purely on the basis of the available evidence, but will also be conditioned by the quality of the defence and the demeanour of the defendant. On the other hand, if the police are generally racist, there may be a tendency to devalue reports in cases where victims are drawn from ethnic minorities, and they may be less motivated to process these cases. According to the official recorded crime figures in England and Wales, blacks are more likely to be arrested for robbery, while Asians score highly on fraud and forgery. Both blacks and Asians have a high rate of arrest for drug-related offences as well as for violence against the person and sexual offences (see Table 9.1).

Table 9.1   Percentage breakdown by ethnic appearance of those arrested for notifiable offences by offence group, 2004–05 (England and Wales)

	White	*Black*	*Asian*	*Other*	*Not known*	*Total no.*
Violence against the person	85.3	7.8	5.0	1.3	0.6	386,312
Sexual offences	79.5	9.7	7.4	2.5	0.8	30,190
Robbery	61.2	29.4	7.0	1.8	0.6	32,601
Burglary	89.4	6.9	2.6	0.7	0.5	96,518
Theft and handling	85.4	8.3	4.4	1.4	0.6	362,776
Fraud and Forgery	65.9	18.3	10.9	4.2	0.7	36,144
Criminal Damage	91.1	5.0	2.7	0.7	0.6	156,248
Drugs	78.4	13.4	6.4	1.3	0.5	83,355
Other	80.4	9.2	6.8	2.7	0.8	145,909

Source: Ministry of Justice (2007b)

Table 9.2 provides a general overview of the progress of different minority ethnic groups through the different stages of the criminal justice system. It indicates a high level of stop and searches directed at those described as 'black'. The same group have relatively high number of cases which go to the Crown Court and constitute a disproportionate percentage of the prison population. Overviews of this type are used to try to identify whether there are particular stages of the criminal justice system where discriminatory practices arise.

Table 9.2   Percentage of people at different stages of the criminal justice process by ethnic group, 2005–06 (England and Wales)

		Ethnicity		
	White	Black	Asian	Unknown/not recorded
Stop and searches	74.7	14.1	7.1	2.6
Arrests	84.3	8.8	4.9	0.6
Cautions	83.8	6.4	4.4	4.2
Youth offences	84.7	6.0	3.0	3.3
Crown Court	75.7	13.0	7.4	–
Prison population	76.8	13.5	5.4	0.7
Prison receptions	80.8	10.2	5.4	0.5
General population (aged 10 and over, 2001)	91.3	2.8	4.7	0.0

Source: Ministry of Justice (2007b)

Courts and sentencing

The decision-making process in the courts has been identified as a pivotal stage in the criminal justice process, since it is at this point that previous decisions can effectively be modified or reversed and critical decisions in relation to the use of custody are made. The sentencing process, however, involves wider issues of justice and public safety. It is therefore not just a 'tap' for regulating the flow of offenders into prison or community-based sanctions, but it is also a point at which justice must be seen to be done (Ashworth, 1983).

The Race Relations Act (1968) and subsequent amendment in 2000 has made it unlawful to discriminate on the grounds of race, colour or nationality, and consequently the courts themselves must be seen to act in non-discriminatory ways. Since the makeup of the judiciary is overwhelmingly white, middle class and conservative, it might be assumed that sentencing decisions would tend to work systematically against ethnic minorities. In 1994 there were only four judges in England and Wales who were either African Caribbean or Asian. However, although the research on this issue has found a number of specific examples of racist bias in sentencing, in general it has been found that if the seriousness of the case and the defendant's previous history are taken into account, there is a rough parity in the sentences handed out to offenders from different ethnic minority groups (Blumstein, 1982; Hood, 1992). By the time offenders from different ethnic groups appear in court, they appear to be roughly similar in terms of socio-economic characteristics, although some discrepancies remain which may have an impact upon sentencing decisions. For example, in the study carried out by Imogen Brown and Roy Hullin (1992) which examined the decision-making process in relation to over 3,000 defendants, they noted that over 50 per cent of the African Caribbean defendants were unemployed, and that this was almost twice that of the white and Asian defendants (Crow and Cove, 1984; Moxon, 1988).

One influential piece of research which has attempted to come to terms with the considerable methodological difficulties involved in developing comparisons between different ethnic groups is a study based on a sample of 2,884 defendants who appeared in Crown Courts in the West Midlands. This piece of research, carried out by Roger Hood (1992), employed multivariate analysis. By developing a 'risk of custody' score, which was designed to calculate the probability of custody for different groups, the aim was to identify the 'race effect' of sentencing. That is, on the basis of 15 selected variables, excluding race, the study was designed to identify the variation in the use of custody for each ethnic group.

In line with previous research, Hood (1992) found that the racial disparity in sentencing is less than might have been assumed, with blacks on average being about 5 per cent more likely than whites to be given a custodial sentence, while the Asian group were about 5 per cent less likely to receive a custodial sentence than the white group. Criminal histories, it was found, and the severity of the offence accounted for approximately 80 per cent of the over-representation of black male offenders in prison, and the remaining 20 per cent was largely accounted for by the fact that a significant percentage of black offenders opted for Crown Court and pleaded not guilty, with the consequence that if they were convicted they were more likely to receive a prison sentence and probably a longer prison sentence.

Hood also noted that black offenders were more likely to have been remanded in custody by magistrates. Being already in custody, pleading not guilty and consequently not having a Social Inquiry Report written on them, they were more likely to receive a custodial sentence if convicted. A higher proportion of black and Asian defendants received sentences of over three years, and there were significant differences in the deployment of non-custodial options, with black offenders receiving generally higher-tariff alternatives than whites. Other research has shown that blacks were also less likely to be given a probation order or a community service order than whites (Mair, 1986).

Although Hood's study (1992) addresses some of the methodological issues involved in making comparisons of this type, there are a number of problems which remain and which tend to limit the validity of his overall research findings. Despite the fact that Hood is critical of earlier studies which lump together different ethnic groups under two or three general headings, he adopts a similar strategy and divides his sample into the familiar categories of black, Asian and white. Relatedly, there are issues about the choice of location and the representativeness of the sample, as well as the ability to generalise from these specific findings to the whole country.

In relation to the representativeness of the survey, it should be noted that there were significant differences in the sentencing practices of the five different Crown Courts which Hood investigated, with the Dudley Courts, in particular, generating much higher rates of racial disparity. Whereas in Birmingham Crown Court, which involved the largest percentage of the total sample, a black offender had a one in three probability of receiving a custodial sentence, in Dudley a black offender had a one in two chance. Thus, if the distribution of cases had been different, with more cases taken from Dudley, the study would have shown a much greater racial bias. Consequently, the conclusion that there were only a few percentage points difference in the sentencing of different ethnic groups would have to be revised. Hood's conclusion that the decision to plead not guilty and the lack of Social Inquiry Reports suggests that the question of disparity is largely a procedural and technical issue, on the one hand, and a consequence of adopting the high-risk strategy of choosing to be tried in the Crown Court by black defendants, on the other. The question of why so many choose Crown Court and decided to plead guilty is not, however, addressed.

There are fundamental methodological issues related to the use of a prediction scale which is only accurate in 75 per cent of cases, while the 'risk of custody' score is limited to legally 'relevant' factors and excludes factors such as unemployment. The exclusion of this particular factor is surprising, to the extent that Hood himself in the course of his analysis of the operation of different Crown Courts makes repeated reference to the significance of unemployment, but nevertheless treats it as an extraneous independent variable. At the same time he refers to the higher use of fines for Asians and implies that this might be a function of a generally higher level of employment among this group.

A major difference between the black and white offenders who appeared before the Dudley Courts, according to Hood (1992), was that 'the proportion of black offenders given a custodial sentence was significantly higher for those who were employed' (1992: 64). He points out that at Birmingham Court, where the disparities in sentencing were at a minimum, there were no significant difference between the proportion of blacks and whites who were known to be unemployed or in receipt of welfare. In his explanation for ethnic variation in sentencing patterns in Coventry, Hood states that 'The reason for their different practice appeared to be the much greater use of custody at Coventry for offenders who were unemployed' (1992: 93), and he notes in another passage that 'Being unemployed was a factor significantly correlated with receiving a custodial sentence if the defendant was black but not if he was white or Asian' (1992: 86).

This is not to argue that unemployment is necessarily one of the main factors influencing the use of custody, or that it operates in some direct and unmediated way to affect rates of imprisonment. Rather, it is to suggest that there may be causal links between unemployment and imprisonment, and therefore there is good reason for including it among the key variables (Halevy, 1995; Hood, 1995). The point is that not all variables that might possibly affect sentencing can be included in the analysis, while the influence of excluded variables that do have a racial correlation may be mistakenly attributed to those variables which are included. As Hood (1995) himself admits, his study does not aim to provide a causal explanation but operates at the level of aggregates and concludes by stating that the reasons for the disparities in the treatment of black and white males must remain open to speculation. The main weakness, however, of Hood's study is the assumption that factors such as previous offending or convictions are themselves racially neutral (Bowling and Philips, 1999).

Although the percentages are not very large, Hood's study does provide evidence of both 'direct' and 'indirect' discrimination in Crown Courts. Direct discrimination was evident in terms of bail decisions, the rate at which blacks were sentenced to custody and the length of custodial sentence imposed. Indirect discrimination is seen to occur in relation to the decision to plead not guilty and the use of Social Inquiry Reports. However, Hood's general argument is that discrimination in relation to sentencing in Crown Courts is neither systematic nor universal (FitzGerald, 1993).

A subsequent study conducted by Martina Feilzer and Roger Hood (2004) which focused on discrimination in relation to young people has encountered similar methodological difficulties. Although it involves over 1,700 cases and includes a wide range of variables, it operates with a limited set of categories which limit the explanatory potential of the research. Using the now familiar distinctions between black, white, Asian, mixed and other, variations between specific ethnic groups remains unclear. The use of the category 'mixed parentage' raises important issues of definition and categorisation since there appears to be widespread tendency to define those with 'mixed parentage' as a 'black' which potentially skews the sample, particularly since those with 'mixed parentage' tend to be overrepresented amongst those given custody and tend to be given more restrictive community sentences according to Feilzer and Hood. Significantly, one study by Modood and Berthoud (1997) on ethnic minorities in Britain found that 40 per cent of children identified as 'Caribbean' had one white parent. All sentencing research of this type faces the same problems of sample size and the use of categories, as well as the selection of variables, and these choices can seriously affect the findings. As Feilzer and Hood (2004) admit, they were 'unable to measure all the variables that might have had an effect on the decision made'. Thus, their overall finding that there is little variation in the use of custody between blacks and whites has to be treated with caution (Mhlanga, 1997; Bowling and Phillips, 2002).

Hood's (1992) conclusion in his West Midlands study that 80 per cent of custodial decisions among the black group of offenders is accounted for by the nature and severity of the offence is similar to that presented in Alfred Blumstein's influential American study on sentencing and racial disproportionality in prisons. Blumstein (1982) arrives at a similar conclusion to Hood, but adopts a different mode of analysis. He compares arrest and imprisonment patterns using a four-stage model. Having divided the prison population into eleven categories, he then proceeded to examine what percentage of each category of sentenced prisoners was black. Using FBI data on arrests, he then proceeded to find out what proportion of persons arrested for the same eleven categories of offence were black. His analysis is based upon the assumption that in a non-biased system the racial proportions in arrests would be mirrored in the racial proportions imprisoned. Thus, for example, he found that 52.3 per cent of those imprisoned for homicide were black and that 51.6 per cent of those arrested for homicide were black. He thereby concluded that 97.2 per cent of the racial disproportionality for that offence could be accounted for by the black homicide arrest rates. Interestingly, like Hood, Blumstein found that there was evidence of discrimination among the less serious offences and in those cases in which there was room for judicial discretion. Thus the implication of both Blumstein and Hood's analysis is that reducing racism in the criminal justice system is unlikely to have much effect on the size or the racial composition of the prison population and that the only way to change the present level of racial disproportionality in prison would be to reduce the involvement of black people in serious crime.

Blumstein (1988), however, does raise an important point about the possibility of comparing like with like in relation to different categories of offence, particularly if institutional racism is prevalent:

> If, for example, a prosecutor was systematically favouring whites by dropping less serious cases for them, then the whites convicted of a particular offence would have committed more serious crimes than non-whites; judges who were perfectly race blind in their sentencing would impose harsher sentences on white offenders than non-white offenders. This apparently harsher treatment of whites (as it might be seen by people who did not understand the prosecutor's screening policies) would camouflage a systematic bias against non-whites. This is merely one of the ways by which discrimination that did exist could be masked. (Blumstein, 1988: 249)

This problem of masking discrimination can also be affected by the possibility of 'victim discounting' if the victim is black. This process has implications for the validity of statistical inferences which Hood presents. Given the evidence of racist attitudes among the police, the differential use of cautioning and bail for certain ethnic minority groups appears to be the product of precisely the process which Blumstein identifies, such that discrimination is not only masked but compounded by an apparently 'neutral' judiciary. This problem arises in part from the attempt to investigate racial discrimination in the criminal justice system through a series of snapshots, rather than attempting to examine it as part of a process which is both subtle and opaque. There is a complex interaction between the social characteristics of different groups of offenders, their offending histories, the type of offence they commit, the decision to remand offenders in custody and ultimately the deployment of custodial and non-custodial sentences. As Marian FitzGerald and Peter Marshall point out in relation to Hood's study:

> [So] the factors which drive up the remand rate for black defendants go beyond their offending histories and the characteristics of the offences with which they have been charged; they appear to include evidence of both direct and indirect discrimination. What is particularly striking is that the amount of unexplained difference in the bail/remand decision was at least twice as large as the difference found at the point of sentencing. That is, there is a strong inference of discrimination in the

decision to bail or remand. Yet this decision is one of the apparently 'race neutral' or strictly legal factors which 'explains' ethnic disparities at the sentencing stage, minimizing any possible inference of discrimination at this point. (FitzGerald and Marshall, 1996: 153)

Thus, given that socioeconomic variables such as unemployment, homelessness and single-parent households have all been held to influence the remand/bail decision, removing these considerations from the analysis may provide a more sanitised form of analysis which allow the construction of a more comfortable set of conclusions, but does not do justice to the complex interplay of socio-economic and decision-making processes at the various stages of the criminal justice process.

Race and the experience of incarceration

There has been considerable debate about whether black and white offenders experience imprisonment in different ways. The experience of confinement will be conditioned by the levels of solidarity among different ethnic groups, their subcultural backgrounds and the power relations within the prison itself, involving not only interpersonal relations and systems of control but also the design and management of the prison. The internal power relations among prisoners will affect the distribution of work, the forms of interpersonal support, and the experience of bullying and intimidation.

The pains of imprisonment are felt most acutely by non-nationals. The intensification of the problems of imprisonment among this group are often a result of problems of language and communication, the lack of information, isolation from family and friends, and in particular the uncertainty which is associated with knowing little about the operation of the criminal justice system and as a consequence being unsure about procedures and the length of time involved for cases to be heard and decided. There are related problems of organising good legal representation and following through the developments of the case. Foreign nationals are less likely to be given bail and may not be eligible for home release or benefit from early release policies. For these reasons foreign prisoners tend to become marginalised in the world of the marginalised. Foreign prisoners on remand experience specific difficulties in relation to the initial notification to their families, the general lack of outside contact, and in particular not knowing how long they will remain in custody (Cheney, 1993; Matthews, 1994).

In England and Wales the geographical concentration of ethnic minority populations in the inner-city areas of London and the West Midlands means that prisoners from these groups are not evenly distributed across the country but tend to be located mainly in the South East, where they make up between a quarter and a half of the prison population (Genders and Player, 1989). Relations between rank-and-file prison staff and ethnic minority prisoners is mediated by certain widely held stereotypes, in which African Caribbean prisoners are described as being aggressive, difficult, lazy and as having a 'chip on their shoulder'. Probably, not surprisingly, black prisoners tend to keep their distance from white prison officers and are suspicious of them. In contrast, Asian prisoners are portrayed by prison officers as 'model prisoners'. Consequently, whereas prison officers are reported to be generally hostile and unsympathetic towards black prisoners, they are more sympathetic towards Asian prisoners, who are frequently described as 'scapegoats', and are seen as suffering from bullying and intimidation. Asian prisoners are also seen to suffer from a lack of adequate facilities in prison to meet their dietary needs and to enable them to practice their religion.

Elaine Genders and Elaine Player (1989) found evidence of different degrees of solidarity between both black and Asian groups which provided some degree of support. However, the type of organised political groupings of black prisoners which has been reported in some American prisons was not evident in the prisons they visited. According to the *National Prison Survey, 1991* (Walmsley, *et al.*, 1992), there are significant differences between different ethnic groups in prison terms regarding the offences they have committed. Black inmates tend to have a much higher rate of conviction for robbery than whites or Asians, but a lower rate for burglary. Over 40 per cent of the adult black prison population had been convicted of drug offences, although black prisoners are less likely to have either very short or long sentences.

Race and imprisonment in America

The debates around race and imprisonment in Britain have been influenced to a large extent by developments in America. This is partly because this issue has been more widely discussed and partly because statistics on the ethnicity of offenders and prisoners have been collected over a much longer period of time. Also, the politicisation of race and imprisonment during the 1960s and 1970s through the writings of black activists like George Jackson (1970) and Eldridge Cleaver (1968) brought attention to the plight of black people within the American prison system.

Although the debate on race and imprisonment in America has been extensive, and at times heated, it has in some respects been peculiarly narrow, in the sense that ethnic and racial differences are condensed within much of the academic and official literature into a direct 'black–white' or 'white–non-white' opposition. As a consequence the experiences of other ethnic groups tends to be marginalised or ignored, which in turn has consequences not only for the way in which the race and incarceration issue is conceived and discussed, but also that the differences between different minority groups remains largely unexamined. This black/white opposition has been described as monochromatic criminology (Anderson, 2002; Matthews, 2009).

Of particular significance are Hispanics, who currently constitute the second largest ethnic minority group in the United States, making up 9 per cent of the population – compared to blacks, who make up approximately 12 per cent at present. In the next decade or so, however, Hispanics are destined to become the largest ethnic minority group in America. Hispanics currently constitute the largest ethnic minority group in some of America's largest cities, including Detroit, Chicago and Los Angeles. Moreover, Hispanics have been the fastest growing ethnic minority group among the prison population in recent years, increasing from 163 per 100,000 in 1980 to 622 per 100,000 in 1995, to 1,220 per 100,000 in 2005 (Bureau of Justice, 1996, 2006).

Despite these trends, the predominant focus among American criminologists in relation to race is on black offenders and prisoners. Indicatively, Hispanics can be classified as either 'black' or 'white', and in some of the literature and statistical presentations they are divided into blacks and whites, although the basis of this decision if rarely clear. In some studies they are classified as 'non-white', which is often read as 'black'. Although Hispanics are identified as an ethnic group with a common language, they are seen to be made up of different 'races' (Irwin and Austin, 1994). In the attempt to explain the apparently arbitrary and inconsistent nature of racial classification, Robert Sampson and Janet Lauritsen (1997) inform us that:

> Not sharing a common culture, the myriad groups classified as Hispanics thus fail to meet the criteria we typically think of as constituting an ethnic group. For these and other reasons the construction of Hispanics has been criticised as a political definition which has little meaning, with many preferring the label 'Latino' instead. (Sampson and Lauritsen, 1997: 315)

It is strange that whereas the term 'Hispanic' is seen to be politically loaded, it is apparently less problematic than 'Latino'. However, the authors use the term 'black' as if it were neither politically loaded nor problematic. To some extent there is a rationale for adopting the term 'black' less critically than other ethnic designations, because of the nature of social and spatial segregation in America, but it is evident that the notion of 'black' also needs to be critically deconstructed and treated with caution if it is to have any real policy relevance.

The attitudes towards Hispanics and the methods of classification say a great deal about how the issue of race is seen in America. Clearly, for many writers, 'race' is synonymous with 'black'. This form of racialisation is no doubt a function of the social and geographical concentration of large segments of the black population in inner-city ghettos. For many Americans the issue of crime and the fear of crime is translated into a fear of black crime (Skogan, 1995). As Andrew Hacker (1992) has pointed out: 'The dread whites feel of black crime goes beyond actual risks and probabilities.' The predominant focus on black crime is, however, not presented only in terms of white fears but also, it is argued, because the victims of black crime are disproportionately black.

For many conservative critics the translation of the problem of crime into the problem of race is politically convenient. Punitive interventions are justified against blacks in general, since criminality is seen to be endemic in this group. Getting tough on black crime is rationalised not only in terms of the extent and seriousness of the transgression, but also in terms of protecting the public (Dilulio, 1994). Liberals, on the other hand, although they largely agree that black crime is a major problem, argue that blacks are subject to processes of criminalisation whereby the types of activities they are involved in receive undue attention from crime control agencies. Michael Tonry (1995), for example, in his book *Malign Neglect*, argues that the rapid growth of the prison population in America in recent years has been largely a consequence of the 'war on drugs' and that this war has been largely waged against inner-city blacks.

He produces evidence to show that drug use during the 1980s was widespread among different sections of the population, but that the 'war on drugs' was aimed at crack cocaine users, who were overwhelmingly young and black. The implementation of this selective policy was not accidental and its consequences were predictable. According to Tonry:

> The 'War on Drugs' foreseeably and unnecessarily blighted the lives of hundreds of thousands of young disadvantaged black Americans and undermined decades of effort to improve life chances of members of

the urban black underclass. The war was fought largely from partisan political motives to show that the Bush and Reagan administrations were concerned about public safety, crime prevention, and the needs of victims (as if Democrats or any responsible mainstream figures were not). The bodies counted in this war, as they lay in their prison beds, however, are even more disproportionately black than prisoners already were. War or no war, most people are saddened to learn that for many years 30 to 40 per cent of those admitted to prison were black. The War on Drugs was a calculated effort foreordained to increase those percentages and this is what happened. (Tonry, 1995: 82)

Tonry makes the important point that the effects of crime control policies during the 1980s have made a major contribution to declining levels of lawful employment among young black males. It is estimated that one in twelve young black males is incarcerated in America at any one time, while one in four is under the control or supervision of the criminal justice system ((Mauer, 1999). The stigmatising and marginalising effects of imprisonment, combined with the probabilities of recidivism, means that the possibilities of legitimate employment for a significant number of black males is greatly reduced, while their dependants and partners are destined to a life of welfare dependency. At the same time, of course, it means that the experience of imprisonment and of prison subcultures is 'exported' back into the urban ghetto. Thus the conclusion of Tonry's study is that, however ineffectual the 'war on drugs' might have been in reducing drug use, it was very effective in increasing the level of black incarceration. Through selective intervention the police were able to target blacks and thereby be seen to be effectively fighting the 'war on drugs' by maintaining a high rate of arrest. Tonry's work can therefore be seen as both a critique and an elaboration of Blumstein's (1982) account of the dynamics of racial disproportionality in prisons. Tonry (1995) draws attention to the ways in which arrest figures can be constructed through selective enforcement and how subsequent arrest rates for drug offences help to turn this into a predominantly 'black' issue.

Tonry (1995), however, is critical of Blumstein's (1982) focus on murder, rape and assault and his lack of consideration of the role of drug-related arrests, although Blumstein in a re-examination of this issue does acknowledge the significance of drugs in this process (Blumstein, 1993). Tonry is also critical of Blumstein's use of aggregate data which may well hide important differences in the forms of discrimination experienced by different groups in different locations. There are also, Tonry reminds us, a number of different processes which occur between the point of arrest and prosecution, and Blumstein's analysis suffers from the problem of 'slippage', as the time gap between arrest and prosecution means that the data relating to arrests are from 1978, while the data on the prison population are based on the 1979 figures. Blumstein's analysis also conflates the data on prison admissions with the length of sentence, and he can also be criticised for discounting the considerable degree of discrimination exercised in relation to minor offenders. Given the propensity for offenders to reappear in the criminal justice system at a later date, this discrimination can have a considerable long-term cumulative effect (Bowling and Philips, 1999).

As an examination of the relation between race and crime and race and imprisonment Tonry's study has a number of limitations. First, like many liberal criminologists, Tonry tends to over-racialise crime by presenting the material predominantly in 'black' and 'white' terms, largely leaving out Hispanics and other ethnic minorities, and by presenting his findings in terms of race rather than class. Although he acknowledges the socio-economic position of the black 'underclass', the issue is largely translated into one of race rather than one of poverty or deprivation. This point is best exemplified by Tonry's focus on the discriminatory way in which anti-drugs policies were implemented in the 1980s. He gives a number of reasons to explain why the police focused mainly on black communities. These include vulnerability, visibility, accessibility and the probability of successfully prosecuting those arrested. All these factors relate primarily to the socio-economic nature of the population rather than their race. That is, Tonry does not clearly demonstrate a 'race effect'. Interestingly, poor Hispanics were also targets of the 'war on drugs' and their incarceration rate also increased – not, one suspects, primarily because they were Hispanics, but because, like poor blacks, they were subject to selective enforcement because of their accessibility and vulnerability.

The second major limitation of Tonry's thesis is that he misunderstands the significance of different types of drugs. Crack cocaine does not have the same social meaning and effects of white powdered cocaine. As Philip Bourgois (2003) has pointed out, the significance of drug use cannot be reduced to the pharmaceutical qualities of the substances themselves. The impact of crack cocaine in the late 1980s on the lives, families and neighbourhoods of inner-city black neighbourhoods was devastating. Violence erupted, families were divided and neighbourhoods were destroyed. This did not happen in white middle-class suburban neighbourhoods. Something radical had to be done to stop this process of destruction and interpersonal violence, and although one might question whether large-scale imprisonment was the most appropriate response, it was the case, as always, that liberals like Tonry were conspicuously silent at the time on this issue and failed to offer a viable policy response.

As James Jacobs (2001) has pointed out, liberals prefer to account for the disproportionate imprisonment of African Americans in terms of drugs which they tend to see as a non-victim crime, and this makes the response appear to be overly punitive and discriminatory. However, the available evidence suggests that it is violent offences and not drugs that has been driving up the prison population over the last decade or so in America. At the end of 2004 more than half (52 per cent) of all sentenced inmates in state prisons were sentenced for violent offences in the same year the majority of black (53 per cent) and Hispanic (54 per cent) prisoners were sentenced for violent offences, while the percentage of black and Hispanic prisoners sentenced for drug-related offences was 23 and 21 per cent respectively (Sabol *et al.*, 2007).

Confining ethnic minorities in 'fortress Europe'

Just as the prison systems in Britain and America have undergone profound changes in relation to their ethnic composition, prisons across Western Europe experienced parallel developments. The major and immediate difference, however, is that although there have been profound changes in recent years in relation to the ethnic composition of those incarcerated in Western Europe, the majority of these ethnic groups are 'white'. In many cases they are immigrants, transient workers and refugees from Eastern Europe who have become caught up in the criminal justice systems of their country of residence.

In the majority of Western European countries the percentage of foreign nationals has grown steadily over the last decade and in a number of countries over 30 per cent of the prison population is made up of non-nationals. In certain prisons, particularly those located in industrial centres, foreigners make up over half of the prison population. The increased number of foreign nationals in prison across Western Europe has been widely attributed to their growing involvement in crime. However, an examination of prison statistics indicates that a significant percentage of foreigners are detained on migration-related, rather than criminal grounds (Tomasevski, 1994). The growing proportion of foreigners held in Western European prisons, particularly where overcrowding is already present, has raised a number of human rights issues since the conditions under which foreign prisoners are held and the abuses which they suffer have been reported by organisations such as Amnesty International and by the Council of the European Committee for the Prevention of Torture and Inhuman or Degrading Treatment or Punishment (Morgan and Evans, 1994; Spinellis *et al.*, 1996).

The principal reasons given for the increase in the proportion of foreign nationals in prisons throughout Western Europe is migration and the attempts to control it, on one hand and the internationalisation of crime – particularly drugs and fraud – on the other. Many migrants living in Western Europe live under conditions that are depressingly familiar:

> The large concentration of migrants in urban ghettos makes their presence – and also their problems – particularly visible: levels of unemployment are regularly higher than amongst citizens, and the prevalence of low skilled workers diminishes prospects of employment. Migrant communities inhabit the worst housing in the poorest areas of inner cities. Mutual accusations between the native and migrant populations abound; the former object that migrants reject integration by transferring their own lifestyle to the host country; the latter object that they are rejected, stigmatised and discriminated against, often because of their race, colour, ethnicity, or religion, or all of these. Nationals often equate migrants with increased criminality, while migrants see themselves as targets of racist violence, harassment, or at least prejudice. (Tomasevski, 1994: 36)

As with the black–white dichotomy which informs so much of the British and American literature, the distinction national–foreigner has been found to be inadequate and unable to account for variations in status between, for example, visitors, residents, asylum-seekers and tourists. There are now a number of emerging groups in Western Europe who are not foreigners and are not citizens, and are variously referred to as the 'new minorities' or as 'non-native ethnic groups'.

Interestingly, the recording of race has been discontinued in a number of Western European countries, both outside and inside the prison system, in order to overcome the ideological separation of diverse populations into races. However, the abolition of these categories of race has not, it would appear, had the effect of reducing racism. Racism has been flourishing throughout Western Europe in recent years, and foreigners and the 'new minorities' are not subject to the same legal protections and safeguards as the indigenous population; rights and freedoms are normally only accorded to citizens. Thus the general prohibitions against discrimination, which are designed to protect the human rights of minorities, seldom apply to foreigners.

Foreign nationals detained in prisons have the familiar problems of isolation and lower levels of legal and personal support. The growing proportion of non-nationals in prisons is also creating new problems for prison administrators in different countries. The aims of reintegration into society do not readily apply to foreigners, and the lack of rehabilitative purpose tends towards warehousing in prisons, which are often overcrowded. The net effect of the growing racial disproportionality in prisons is that there appears to be developing a two-tier system of imprisonment in Western Europe: one for citizens and one for foreign nationals. These two systems of imprisonment, although occurring in the same building, mean that the experiences, purposes and effects of incarceration are likely to be very different for the two groups.

Thus a review of recent developments in Britain, America and Western Europe reveals that in each location there is a growing racial disproportionality among the prison population and that prisons are filling up with members of different minority groups who tend to be socially and economically disadvantaged, and drawn mainly from deprived inner city areas. There is also an indication that the prison system itself is becoming divided and reconstructed along racial lines (Faugeron, 1996).

Conclusion

In the attempt to explain the growing racial disproportionality in prisons in different countries it has been necessary to trace the process back to its source. As always, it is a case of thinking backwards and writing forwards. In this process of reflection it has been necessary to problematise the very terms 'race', 'black', 'white' and the like and to treat them as if they were always in parentheses. At the same time it has also been necessary to explore critically the methods of classification adopted, since they provide the conceptual grids through which the debate is structured.

At the core of the debate on race, crime and imprisonment, the three recent contributions by Alfred Blumstein (1982), Roger Hood (1992) and Michael Tonry (1995) provide accounts which are complementary, on one level, and contradictory, on another. Whereas Blumstein's study focuses on the relation between arrests and convictions and concludes that approximately 80 per cent of the racial disproportionality in prisons can be accounted for by differential arrest rates between ethnic groups for serious crime, Tonry's analysis qualifies Blumstein's approach by emphasising the ways in which crime control policies can be selectively enforced, with the result that 'indirect racism' is a contributory component of arrest data. But Tonry agrees with Blumstein and Hood that the sentencing process is much less discriminatory than is often assumed, and that although racism is not totally absent, the 'race effect' in sentencing is probably less than 10 per cent. The implications of this conclusion for Blumstein is that reducing racism among criminal justice agencies will make little real difference to the numbers of people in prison or to the level of racial disproportionality. To make any real difference to the composition of the prison population, the socio-economic basis of offending would have to be addressed. Hood, on the other hand, suggests a number of largely administrative strategies which would minimise the adverse consequence of pleading not guilty, as well as calling for a reconsideration of the sanctions for trading in cannabis. All three authors, however, would probably agree with Marian FitzGerald and Peter Marshall (1996), who point out that the construction of crime is a process of action and reaction and that it is difficult to operate in the real world with a clear-cut distinction between recorded patterns of offending and strategies of law enforcement. It is not always easy in specific cases to disentangle the offender from the offence, or the offence from the response.

Michael Tonry (1995) takes the issue further by arguing that sentencing policy, rather than simply endorsing discriminatory practices which have occurred at an earlier stage in the process, should attempt to compensate in some form for social adversity. If it is the case, he argues, that the reason for the disproportionate involvement in serious crime is a consequence of the socio-economic pressures which different groups experience and the range of temptations and disincentives to which different groups of people are subject, then rather than treat all offenders as if they were alike, greater recognition should be paid to their circumstances and the context in which the offending takes place. In essence, Tonry's argument raises the classicist dilemma of whether it is correct to treat people who are unequal as if they were equal, since this tends to compound inequality. Interestingly, Hood's (1992) analysis demonstrated how, in Dudley Crown Court, it was the lack of consideration given to mitigating circumstances which resulted in more black offenders being given a custodial sentence (Zatz, 1984). However, as Andrew von Hirsch and Julian Roberts (1997) point out, Tonry's suggestion that black people who are unemployed should be given some consideration in relation to the severity of their sentence could serve by implication to penalise those black offenders who are employed. Thus the extent to which we should take mitigating factors into account rather than focus on 'just desserts' needs to be seriously considered. The implications of Tonry's own analysis, however, are that it is discretionary law enforcement, which should be the primary object of intervention rather than decision-making at the sentencing stage.

Despite these differences and controversies, the debate around the racial disproportionality in prison has, however, taken on a strangely reassuring quality in which virtually all parties can claim some degree of correctness. There is considerable evidence of both direct and indirect racism at different stages of the criminal justice process. There is also evidence of cumulative racism operating at different points of the process; of stereotyping and scapegoating; and of specific forms of racism operating in the major criminal justice agencies, particularly among the police and sections of the judiciary. On the other hand, evidence can also be mobilised to show a disproportionate involvement of certain ethnic minority groups in particular forms of offending, and that whatever the material and social basis of these patterns of offending, it has real effects and consequences on individual victims and communities. At the same time, however, it is a debate that operates with restrictive and inconsistent categories. At one moment processes are over-racialised, while at other times racial factors are played down or ignored altogether. It is a debate which both conflates and confuses ethnic and national differences and in which the major criminal justice agencies appear equally culpable and equally neutral in processing offenders from different ethnic groups.

What is left unresolved in this debate is the 'race effect'. The tendency to talk in terms of race rather than class not only over-racialises offending and victimisation, but also lends weight to the notion that the problem is 'black crime' and is therefore primarily or exclusively a race issue. It is a short step from this point to the identification of all blacks, or another minority group, with crime, and once having 'demonstrated' this relation to use it as a basis for directing 'get tough' crime control policies at this group. If we are to overcome the current mixture of complacency and uncertainty there is a need to identify more clearly how race fits into the equation and thereby to begin to uncover the forms which racism takes in different contexts.

10
The Future of Imprisonment

Introduction

The modern prison, which emerged at the beginning of the nineteenth century, has been closely linked by social historians to modernism. As a form of punishment it embodied the central tenets of Enlightenment thought with its emphasis on the application of rational and scientific principles to social problems such as crime and disorder. In this way, the prison was conceived of as a social laboratory in which individuals could be transformed and social progress could be achieved. Embracing the guiding notions of proportionality and penal economy, Enlightenment thinkers sought to provide a mode of punishment which would remove errant individuals from the corrupting influence of their environment. By placing them in segregative institutions and subjecting them to the rigours of labour discipline, it was believed that it would be possible to instil the habits of industry, thereby turning unproductive and recalcitrant individuals into useful law-abiding subjects.

The modern prison was an institution that embodied the coercive powers of the developing democratic state in ways which accommodated classicist notions of justice, emphasising due process and equality before the law. This new social experiment differed from previous forms of confinement in that its objective was to punish individuals by removing that commodity which all free citizens held in equal amounts – time. But critics like Karl Marx began to argue in the mid nineteenth century that underneath the appearance of freedom and equality was a system of exploitation, inequality and wage slavery (Berman, 1983). The modernist project was, according to Marx, deeply flawed because underlying the sphere of formal equality were substantive inequalities. The social revolutions, civil wars and other forms of class struggle which occurred across Europe in the mid nineteenth century called into question the legitimacy of the social system and its ability to realise the ideals of individual freedom and social justice.

The mounting critiques of the modernist project in this revolutionary period were specifically applied to those newly fashioned regulatory state institutions such as the prison. As a mechanism for controlling or transforming the 'dangerous classes' and 'criminal classes' into docile and useful citizens, it appeared to be of limited utility. The evidence which emerged during the second half of the nineteenth century of growing levels of recidivism, violent disturbances, strikes against prison workshops, disagreements over wages and rewards for prison work, as well as the increasing costs of running penal institutions, strongly suggested that either the penal project was failing or that it needed considerable rethinking to make it work. There were also growing problems of overcrowding and the spread of disease in prisons, as well as disturbing and frequent reports of suicide and insanity among prisoners. Rather than produce a steady stream of reformed offenders, the prison succeeded in producing, as Foucault (1977) has argued, a manageable population of recidivists, as well as the 'delinquent' as an individual existing before and outside the criminal act. By providing a social laboratory for the study of the delinquent the prison succeeded in producing a new science: the science of criminology. 'Delinquency', as Foucault put it, 'is the vengeance of the prison on justice.'

The various strands of criticism which began to appear towards the end of the nineteenth century tended to oscillate between the question of the effectiveness of the prison in reforming individuals and concerns about its economic and social cost. Thus:

> It should be noted that this monotonous critique of the prison always takes one of two directions; either that the prison was insufficiently corrective, and that the penitentiary critique was still at the rudimentary stage; or that in attempting to be corrective it lost its power as punishment, that the true penitentiary technique was rigour, and the prison was a double economic error; directly by its intrinsic cost and indirectly by the cost of the delinquency that it did not abolish. (Foucault, 1977: 268)

The ostensible 'failure' of the prison to achieve its various objectives promoted a range of penal reforms and led to the decreasing scale of imprisonment across Europe and America from the end of the nineteenth century to the first half of the twentieth century. These developments were complex and diverse and took different forms in different countries, but they can be broadly summarised as being conditioned by three central determinants. The first involved changes in the nature of the capitalist state which had taken on responsibility for financing and running the prison system. The development of the welfare state towards the end of the nineteenth century marks a major shift in the mode of regulation (Garland, 1985). The second development of some consequence was the introduction of a system of mass production based on assembly-line principles known as 'Fordism' (after the famous car manufacturer Henry Ford). This changed the nature of labour discipline by building factory discipline into the assembly line itself (Lea, 1979). Also, by the end of the nineteenth century the habits of work were widely established and class struggle had become increasingly mediated by national trade union organisations. Third, the emerging discipline of criminology encouraged and attracted a growing range of experts – psychiatrists, doctors, lawyers, criminologists – who aimed to develop a more scientific system through which the rehabilitation of offenders could be achieved (Ignatieff, 1978). These approaches relied less on the punitive strategies of arduous prison labour and more on medical and psychological techniques which could identify and reform offenders who were considered salvageable. This form of intervention was more likely to succeed if special reformatory institutions were established and if the 'experts' were given enough time to allow deviants to benefit from their expertise. The possibility of the prison exacting a 'just measure of pain' was increasingly called into question as more details about offenders became known and as systems of punishment were seen to require more flexibility in the period of time served. The adoption of indeterminate sentencing and parole provided prison administrators with powers which were more flexible and wide-ranging.

Thus, at the end of the nineteenth century, a marked shift in emphasis took place involving a decreasing preoccupation with the problems of production and labour discipline and an increasing focus on issues associated with biological and social reproduction and the 'quality' of labour power. Through the development of welfare capitalism the prison increasingly became a punishment of last resort, acting as a backup sanction to the emerging range of community-based punishments. The decline in the use of the prison in various countries during the first half of the twentieth century encouraged Rusche and Kirschheimer (1939 [2003]), who were writing in the 1930s, to conclude that the modern prison had initially been the product of industrial capitalism and post-Enlightenment thought and that the contradictory developments of modernity had turned the prison into an increasingly anachronistic institution, such that in advanced capitalist societies it would become a subordinate sanction in relation to other penalties such as the fine.

However, the expected demise of the prison has not occurred in the postwar period. On the contrary, the prison has maintained its central role within the penal system, and in many countries the number of those imprisoned has increased. This development has occurred against a backdrop of what are widely seen as major changes in the nature of work, culture and social organisation. Increasingly, references are made to terms such as post-industrialisation, postmodernism and post-Fordism, and these terms are deployed to suggest that we are currently undergoing a major transformation in social and economic relations. Since it has been suggested that the development of the modern prison was closely associated with modernity and modernism, then it might be expected that the shift towards postmodernism would have profound implications for the future of imprisonment.

Modernism and postmodernism

If modernism is associated with the rational control of society through the application of scientific principles aimed at achieving individual and social transformation in the pursuit of progress, justice and equality, postmodernism emphasises the opposite. Thus the postmodernists question the rationality of science and the possibility of achieving progress through the application of scientific techniques. Rather than serving as an instrument for illumination and clarification, science is seen to operate as a tool of oppression and control. The evidence of the gulags and the Holocaust is presented as a damning critique of the modernist project and of its ability to realise the ideals of freedom and justice. Postmodernists are suspicious of 'grand narratives' and their emphasis on the totality. Instead they argue for recognition of difference, autonomy and for local and specific interventions, rather than aiming for all-encompassing forms of change (Harvey, 1989; Lyotard, 1986; Smart, 1992).

In the review of the supposed transformation from penal modernism to postmodernism, David Garland (1990) notes that there have been changes in recent years in relation to be the rehabilitative ideal, the rise of the 'back to justice' movement, the growth of community-based corrections, and an emphasis upon new forms of managerialism which reflect a growing concern with aggregate groups rather than with individual offenders. He concludes, however, that the description of penality as being 'post-rehabilitative', 'post-disciplinary', or 'post-institutional' and ultimately postmodern is not supported by the evidence. The experience of the gulags, Garland argues, does not signal the collapse of the modernist project but rather exposes the dangers or the 'dark side' of modernism. Moreover, he suggests that contradiction and critique are essential and indispensable features of the modernist project. Although the development of modernity is uneven and there had been various shifts of emphasis as well as ongoing conflicts concerning the meaning and significance of imprisonment, Garland argues that neither the prison apparatus nor penal practice is currently undergoing major change. In addition, he points out that the professional groups that staff the penal apparatus have remained essentially the same throughout the twentieth century. Thus, in opposition to the claims of postmodernists, he argues that:

> The age of penal modernism is not yet over. Nor is penal modernity about to fade. Instead, what we have been witnessing since the late 1960s is that transformation of penal modernism from being a critical, reforming program to being itself but part of the fabric of modern penality, and hence a target for other critical, reforming movements. With this shift, one sees the closing of a long period of a naïve enthusiasm and optimism regarding the modernist project and the emergence of a more mature, more informed, more ambivalent understanding of what it entails. Modernism has come to understand itself better and to appreciate the program of modernist penality has serious limitations and is riven with deep moral ambiguity. (Garland, 1995: 203)

Thus, despite the postmodernist critiques and a series of internal rumblings within the penal system itself, Garland argues that the modernist project remains intact, although he concedes that it is becoming increasingly pragmatic, managerialist and directionless. Although Garland claims that changes occurring in the penal sphere may be more to do with the rhetoric than changes in material practices, there is an abiding feeling among those working both inside and outside the penal system that significant changes are under way. The continual reference to the penal 'crisis' in both academic and popular literature suggests that the prison currently faces a number of deep-seated problems that go beyond poor conditons and overcrowding and raise issues about the legitimacy of the prison itself (Fitzgerald and Sim, 1979; Sparks, 1994). There are also those like Malcolm Feeley and Jonathan Simon (1992, 1994) who argue that the prison is undergoing a fundamental transformation based on the adoption of actuarial justice that is in the process of replacing the 'Old

Penology' based on the rehabilitation and reform of individual offenders by a 'New Penology' based on risk assessment and the management of the 'underclass'.

Rather than examine these options directly in terms of claims and counter-claims by modernists and postmodernists, with the danger of becoming enmeshed in this unresolved polemic (Hallsworth, 2002; Lucken, 1998; Penna and Yar 2003; Russell, 1997), it may be more useful to examine current developments in terms of what have been identified as the three essential elements which have shaped the development of the modern prison – space, time and labour. Examining changes in the nature of penality allows the development a more nuanced understanding of current developments. In the process it is suggested that seeing recent developments in terms of a shift from modernism to postmodernism is limited and that it is more instructive to see recent changes in light of the transition from Fordism to post-Fordism.

Fordism and post-Fordism

The perceived shift in the balance in recent years from industrial production based on Fordist principles towards more flexible forms of accumulation has a number of important consequences both in relation to participation in the production process and also in relation to the organisation of the labour market itself (Amin, 1994; Lea, 1997). These changes have been well-documented and can be briefly summarised as having three general characteristics: a general decline in manufacturing and a consequent shift of personnel from the industrial to the service sector; the restructuring of the workforce leading to greater job insecurity, not only for the young but also for the older sections of the community who may have worked for a number of years previously; and the 'feminisation' of the labour force, with a greater proportion of women engaging in paid work, although often involving low-paid, temporary, contracts.

How do these changes impact upon the process of imprisonment? These developments may be seen to influence the scale of imprisonment both by fostering disruption and fragmentation of social relations and informal controls, on one hand, and by simultaneously undermining and transforming the two main regulatory mechanisms that were established in the Fordist era – the modern family and the Keynesian welfare state – on the other. In this process of restructuring, the long-held assumption that the sovereign state is capable of providing security and law and order is being called into question (Garland, 1996). Faced with these difficulties, it is probably not surprising that the main criminal justice agencies appear to be adopting a more pragmatic approach, geared to managerialist principles, and have become preoccupied with the development of performance indicators and measurable outputs. The growing interest in risk assessment in relation to crime control and penality can be seen to arise from the promise of rationalising resources by targeting potentially difficult and dangerous populations, while providing struggling agencies with a new set of pseudo-scientific rationales (Feeley and Simon, 1992; Jones, 1996).

Another favoured option of the reconstituted state is privatisation. This involves not only the handing over of the management of prisons but also the development of interagency alliances involving the private and voluntary sectors (Beyens and Snacken, 1996; Matthews, 1989a). The management of prisons by private agencies has become an established practice over the past decade, although the actual savings to the taxpayer of this option remain uncertain. There are also important issues of accountability (Harding, 1997). Privatisation in its various forms has rendered the conventional divisions between 'public' and 'private' problematic and in turn has invited a re-examination of the adequacy of state-centred approaches for the management of crime control. At the same time the attempt to devolve responsibility for crime control onto local communities is undermined by the fact that it is precisely in those communities in which the level of crime and disorder are highest that neighbourhoods are fragmented and where informal controls are at their weakest, and therefore are more difficult to mobilise.

Another way of reading recent developments is that in the wake of rapid social change, social fragmentation and disruption, traditional institutions such as the prison are being re-mobilised to absorb a growing array of social problems and to provide a semblance of stability. The re-mobilisation of the prison becomes the preferred option in a climate of growing uncertainty and provides policy-makers with a convenient way in which to respond to public demands for greater security and protection in a world which is increasingly uncertain and unpredictable – even if it is recognised that as a mechanism of discipline and reform it has limited utility. Such a reading might help us to resolve the paradox of the increasing scale of imprisonment in England and Wales and the US at a time when it is very difficult to find anyone advocating the use of imprisonment or claiming that prison works. As Michael Jacobson (2005) has argued, it is very difficult these days to find people who are arguing for prison expansion, and policy-makers tend to be apologetic and defensive when they announce an increase in prison populations or the building of new prisons.

One of the most disturbing developments that has taken place in parts of America where the legitimate economic livelihoods of communities have declined has been the tendency to lobby for the construction of a prison in the locality in order to provide some form of employment for local population. As Nils Christie (1993) has argued, there is a real danger of crime control becoming an industry which serves to replace those industries which have declined or disappeared. Thus, in as much as there are causal links between unemployment, crime and imprisonment, it is possible to conceive of a scenario in which, as structural unemployment occurs in certain areas, the level of crime and imprisonment increases, and as a consequence more prisons are built. Thus the prison becomes both a product of and a solution to the problem of increasing unemployment. In this context the distinction between the 'respectable' and the 'disorganised' working class is likely to become more pronounced (Platek, 1996).

A closely related development is the decanting of prisoners back into the poor inner-city neighbourhoods from which many of them lived before entering prison. This has resulted in a growing concentration of ex-prisoners in run-down neighbourhoods such that high levels of incarceration not only have an impact on the prisoner's family but can also have adverse effects on the economic and social stability of neighbourhoods (Clear, 2002; Fagan, 2004). There has been a growing focus in recent years on the 'collateral damage' associated with imprisonment and the ways in which imprisonment not only affects the life chances and job prospects of those sent to prison but also how it impacts upon their partners and dependents. The suggestion is that the 'pains of imprisonment' go far beyond the prison walls, creating cycles of disadvantage, and thereby nurturing new generations of offenders.

Relatedly, there is a growing concern about recidivism and the way in which the prison system recycles the same people though the system over time. The statement by the Home Office (1990) that 'prison can be an expensive way of making bad people worse' appears to acknowledge this limitation while strategically decreasing public expectations. The perennial problem of organising meaningful work and training programmes in prison and the continued decline of prison industries in part reflect the problems of production in the outside world, despite the repeated attempts to increase the profitability of work in prison. The issue of 'less eligibility' also appears be becoming less relevant as the conditions of the poorest sections of the general population decline, while the standards of civilised society demand that prisons are maintained to prescribed standards of comfort and hygiene.

Thus the shift to post-Fordism – which should not be over-exaggerated, since manufacturing remains a major part of the production process in many Western countries – has a contradictory impact on the development of incarceration (Harris and McDonald, 2000). On one hand, the shift towards short-term contracts has created greater uncertainty, the fragmentation of communities, the breakdown of informal controls and changes in the nature and role of the national state. At the same time the cost-effectiveness of imprisonment is increasingly called into question, while changes in the nature of the labour market, employment opportunities and the nature of work have increasingly undermined the role of the prison as a disciplining and reforming institution.

The deinstitutionalisation of work and the increasing use of electronic communication mean that a growing proportion of the population work from home Indeed, labour becomes more mobile and more flexible. As the manufacturing sector declines in countries like Britain and America and the service sector grows, the confinement of labour within the factory becomes less of a necessity. An instructive example of the growing flexibility of labour services and the transcendence of space by modern communication systems is apparent in the case of the Californian prison where inmates book flights for an American airline. Facilitating the movement of others while in confinement and at the same time transcending the prison walls with the use of electronic media is a double irony which, no doubt, is not lost on the prisoners themselves.

The growing significance of migrant labour in a period of globalisation has been discussed at length in previous chapters. In many ways migrant labour represents the mobility and insecurity of post-Fordism. It is also the case that migrant workers often lack the safeguards of employment rights and citizenship and are vulnerable to discriminatory treatment by the criminal justice system in different countries. This treatment does not necessarily have to be deliberate or racist, but arises from the fact that as non-citizens or semi-citizens they lack the rights and securities that provide full citizens with a degree of protection. Having no fixed accommodation, and no family support or access to legal services all work against the migrant, and these and related services serve to propel migrants more readily into the prison. The migrant, as Bauman (2000) argues, stands in stark contrast to the tourist who, as an affluent consumer, represents the acceptable face of international mobility (Weber and Bowling, 2008). The migrant worker, on the other hand, is viewed with ambivalence and is tolerated as long as he or she engages in poorly paid or essential work without making too many demands. The growing number of foreigners in prisons in Europe is a cause for international concern, since 20–60 per cent of inmates in different countries are non-nationals.

Space and spacism

Modern forms of capitalist production incorporating unparalleled advances in communication have intensified and fragmented the ordering of time and space whereby split-second capital transactions traverse space literally in 'no time'. (Bauman, 2000). As Anthony Giddens (1984) has suggested, the separation and commodification of time and space was one of the defining features of industrial capitalism, while David Harvey (1989) depicts the shift towards 'flexible accumulation' as involving the 'annihilation of space through time', which he sees as resulting in greater 'time–space compression' in Western capitalism since the 1960s. The processes which Harvey (1994) outlines also involve a changing relation between time and labour. He suggests that the processes of globalisation and consequent changes in the international division of labour are connected to the development of the 'information society', involving the speeding up of communications, changing forms of individual and national identity and, importantly, the changing role of the state, as well as other regulatory institutions of modern society such as the family and the prison. Most critically, the shifting emphasis from Fordism to flexible accumulation, which Harvey and others see as one of the most significant developments in the last three decades, not only involves profound changes in the organisation of the production process but also has implications for the process of socialisation and the nature of discipline.

One of the major effects of post-Fordist forms of flexible accumulation and the associated decline in manufacturing is that they have a different impact on different regions and particularly on different urban areas. Urban sociologists tend to distinguish between three types of urban area: the deindustrialised city, characterised by a decline in manufacturing, rising unemployment and growing levels of deprivation; the reconstructed city, characterised by the introduction of new forms of manufacturing, such as chemical plants or computer companies, which have been introduced to replace the declining traditional industries; and the global city, which has become more service-orientated and linked more directly to international financial markets (Lasch and Urry, 1994).

In each of these three urban areas there are differences in the nature and availability of work as well as in lifestyle and in the pace of life. The feminisation of the labour market and the rise of the women's movement

have also significantly changed the face of cities through the transformation of households and through the domestic division of labour, as well
as through the use of public space. Women are increasingly becoming
involved in disputes over the use of space between business, commercial
and residential interests (Massey, 1997).

Disputes over the 'ownership' of urban space are also played out along
racial lines (Webster, 2007). Alternatively, minority groups are managed
through forms of spatial control by which work, leisure and shopping
activities are relocated into suburban areas which are inaccessible to
the poorer ethnic-minority communities. Although the strategy of
ethnic segregation and exclusion by design – spacism – is widely used,
particularly in America, the limits of this strategy as a mechanism of
social control are reflected in the fact that it is from this population that
a disproportionate percentage of the prison population is drawn. This is
largely because spacism serves not to solve the problems of poverty and
deprivation, but rather to intensify and compound them.

Social and geographical space within the city is restructured in relation
to growing social divisions, together with new demands for autonomy,
privacy and the recognition of difference (Sennett, 1991; Soja, 1989).
This reorganisation of urban space allows for the development of new
strategies of spatial regulation, which are able to target more accurately
selected problems and particular populations (Nellis, 2005). Forms of
regulation which embrace technological and informational systems are
able to permeate the concrete structures of modernity. Within this milieu,
private security police are able to operate alongside the proliferation
of the glittering array of technology which has been made available
by this growing body of private providers. Crime prevention through
environmental design, together with increasingly privatised forms of
policing, has displaced crime and helped to construct what Mike Davis
(1990) calls 'fortress cities'. As he suggests, these tendencies are nowhere
more evident than in Los Angeles, the 'the city of the future', where
designer prisons have been constructed by celebrity architects:

> An extraordinary example, the flagship of the emergent genre, is Welton
> Becket Associates, new Metropolitan Detention Center in Downtown
> Los Angeles. Although this ten-story Federal Bureau of Prisons facility is
> one of the most visible new structures in the city, few of the hundreds
> of thousands of commuters who pass by every day have even an inkling
> of its function as a holding center for what has officially been described
> as the 'managerial elite of narco-terrorism'. This postmodern Bastille

– the largest prison built in a major US urban center in decades – looks instead like a futuristic hotel or office block, with artistic flourishes (for example, the high-tech trellises on its bridge-balconies) that are comparable to Downtown's best designed recent architecture. In contrast to the human inferno of the desperately overcrowded County Jail a few blocks away, the Becket structure appears less of a detention center than a convention center for federal felons – a distinguished addition to Downtown's continuum of security and design. (Davis, 1992: 176)

The creation of a number of smaller local prisons in urban centres where they may take the form of high-rise tower blocks or purpose-built constructions designed to mesh in with the wider environment appears to be gaining considerable support among prison administrators and penal reformers alike. There is also a growing interest in 'community prisons', which is linked to the increasing preoccupation with localism. Community prisons are also rationalised in terms of the need for greater accessibility of prisoners' friends and families, as well as in relation to the calls for the construction of a number of different types of prison that can accommodate the interests, needs and demands of different populations (Tumim, 1996).

Another major contribution to the theorisation of spatial control is Stanley Cohen's *Visions of Social Control* (1985), which provides a reconceptualisation of the relation between inclusive and exclusive strategies. In essence, Cohen argues that all societies involve a mixture of inclusive and exclusive strategies in which inclusion means integration, assimilation, accommodation, toleration, absorption and incorporation, while exclusion means banishment, expulsion, segregation and isolation. Importantly, although we tend to think of exclusion in negative terms and inclusion as something positive, there is no necessary reason why inclusive or informal strategies of control are necessarily any more benign or just than exclusive ones. This mistaken assumption was always too uncritically embraced by the first-generation abolitionists, who saw informal or non-state forms of control as intrinsically benign and progressive and were always faced with the problem of how to deal with vigilante groups and 'citizen patrols' (de Haan, 1990). Moreover, Cohen points out that the destructuring impulses which surfaced in the 1960s, which were designed to promote inclusionary strategies, ultimately fed back into exclusionary processes. Drawing on Cohen's analysis, it is evident that it is not sufficient to think solely in terms of inclusion versus exclusion and that there are a number of different cross-cutting axes along which control strategies operate.

The prison, along with social control strategies in general, can be located along the various dimensions shown in Figure 10.1. At the same time these different options can combine in a number of different ways. Control can be state-sponsored but decentralised, informal and punitive, or can operate in ways which are visible and accountable but privatised, and so on. Currently it would seem that the prison system is becoming increasingly decentralised, but more punitive and less protective. The degree of segregation has also been reduced through the development of links with community organisations, while forms of accountability are becoming less transparent as a result of privatisation (Harding, 1997).

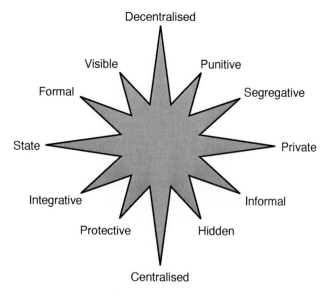

Figure 10.1   Polarities of social control strategies

John Braithwaite (2002) takes issue with Cohen's (1985) scepticism about the viability of inclusionary modes of control, and particularly with Cohen's contention that 'inclusionary controls are ill-equipped to foster social integration', and that since 'rituals of blaming are difficult to sustain, they lose their moral edge'. Braithwaite claims that informal rituals of shaming can be effective as long as they aim to be reintegrative rather that stigmatising. Although at first sight Braithwaite's response appears as a useful corrective to the excesses of labelling theory, it fails to recognise that informal control is double-edged and that it can be destructive and demeaning as well as supportive and instructive. Moreover, the rational, coherent, honest world which Braithwaite (1993) presents as a basis for applying shaming rituals is far removed from the urban realities of modern life.

Significantly, he cites Japan as a society which widely employs reintegrative shaming and consequently has, he claims, 'safe streets and empty jails'. However, Braithwaite admits that, 'as much as I admire the crime control achievement of Japan, I would not want to live there because I think I would find the informal pressures of conformity oppressive'. This statement seems to confirm the point made by Cohen about the limits and disadvantages of 'inclusive' forms of control. It is also evident that Braithwaite's theory of reintegrative shaming avoids facing the central issue of the mutual relationship and interdependence of inclusive and exclusive strategies and that the threat of exclusion is an ever-present dimension of reintegrative strategies. Thus reintegrative shaming does not stand in opposition to segregative and exclusionary sanctions but forms part of an interdependent relation. Indeed, Braithwaite's call for a shift in the moral balance towards more informal forms of regulation was written at a time when the capacities of neighbourhoods to engage in such moralising practices was becoming progressively more limited. In short, Braithwaite's plea for reintegrative shaming appears to have occurred precisely at the point at which changing economic and social relations were making such choices increasingly untenable (Matthews, 2006).

There is a sense, therefore, in which those arguing for inclusion in the form of developing more expansive forms of informal control and those who see the drift in the present period towards exclusionary strategies are both wide of the target. Although it is the case that in the current period both prisons and community based sanctions are expanding for certain categories of offenders, what also appears to be happening, as Cohen (1985) has intimated, is the development of strategies of social control which are neither genuinely inclusive, in that they do not involve forms of incorporation or reintegration back into the community, and nor, at the same time, are they properly exclusive in that they do not involve segregation or expulsion. Thus the bulk of deviants and offenders are not 'swallowed up' or 'spewed out', to use Lévi-Strauss's (1992) analogy. Instead, they are subject to forms of intervention which are organised through a changing combination of state and non-state agencies and are subject to penalties which have little relation to the mores of the community in which they live (Young, 1999). Indeed, they may involve a minimum degree of interpersonal contact and are more likely to be administrative. Forms of intervention tend increasingly to be directed towards the control of behaviour or involve low-level monitoring. Alternatively, the aim is to deter prospective offenders through the increased use of surveillance, the deployment of private security police, or simply to prevent crime through environmental design.

It's about time

Reference has already been made to the time–space compression which has been a feature of 'information society' in recent decades. David Harvey (1989) has outlined some of the implications of this process. Just as notions of space have been transformed through the creation of the 'global village', notions of 'hyperspace', 'cyberspace' and the use of new forms of electronic communication, so time has accelerated such that contemporary life is generally experienced as speeding up. The impact of time–space compression is nowhere more evident than in the operation of international financial markets. A week may be a long time in politics but, as they say, it is a lifetime on the stock exchange.

Alongside the acceleration of time and the consequent speeding up of decision-making processes, there is a simultaneous propensity to 'freeze' and repackage time through films and videos as well as by means of television and computer link-ups. Regular exposure to these forms of media reorganises the time–space relation and creates a constant interplay between fantasy and reality. Thus, throughout the average day, time is accelerated, suspended, frozen and then re-spent. Not surprisingly, the mass media itself is fascinated by this changing sense of time, and various popular programmes and films have explored this theme in different ways.

Time also appears to be taking on an increasingly cyclical quality, with a tendency to oscillate continuously between the present and the past. Fashions, ideas and cultural artefacts are continuously recycled, and as the past fuses with the present, even nostalgia is no longer available in the way in which it once was. This oscillation between the past and the present is in part a consequence of the fact that, politically, the future has been suspended. The prospect of a qualitative social transformation in the form of socialism has dissolved with the gradual collapse of Russian communism. The future appears only to offer more of the same and, as many postmodernists argue, global change appears less possible and only local political change is realistic. Utopia has been abolished and we appear to have been sentenced to an ever-recurring present. In this context the functions of imprisonment are likely to shift towards deterrence and incapacitation. Moreover, the growing preoccupation of risk analysis is a strategy for distilling the future into the present.

In effect, what we appear to witnessing is the dissolution of time as a linear and universal process, that can be tied to strict calibration and which has a fixed direction. Thus:

> Linear, irreversible, measurable, predictable time is being shattered in the network society, in a movement of extraordinary historical significance. But we are not just witnessing a relativization of time ... The transformation is more profound: it is the mixing of tenses to create a forever universe, not self-expanding but self-maintaining, not cyclical but random, not recursive but inclusive; timeless time using technology to escape the context of its existence, and to appropriate any value each context could offer to the ever-present. (Castells, 1996: 433)

Thus, whereas industrialisation brought linear synchronicity to the assembly lines of Fordist factories in which clock time was heralded as the organising principle of production, these forms of linear, predictable time are being radically challenged in the 'network society'. Post-Fordism allows for flexi-time and generally encourages flexible working arrangements, although there are gender differences in the application which has implications for the formation of gender identities (Odih, 2003). Castells also argues that advances in information technology have made possible the globalisation of the economy as well as the fragmentation of power which, he argues, is no longer concentrated in institutions (the state) or organisations (capitalist firms), while power is diffused through the global networks of capital and information is transmitted through a growing array of real and virtual images. In this way, events that are distributed across time and space can appear as if they were simultaneous, while simultaneous events can appear as intermittent.

Time, however, is not accelerating at the same rate for all sections of the population. Although, among the informational elite, there are never enough hours in the day, among those who live in declining deindustrialised urban areas or in the segregated urban ghettos, the experience of time is very different (Massey, 1997). Days are long, and individuals are likely to find themselves with a great deal of time on their hands. Since it is from this population that the prison population is disproportionately drawn, it may be the case paradoxically that if a time-based punishment is to have a deterrent value, it needs to be of a considerable duration. By the same token, the decline of indeterminate sentencing and the movement towards determinate, mandatory and so-called 'honest' sentencing can all be seen as attempts to reinstate some degree of consistency in time-based punishments against a background in which the notion of time itself appears more differentiated and uncertain. This has, in turn, destabilised the notion of proportionality in sentencing. Moreover, where time-based punishments continue to be used, they are increasingly concerned with the curtailment of 'spare' time and 'leisure' time.

Thus time itself appears to be losing its universality. It has different meanings for different individuals and groups as a consequence of variations in relation to work, life expectancy and identity. Castells (1996) argues that the new forms of flexible labour based on fixed-term contracts, casual seasonal labour-agency labour, freelancers and outsourcing have a differential impact on men and women which serves to unsettle the formation of gender identities (Odih, 2003). To be sure, time was always a less universal measure than is often assumed, and was in fact always a commodity upon which different groups had a different purchase. But over the last few decades these differences have become more pronounced, and as a consequence time is becoming an increasingly uncertain measure. Thus changes in the experience and meaning of time, like the changing nature of space and labour, are likely to have a mixed impact upon imprisonment. There are movements to reassert time-based punishments, while the belief in a never-ending present serves to assure us that the prison will always be with us. However, by the same token, the denial of the possibility of social progress serves to undermine the basic rationale on which the modern prison rests. It is the gradual undermining of the perceived 'naturalness' of imprisonment that presents the prison as increasingly being in a state of 'crisis', and raises issues of legitimacy even while its use increases.

The use of imprisonment and other forms of confinement, however, has not increased in all countries in recent years. In Ireland, for example, there has been a noticeable decrease in the number of individuals coercively confined over the last 50 years. It has been estimated that in 1951 approximately 1 per cent of the population were subject to some form of coercive confinement – prisons, borstals, reformatories, industrial schools, psychiatric institutions and homes for unmarried mothers. The number confined to these institutions was eight times higher in 1951 than it is today (O'Sullivan and O'Donnell, 2007). In opposition to the current liberal claim that society is constantly expanding and intensifying confinement, the experience in Ireland, as well as some other countries, is that they appear to be moving away from forms of coercive confinement. If we accept that the social and economic foundations of the modern prison are subsiding, and if the prison was primarily a disciplinary institution, the question arises of whether we are moving into a post-disciplinary society.

Towards a post-disciplinary society?

There are two readings of Foucault's *Discipline and Punish*. In the first reading the disciplinary practices that were developed in the modern prison during the nineteenth century have subsequently spread beyond the prison and become dispersed through the social body. Central to this 'dispersal of discipline' thesis is the concept of the Panopticon, which is seen as the model of surveillance society. The alternative reading is that the disciplinary practices were associated with modernity and that in the era of late modernity we are moving into a post-disciplinary society.

Stanley Cohen (1985) has presented a version of the 'dispersal of discipline' thesis which suggests that the forms of scientific knowledge, treatment and evaluation, as well as the systems of classification, which had originally been developed in the closed fortress of the prison were at a later date taken up and adapted by the growing body of professionals who organise community-based sanctions. Through the widespread adoption of these procedures, in the name of either science, progress or humanitarianism, the state is seen to engage in the more subtle, systematic and ultimately more invidious control of everyday life. The Orwellian nightmare of the totally controlled society is closely associated with this vision of discipline, gradually but relentlessly spreading through the social body (Cohen, 1979).

As Anthony Bottoms (1983) has argued, there are both conceptual and empirical limitations to the dispersal of discipline thesis. First, he suggests that Cohen and others have conflated corporal, judicial and carceral systems of punishment and consequently have assumed that all dispersed forms of social control are 'disciplinary' in the Foucauldian sense. Second, there are a range of penalties including fines, compensation orders and community service orders which are becoming more widely used but which are not 'disciplinary' techniques as such. Third, the 'dispersal of discipline' thesis tends to refer to discipline in an undifferentiated way, with the consequence that the specificity of particular disciplinary practices, as well as the way in which they are used in relation to different groups, is overlooked. Finally, Cohen and others tend to equate social control with 'state control', which they see as being exercised as a negative 'top down' strategy rather than seeing it, in some instances at least, as incorporating a series of defensive and adaptive measures.

The important point which Bottoms is making here is that some of the more prominent current crime control strategies do not involve 'discipline' in the sense that Foucault outlines it, but rather low-level monitoring and supervision, often accompanied by forms of non-intervention, neglect and indifference. In a rejoinder, Cohen (1983) has referred to these developments as constituting what he calls the 'new behaviourism', which aims not to reform, rehabilitate or confront the values of offenders, but more simply aims to monitor their movements and regulate their activities. This strategy, Cohen suggests, is associated with a 'minimal statism' that is also less concerned with changing people than with limiting the range and costs of state intervention to particular types of offences or offenders. Alongside these modalities of action and inaction there are other developing control strategies which involve the expansion of bureaucratic and administrative measures, a shift away from the purely offender-orientated approaches towards a greater consideration of the victim and their claims for compensation and support, as well as a growing emphasis on both restitutive and restorative sanctions (Dutton, 1992; Pratt, 1990).

The most significant and probably the most neglected feature of contemporary control systems, Bottoms (1983) points out, is the decrease in the proportionate use of imprisonment. He emphasises that successive governments in Britain and other European countries, whatever they may have said publicly about 'getting tough', have been practically committed to a policy of decarceration over the past 30 years or so by developing 'alternatives to imprisonment' or expanding the use of existing non-custodial sanctions, such that the proportion of convicted defendants sentenced to imprisonment has fallen consistently over this period.

Other versions of the 'dispersal of discipline' thesis tend to focus on Foucault's emphasis on the model of the Panopticon as the basis for the development of the surveillance society. The growing use of CCTV and other monitoring techniques is widely seen as part of a system of endless surveillance (Lyon, 2006). However, Zygmunt Bauman (1998) has argued that the Panopticon only works in societies whose inhabitants have fixed places, functions and appetites, and that in more fluid 'liquid' societies involving greater movement and diversity, surveillance performs a limited regulatory function. In a similar vein, Mike Davis's (1990) account of the changing social and geographical relations in Los Angeles suggests that surveillance is not so much focused on the activities of the mass of the population but is used to control the borders of the different city districts.

But surveillance, as Anthony Giddens (1981) has pointed out, refers not only to the sphere of supervision but also to the collection of information and the ordering and deployment of that knowledge. Thus surveillance can also include the collection of personal data, monitoring use of the internet, scrutinising the form and content of emails, as well as gathering information on telephone usage, with or without the user's consent. Increasingly the police have access to much of this data and the police themselves are busy collecting data of their own. It is not difficult to find examples of the ways in which information can be used as the basis for regulatory practices. In some cases, information can be used for political purposes to identify 'problem groups or individuals', and there are a growing number of agencies, besides the police, that have access to detailed personal data. As Thomas Mathieson (2003) has pointed out, elaborate information systems are being developed across Europe which gather details not only of those involved in crime who may be given a 'danger rating', but also on their associates and victims. This information can be cross-referenced with national databases that keep information on criminals and suspected criminals as well as gathering details of their movements, interests, associates, patterns of consumption and financial standing.

There are, however, four main arguments against the claims that we are moving towards a surveillance society associated with the model of the Panopticon. The first type of objection has been suggested by Bauman, who argues that surveillance is too remote and technological to engage the 'hearts and minds' of the general population, and as a mechanism of regulation it does not seduce them in the ways in which consumption and enjoyment imperatives are able to do. Second, the surveillance and monitoring of the population in order to identify and respond to transgressions is increasingly being superseded by a growing interest in preventing or anticipating anti-social behaviour through the use of actuarial risk-based analysis (Zedner, 2004). In this way, it is argued, we are moving into a pre-crime rather than post-crime society, in which the established system of criminal justice itself is undergoing a radical transformation. Third, the original aim of the Panopticon involving the surveillance of the many by the few is being reversed in the 'viewer society' such that it is increasingly the many watching the few (Mathieson, 1997). The advent of the mass media and the information society means that surveillance becomes an increasingly two-way process, which is at odds with a state-centred, hierarchical model of surveillance (Boyne, 2000). Fourth, there are problems of information management, involving storage, indexation and restrictions on data sharing. Problems of 'information overload' and of sorting and sharing data mean that a system of regulation faces problems of co-ordination and organisation.

It may well be, however, that the significance of contemporary forms of surveillance is that they are converging into what has been called a 'surveillant assemblage' (Bogard, 2006). Indeed, Kevin Haggerty and Richard Ericson (2000) have argued that the hierarchical systems of surveillance which feature in Orwell's *Nineteen Eighty-Four* and Foucault's depiction of the Panopticon are being superseded by non-hierarchical forms of information gathering and monitoring that combine a wide range of information systems with the aim of gathering information on human subjects rather than manipulating and ordering them. Thus:

> The surveillant assemblage does not approach the body in the first instance as a single entity to be molded, punished or controlled. First it must be known, and to do so it is broken down into a series of discrete signifying flows. Surveillance commences with a space of comparison and the introduction of breaks in the flows that emanate from and circulate within the human body. For example, drug testing striates flows of chemicals, photography captures flows of reflected lightwaves and lie detectors align and compare assorted flows of respiration, pulse and electricity. The body is itself then an assemblage comprised of myriad component parts and processes that are broken down for purposes of observation. (Haggerty and Ericson, 2000: 612–13)

By breaking the body down into a series of functions and processes through the use of different technologies of surveillance it is possible to transform the body of individual subjects into information sets that can then be used as a basis for intervention. In this process, privacy and anonymity are systematically eroded.

Nancy Fraser (2003) has argued that up until the last quarter of the twentieth century, the mode of discipline associated with Fordism was dispersed through the social body, but since the mid 1970s, post-Fordist flexibilisation has gained ascendancy. This involves a process of decentredness, deregulation and destructuring. It signals greater flexibility and open-endedness, as well as a shift towards globalisation and transnationalism. This, in turn, involves a shifting focus of social control towards terrorism, organised crime and trafficking. In line with other theorists, Fraser suggests that this has implications for the role of the national state and the mobilisation of power relations which, she argues, increasingly involve systems of networked governance involving different forms of interagency working and the increased prominence of non-governmental organisations, as well as a changing relation between the national and local state (Crawford, 2006). These changing configurations of governance involve a reconfiguration of the spatial and temporal dimensions. As Fraser argues, what networks are to space, flexibilisation is to time.

In a similar vein, Nick Rose (1996) argues that we are experiencing the 'death of the social' and that the welfare state that was based upon a nexus of collective solidarities and dependence is now in decline. We no longer govern through 'society' but through the regulated choices of individuals, and in this way we are governed through the exercise and pursuit of our 'freedom'. The aim is now for each individual to maximise his or her quality of life through his/her own acts and choices, and to 'enterprise' or 'responsibilise' him/herself and thereby create the actively responsible citizen.

In an important contribution to this debate, Gilles Deleuze (1995) has suggested that we are moving towards a post-disciplinary 'control society'. Deleuze claims that Foucault associated disciplinary societies with the eighteenth and nineteenth centuries, reaching their apogee at the beginning of the twentieth century. Disciplinary societies are characterised by major sites of confinement – the family, the school, the prison and the factory. This involved a particular ordering of space-time, but after the Second World War we see the general breakdown of these sites of confinement and a movement to new forms of deinstitutionalisation. Whereas confinement aims to mould individuals, the logic of the control society is modulation (alterations according to circumstances). We move from the confinement of the factory where the masses could be monitored and the wage packet was largely fixed, to a more fluid business model of rewards and incentives based on continuous assessments of efforts and productivity.

The process of deinstitutionalisation Deleuze suggests is gathering pace. The decarceration of the mentally ill in the 1970s and 1980s; the movement in education towards lifelong learning, distance learning and the Open University; the attempt to develop alternatives to custody and intermittent custody, and the emergence of new strategies for the delivery of medicine through helplines and home-based services, all serve as examples of this process. We are also witnessing the demise of the factory and even the office and a shift towards new forms of self-employment, outsourcing, franchising and home-based working. These changes, according to Deleuze, signal the movement from disciplinary to control societies. In control societies, control is managed not through confinement but through forms of continuous control and instant communication. This involves the monitoring and examination of communications, of patterns of consumption, and in particular the use of credit. Thus, whereas it was the case that disciplinary society was organised around the crime–punishment relation in which the punishment would be designed to be for a fixed duration after which offenders can return to the community having paid for their crimes, in the control society the focus is on prevention and building the cost of transgression into the self-regulating behaviour of the individual. Thus individuals become aware that detailed personal files collated by faceless agencies carry information on a range of different aspects of their lives, and it becomes clear at an early age that this information will follow you throughout your life and can have a significant impact on your employment prospects and the availability of credit or loans. In the same way, peer reviews and appraisals at work, as well as gathering details on relational and health issues, can seriously impact one's life chances. In the control society, regulation, Deleuze argues, will be subtle, pervasive and relentless. Thus:

> Compared with the approaching forms of ceaseless control in open sites, we may come to see the harshest confinement as part of a wonderful happy past. (Deleuze 1995: 175)

Conclusion

We are in a period of transition and uncertainty. The widespread use of the prefix 'post' in relation to post-disciplinary, post-Panopticon and post-social, as well as postmodernity and post-Fordism, all suggest that the apparently solid structures of the nineteenth and twentieth centuries are in the process of transformation. In times of radical change there is a tendency, on one hand, to exaggerate the importance of events or processes that turn out in the longer term to be of relatively minor significance. On the other hand, there is also a tendency to fail to recognise change and to see any continuing trace of traditional structures as an indication that nothing is really changing and that it is 'business as usual'.

When change is recognised, there is a danger of seeing the emerging forms of regulation being driven mainly by political imperatives. As has been suggested in previous chapters, the changing use of the prison is conditioned not so much by a 'populist punitiveness', as many liberal criminologist suggest, but by socio-economic and cultural forces. We are, however, left with the problem of explaining the growth of the prison in different countries if it is the case that we are moving toward a post-disciplinary control society. It has been suggested above that the resolution to this paradox is to be found in the attempt to remobilise established regulatory mechanisms in a period in which new post-disciplinary forms of regulation have not as yet become fully established. In the same way, we are seeing the demise of the modern family and the simultaneous attempts by governments to shore it up and reform it while responsibilising parents. However, despite these efforts, we know that the modern 'cornflake' family that was associated with Fordism is a failing institution that is undergoing radical transformation.

These observations leave us with the perplexing issue of penal reform. It is not surprising in the current period that there are very few voices claiming that prison works or presenting a case for prison expansion. The building of new prisons is largely justified by the need to reduce overcrowding and to accommodate the growing number of offenders coming through the courts. In response, the vast majority of liberal and radical criminologists are arguing for either reductionism or some form of abolitionism. There are growing calls for the use of alternatives to custody but, as we have seen, this is no panacea, and the proliferation of so-called 'alternatives' has occurred alongside the growth of imprisonment in many countries and has arguably contributed to penal expansion. As suggested in earlier chapters, we have, through the process of reform and adaptation, created an increasingly complex network of agencies and institutions that make up an extended punishment–welfare continuum. It has also been suggested that any form of intervention in the penal sphere requires a systems approach that can identify the flow of offenders through an extended criminal justice system and identify how the different elements of the system work to produce unexpected and in some cases undesirable outcomes. If, however, current changes in the nature of productive relations are undermining the basis of disciplinary society and its preoccupation with confinement, as a number of theorists suggest, it would seem that the scope and potential for penal reform is increasing, and if we can learn the lessons of past failures and develop a realistic strategic approach, there is much that can be achieved. Opposition to incarceration as the dominant form of punishment is becoming more resolute, while its conceptual foundations are contracting and the prison walls are becoming increasingly permeable.

Websites

Organisation of this directory

This gives a list of websites having information relating to prisons and prisoners. It is organised according to country. To make it as user-friendly as possible, England and Wales are given first, followed by the United States, and then international sites. Following these, countries are listed alphabetically.

Within each country, general websites pertaining to all issues are given (both government and independent organisations' websites). This is followed by a list of websites that give information on specific issues such as female prisoners, population data and youth issues. It has not been possible to do this for all countries, but as full a list as possible has been compiled.

England and Wales

General sites

Crime Reduction, www.crimereduction.gov.uk
Prison Service, www.hmprisonservice.gov.uk
Research Development and Statistics Directorate, www.homeoffice.gov.uk/rds/index/htm

Independent organisations

Prisoners Abroad, www.prisonersabroad.org.uk

Youth issues

Youth Justice Board, www.youth-justice-board.gov.uk

Ex-offenders

Nacro, www.nacro.org.uk
Unlock, www.tphbook.dircon.co.uk/unlock.html

Publications

RDS, www.homeoffice.gov.uk/rds/pubsintro1.html

Classifications

Prison Classification, www.postcardsfromprison.com/research/indextwo.htm

United States

General sites

Government sites
Bureau of Justice Statistics, www.ojp.usdoj.gov/bjs

Bureau of Prisons library, http://bop.library.net
National Institute of Justice, www.ojp.usdoj.gov/nij/new.htm
US Department of Justice, Federal Bureau of Prisons, www.bop.gov

Independent organisations

Justice Information Centre, www.ncjrs,org
National Institute of Corrections, Prisons Division, www.nicic.org/about/divisions/
    prisons.htm
Prison Information, http://sun.soci.niu.edu/~critcrim/prisons/prisons.html
Prison links, http://web.syr.edu/~tckerr/PrisonLinks.html

Specific sites

Population data

Bureau of Justice Statistics, www.ojp.usdoj.gov/bjs/prisons.htm
Federal Bureau of Prisons Quick Facts, www.bop.gov.fact0598.html
General Prison Statistics, http://sun.soci.niu.edu/~critcrim/prisons/prisons/html
US Department of Justice, Federal Bureau of Prison, www.bop.gov

Female prisoners

General Prisons Statistics, http://sun.soci.niu.edu/~critcrim/prisons/prisons.
    html

Ethnicity

Bureau of Justice Statistics, www.ojp.usdoj.gov/bjs/abstract/aic.htm
Bureau of Justice Statistics, www.ojpusdoj.gov/bjs/glance/cprace.htm
Sourcebook of Criminal Justice Statistics, www.albany.edu/sourcebook/1995/
    tost_6html#_a

Prison details

Prison Law Links, http://links.prisonwall.org

Drugs

Bureau of Prisons, www.bop.gov

Youth issues

Bureau of Justice Statistics, www.ojp.usdoj.gov/bjs/abstract/pspa1897.htm
Juvenile Net, www.juvenilenet.org/

Publications

American Corrections Association, www.corrections.com/aca/
American Jail Association, www.corrections.com/aja/

International Sites

Basic Principles for the Treatment of Prisoners, www.hri.ca/uninfo/treaties/35.shtml
Council of Europe, www.coe.int ; www.coe.fr/cm/ta/rec/1999/99r22.htm
Council of Juvenile Corrections Administrators, www.corrections.com/cjca/index.
    html

HIV Corrections, www.hivcorrections.org
Home Office, www.homeoffice.gov.uk/rds/pdrs/r88.pdf
Human Rights Watch, www.hrw.org/hrw/advocacy/prisons/index.htm
International Centre for Prison Studies, London, www.kcl.ac.uk/depsta/rel/icps
International Corrections and Prisons Association, www.icpa.ca/home.html
International Criminal Justice, www.justiceaction.org.au/Links/worldcjlinks.
    html
Office of International Criminal Justice, www.oicj.org
Penal Reform International, www.penealreform.org/
United Nations Crime and Justice Information Network, www.uncjin.org
WHO Health in Prisons Project, www.hipp-europe.org

Africa

UNAFRI, www.unafri.or.ug/index.htm

Australia

General sites

Government sites

Australian Bureau of Statistics, www.abs.gov.au
Australian Institute of Criminology, www.aic.gov.au ; www.aic.gov.au/research/
    corrections/index/html; www.aic.gov.au/research/corrections/stats/index.
    html
Australian Ministry of Justice, Offender Management, www.justice.wa.gov.au/
    home.asp

Specific sites

Youth issues

Australian Institute of Criminology, www.aic.gov.au/research/corrections/juvenile/
    index.html and www.aic.gov.au/research/corrections/stats/rpp20-ext/index.
    html

Canada

General sites

Government sites

Correctional Service of Canada, www.csc-scc.gc.ca/text/home_e.shtml

Independent organisations

Justice Network, www.acjnet.org

Specific sites

Female prisoners

Canadian Association of Elizabeth Fry Societies, www.web.apc.org/~kpate/caefs_
    e.htm

Eire

Irish Prisons Service, www.irishprisons.ie

Finland

Finland Prison Service, www.vankeinhoito.fi/5141.htm

France

Government sites
Ministere de la Justice, www.justice.gouv.fr/minister/sceri/indexgb.htm

Independent organisations
CESDIP, www.cesdip.msh-paris.fr

Germany

Kriminologische Zentralstelle, Wiesbaden, www.krimz.de

Holland

Justice Department, www.minjust.nl:8080/
Punishment in the Netherlands, www.minijust.nl:8080/a_beleid/thema/execut/
  execut.htm

Japan

Amnesty International, www.web.amnsesty.org/ai.nsf/index/ASA220041998

New Zealand

Department of Corrections, www.corrections.govt/nz; www.corrections.govt.nz/
  facts/key.html; www.corrections.govt.nz/facts/statistics.html

Northern Ireland

Northern Ireland Prison Service, www.niprisonservice.gov.uk

Scotland

Scottish Prison Service, www.sps.gov.uk

Miscellaneous

Home Office, www.homeoffice.gov.uk/
HM Prison Service, www.hmprisonservice.gov.uk/

HM Chief Inspector of Prisons for England and Wales, http://inspectorates. homeoffice.gov.uk/hmiprisons/

HM Chief Inspector of Prisons for Scotland, www.scotland.gov.uk/Topics/Justice/ Prisons/17208

Lord Chancellor's Department, www.parliament.uk/parliamentary_committees/ lcdcom.cfm

National Probation Service for England and Wales, www.probation.homeoffice. gov.uk/output/Page1.asp

Northern Ireland Prison Service, www.niprisonservice.gov.uk/

Prisons and Probation Ombudsman for England and Wales, www.ppo.gov.uk/

Scottish Prison Service, www.sps.gov.uk/default.aspx

Youth Justice Board, www.youth-justice-board.gov.uk/

Action for Prisoner's Families, www.prisonersfamilieshelpline.org.uk/php/bin/ readarticle.php?articlecode=9241

Apex Trust, www.apextrust.com/

Inside Out Trust www.ccjf.org/whatcanido/projects/inside.html

Inquest, www.inquest.org.uk/

Irish Prison Reform Trust, www.iprt.ie/

Liberty, www.liberty-human-rights.org.uk/

Nacro, www.nacro.org.uk/

National Association for Youth Justice, http://nayj.org.uk/website/

National Children's Bureau, www.ncb.org.uk/Page.asp

Penal Reform International, www.penalreform.org/

Prisoners Abroad, www.prisonersabroad.org.uk/

Women In Prison, www.womeninprison.org.uk/

Prison Privatisation Report International from the University of Greenwich, www. psiru.org/ppri.asp

Bibliography

Aas, K.-J. (2007) *Globalization and Crime* (London: Sage).

Adams, B. (1990) *Time and Social Theory* (Cambridge: Polity Press).

Adams, R. (1992) *Prison Riots in Britain and the USA* (London: Macmillan).

Adler, F. (1975) *Sisters in Crime: The Rise of the New Female Criminal* (New York: McGraw-Hill).

Allen, R. (1991) 'Custody for Juveniles – From Elimination to Abolition?', *Youth and Policy*, **32** (March): 10–18.

All Party Parliamentary Penal Affairs Group (1980) *Too Many Prisoners: An Examination of Ways of Reducing the Prison Population* (London: HMSO).

Amin, A. (1994) *Post-Fordism: A Reader* (Oxford: Blackwell).

Anderson, E. (2002) 'The Ideologically Driven Critique', *American Journal of Sociology*, **6**: 1533–60.

Ashworth, A. (1983) *Sentencing and Penal Policy* (London: Weidenfeld & Nicolson).

Audit Commission (1996) *Misspent Youth: Young People and Crime* (London).

Austin, J., M. Bruce, L. Carroll, P. McCall and S. Richards (2001) 'The Use of Incarceration in the United States', *Critical Criminology*, **10**: 17–41.

Austin, J., J. Clarke, P. Hardyman and D. Henry (1999) 'The Impact of Three Strikes and You're Out', *Punishment and Society*, **1** (2): 131–62.

Austin, J., S. Cuvelier and A. McVey (1992) 'Projecting the Future of Corrections: The State of the Art', *Crime and Delinquency*, **38** (2): 285–309.

Austin, R. (1981) 'Liberation and Female Criminality in England and Wales', *British Journal of Criminology*, **31** (4): 371–4.

Australian Institute of Criminology (2009) *Crime Facts and Figures 2008* (Canberra: Australian Institute of Criminology), www.aic.gov.au.

Back, L. (1996) *New Ethnicities and Urban Culture* (London: UCL Press).

Bailey, V. (1987) *Delinquency and Citizenship* (Oxford: Clarendon Press).

Barak-Glantz, I. (1981) 'Toward a Conceptual Schema of Prison Management Styles', *Prison Journal*, **61** (2): 42–60.

Barrett, N. (1991) *The Politics of Truth* (Cambridge: Polity Press).

Bateman, T. (2006) 'Levels of Self-Harms in Custody Rise', *Youth Justice*, **6** (3): 223–24.

Bauman, Z. (1989) *Modernity and the Holocaust* (Oxford: Blackwell).

Bauman, Z. (1998) *Globalization: The Human Consequence* (Cambridge: Polity Press).

Bauman, Z. (2000) *Liquid Modernity* (Oxford: Blackwell).

Beccaria, C. (1764) *An Essay on Crimes and Punishments* (reprinted Indianapolis: Bobbs Merrill, 1963).

Beck, A. and L. Glaze (2001) *Correctional Populations in the United States 1980 to 2000* (Washington, DC: Bureau of Justice Statistics, Department of Justice).

Beck, A. and B. Shipley (1989) Recidivism of Prisoners Released in 1983 (Washington, DC: Bureau of Justice Statistics Special Report, Department of Justice).

Beckett, K. and B. Western (2001) 'Governing Social Marginality: Welfare, Incarceration and the Transformation of State Policy', *Punishment & Society*, **3** (1): 43–59.

Beetham, D. (1991) *The Legitimation of Power* (London: Macmillan).

Begum, N. (2004) *Characteristics of the Short-Term and Long-Term Unemployed* (London: Office of National Statistics, Labour Market Division).

Bentham, J. (1791) *Panopticon* (London).

Berman, M. (1983) *All That Is Solid Melts Into Air: The Experience of Modernity* (London: Verso).

Bettelheim, B. (1960) *The Informed Heart* (New York: Free Press).

Beyens, K. and S. Snacken (1996) 'Prison Privatisation: An International Perspective', in R. Matthews and P. Francis (eds), *Prisons 2000* (London: Macmillan).

Blau, R. and W. Scott (1963) *Formal Organisations: A Comparative Approach* (London: Routledge & Kegan Paul).

Blumstein, A. (1982) 'On the Racial Disproportionality of the United States Prison Population', *Journal of Criminal Law and Criminology*, **73**: 1259–81.

Blumstein, A. (1988) 'Prison Populations: A System Out of Control', in M. Tonry and N. Morris (eds), *Crime and Justice: A Review of Research*, Vol. 10 (Chicago: University of Chicago Press).

Blumstein, A. (1993) 'Racial Disproportionality of the US Prison Population Revisited', *University of Colorado Law Review*, **64**: 743–60.

Blumstein, A. and A. Beck (1999) 'Population Growth in the US Prisons, 1980–1996' in M. Tonry and J. Petersilia (eds), *Prisons* (Chicago: University of Chicago Press).

Blumstein, A., M. Tonry and A. Van Ness (2005) 'Cross National Measures of Punitiveness', in M. Tonry and D. Farrington (eds), *Crime and Punishment in Western Countries 1980–1999* (Chicago: University of Chicago Press).

Blumstein, A. and J. Wallman (2000) *The Crime Drop in America* (Cambridge: Cambridge University Press).

Blyth, M. and R. Newman (2008) 'Sentenced to Education: The Case for A Hybrid Custodial Sentence', in M. Blyth, R. Newman and C. Wright (eds), *Children and Young People in Custody: Managing the Risk* (Bristol: The Policy Press).

Bogard, W. (2006) 'Surveillant Assemblages and Lines of Flight', in D. Lyon (ed.), *Theorising Surveillance: The Panopticon and Beyond* (Cullompton: Willan).

Boin, A. and W. Rattray (2004) 'Understanding Prison Riots: Towards a Threshold Theory', *Punishment & Society*, **6** (1): 47–65.

Boland, B. (1980) 'Fighting Crime: The Problem of Adolescents', *Journal of Criminal Law and Criminology*, 71 (2): 94–7.

Boland, B. and J. Q. Wilson (1978) 'Age, Crime and Punishment', *Public Interest*, **51**: 22–34.

Bonta, J. (1996) 'Risk Needs Assessment and Treatment', in A. Harland (ed.), *Choosing Correctional Options That Work* (Thousand Oaks, Calif.: Sage).

Booth, W. (1890) *In Darkest England and the Way Out* (London: Salvation Army).

Bosworth, M. (1999) *Engendering Resistance: Agency and Power in Women's Prisons* (Aldershot: Ashgate).

Bottomley, K. (1984) 'Dilemmas of Parole in a Penal Crisis', *Howard Journal*, **23** (1): 24–40.

Bottoms, A. (1974) 'On the Decriminalisation of the English Juvenile Courts', in R. Hood (ed.), *Crime, Criminology and Policy* (London: Heinemann).

Bottoms, A. (1977) 'Reflections on the Renaissance of Dangerousness', *Howard Journal*, **16**: 70–96.

Bottoms, A. (1980) 'An Introduction to the Coming Crisis', in A. Bottoms and R. Preston (eds), *The Coming Penal Crisis* (Edinburgh: Scottish Academic Press).

Bottoms, A. (1983) 'Neglected Features of Contemporary Penal Systems', in D. Garland and P. Young (eds), *The Power to Punish* (London: Heinemann).

Bottoms, A. (1987) 'Limiting Prison Use: Experience in England and Wales', *Howard Journal*, **26** (3): 177–202.

Bottoms, A. (1995) 'The Philosophy and Politics of Punishment and Sentencing', in C. Clarkson and R. Morgan (eds), *The Politics of Sentencing Reform* (Oxford: Clarendon Press).

Bottoms, A. (1999) 'Interpersonal Violence and Social Order in Prisons', in M. Tonry and J. Petersilia (eds), *Prisons* (Chicago: University of Chicago Press).

Bottoms, A., S. Rex and G. Robinson (2004) 'How Did We Get Here?', in A. Bottoms, S. Rex and G. Robinson (eds), *Alternatives to Prison: Options for an Insecure Society* (Cullompton: Willan).

Bottoms, A. and P. Wiles (1992) 'Housing Markets and Residential Community Care Careers', in D. Evans, R. Fyfe and D. Herbert (eds), *Crime, Policing and Place* (London: Routledge).

Bottoms, A. and P. Wiles (1997) 'Environmental Criminology', in M. Maguire, R. Morgan and R. Reiner (eds), *The Oxford Handbook of Criminology* (2nd edn) (Oxford: Clarendon Press).

Bourgois, P. (2003) *In Search of Respect: Selling Crack in El Barrio* (2nd edn) (Cambridge: Cambridge University Press.

Bowker, L. (1977) *Prisoner Subcultures* (Lexington, Mass.: Lexington Books).

Bowling, B. and C. Phillips (1999) *'Race' and Criminal Justice* (London: Longman).

Bowling, B. and C. Phillips (2002) *Racism, Crime and Justice* (Harlow: Longman).

Box, S. (1957) *Recession, Crime and Punishment* (London: Macmillan).

Box, S. and C. Hale (1983) 'Liberation and Female Criminality in England and Wales', *British Journal of Criminology*, **23** (1): 35–49.

Boyne, R. (2000) 'Post Panopticonism', *Economy and Society*, **29** (2): 285–307.

Braithwaite, J. (1989) *Crime, Shame and Reintegration* (Cambridge: Cambridge University Press).

Braithwaite, J. (1993) 'Shame and Modernity', *British Journal of Criminology*, **33** (1): 1–18.

Braithwaite, J. (2000) 'The New Regulatory State and the Transformation of Criminology', *British Journal of Criminology*, **40** (2): 222–38.

Braithwaite, J. (2002) *Crime, Shame and Reintegration* (Cambridge: Cambridge University Press).

Braithwaite, J. (2003) 'What's Wrong with the Sociology of Punishment?', *Theoretical Criminology*, **7** (1): 5–28.

Brewer, D., J. Hawkins, B. Catalano and H. Neckerman (1995) 'Preventing Serious Violent and Chronic Juvenile Offending', in J. Howell, B. Krisberg, J. Hawkins and J. Wilson (eds), *Serious, Violent and Chronic Juvenile Offenders* (London: Sage).

Bright, M. (2003) 'One in 100 Black Adults Now in Jail', *Guardian*, 30 March.

Brillon, Y. (1988) 'Punitiveness, Status and Ideology in Three Canadian Provinces', in N. Walker and M. Hough (eds), *Public Attitudes to Sentencing Surveys from Five Countries* (Aldershot: Gower).

Brown, E. (2006) 'The Dog That Did Not Bark: Punitive Social Views and the Professional Middle Classes', *Punishment & Society*, **8** (3): 287–312.

Brown, I. and R. Hullin (1992) 'A Study of Sentencing in Leeds Magistrates Courts: The Treatment of Ethnic Minority and White Offenders', *British Journal of Criminology*, **32** (1): 41–54.

Brownlee, I. (1998) 'New Labour – New Penology?: Punitive Rhetoric and the Limits of Managerialism in Criminal Justice Policy', Journal of Law and Society, **25** (3): 313–35.

Bullock, K. and B. Jones (2004) *Acceptable Behaviour Contracts: Addressing Anti-social Behaviour in the London Borough of Islington* (London: Home Office).

Bureau of Justice (1996) *Prisoners in 1996*. NCJ 164619. US Department of Justice.

Bureau of Justice (1997) *Lifetime Likelihood of Going to State or Federal Prison*, US Department of Justice Special Report, NCJ-160092.

Bureau of Justice (2002) 'In a 15 State Study over Two Thirds of Released Prisoners Were Rearrested Within Three Years', www.ojp.gov/bjs/reentry/recidivism/htm.

Bureau of Justice (2006) *Prisoners in 2006*. NCJ 219416. US Department of Justice.

Bureau of Justice (2007) 'Direct Expenditure for Each of The Major Criminal Justice Functions: Key Facts', www.ojp.usdoj.gov/bjs/glance/exptyp.htm.

Bureau of Justice (2008) 'Adult Correctional Population 1980–2007', www.ojp.gov/bjs/glance/covr2.htm.

Burnett, R. and C. Appleton (2004) *Joined Up Youth Justice: Tackling Youth Crime in Partnership* (Lyme Regis: Russell House Publishing).

Burney, E. (1985) *Sentencing Young People* (Aldershot: Gower).

Burney, E. (1990) *Putting Street Crime in its Place, Report for the Police Consultative Group for Lambeth* (London Borough of Lambeth).

Byrne, R. (1992) *Prisons and Punishments of London* (London: Grafton).

Byrne, J., A. Lurigio and J. Petersilia (1992) *Smart Sentencing: The Emergence of Intermediate Sanctions* (Thousand Oaks, Calif.: Sage).

Caddle, D. and D. Crisp (1996) *Imprisoned Women and Mothers*, Home Office Research Study No. 162 (London: HMSO).

Campbell, B. (1993) *Goliath: Britain's Dangerous Places* (London: Methuen).

Campbell, D. (2008) 'Give Prisoners Right to Vote Says UN', *Guardian*, 19 September.

Canter, D. (1987) 'Implications for "New Generation" Prisons of Existing Psychological Research into Prison Design and Use', in A. Bottoms and R. Light (eds), *Problems of Long Term Imprisonment* (Aldershot: Gower).

Caplow, T. and J. Simon (1999) 'Understanding Prison Policy and Population Trends', in M. Tonry and J. Petersilia (eds), *Prisons* (Chicago: University of Chicago Press).

Carlen, P. (1983) *Women's Imprisonment* (London: Routledge & Kegan Paul).

Carlen, P. (1990) *Alternatives to Women's Imprisonment* (Milton Keynes: Open University Press).

Carlen, P. (1992) 'Criminal Women and Criminal Justice: The Limits to and Potential of Left Realist Perspectives', in R. Matthews and J. Young (eds), *Issues in Realist Criminology* (London: Sage).

Carlen, P. (ed.) (2002a) *Women and Punishment: The Struggle for Justice* (Cullompton: Willan).

Carlen, P. (2002b) 'Carcereal Clawback: The Case of Women's Imprisonment in Canada', *Punishment & Society*, **4** (1): 115–21.

Carlen, P. (2002c) 'Introduction: Women and Punishment', in P. Carlen (ed.), *Women and Punishment: The Struggle for Justice* (Cullompton: Willan).

Carlen, P. and C. Tchaikovsky (1996) 'Women's Imprisonment in England at the End of the Twentieth Century: Legitimacy, Realities and Utopias', in R. Matthews and P. Francis (eds), *Prisons 2000* (London: Macmillan).

Carlen, P. and Tombs, J. (2006) 'Reconfiguration of Penality: The Ongoing Case of Women's Imprisonment and Reintegration Industries', *Theoretical Criminology*, **10** (3): 337–60.

Carlen, P. and A. Worrall (2004) *Analysing Women's Imprisonment* (Cullompton: Willan).

Carpenter, M. (1851) *Reformatory Schools for the Children of the Perishing and Dangerous Classes and for Juvenile Offenders* (London: Gilpin).

Carrabine, E. (2005) 'Prison Riots, Social Order and the Problems of Legitimacy', *British Journal of Criminology*, **45** (6): 896–913.

Carter, Lord (2007) *Securing the Future: Proposals for the Efficient and Sustainable Use of Custody in England and Wales* (The Carter Report) (London: Home Office).

Casale, S. (1989) *Woman Inside: The Experience of Women Remand Prisoners in Holloway* (London: Civil Liberties Trust).

Castells, M. (1994) 'European Cities, the International Society and the Global Economy', *New Left Review* 204: 18–32.

Castells, M. (1996) *The Rise of The Network Society: The Information Age*, Vol. 1 (Oxford: Blackwell).

Cavadino, M. and J. Dignan (2006) 'Penal Policy and Political Economy', *Criminology and Criminal Justice*, **6** (4): 435–56.

Cheliotis, L. (2006) 'Penal Managerialism from Within: Implications for Theory and Research', *International Journal of Law and Psychiatry*, **29**: 397–404.

Cheney, D. (1993) *Into the Dark Tunnel* (London: Prison Reform Trust).

Chesney-Lind, M. (1991) 'Patriachy, Prisons and Jails: A Critical Look at Trends in Women's Incarceration', *Prison Journal*, **71**: 51–67.

Chesney-Lind, M. (2004) *Girls and Violence: Is the Gender Gap Closing?* National Electronic Network on Violence Against Women, Applied Research Forum, www.vawnet.org.

Chesney-Lind, M. (2006) 'Patriarchy, Crime and Justice: Feminist Criminology in an Era of Backlash', Feminist Criminology, **1** (1): 6–26.

Chesney-Lind, M. and V. Paramore (2001) 'Are Girls Getting More Violent? Exploring Juvenile Robbery Trends', *Journal of Contemporary Criminal Justice*, **17** (2): 142–66.

Christie, N. (1993) *Crime Control as Industry: Toward Gulags Western Style* (London: Routledge).

Civitas (2004) *Prison is a Bargain* (London: Civitas).

Clark, J. (1995) 'The Impact of Prison Environment on Mothers', *Prison Journal* **75** (3): 306–29.

Clarke, J., *et al.* (1975) 'Subcultures, Cultures and Class', *Working Papers in Cultural Studies* **7** and **8** (Summer): 9–75.

Clarke, R. (1992) *Situational Crime Prevention: Successful Case Studies* (New York: Harrow & Heston).

Clarke-Hall, W. (1926) *Children's Courts* (London: George Allen & Unwin).

Clear, T. (2002) 'The Problem with Addition by Subtraction: The Prison Crime Relationship in Low Income Communities', in M. Mauer and M. Chesney-Lind (eds), *Invisible Punishment: The Collateral Consequences of Mass Imprisonment* (New York: The New Press).

Clear, T., D. Rose and J. Ryder (2001) 'Incarceration and the Community: The Problem of Removing and Returning Offenders', *Crime and Delinquency*, **47** (3): 335–51.

Cleaver, E. (1968) *Soul on Ice* (New York: McGraw-Hill).

Clegg, S. (1990) *Modern Organisations: Organisation Studies in the Postmodern World* (London: Sage).

Clemmer, D. (1940) *The Prison Community* (New York: Holt, Rinehart & Winston).

Cohen, S. (1977) 'Prisons and the Future of Control Systems', in M. Fitzgerald *et al.* (eds), *Welfare in Action* (London: Routledge & Kegan Paul).

Cohen, S. (1979) 'The Punitive City: Notes on the Dispersal of Social Control', *Contemporary Crisis*, **3**: 339–63.

Cohen, S. (1983) 'Social Control Talk: Telling Stories of Correctional Change', in D. Garland and P. Young (eds), *The Power to Punish* (London: Heinemann).

Cohen, S. (1985) *Visions of Social Control* (Cambridge: Polity Press).

Cohen, S. (1992) *The Evolution of Women's Asylums Since 1500* (Oxford: Oxford University Press).

Cohen, S. and L. Taylor (1972) *Psychological Survival* (Harmondsworth: Penguin).

Connell, R. (1987) *Gender and Power* (Cambridge: Polity Press).

Cooke, D. (1989) 'Containing Violent Prisoners: An Analysis of the Barlinnie Special Unit', *British Journal of Criminology*, **29** (2): 129–43.

Cooper, M. and R. King (1965) 'Social and Economic Problems of Prisoners Work', *Sociological Review* Monograph No. 9: 145–73.

Correctional Services Canada (1990) *Creating Choices: Report of the Task Force on Federally Sentenced Women* (Ottawa), www.csc-scc.gc.ca/text/prgm/fsw/choices/toce-eng.shtml.

Council of Europe (1995) *European Sourcebook of Crime and Criminal Justice Statistics* (Strasbourg: Council of Europe).

Crawford, A. (2001) 'Joined Up but Fragmented: Contradiction, Ambiguity and Ambivalence in the Heart of New Labour's "Third Way"', in R. Matthews and J. Pitts (eds), *Crime, Disorder and Community Safety* (London: Routledge).

Crawford, A. (2003) 'Contractual Governance and Deviant Behaviour', *Journal of Law and Society*, **30** (4): 479–505.

Crawford, A. (2006) 'Networked Governance and the Post Regulatory State', *Theoretical Criminology*, **10** (4): 449–80.

Crewe, B. (2007) 'Power Adaptation and Resistance in the Late Modern Prison', *British Journal of Criminology*, **47** (2): 256–75.

Crow, I. and J. Cove (1984) 'Ethnic Minorities and the Courts', *Criminal Law Review*: 413–17.

Crowther, C. (2000) 'Thinking About The "Underclass": Towards a Political Economy of Policing', *Theoretical Criminology*, **4** (2): 149–65.

Cullen, F., P. Gendreau, R. Jarjoural and J. Wright (1997) 'Crime and the Bell Curve: Lessons From Intelligent Criminology', *Crime and Delinquency*, 43 (4): 387–411.

Cullen, F. and K. Gilbert (1982) *Reaffirming Rehabilitation* (Cincinnati, Ohio: Anderson).

Cullen, F., P. Wright and B. Applegate (1996) 'Control in the Community: The Limits of Reform', in A. Harland (ed.), *Choosing Correctional Options that Work* (Thousand Oaks, Calif.: Sage).

Currie, E. (1998) *Crime and Punishment in America* (New York: Metropolitan Books).

Daly, K. (1994) *Gender, Crime and Punishment* (New Haven, Conn.: Yale University Press).

Daly, K. and M. Tonry (1997) 'Gender, Race and Sentencing', in M. Tonry (ed.), *Crime and Justice: A Review of Research*, Vol. 22 (Chicago: University of Chicago Press).

Dandeker, C. (1990) *Surveillance, Power and Modernity* (Oxford: Polity Press).

Davies, N. (2004) 'Scandal of Society's Misfits Dumped in Jail', *Guardian*, 6 December.

Davis, G., J. Boucherat and D. Watson (1989) 'Pre-Court Decision-Making in Juvenile Justice', *British Journal of Criminology*, **29** (3): 219–36.

Davis, M. (1990) *City of Quartz: Excavating the Future in Los Angeles* (London: Vintage).

Davis, M. (1992) 'Fortress Los Angeles: The Militarisation of Urban Space', in M. Sorokin (ed.), *Variations on a Theme Park* (New York: Hill & Wang).

Defoe, D. (1728) *Street Robberies Considered* (London).

de Haan, W. (1990) *The Politics of Redress: Crime, Punishment and Penal Abolition* (London: Unwin Hyman).

de Koster, W., J. van der Waal, P. Achterberg and D. Hontman (2008) 'The Rise of The Penal State: Neoliberalisation or New Political Culture', *British Journal of Criminology*, **48** (6): 720–34.

Deleuze, G. (1995) *Negotiations* (New York: Columbia University Press).

de Mandeville, B. (1725) *An Enquiry into the Causes of the Frequent Executions at Tyburn* (London).

Devlin, A. (1998) *Invisible Women: What's Wrong With Women's Prisons?* (Winchester: Waterside Press).

Dews, P. (1979) 'The Nouvelle Philosophie of Foucault', *Economy and Society*, **8** (2): 127–71.

DiGiorgi, A. (2006) *Re-Thinking the Political Economy of Punishment: Perspectives on Fordism and Penal Politics* (Aldershot: Ashgate).

Dignan, J. (1999) 'The Crime and Disorder Act and the Prospects for Restorative Justice', *Criminal Law Review* (January): 48–60.

Dilulio, J. (1987) *Governing Prisons* (New York: Free Press).

Dilulio, J. (1994) 'The Question of Black Crime', *Public Interest* (Fall): 3–32.

Ditchfield, J. (1990) *Control in Prisons: A Review of the Literature*, Home Office Research Study No. 118 (London: HMSO).

Ditton, P. and Wilson, D. (1999) *Truth in Sentencing in State Prisons*, Bureau of Justice Statistics, NCJ 170032, Department of Justice.

Dobash, R. P., R. E. Dobash and S. Gutteridge (1986) *The Imprisonment of Women* (Oxford: Blackwell).

Dobkin, J. (2005) 'Where do Prisoners Come From?', http://gothamist.com/2005/11/27/where_do_prison.php.

Dodd, A. and J. Roberts (1988) 'Public Punitiveness and Public Knowledge of the Facts: Some Canadian Surveys', in N. Walker and M. Hough (eds), *Public Attitudes to Sentencing* (Aldershot: Gower).

Donzelot, J. (1979) *The Policing of Families* (London: Hutchinson).

Doob, A. and C. M. Webster (2006) 'Countering Punitiveness: Understanding Stability in Canada's Imprisonment Rate', *Law and Society Review*, **40** (2) 325–67.

Dow, M. (2004) *American Gulag: Inside US Immigration Prisons* (Berkeley: University of California Press).

Downes, D. (1966) The Delinquent Solution (London: Routledge & Kegan Paul).

Downes, D. (2001) 'The Macho Political Economy: Mass Incarceration in the USA: A European Perspective', *Punishment & Society*, 3: 61–80.

Dreyfus, H. and P. Rabinow (1982) *Michel Foucault: Beyond Structuralism and Hermeneutics* (Brighton: Harvester Press).

Dunlop, A. (1974) *The Approved School Experience*, Home Office Research Unit Report (London: HMSO).

Durham, A. (1993) 'Public Opinion Regarding Sentences for Crime: Does it Exist?', *Journal of Criminal Justice*, 21: 1–11.

Durkheim, E. (1952) *Suicide: A Study in Sociology* (London: Routledge & Kegan Paul).

Durose, M. and C. Murnola (2004) *Profile of Non-Violent Offenders Exiting State Prisons*, NCJ 207081, Bureau of Justice Fact Sheet, Department of Justice.

Dutton, M. (1992) 'Disciplinary Projects and Carceral Spread: Foucauldian Theory and Chinese Practice', *Economy and Society*, 21 (3): 274–94.

Dwyer, J., J. Wilson and P. Carlen (1987) 'Women's Imprisonment in England and Wales and Scotland: Recurring Issues', in P. Carlen and A. Worral (eds), *Gender, Crime and Justice* (Milton Keynes: Open University Press).

Dyer, J. (2000) *The Perpetual Prison* Machine (Boulder, Colo.: Westview Press).

Easton, H. (2009) *Looking Forward: Volunteer Mentoring Pathfinder Evaluation*, London Probation.

Easton, S. and Piper, C. (2005) *Sentencing and Punishment: The Quest for Justice* (Oxford: Oxford University Press).

Eaton, M. (1993) *Women After Prison* (Milton Keynes: Open University Press).

Edgar, K., I. O'Donnell and C. Martin (2003) *Prison Violence: The Dynamics of Conflict and Power* (Cullompton: Willan).

Ekblom, P. and N. Tilley (2000) 'Going Equipped: Criminology, Situational Crime Prevention and the Resourceful Offender', *British Journal of Criminology*, 40: 376–98.

Elias, N. (1982) *The Civilising Process: State Formation and Civilisation* (originally publ. 1939) (Oxford University Press).

Epstein, R. (1996) 'Imprisonment For Non-Payment of Fines', *Justice of the Peace and Local Government Law*, 3 August: 160–2.

Evans, R. (1982) *The Fabrication of Virtue: English Prison Architecture 1750–1840* (Cambridge: Cambridge University Press).

Fagan, J. (2004) 'Crime Law and the Community: Dynamics of Incarceration in New York City', in M. Tonry (ed.), *The Future of Imprisonment* (Oxford: Oxford University Press).

Farrington, D. (1992) 'Trends in English Juvenile Delinquency and Their Explanation', *International Journal of Comparative and Applied Criminal Justice*, **16** (2): 151–63.

Farrington, D., J. Ditchfield, P. Howard and D. Joliffe (2002) *Two Intensive Regimes for Young Offenders: A Follow Up Evaluation*, Findings 163 (London: Home Office).

Farrington, D., G. Hancock, M. Livingston, K. Painter and G. Towl (2000) *Evaluation of Intensive Regimes for Young Offenders*, Research Findings 121, (London: Home Office).

Farrington, D. and D. Joliffe (2005) 'Crime and Punishment in England and Wales 1981–1999', in M. Tonry and D. Farrington (eds), *Crime and Punishment in Western Countries 1980–1999* (Chicago: University of Chicago Press).

Farrington, D., P. Langan and M. Tonry (eds) (2004) *Cross National Studies in Crime and Justice* (Washington, DC: US Bureau of Justice Statistics).

Farrington, D., P. Langan and P. Wikstrom (1994a) 'Changes in Crime and Punishment in England, America and Sweden in the 1980s and 1990s', *Studies in Crime and Crime Prevention*, **3**: 104–31.

Farrington, D., P. Langan and P. Wikstrom (1994b) 'Changes in Crime and Punishment in England and America in the 1980s', *Justice Quarterly*, **9** (1): 5–31.

Faugeron, C. (1996) 'The Changing Functions of Imprisonment', in R. Matthews and P. Francis (eds), *Prisons 2000* (London: Macmillan).

Fawcett Society (2004) Commission of Women and the Criminal Justice System, www.fawcettsociety.org.uk.

Fawcett Society (2007) *Women and Justice: Third Annual Review of the Commission on Women and the Criminal Justice System* (London: Fawcett Society).

Feeley, M. and J. Simon (1992) 'The New Penology: Notes on the Emerging Strategy of Corrections and its Implications', *Criminology*, **30**: 449–74.

Feeley, M. and J. Simon (1994) 'Actuarial Justice: The Emerging New Criminal Law', in D. Nelken (ed.), *The Futures of Criminology* (London: Sage).

Feest, J. (1991) 'Reducing the Prison Population: Lessons from the West German Experience', in J. Muncie and R. Sparks (eds), *Imprisonment: European Perspectives* (London: Harvester Wheatsheaf).

Feilzer, M., R. Appleton, C. Roberts and C. Hoyle (2004) *The National Evaluation of the Youth Justice Board's Cognitive Behaviour Projects* (London: Youth Justice Board).

Feilzer, M. and R. Hood (2004) *Differences or Discrimination? Minority Ethnic Young People in the Youth Justice System* (London: Youth Justice Board).

Fellner, J. and M. Mauer (1998) *Losing the Vote: The Impact of Felony Disenfranchisement Laws in the United States*. New York: Human Rights Watch, and Washington, DC: The Sentencing Project), www.hrw.org and www.sentencingproject.org.

Ferdinand, T. (1989) 'Juvenile Delinquency and Juvenile Justice: Which Came First?', *Criminology*, **27** (1): 79–106.

Field, S. (1990) *Trends in Crime and Their Interpretation*, Home Office Research Study 119 (London: Home Office).

Field, S. (1995) 'Economic Cycles and Crime in Europe', in *Crime and the Economy, Report of the 11th International Council of Europe Colloquium on Crime* (Strasbourg: Council of Europe).

Field, S. (1999) *Trends in Crime Revisited*, Home Office Research Study 195 (London: Home Office).

Fielding, H. (1751) *An Enquiry into the Causes of the Late Increase of Robbers* (2nd edn) (London).

Fitzgerald, M. (1977) *Prisoners in Revolt* (Harmondsworth: Penguin).

Fitzgerald, M. and J. Sim (1979) *British Prisons* (Oxford: Blackwell).

FitzGerald, M. (1993) *Racial Discrimination in the Criminal Justice System*, Home Office Research and Statistics Department Research Bulletin No. 34: 43–8 (London: Home Office).

FitzGerald, M. (1995) 'Ethnic Differences', in M. Walker (ed.), *Interpreting Crime Statistics* (Oxford Science Publications).

FitzGerald, M. and P. Marshall (1996) 'Ethnic Minorities in British Prisons', in R. Matthews and P. Francis (eds), *Prisons 2000* (London: Macmillan).

Flanagan, T. (1995) *Long Term Imprisonment* (London: Sage).

Flood-Page, C., S. Campbell, V. Harrington and J. Miller (2000) *Youth Crime: Findings from the 1998/99 Youth Lifestyles Survey.* Home Office Research Study 209 (London: Home Office).

Ford, R. (2005) 'Prisoners May be Set Free to Ease Jail Numbers', *Sunday Times*, 31 May.

Forsythe, W. (1990) *Penal Discipline, Reformatory Projects and the English Prison Commission 1985–1939* (Exeter: University of Exeter Press).

Foucault, M. (1971) *Madness and Civilisation* (London: Tavistock).

Foucault, M. (1977) *Discipline and Punish: The Birth of the Prison* (London: Allen Lane).

Foucault, M. (1979) *The History of Sexuality Volume 1: An Introduction* (London: Allen Lane).

Foucault, M. (1982) 'The Subject of Power', in H. Dreyfus and P. Rabinow (eds), *Michel Foucault: Beyond Structuralism and Hermeneutics* (Brighton: Harvester).

Fox, J. and A. Piquero (2003) 'Deadly Demographics – Population Characteristics and Forecasting Homicide Trends', *Crime and Delinquency*, **49** (3): 339–59.

Franke, H. (1992) 'The Rise and Decline of Solitary Confinement: Social History Explorations of Long Term Penal Changes', *British Journal of Criminology*, **32** (2): 125–43.

Fraser, N. (2003) 'From Discipline to Flexibilisation? Re-Reading Foucault in the Shadow of Globalisation', Constellations, **10** (2): 160–71.

Freedman, E. (1984) *Their Sisters' Keepers: Women's Prison Reform in America 1830–1930* (Ann Arbor: University of Michigan Press).

Friendship, C., L. Blud, M. Ericson and R. Towers (2002) *An Evaluation of Cognitive Behavioural Treatment of Prisoners*, Findings 161 (London: Home Office).

Frost, N. (2008) 'The Mismeasure of Punishment: Alternative Measures of Punitiveness and Their (Substantial) Consequences', *Punishment & Society*, 10 (3): 277–300.

Fry, E. (1827) *Observations on Visiting, Superintending and Government of Female Prisons* (London: John & Arthur).

Fyfe, N. (1997) 'Crime', in M. Pacione (ed.), *Britain's Cities: Geographies of Division in Urban Britain* (London: Routledge).

Galstar, G. and L. Scaturo (1985) 'The US Criminal Justice System: Unemployment and the Severity of Punishment', *Journal of Research in Crime and Delinquency*, **22** (2): 163–89.

Garland, D. (1981) 'The Birth of the Welfare Sanction', *British Journal of Law and Society*, 8 (Summer): 29–45.

Garland, D. (1985) *Punishment and Welfare: A History of Penal Strategies* (Aldershot: Gower).

Garland, D. (1990) *Punishment and Modern Society* (Oxford University Press).

Garland, D. (1995) 'Penal Modernism and Postmodernism', in T. Blomberg and S. Cohen (eds), *Punishment and Social Control* (New York: Aldine de Gruyter).

Garland, D. (1996) 'The Limits of the Sovereign State: Strategies of Crime Control in Contemporary Society', *British Journal of Criminology*, **36** (4): 445–72.

Garland, D. (2001) *Culture of Control* (Oxford: Oxford University Press).

Garland, D. (2006) 'Concepts of Culture in the Sociology of Punishment', *Theoretical Criminology*, **10** (4): 419–48.

Gelb, K. (2003) 'Women in Prison – Why the Rate of Incarceration is Increasing?' Paper presented at the 'Evaluation in Crime and Justice; Trends and Methods' Conference, Canberra, March, Australian Institute of Criminology.

Gelsthorpe, L. (2004) 'Female Offending: A Theoretical Overview' in G. McIvor (ed.), *Women Who Offend: Research Highlights in Social Work* (London: Jessica Kingsley).

Gelsthorpe, L. and A. Morris (2002a) 'Women's Imprisonment in England and Wales: A Penal Paradox', *Criminal Justice*, **2** (3): 277–301.

Gelsthorpe, L. and A. Morris (2002b) 'Restorative Youth Justice: The Last Vestiges of Welfare?', in J. Muncie, G. Hughes and E. McLaughlin (eds), *Youth Justice: Critical Readings* (London: Sage).

Gelsthorpe, L., C. Sharpe and J. Roberts (2007) *Provision for Women Offenders in the Community* (London: Fawcett Society), www.fawcettsociety.org.uk.

Genders, E. and E. Player (1986) 'Women's Imprisonment: The Effects of Youth Custody', *British Journal of Criminology*, **26** (4): 357–70.

Genders, E. and E. Player (1989) *Race Relations in Prison* (Oxford: Clarendon Press).

Genders, T. and E. Player (1995) 'Women Lifers: Assessing the Experience', in T. Flanagan (ed.), *Long-Term Imprisonment* (Thousand Oaks, Calif.: Sage).

Giddens, A. (1981) *Contemporary Critique of Historical Materialism: Power, Poverty and the State* (London: Macmillan).

Giddens, A. (1984) *The Constitution of Society* (Cambridge: Polity Press).

Giddens, A. (1987) 'Time and Social Organisation', in *Social Theory in Modern Society* (Cambridge: Polity Press).

Giddens, A. (1990) *The Consequences of Modernity* (Cambridge: Polity Press).

Giller, H. and A. Morri (1983) *Providing Criminal Justice for Children* (London: Edward Arnold).

Gilligan, C. (1982) *In a Different Voice* (Cambridge, Mass.: Harvard University Press).

Gillis, J. (1974) *Youth and History* (London: Academic Press).

Gilroy, P. (1987) *There Ain't No Black in the Union Jack* (London: Routledge).

Glaze, L. and T. Bonczar (2007) *Probation and Parole in the United States 2006*, Bureau of Justice Statistics Bulletin.

Glaze, L. and L. Maruschak (2008) *Parents in Prison and Their Minor Children*, NCJ 222984, US Department of Justice, www.ojp.usdoj.gov/bjs/abstract/pptmc. htm.

Goffman, E. (1968) *Asylums: Essays on the Social Situation of Mental Patients* (Harmondsworth: Pelican).

Goldson, B. (2002a) *Vulnerable Inside: Children in Secure and Penal Settings* (London: The Children's Society).

Goldson, B. (2002b) 'New Punitiveness: The Politics of Child Incarceration', in J. Muncie, G. Hughes and E. McLaughlin (eds), *Youth Justice Critical Readings* (London: Sage).

Gormally, B., K. McEvoy and D. Wall (1993) 'Criminal Justice in a Divided Society: Northern Ireland Prisons', in M. Tonry (ed.), *Crime and Justice: A Review of Research*, Vol. 17 (Chicago: University of Chicago Press).

Gottfredson, S. and R. Taylor (1987) 'Attitudes of Correctional Policy Makers and the Public', in S. Gottfreson and S. McConville (eds), *America's Correctional Crisis* (New York: Greenwood Press).

Gouldner, A. (1954) *Patterns of Industrial Bureaucracy* (Glencoe, Ill.: Free Press).

Gouldner, A. (1968) 'The Sociologist as Partisan: Sociology and the Welfare State', *American Sociologist* (May): 103–16.

Graham, J. (1990) 'Decarceration in the Federal Republic of West Germany', *British Journal of Criminology*, **30** (2): 150–70.

Green, P. (1991) *Drug Couriers* (London: Howard League).

Greenberg, D. (2001) 'Novus Ordo Saeclorum? A Commentary on Downes and on Beckett and Western', *Punishment & Society*, **3** (1): 81–93.

Greene, J. (2002) 'Entrepreneurial Corrections: Incarceration as a Business Opportunity', in M. Mauer and M. Chesney-Lind (eds), *Invisible Punishment: The Collateral Consequences of Imprisonment* (New York: The New Press).

Greene, J., K. Pranis and N. Frost (2006) *Hard Hit: The Growth of the Imprisonment of Women 1977–2004*. NCJ 217185 (New York: Department of Justice and Institute on Women and Criminal Justice United States), www.ncjrs.gov/App/Publications/abstract.aspx?ID=238811.

Hacker, A. (1992) *Two Nations* (New York: Scribner).

Hagan, J. and R. Dinovitzer (1999) 'Collateral Consequences of Imprisonment for Children, Communities and Prisoners', in M. Tonry and J. Petersilia (eds), *Prisons* (Chicago: University of Chicago Press).

Haggerty, K. and Ericson, R. (2000) 'The Surveillant Assemblage', *British Journal of Sociology*, **51** (1): 605–22.

Hale, C. (1998) 'Crime and the Business Cycle in Post War Britain', British Journal of Criminology, **38** (4): 681–98.

Halevy, T. (1995) 'Racial Discrimination in Sentencing? A Study with Dubious Conclusions', *Criminal Law Review*: 267–71.

Hall, S., C. Critcher, T. Jeffersson, J. Clarke and B. Roberts (1978) *Policing the Crisis: Mugging, the State, Law and Order* (London: Macmillan).

Halliday Report (2001) *Making Punishments Work: Report of a Review of the Sentencing Framework in England and Wales* (London: Home Office).

Hallsworth, S. (2002) 'The Case for Postmodern Penality', *Theoretical Criminology*, **6** (2): 145–64.

Hancock, L. (2004) 'Criminal Justice, Public Opinion, Fear and Popular Politics', in J. Muncie and D. Wilson (eds), *The Cavendish Student Handbook of Criminal Justice and Criminology* (London: Cavendish).

Hannah-Moffat, K. (1995) 'Feminine Fortresses: Woman-Centred Prisons', *Prison Journal*, 75 (2): 135–65.

Hannah-Moffatt, K. (2002) 'Creating Choices: Reflecting on Choices' in P. Carlen (ed.), *Women and Punishment: The Struggle for Justice* (Cullompton: Willan).

Hannah-Moffatt, K. (2005) 'Criminogenic Needs and the Transformative Risk Subject: Hybridizations of Risk/Need in Penality', *Punishment & Society*, 7 (1): 24–51.

Harding, R. (1997) Private Prisons and Public Accountability (Buckingham: Open University Press).

Harer, M. and D. Steffensmeier (1996) 'Race and Prison Violence', *Criminology*, 34 (3): 323–50.

Harlow, Wolf C. (2003) *Education and Correctional Populations*, NCJ 195670, US Department of Justice, www.ojp.usdoj.gov/bjs/abstract/ecp.htm.

Harries, R. (1999) *The Cost of Criminal Justice*, Research Findings No. 103 (London: Home Office).

Harris, J. and C. McDonald (2000) 'Post-Fordism, The Welfare State and the Personal Social Services: A Companion of Australia and Britain', *British Journal of Social Work*, 30: 51–70.

Harris, K. (1987) 'Moving into the New Millennium: Toward a Feminist Vision of Justice', *Prison Journal*, 10: 27–38.

Harris, R. (1985) 'Towards Just Welfare', *British Journal of Criminology*, 25 (1): 31–45.

Harris, R. and D. Webb (1987) *Welfare, Power and Juvenile Justice* (London: Tavistock).

Hartsock, N. (1987) 'Rethinking Modernism: Minority vs Majority Theories', *Cultural Critique*, 7: 187–206.

Harvey, D. (1989) *The Condition of Postmodernity* (Oxford: Blackwell).

Harvey, D. (1994) 'Flexible Accumulation Through Urbanisation: Reflections on Post-Modernism in the American City', in A. Amim (ed.), *Post-Fordism: A Reader* (Oxford: Blackwell).

Hawkins, G. (1983) 'Prison Labour and Prison Industries', in M. Tonry and N. Morris (eds), *Crime and Social Justice: A Review of Research*, Vol. 5 (Chicago: University of Chicago Press).

Hayman, S. (1996) *Community Prisons for Women* (London: Prison Reform Trust).

Hayward, K., J. Ferrall and J. Young (2008) *Cultural Criminology* (London: Sage).

Hayward, K. and M. Yar (2006) 'The Chav Phenomenon: Consumption, Media and the Construction of a New Underclass', *Crime, Media and Culture*, 2 (1): 9–28.

Hedderman, C. and L. Gelsthorpe (1997) 'Understanding the Sentencing of Women', Home Office Research Study No. 170 (London: HMSO).

Hedderman, C. and M. Hough (1994) *Does the Criminal Justice System Treat Men and Women Differently?*, Research Findings No. 10, Home Office Research and Statistics Department (London: HMSO).

Hebdidge, D. (1979) *Subculture: The Meaning of Style* (Andover: Methuen & Co.).

Heidensohn, F. (1975) 'The Imprisonment of Females', in S. McConville (ed.), *The Use of Imprisonment* (London: Routledge).

Heidensohn, F. (1986) 'Models of Justice: Portia or Persephone? Some Thoughts on Equality, Fairness and Gender in the Field of Criminal Justice', *International Journal of the Sociology of Law*, **14**: 287–98.

Herrnstein, R. and C. Murray (1994) *The Bell Curve* (New York: The Free Press).

Hill, G. and P. Harrison (2005) *Female Prisoners Under State and Federal Jurisdiction*, Bureau of Justice Statistics.

Hinds, L. (2005) 'Crime Control in Western Countries 1970–2005', in J. Pratt, D. Brown, M. Brown, S. Hallsworth, and W. Morrison (eds), *The New Punitiveness: Trends, Theories, Perspectives* (Cullompton: Willan).

Hirst, J. (1995) 'The Australian Experience: The Convict Colony', in N. Morris and D. Rothman (eds), *The Oxford History of the Prison* (New York: Oxford University Press).

Hirst, P. and G. Thompson (1992) 'The Problem of Globalisation', *Economy and Society*, **21** (4): 360–95.

HM Chief Inspector of Prisons (2001) *Report of Her Majesty's Chief Inspector of Prisons December 1999–November 2000* (London: Home Office).

HM Chief Inspector of Prisons (2008a) *No Problems – Old and Quiet: Older Prisoners in England and Wales* (London: Home Office).

HM Chief Inspector of Prisons (2008b) *Annual Report 2006/2007* (London: Home Office).

HM Chief Inspector of Prisons (2009) *Annual Report 2007–08* (London: The Stationery Office).

HM Inspectorate of Prisons (1997a) *Young Prisoners: A Thematic Review* (London: HMSO).

HM Inspectorate of Prisons (1997b) *Women in Prison: A Thematic Review* (London: HMSO).

HM Inspectorate of Prisons (2004) '*No Problems – Old and Quiet': Older Prisoners in England and Wales. A Thematic Review by HM Chief Inspector of Prisons* (London: Home Office).

HM Inspectorate of Prisons (2008) *Older Prisoners in England and Wales: A Follow-Up to the 2004 Thematic Review by HM Chief Inspector of Prisons* (London: Home Office).

Holdaway, S. (1996) *The Racialisation of British Policing* (London: Macmillan).

Home Office (1933) *Children and Young Persons Act* (London: HMSO).

Home Office (1945) *Prisons and Borstals* (London: HMSO).

Home Office (1968) *Children in Trouble* (London: HMSO).

Home Office (1969) *People in Prison*, Cmnd. 4214 (London: HMSO).

Home Office (1970) *Detention Centres: Report of the Advisory Council on the Penal System* (London: HMSO).

Home Office (1984) *Suicide in Prison: A Report by HM Inspector of Prisons* (London: HMSO).

Home Office (1985) *New Directions in Prison Design: Report of a Home Office Working Party on American New Generation Prisons* (London: HMSO).

Home Office (1986) *The Report of the Working Party on Suicide in Prison* (London: HMSO).

Home Office (1990) *Report of a Review by Her Majesty's Chief Inspector of Prisons for England and Wales of Suicide and Self-harm in Prison Service Establishments* (London: HMSO).

Home Office (1995) *Review of the Prison Service Security in England and Wales* (The Learmont Report), Cmnd. 3020 (London: HMSO).

Home Office (1996a) *Probation Statistics, England and Wales 1995* (London: HMSO).

Home Office (1996b) *Report on the Work of the Prison Department* (London: HMSO).

Home Office (1998) *Summary Probation Statistics England and Wales 1997*, Statistical Bulletin Issue 12/98 (London: Home Office).

Home Office (1999) *Projections of Long-Term Trends in the Prison Population to 2006*, Statistical Bulletin, January (London: HMSO).

Home Office (2001a) *Making Punishment Work: Report of the Review of the Sentencing Framework for England and Wales* (The Halliday Report) (London: Home Office).

Home Office (2001b) *Probation Statistics, England and Wales* (London: Home Office).

Home Office (2002) *Statistics on Women and the Criminal Justice System* (London: Home Office).

HM Inspectorate of Prisons (2005) *Recalled Prisoners: A Short Review of Recalled Adult Male Determinate Sentenced Prisoners* (London: Home Office).

Home Office (2006a) *Sentencing Statistics 2005, England and Wales*. Ministry of Justice Statistics Bulletin (London: Home Office).

Home Office (2006b) *Rebalancing the Criminal Justice System in Favour of the Law Abiding Majority* (London: Home Office).

Home Office (2007) *A Summary of Findings on Enforcement of Community Penalties in Three Joint Area Inspections* (London: Home Office).

Hood, R. (1965) *Borstal Re-Assessed* (London: Heinemann).

Hood, R. (1992) *Race and Sentencing* (Oxford: Clarendon Press).

Hood, R. (1995) 'Race and Sentencing: A Reply', *Criminal Law Review*: 272–9.

Hood, R. and Shute, S. (2000) *The Parole System at Work: A Study of Risk Based Decision Making*, Home Office Research Study No. 202 (London: Home Office).

Hood, R. and S. Sparks (1969) *Community Homes and the Approved School System* (Cambridge: Institute for Criminology, University of Cambridge).

Hough, M. and P. Mayhew (1984) *Taking Account of Crime: Findings from the British Crime Survey* (London: HMSO).

Hough, M., R. Allen and E. Solomon (2008) *Tackling Prison Overcrowding* (Bristol: The Policy Press).

Howard, J. (1777) *The State of Our Prisons* (Warrington; republ. Montclair, NJ, 1973).

Howard, L. (1994) 'Where Do Prisoners Come From? Some Information About the Home Areas of Prisoners in England and Wales', *Research Bulletin* No. 36, Research and Statistics Department, Home Office (London: HMSO).

Howard League (1997) *Lost Inside – The Imprisonment of Teenage Girls* (London: Howard League).

Howe, A. (1994) *Punish and Critique: Towards a Feminist Analysis of Penalty* (London: Routledge).

Hudson, B. (1987) *Justice Through Punishment* (London: Macmillan).

Hudson, B. (2002) 'Gender Issues and Penal Policy' in P. Carlen (ed.), *Women and Punishment: The Struggle for Justice* (Cullompton: Willan).

Hughes, R. (1987) *The Fatal Shore: A History of Transportation of Convicts to Australia 1787–1858* (London: Collins Harvill).

Hughes, T. and J. Wilson (2003) *Reentry Trends in the United States*. Bureau of Justice Statistics, US Department of Justice.

Human Rights Watch (2003) *Ill Equipped: US Prisons and Offenders with Mental Illness* (New York: Human Rights Watch).

Hunter, G., I. Hearnden and T. Gyateng (2009) *Statistics on Women and the Criminal Justice System* (London: Ministry of Justice), www.justice.gov.uk/publications/statistics.htm.

Hutton, N. (2005) 'Beyond Populist Punitiveness?', *Punishment & Society*, **7** (3): 243–58.

IEA (1996) *Charles Murray and the Underclass: The Developing Debate* (London: Institute of Economic Affairs).

Ignatieff, M. (1978) *A Just Measure of Pain: The Penitentiary in the Industrial Revolution 1750–1850* (London: Macmillan).

Ignatieff, M. (1981) 'State, Civil Society, and Total Institutions: A Critique of Recent Social Histories of Punishment', in M. Tonry and N. Morris (eds), *Crime and Justice*, Vol. 3 (Chicago: University of Chicago Press).

Innes, J. (1987) 'Prisons for the Poor: English Bridewells 1555–1800', in F. Snyder and D. Hay (eds), *Labour, Law and Crime* (London: Tavistock).

Innis, M. (2003) *Understanding Social Control: Deviance, Crime and Social Order* (Buckingham: Open University Press).

Irish Penal Reform Trust (2008) *Plans for Transfer of the Dochas Centre*, Dublin, www.iprt.ie.

Irish Prisons Inspectorate (2003) *Mountjoy Prison and Dochas Centre*. Mountjoy Inspection, January (Dublin: Irish Prisons Inspectorate).

Irwin, J. (1970) *The Felon* (Englewood Cliffs, NJ: Prentice Hall).

Irwin, J. and J. Austin (1994) *It's About Time: America's Imprisonment Binge* (Belmont, Calif.: Wadsworth).

Irwin, J., V. Strivaldi and J. Ziedenberg (1999) *America's One Million Non-Violent Prisoners* (Washington, DC: Justice Policy Institute).

Jackson, G. (1970) *Soledad Brother: The Prison Letters of George Jackson* (New York: Coward & McCann).

Jacobs, J. (1977) *Stateville: The Penitentiary in Mass Society* (Chicago: University of Chicago Press).

Jacobs, J. (1979) 'Race Relations and the Prisoner Subculture', in N. Morris and M. Tonry (eds), *Crime and Justice: A Review of Research*, Vol. 1 (Chicago: University of Chicago Press).

Jacobs, J. (2001) 'Facts, Values and Prison Policies: A Commentary on Zimring and Tonry', *Punishment & Society*, **3** (1): 183–8.

Jacobson, J., Roberts, J. and Hough, M. (2008) 'Towards More Consistent and Predictable Sentencing in England and Wales', in M. Hough, R. Allen and E. Solomon (eds), Tackling Prison Overcrowding (Bristol: The Policy Press).

Jacobson, M. (2005) *Downsizing Prisons: How to Reduce Crime and Mass Incarceration* (New York: New York University Press).

Jacobson, M. (2006) 'Reversing the Punitive Turn: The Limits and Promise of Current Research', *Criminology and Public Policy*, **5** (2): 277–84.

Jancovic, I. (1977) 'Labour Market and Imprisonment' *Crime and Social Justice* (Fall/Winter): 17–31.

Jay, M. (1973) *The Dialectical Imagination* (London: Heinemann).

Jessop, B. (1994) 'Post-Fordism and the State', in A. Amim (ed.), *Post-Fordism: A Reader* (Oxford: Blackwell).

Joliffe, D. and D. Farrington (2007) *A Rapid Evidence Assessment of the Impact of Monitoring on Reoffending* (London: Home Office).

Jones, P. (1996) 'Risk Prediction in Criminal Justice', in A. Harland (ed.), *Choosing Correctional Options that Work* (Thousand Oaks, Calif.: Sage).

Jones, S. (1993) *The Language of Genes* (London: Flamingo).

Kalmthout, A. and F. Hofstee-van der Meulen (2007) Foreigners in European Prisons, European Prisoners Project, www.foreignersinprison.en.

Karmen, A. (2000) *The New York Murder Mystery: The True Story Behind the Crime Crash of the 1990s* (New York: New York University Press).

Keith, M. (1993) 'From Punishment to Discipline: Racism, Racialism and the Policing of Social Control', in M. Cross and M. Keith (eds), *Racism, the City and the State* (London: Routledge).

Kelling, G. and C. Coles (1996) *Fixing Broken Windows: Restoring Order and Reducing Crime in Our Communities* (New York: Free Press).

Kempf-Leonard, K. and E. Peterson (2000) 'Expanding Realms of the New Penology: The Advent of Actuarial Justice for Juveniles', *Punishment & Society*, 2 (1): 66–97.

Kendall, K. (2002) 'Time to Think Again About Cognitive Behavioural Programmes' in P. Carlen (ed.), *Women and Punishment: The Struggle for Justice* (Cullompton: Willan).

Kilbrandon Committee (1964) *Report of the Committee on Children and Young Persons* (Scotland), Cmnd. 2306 (Edinburgh: HMSO).

King, M. and C. Piper (1990) *How the Law Thinks About Children* (Aldershot: Gower).

King, R. (1987) 'New Generation Prisons, The Prison Building Programme and the Future of the Dispersal System', in A. Bottoms and R. Light (eds), *Problems of Long-Term Imprisonment* (Aldershot: Gower).

King, R. (1991) 'Maximum Security Custody in Britain and The USA: A Study of Gartree and Oak Park Heights', *British Journal of Criminology*, 31 (2): 125–93.

King, R., M. Mauer and M. Young (2005) *Incarceration and Crime: A Complex Relationship* (Washington, DC: The Sentencing Project).

King, R. and K. McDermott (1989) 'British Prisons 1970–1987: The Ever-Deepening Crisis', *British Journal of Criminology*, 29 (2): 107–28.

King, R. and R. Morgan (1980) *The Future of the Prison System* (Farnborough: Gower).

Kong, R. and K. AuCoin (2008) 'Female Offenders in Canada'. *Juristat*, 28 (1), Catalogue no. 85–002-XIE. Canadian Centre for Justice Statistics.

Landau, S. and G. Nathan (1983) 'Selecting Delinquents For Cautioning in the London Metropolitan Area', *British Journal of Criminology*, 23 (2): 128–49.

Langan, P. (1985) 'Racism on Trial: New Evidence to Explain the Racial Composition of Prisons in the United States', *Criminology*, 76 (3) 666–83.

Langan, P. (1991) 'America's Soaring Prison Population', *Science*, 251 (29 March): 1568–73.

Langan, P. and D. Levin (2002) *Recidivism of Prisoners Released in 1994*, Bureau of Justice Special Report, US Department of Justice.

Lapido, D. (2001) 'The Rise of America's Prison Industrial Complex', *New Left Review*, 7: 109–23.

Lasch, S. and J. Urry (1994) *Economics of Signs and Space* (London: Sage).

Lawrence, S. and J. Travis (2004) *The New Landscape of Imprisonment: Mapping America's Prison Expansion* (Washington, DC: Urban Institute, Justice Policy Center).

Lawson, D. (1970) *City Lads in Borstal* (Liverpool: Liverpool University Press).

Lea, J. (1979) 'Discipline and Capitalist Development', in B. Fine *et al.* (eds), *Capitalism and the Rule of Law* (London: Hutchinson).

Lea, J. (1986) 'Police Racism: Some Theories and Their Policy Implications', in R. Matthews and J. Young (eds), *Confronting Crime* (London: Sage).

Lea, J. (1992) 'The Analysis of Crime' in R. Matthews and J. Young (eds), *Rethinking Criminology: The Realist Debate* (London: Sage).

Lea, J. (1997) 'Post-Fordism and Criminality' in N. Jewson and S. MacGregor (eds), *Transforming Cities: Contested Governance and New Spatial Divisions* (London: Routledge).

Lea, J. (1998) 'Criminology and Postmodernity' in P. Walton and J. Young (eds), *The New Criminology Revisited* (London: Macmillan).

Lea, J. and J. Young (1984) *What Is To Be Done About Law and Order?* (Harmondsworth: Penguin).

Leander, K. (1995) 'The Normalisation of Swedish Prisons', in V. Ruggiero, M. Ryan and J. Sim (eds), *Western European Prison Systems* (London: Sage).

Lefebvre, H. (1991) *The Production of Space* (Oxford: Blackwell).

Lemert, E. (1970) 'Juvenile Justice Italian Style', *Law and Society Review*, 20 (4): 509–44.

Leonard, E. (1982) *Women, Crime and Society: A Critique of Criminological Theory* (London: Longman).

Lerman, P. (1982) *Deinstitutionalisation and the Welfare State* (New Brunswick, NJ: Rutgers University Press).

Lévi-Strauss, C. (1992) *Tristes Tropiques* (Harmondsworth: Penguin).

Levitas, R. (1996) 'Fiddling While Britain Burns? The Measurement of Unemployment', in R. Levitas and W. Guy (eds), *Interpreting Social Statistics* (London: Routledge).

Levitt, S. (1996) 'The Effect of Prison Population Size on Crime Rates: Evidence from Prison Overcrowding Litigation', *Quarterly Journal of Economics*, 111: 319–51.

Liebling, A. (1992) *Suicides in Prison* (London: Routledge).

Liebling, A. (1999) 'Prison Suicide and Prison Coping', in M. Tonry and J. Petersilia (eds), *Prisons* (Chicago: University of Chicago Press).

Liebling, A. and T. Ward (1994) *Deaths in Custody: International Perspectives* (London: Whiting & Birch).

Lilly, R. and M. Deflem (1996) 'Profit and Penalty: An Analysis of the Corrections Commercial Complex?', *Crime and Delinquency*, 42 (1): 3–20.

Linebaugh, P. (1977) 'The Tyburn Riot Against the Surgeons', in D. Hay *et al.* (eds), *Albion's Fatal Tree* (Harmondsworth: Penguin).

Lloyd, C. (1990) *Suicide and Self Injury in Prison: A Literature Review*, Home Office Research Study No. 115 (London: HMSO).

Longford Committee (1964) *Crime – A Challenge To Us All* (London: Labour Party).

Lowman, J., R. Menzies and T. Palys (1987) *Transcarceration: Essays in the Study of Social Control* (Aldershot: Gower).

Lucken, K. (1998) 'Contemporary Penal Trends: Modern or Postmodern?', *British Journal of Criminology*, 38 (1): 106–23.

Lynch, J. (1983) 'A Comparison of Prison Use in England, Canada, West Germany and the United States', *Journal of Criminal Law and Criminology*, **79**: 108–217.

Lynch, J. (1993) 'A Cross National Comparison of Length of Custodial Sentences for Serious Crimes?', *Justice Quarterly*, **10** (4): 639–60.

Lyon, J. (2006) 'The Foreigners Still Locked in Our Jails and Other Scandals', *Guardian*, 27 April.

Lyotard, J. (1986) *The Postmodern Condition* (Manchester: Manchester University Press).

MacKinnon, C. (1987) *Feminism Unmodified: Discourses on Life and Law* (Cambridge, Mass: Harvard University Press).

Maden, A., M. Swinton and J. Gunn (1992) 'The Ethnic Origin of Women Serving a Prison Sentence', *British Journal of Criminology*, **32** (2): 218–22.

Maguire, M., J. Vagg and R. Morgan (1985) *Accountability and Prisons* (London: Tavistock).

Mahoney, D. and J. Doak (2004) 'Restorative Justice – Is More Better? The Experience of Police Led Restorative Cautioning Projects in Northern Ireland', *Howard Journal*, **43** (5): 484–505.

Mair, G. (1986) 'Ethnic Minorities, Probation and the Magistrates Courts', *British Journal of Criminology*, **26** (2): 147–55.

Mair, G. and C. Nee (1990) *Electronic Monitoring: The Trials and Their Results*, Home Office Research Study No. 120 (London: HMSO).

Mallory, J. (2006) 'Globalisation, Prisons and the Philosophy of Punishment', *Women's Studies*, **35**: 529–43.

Marion, N. (1992) 'Presidential Agenda Setting in Crime Control', *Criminal Justice Policy Review*, **6** (2): 159–84.

Martens, P. (1997) 'Immigrants Crime and Criminal Justice in Sweden' in M. Tonry (ed.), *Ethnicity, Crime and Immigration: Crime and Justice*, Vol. 21 (Chicago: University of Chicago Press).

Martinson, R. (1979) 'Symposium on Sentencing', *Hofra Law Review*, **7** (2): 243–58.

Marvell, T. (1994) 'Is Further Prison Expansion Worth the Costs?', *Federal Probation*, **58** (4): 59–62.

Marvell, T. and C. Moody (1994) 'Prison Population Growth and Crime Reduction', *Journal of Quantitative Criminology*, **10**: 109–40.

Marvell, T. and C. Moody (1997) 'Age-Structure Trends in Prison Populations', *Journal of Criminal Justice*, **25** (2): 115–24.

Marx, K. (1970) *A Contribution to the Critique of Political Economy* (London: Lawrence & Wishart).

Marx, K. (1984) *Capital*, Vol. 1 (London: Lawrence & Wishart).

Marx, K. and F. Engels (1975) 'Debates on the Law of the Thefts of Wood', in K. Marx and F. Engels, *Collected Works*, Vol. 1 (London: Lawrence & Wishart).

Mason, B. (2006) ' A Gendered Irish Experiment: Grounds for Optimism', in F. Heidensohn (ed.), *Gender and Justice* (Cullompton: Willan).

Mason, P. (2003) *Criminal Visions: Media Representations of Crime and Justice* (Cullompton: Willan).

Massey, D. (1997) 'Space/Power, Identity/Difference: Tensions in the City', in A. Merrifield and E. Swyngedouw (eds), *The Urbanisation of Injustice* (New York: New York University Press).

Mathieson, T. (1974) *The Politics of Abolition* (Oxford: Martin Robertson).

Mathieson, T. (1990) *Prison on Trial* (London: Sage).

Mathieson, T. (1997) 'The Viewers Society: Michel Foucault's Panopticon Revisited', *Theoretical Criminology*, 1 (2): 215–34.

Mathieson, T. (2003) 'The Rise of the Surveillant State in Times of Globalisation' in C. Sumner (ed.), *The Blackwell Companion to Criminology* (Oxford: Blackwell).

Matthews, R. (1979) 'Decarceration and the Fiscal Crisis', in B. Fine (ed.), *Capitalism and the Rule of Law* (London: Hutchinson).

Matthews, R. (1987) 'Decarceration and Social Control: Fantasies and Realities', in J. Lowman *et al.* (eds), *Transcarceration: Essays in the Study of Social Control* (Aldershot: Gower).

Matthews, R. (ed.) (1988) *Informal Justice?* (London: Sage).

Matthews, R. (ed.) (1989a) *Privatising Criminal Justice* (London: Sage).

Matthews, R. (1989b) 'Alternatives to Prison: A Realist Approach', in P. Carlen and D. Cook (eds), *Paying for Crime* (Milton Keynes: Open University Press).

Matthews, R. (1992) 'Replacing Broken Windows: Crime, Incivilities and Urban Change', in R. Matthews and J. Young (eds), *Issues in Realist Criminology* (London: Sage).

Matthews, R. (1994) *Prisoners Abroad* (London: Centre for Criminology, Middlesex University).

Matthews, R. (1995a) 'Crime and Its Consequences in England and Wales', *Annals of the American Academy of Political and Social Science*, 539 (May): 169–83.

Matthews, R. (1995b) 'The Diversion of Juveniles from Custody: The Experience of England and Wales 1980–1990', in G. Albrecht and W. Ludwig-Mayerhofer (eds), *Diversion and Informal Social Control* (Berlin: Walter de Gruyter).

Matthews, R. (1999) *Doing Time: An Introduction to the Sociology of Imprisonment* (1st edn) London: Palgrave Macmillan.

Matthews, R. (2003) 'Rethinking Penal Policy: Towards a Systems Approach' in R. Matthews and J. Young (eds), *The New Politics of Crime and Punishment* (Cullompton: Willan).

Matthews, R. (2005) 'The Myth of Punitiveness', *Theoretical Criminology*, 9 (2): 175–202.

Matthews, R. (2006) 'Reintegrative Shaming and Restorative Justice: Reconciliation or Divorce?', in I. Aertson, J. Daems and Luic Robert (eds), *Institutionalising Restorative Justice* (Cullompton: Willan).

Matthews, R. (2009) 'Beyond "So What?" Criminology: Rediscovering Realism', *Theoretical Criminology* (forthcoming).

Matthews, R. and J. Young (1992) 'Reflections on Realism', in J. Young and R. Matthews (eds), *Rethinking Criminology: The Realist Debate* (London: Sage).

Mauer, M. (1999) *Race to Incarcerate* (Washington, DC: The Sentencing Project).

Mauer, M. (1994) *Americans Behind Bars: The International Use of Incarceration* (Washington, DC: The Sentencing Project).

Mauer, M. (2001) 'The Causes and Consequences of Prison Growth in the United States', *Punishment & Society*, 3 (1): 9–20.

Mauer, M. and M. Chesney-Lind (eds) (2002) *Invisible Punishment: The Collateral Consequences of Mass Imprisonment* (New York: The New Press).

May, M. (1973) 'Innocence and Experience: The Evolution of the Concept of Juvenile Delinquency in the Mid-Nineteenth Century', *Victorian Studies*, **18**: 17–29.

Mayhew, H. and J. Binny (1971) *Criminal Prisons of London* (London: Frank Cass & Co.).

McCleary, R. (1961) 'The Governmental Process and Informal Social Control', in D. Cressey (ed.), *The Prison: Studies in Institutionalisation, Organisation and Change* (New York: Holt, Rinehart & Winston).

McConville, S. (1995) 'The Victorian Prison: England, 1865–1965', in N. Morris and D. Rothman (eds), *The Oxford History of the Prison* (Oxford: Oxford University Press).

McConville, S. and S. Hall-Williams (1987) 'The English Response to the Penal Crisis', in S. Gottfredson and S. McConville (eds), *America's Correctional Crisis: Prison Populations and Public Policy* (New York: Greenwood Press).

McGowan, R. (1995) 'The Well Ordered Prison in England 1780–1865', in N. Morris and D. Rothman (eds), *The Oxford History of the Prison* (Oxford: Oxford University Press).

McLaughlin, E. and K. Murji (2001) 'Lost Connections and New Directions: Neo-Liberalism, New Public Managerialism and the Modernisation of the British Police', in K. Stenson and R. Sullivan (eds), *Crime, Risk and Justice* (Cullompton: Willan).

McMahon, M. (1990) 'Net-Widening: Vagaries and the Use of a Concept', *British Journal of Criminology*, **30** (2): 121–50.

McNay, L. (1992) *Foucault and Feminism* (Cambridge: Polity Press).

Melossi, D. (1978) 'Georg Rusche and Otto Kirchheimer: *Punishment and Social Structure*', *Crime and Social Justice*, **9**: 73–95.

Melossi, D. (1979) 'Institutions of Social Control and Capitalist Organisation of Work', in B. Fine *et al.* (eds), *Capitalism and the Rule of Law* (London: Hutchinson).

Melossi, D. (2001) 'The Cultural Embededness of Social Control: Reflections of the Comparison of Italian and North American Cultures Concerning Punishment', *Theoretical Criminology*, **45** (4): 403–24.

Melossi, D. (2003a) 'In a Peaceful Life: Migration and the Crime of Modernity in Europe/Italy', *Punishment & Society*, **5** (4): 371–97.

Melossi, D. (2003b) 'Introduction to the Transaction Edition', in G. Rusche and O. Kirchheimer, *Punishment and Social Structure* (New Brunswick: Transaction Publishers).

Melossi, D. and M. Pavarini (1981) *The Prison and the Factory: The Origins of the Penitentiary System* (London: Macmillan).

Merton, R. (1957) *Social Theory and Social Structure* (New York: The Free Press).

Meyer, J. and P. O'Malley (2005) 'Missing the Punitive Turn? Canadian Criminal Justice, Balance and Penal Modernism', in J. Pratt, D. Brown, M. Brown, S. Hallsworth, and W. Morrison (eds), *The New Punitiveness: Trends, Theories, Perspectives* (Cullompton: Willan).

Mhlanga, B. (1997) *The Colour of English Justice: A Multivariate Analysis* (Aldershot: Avebury).

Miles, R. (1993) *Racism After 'Race Relations'* (London: Routledge).

Millham, S., R. Bullock and P. Cherrett (1975) *After Grace-Teeth: A Comparative Study of the Residential Experiences of Boys in Approved Schools* (London: Human Context Books).

Millham, S., R. Bullock and K. Hosie (1978) *Locking Up Children: Secure Provision Within the Child Care System* (Farnborough: Saxon House).

Millie, A., J. Jacobson and M. Hough (2003) 'Understanding the Growth of the Prison Population in England and Wales', *Criminal Justice*, 3 (4): 369–87.

Mingione, E. (1996) 'Urban Poverty in the Advanced Industrial World: Concepts Analyses and Debates', in E. Mingione (ed.), *Urban Poverty and the Underclass* (Oxford: Blackwell).

Ministry of Justice (2007a) *The Government's Response to the Report by Baroness Corston of a Review of Women with Particular Vulnerabilities in the Criminal Justice System*. Cm 7261 (London: Home Office).

Ministry of Justice (2007b) *Statistics on Race and the Criminal Justice System* (London: Ministry of Justice).

Ministry of Justice (2008a) *Sentencing Statistics 2007 England and Wales*, www.justice.gov.uk/publications/ sentencingannual.htm.

Ministry of Justice (2008b) *Offender Management Caseload Statistics 2007* (London: Home Office).

Modood, T. and R. Berthoud (1997) *Ethnic Minorities in Britain: Diversity and Disadvantage* (London: Policy Studies Institute).

Moore, D. (2007) 'Translating Justice and Therapy: The Drug Treatment Court Networks', *British Journal of Criminology*, 47 (1): 42–60.

Moore, D. and K. Hannah-Moffat (2005) 'The Liberal Veil Revisiting Canadian Penality', in J. Pratt, D. Brown, M. Brown, S. Hallsworth, and W. Morrison (eds), *The New Punitiveness: Trends, Theories, Perspectives* (Cullompton: Willan).

Moore, R., E. Gray, C. Roberts, S. Merrington, I. Waters, R. Fernandez, G. Hayward and R. Rogers (2004) *ISSP: The Initial Report* (London: Youth Justice Board).

Morgan, R. (1991) 'Woolf: In Retrospect and Prospect', *Modern Law Review*, 54 (5): 713–25.

Morgan, R. (1997) 'The Aims of Imprisonment Revisited', in A. Liebling and T. Ward (eds), *Deaths in Custody: International Perspectives* (London: Whiting & Birch).

Morgan, R. (2002) 'Privileging Public Attitudes to Sentencing', in J. Roberts and M. Hough (eds), *Changing Public Attitudes to Punishment* (Cullompton: Willan).

Morgan, R. and M. Evans (1994) 'Inspecting Prisons: The View from Strasbourg', in R. King and M. Maguire (eds), *Prisons in Context* (Oxford: Clarendon Press).

Morris, A. and H. Giller (1987) *Understanding Juvenile Justice* (London: Croom Helm).

Morris, A., H. Giller, E. Szwed and H. Geach (1980) *Justice for Children* (London: Macmillan).

Morris, A. and M. Tonry (1990) *Between Prison and Probation* (New York: Oxford University Press).

Morris, A. and C. Wilkinson (1995) 'Responding to Female Prisoners' Needs', *Prison Journal*, 75 (3): 295–306.

Morris, N. (1974) *The Future of Imprisonment* (Chicago: University of Chicago Press).

Morris, T. and P. Morris (1963) *Pentonville: A Sociological Study of an English Prison* (London: Routledge & Kegan Paul)

Morrison, W. (1996) 'Modernity, Imprisonment and Social Solidarity', in R. Matthews and P. Francis (eds), *Prisons 2000* (London: Macmillan).

Mountbatten, Lord (1966) *Report of the Inquiry into Prison Escapes and Security* (London: HMSO).

Moxon, D. (1988) *Sentencing Practice in the Crown Court*, Home Office Research Study No. 102 (London: HMSO).

Moxon, D. and C. Whittaker (1996) *Imprisonment for Fine Default*, Research Findings No. 35, Home Office Research and Statistics Directorate (London: HMSO).

Muncie, J. (1999) 'Institutional Intolerance: Youth Justice and the 1998 Criminal Justice Act', Critical Social Policy, **19** (2): 147–75.

Muncie, J. (2005) 'The Globalisation of Crime Control – The Case of Youth and Juvenile Justice', *Theoretical Criminology*, **9** (1): 35–64.

Murray, C. (1990) *The Emergence of The British Underclass* (London: Institute of Economic Affairs).

Murray, C. (1994) *Underclass: The Crisis Deepens* (London: Institute of Economic Affairs).

Murray, C. (1997) *Does Prison Work?* (London: Institute of Economic Affairs).

Mylanga, B. (1997) *The Colour of English Justice: A Multivariate Analysis* (Aldershot: Avebury).

NACRO (1991) *Seizing the Initiative: Final Report on the DHSS Intermediate Treatment Initiative to Divert Juvenile Offenders from Care and Custody, 1983–1989* (London: NACRO).

Naffine, N. (1997) *Feminism and Criminology* (Cambridge: Polity Press).

Nathan, S. (2005) 'Prison Privatisation: Some Recent Developments and Issues', Paper Presented to Eleventh United Nations Congress on Crime Prevention and Criminal Justice, Bangkok, www.psiru.org/justice.

National Audit Office (1985) *Home Office and Property Services Agency: Programme for the Provision of Prison Places* (London: HMSO).

Neale, K. (1991) 'European Prison Rules: Contextual, Philosophical and Practical Aspects', in J. Muncie and R. Sparks (eds), *Imprisonment: European Perspectives* (London: Harvester Wheatsheaf).

Nelken, D. (2005) 'When is Society Non-Punitive: The Italian Case', in J. Pratt, D. Brown, M. Brown, S. Hallsworth, and W. Morrison (eds), *The New Punitiveness: Trends, Theories, Perspectives* (Cullompton: Willan).

Nellis, M. (2005) 'Electronic Monitoring, Satellite Tracking and the New Punitiveness in England and Wales', in J. Pratt, D. Brown, M. Brown, S. Hallsworth, and W. Morrison (eds), *The New Punitiveness: Trends, Theories, Perspectives* (Cullompton: Willan).

Newburn, T. (1997) 'Youth, Crime and Justice', in M. Maguire, R. Morgan and R. Reiner (eds), *The Oxford Handbook of Criminology* (2nd edn) (Oxford: Clarendon Press).

Newman, C. (2003) *Last Chance: Older Women Through the Criminal Justice System* (London: The Griffins Society), www.thegriffinssociety.org

Nicholas, S., C. Kershaw and A. Walker (2008) *Crime in England and Wales 2006/07* (London: Home Office).

Nottingham Juvenile Liaison Bureau (1985) *The Limits of Diversion*, Second Annual Report (Nottingham: NJLB).

Nuttall, C. and K. Pease (1994) 'Changes in the Use of Imprisonment in England and Wales 1950–1991', *Criminal Law Review*: 316–21.

O'Brien, P. (1982) *The Promise of Punishment: Prisons in Nineteenth Century France* (Princeton, NJ: Princeton University Press).

Odih, P. (2003) 'Gender, Work and Organisation in the Time Space Economy of "Just in Time" Labour', *Time and Society*, **12** (2/3): 293–314.

Offe, C. (1984) *Contradictions of the Welfare State* (London: Hutchinson).

Offe, C. (1985) 'Work: The Key Sociological Category?', in *Disorganised Capitalism* (Cambridge: Polity Press).

O'Mahoney, D. and J. Doak (2004) 'Restorative Justice – Is More Better? The Experience of the Police Led Cautioning Pilots in Northern Ireland', *Howard Journal*, **43** (5): 484–505.

O'Malley, P. (1999) 'Volatile and Contradictory Punishment', *Theoretical Criminology*, **3** (2): 175–196.

O'Malley, P. (2004) *Risk Uncertainty and Government* (London: The Glasshouse Press).

O'Malley, P. (2009) 'Theorizing Fines', *Punishment & Society*, **11** (1): 67–83.

O'Sullivan, E. and I. O'Donnell (2003) 'Imprisonment and the Crime Rate in Ireland', *Economic and Social Review*, **34** (1): 33–64.

O'Sullivan, E. and I. O'Donnell (2007) 'Coercive Confinement in the Republic of Ireland', *Punishment & Society*, **9** (1): 27–48.

Owen, B. and B. Bloom (1995) 'Profiling Women Prisoners', *Prison Journal*, **75** (2): 165–86.

Page, S. (1993) 'Suicide and the Total Institution', in A. Liebling and T. Ward (eds), *Deaths in Custody: International Perspectives* (London: Whiting & Birch).

Painter, K. (1992) 'Different Worlds: The Spatial, Temporal and Social Dimensions of Female Victimisation', in D. Evans *et al.* (eds), *Essays in Environmental Criminology* (London: Routledge).

Palmer, T. (1992) *The Re-Emergence of Correctional Intervention* (California: Sage).

Parenti, C. (1999) *Lockdown America: Police and Prisons in the Age of Crisis* (London: Verso).

Park, I. (2000) *Review of Comparative Costs and Performance of Privately and Publicly Operated Prisons 1998–1999* (London: Home Office).

Parker, M. (2007) *Dynamic Security: The Demographic Therapeutic Community in Prison* (London: Jessica Kingsley).

Parole Board (2008) *Annual Report 2007/08*, Statistical Annexe.

Parrone, D., and J. Pratt (2003) 'Comparing the Quality and Cost Effectiveness of Public Versus Private Prisons', *Prison Journal*, **83** (3): 301–22.

Pashukanis, E. (1978) *Law and Marxism: A General Theory* (original Russian edition 1924) (London: C. Arthur).

Pawson, R. and N. Tilley (1994) 'What Works in Evaluation Research', *British Journal of Criminology*, **34** (3): 291–306.

Pawson, R. and N. Tilley (1997) *Realistic Evaluation* (London: Sage).

Pearson, G. (1975) *The Deviant Imagination* (London: Macmillan).

Pearson, G. (1983) *Hooligan: A History of Respectable Fears* (London: Macmillan).

Pease, K. (1985) 'Community Service Orders', in M. Tonry and N. Morris (eds), *Crime and Justice: An Annual Review of Research* (Chicago: University of Chicago Press).

Pease, K. (1994) 'Cross National Imprisonment Rates: Limitations of Methods and Possible Conclusions', *British Journal of Criminology*, **34**: 116–30.

Penna, S. and M. Yar (2003) 'From Modern to Postmodern Penality? A Response to Hallsworth', *Theoretical Criminology*, **7** (4): 469–82.

Perrone, D. and T. Pratt (2003) 'Comparing the Quality of Confinement and Cost-Effectiveness of Public Versus Private Prisons: What We Know, Why We Do Not Know More, and Where Do We Go From Here', *Prison Journal*, **83** (3): 301–22.

Petersilia, J. (1985) 'Racial Disparities in the Criminal Justice System', *Crime and Delinquency*, **31** (1): 15–34.

Petersilia, J. (2003) *When Prisoners Come Home: Parole and Prisoner Reentry* (Oxford: Oxford University Press).

Pew Center on the States (2008) *One in a 100: Behind Bars in America*, Public Safety Performance Project, www.pewcenteronthestates.org.

Piehl, A., B. Useem and J. Dilulio (1999) *Right-sizing justice: A Cost Benefit Analysis of Imprisonment in Three States*, Civic Report No. 8, Centre for Civic Innovation at the Manhattan Institute.

Pierson, P. (1994) *Dismantling the Welfare State? Reagan, Thatcher and the Politics of Retrenchment* (Cambridge: Cambridge University Press).

Piper, C. and S. Easton (2006) 'What's Sentencing Got to Do With It? Understanding the Prison Crisis', *Contemporary Issues in Law*, **8** (4): 356–76.

Pitts, J. (1988) *The Politics of Juvenile Crime* (London: Sage).

Pitts, J. (1993) 'Thereotyping: Anti-Racism, Criminology and Black Young People', in D. Cook and B. Hudson (eds), *Racism and Criminology* (London: Sage).

Pitts, J. (1996) 'The Politics and Practice of Youth Justice', in J. Muncie and E. McLaughlin (eds), *Controlling Crime* (London: Sage).

Pitts, J. (1997) 'Youth Crime, Social Change and Crime Control in Britain and France in the 1980s and 1990s', in H. Jones (ed.), *Towards a Classless Society* (London: Routledge).

Pitts, J. (2001) 'Korrectional Karaoke: New Labour and the Zombification of Youth Justice', *Youth Justice*, **1** (2): 3–16.

Pitts, J. (2003) The New Politics of Youth Crime: Discipline or Solidarity?, Lyme Regis: Russell House Publishing.

Pitts, J. (2008) 'Too Grand, Too Bland and Abstract: The Limitations of "Youth Governance" as an Explanatory Schema for Contemporary Governmental Responses to Socially Deviant Young People', *Youth and Policy*, **99** (Spring): 67–89.

Platek, M. (1996) 'We Never Promised Them a Rose Garden', in R. Matthews and P. Francis (eds), *Prisons 2000* (London: Macmillan).

Platt, T. (1969) *The Child Savers* (Chicago: Chicago University Press).

Player, E. (2005) 'The Reduction of Women's Imprisonment in England and Wales: Will the Reform of Short Prison Sentences Help?', *Punishment & Society*, **7** (4): 419–39.

Pollock-Byrne, J. (1992) 'Women in Prison: Why are Their Numbers Increasing?', in J. Benekos and A. Merlo (eds), *Corrections: Dilemmas and Directions* (Cincinnati, Ohio: Anderson Publishing).

Porteous, D. (1998) *Evaluation of CSV Online Mentoring Scheme* (London: Community Service Volunteers).

Poulantzas, N. (1978) *State Power and Socialism* (London: Verso).

Pratt, J. (1985) 'Delinquency as a Scarce Resource', *Howard Journal*, **24**: 93–107.

Pratt, J. (1989) 'Corporatism: The Third Model of Juvenile Justice', *British Journal of Criminology*, **29** (3): 236–55.

Pratt, J. (1990) 'Crime, Time, Youth and Punishment', *Contemporary Crisis*, **14**: 219–42.

Pratt, J. (2007) *Penal Populism* (London: Routledge).

Pratt, J. (2008a) 'The Dark Side of Paradise: Explaining New Zealand's History of High Imprisonment', *British Journal of Criminology*, **46** (4): 541–60.

Pratt, J. (2008b) 'Scandinavian Exceptionalism in an Era of Penal Excess', *British Journal of Criminology*, **48** (3): 275–92.

Pratt, T. and J. Maahs (1999) Are Private Prisons More Cost-Effective than Public Prisons? A Meta-Analysis of Evaluation Research Studies', *Crime and Delinquency*, **45** (3): 358–71.

Preston, P. and M. Perez (2006) 'The Criminalisation of Aliens: Regulating Foreigners', *Critical Criminology*, **14** (1): 43–66.

Prime, J., S. White, S. Liriano and K. Patel (2001) *Criminal Careers of those Born Between 1953 and 1978* (London: Home Office).

Prison Reform Trust (1993) *Women Prisoners on Remand* (London: Prison Reform Trust).

Prison Reform Trust (1997) *The Rising Toll of Prison Suicide* (London: Prison Reform Trust).

Prison Reform Trust (2008) *Bromley Briefings: Prison Factfile* (London: Prison Reform Trust).

Pyle, D. J. and D. F. Deadman (1994) 'Crime and the Business Cycle in Post-War Britain', *British Journal of Criminology*, **34** (3): 339–57.

Rafter, N. (1983) 'Prisons for Women 1970–1980', in M. Tonry and N. Morris (eds), *Crime and Justice: An Annual Review of Research*, Vol. 5 (Chicago: University of Chicago).

Rafter, N. (1985a) 'Gender Prisons and Prison History', *Social Science History*, **9** (3): 233–47.

Rafter, N. (1985b) Partial Justice: Women in State Prisons 1800–1935 (Boston: Northeastern University Press).

Reiman, J. (2004) *The Rich Get Richer and the Poor Get Prison: Ideology, Class and Criminal Justice* (Boston: Allyn and Bacon).

Roberts, J. (2003) 'Public Opinion and Mandatory Sentencing: A Review of International Findings', *Criminal Justice and Behaviour*, **30** (4): 483–508.

Robertson, R. (1995) 'Glocalisation: Time-Space and Homogeneity–Hetrogeneity', in M. Featherstone, S. Hasch and R. Robertson (eds), *Global Modernities* (London: Sage).

Robinson, G. and F. McNeill (2008) 'Exploring the Dynamics of Compliance with Community Penalties', *Theoretical Criminology*, **12** (4): 431–49.

Roche, D. (2003) *Accountability and Restorative Justice* (Oxford: Clarendon Press).

Rock, P. (1996) *Restructuring a Women's Prison* (Oxford: Clarendon Press).

Rose, N. (1987) 'Beyond the Public/Private Division: Law, Power and the Family', *Journal of Law and Society*, **14** (1): 61–77.

Rose, N. (1996) 'The Death of the Social? Reconfiguring the Territory of Government', *Economy and Society*, **25** (2): 173–205.

Rose, N. and P. Miller (1992) 'Political Power Beyond the State: Problematics of Government', British Journal of Sociology, **43** (2): 173–205.

Roshier, B. (1989) *Controlling Crime: The Classical Perspective in Criminology* (Milton Keynes: Open University Press).

Rothman, D. (1971) *The Discovery of the Asylum: Social Order and Disorder in the New Republic* (Boston: Little, Brown & Co.).

Rothman, D. (1973) 'Decarcerating Prisoners and Patients', *Civil Liberties Review*, 1: 8–30.

Rothman, D. (1980) *Conscience and Convenience: The Asylum and its Alternatives in Progressive America* (Boston: Little, Brown & Co.).

Rothman, D. (1981) 'Doing Time: Days, Months and Years in the Criminal Justice System', in H. Gross and A. von Hirsch (eds), *Sentencing* (New York: Oxford University Press).

Rotman, E. (1990) *Beyond Punishment: A New View on the Rehabilitation of Criminal Offenders* (Westport, Conn.: Greenwood Press).

Ruggles-Brise, E. (1921) *The English Prison System* (London: Macmillan).

Rusche, G. and O. Kirchheimer (1939 [2003]) *Punishment and Social Structure* (New Brunswick: Transaction Publishers).

Russell, S. (1997) 'The Failure of Postmodern Criminology', *Critical Criminology*, 8 (2): 61–90.

Rutherford, A. (1983) 'A Statute Backfires: The Escalation of Youth Incarceration in England in the 1970s', in J. Doig (ed.), *Criminal Corrections: Ideals and Realities* (Lexington, Mass.: D. C. Heath & Co.).

Rutherford, A. (1984) *Prisons and the Process of Justice* (London: Heinemann).

Rutherford, A. (1986) *Growing Out of Crime* (Harmondsworth: Penguin).

Rutherford, A. (1995) 'Signposting the Future of Juvenile Justice Policy in England and Wales', in Howard League for Penal Reform, *Child Offenders: UK and International Practice* (London: The Howard League for Penal Reform).

Sabol, W., H. Conture and P. Harrison (2006) *Prisoners in 2006*, Bureau of Justice Statistics, NCJ 219415, US Department of Justice.

Sabol, W., H. Conture and P. Harrison (2007) *Prisoners in America*, Bureau of Justice Statistics NCJ 219416, US Department of Justice.

Said, E. (1993) *Culture and Imperialism* (London: Chatto & Windus).

Sampson, R. and J. Lauritsen (1997) 'Racial and Ethnic Disparities in Crime and Criminal Justice in the United States', in M. Tonry (ed.), *Ethnicity, Crime and Immigration* (Chicago: University of Chicago Press).

Santos, B. (1987) 'Law: A Map of Misreading. Towards a Postmodern Conception of Law', *Journal of Law and Society*, **14** (3): 279–302.

Sayer, A. (1992) *Method in Social Science: A Realist Approach* (2nd edn) (London: Routledge).

Sayer, A. (2000) *Realism and Social Science* (London: Sage).

Scarman, Lord (1982) *The Scarman Report: The Brixton Disorders 10–12 April 1991* (Harmondsworth: Penguin).

Schur, E. (1973) *Radical Non-Intervention: Rethinking the Delinquency Problem* (Englewood Cliffs, NJ: Prentice-Hall).

Scottish Office (1993) *Report on HM Special Unit, Barlinnie* (Edinburgh: HMSO).

Scull, A. (1977) Decarceration: Community Treatment and the Deviant (reprinted 2nd edn 1984) (Englewood Cliffs, NJ: Prentice-Hall).

Seear, N. and E. Player (1986) *Women in the Penal System* (London: The Howard League).

Sennett, R. (1991) *The Conscience of the Eye: The Design and Social Life of Cities* (New York: Knopf).

Shaw, M. (1992) 'Issues in Power and Control: Women in Prison and Their Defenders', *British Journal of Criminology*, **32** (4): 438–53.

Shaw, M. (1996) 'Is There a Feminist Future for Women's Prisons?', in R. Matthews and P. Francis (eds), *Prisons 2000* (London: Macmillan).

Shaw, R. (1992) Prisoners' Children: What are the Issues? (London: Routledge).

Shaw, S. (1985) 'Reflections on "Short Sharp Shock"', *Youth and Policy*, **13** (Summer): 1–5.

Shearing, C. and P. Stenning (1985) 'From the Panopticon to the Disneyworld: The Development of Discipline', in A. Doob and V. Greenspan (eds), *Perspectives in Criminal Law* (Ontario: Canada Law Books Inc.)

Shichor, D. and D. Sechrest (1996) *Three Strikes and You're Out: Vengeance as Public Policy* (Thousand Oaks, Calif.: Sage).

Silver, E. and L. Miller (2002) 'A Cautionary Note on the Use of Actuarial Risk Assessment Tools for Social Control', *Crime and Delinquency*, **48** (1): 138–61.

Silvestri, M. and C. Crowther-Dowey (2008) *Gender and Crime* (London: Sage).

Sim, J. (1994) 'Reforming the Penal Wasteland: A Critical Review of the Woolf Report', in E. Player and M. Jenkins (eds), *Prisons After Woolf: Reform Through Riot* (London: Routledge).

Simon, J. (1972) *Poor Discipline: Parole and the Social Control of the Underclass 1890–1990* (Chicago: University of Chicago Press).

Simon, J. (1999) 'They Died With Their Boots On: The Boot Camp and the Limits of Modern Penality', *Social Justice*, 22: 25–48.

Simon, J. (2001) 'Entitlement to Cruelty: Neo-liberalism and the Punitive Mentality in the United States', in K. Stenson and R. Sullivan (eds), *Crime, Risk and Justice* (Cullompton: Willan).

Simon, J. (2007) *Governing Through Crime* (New York: Oxford University Press).

Skogan, W. (1995) 'Crime and the Racial Fears of White Americans', *The Annals*, **539**: 59–72.

Smart, B. (1983) 'On Discipline and Social Regulation: A Review of Foucault's Geneological Analysis', in D. Garland and P. Young (eds), *The Power to Punish* (London: Heinemann).

Smart, C. (1979) 'The New Female Criminal: Reality or Myth?', *British Journal of Criminology*, **19** (1): 50–9.

Smart, C. (1992) 'Feminist Approaches to Criminology or Postmodern Woman Meets Atavistic Man', in L. Gelsthorpe and A. Morris (eds), *Feminist Perspectives in Criminology* (Buckingham: Open University Press).

Smart, C. (1990) 'Feminist Approaches to Criminology, or Postmodern Woman Meets Atavistic Man', in A. Morris and L. Gelsthorpe (eds), *Feminist Perspectives in Criminology* (Milton Keynes: Open University Press).

Smith, D. (1983) *Police and People in London* (London: Policy Studies Institute).

Smith, D. (1997a) 'Ethnic Origins, Crime and Criminal Justice', in M. Maguire, R. Morgan and R. Reiner (eds), *The Oxford Handbook of Criminology* (2nd edn) (Oxford: Oxford University Press).

Smith, D. (1997b) 'Ethnic Origins, Crime and Criminal Justice in England and Wales', in M. Tonry (ed.), *Ethnicity, Crime and Immigration* (Chicago: University of Chicago Press).

Smith, E. and A. Hattery (2006) 'The Prison Industrial Complex', *Sociation Today*, 4 (2): 1–34, www.ncsociology.org/sociationtoday/v42/prison/htm.

Snider, L. (2003) 'Constituting the Punishable Woman: Atavistic Man Incarcerates Postmodern Woman', *British Journal of Criminology*, 43 (2): 354–78.

Social Exclusion Unit (2002) *Reducing Re-Offending by Ex-Prisoners* (London: Home Office, Social Exclusion Unit).

Soja, E. (1989) *Postmodern Geographies: The Reassertion of Space in Critical Social Theory* (London: Verso).

Solomos, J. and L. Back (1996) *Racism and Society* (London: Macmillan).

Sorensen, J. and Steman, D. (2002) 'The Effect of State Sentencing Policies on Incarceration Rates', *Crime and Delinquency*, 48 (3): 456–75.

Sparks, R. (1994) 'Can Prisons be Legitimate? Penal Politics, Brutalisation and the Timeliness of an Old Idea', in R. King and M. Maguire (eds), *Prisons in Context* (Oxford: Clarendon Press).

Sparks, R. and A. Bottoms (1995) 'Legitimacy and Order in Prisons', *British Journal of Sociology*, 46 (1): 45–62.

Sparks, R., A. Bottoms and W. Hay (1996) *Prisons and the Problem of Order* (Oxford: Clarendon Press).

Spelman, W. (2000) 'The Limited Importance of Prison Expansion' in A. Blumstein and J. Wallman (eds), *The Crime Drop in America* (Cambridge: Cambridge University Press).

Spierenburg, P. (1984) *The Spectacle of Suffering: Executions and the Evolution of Repression* (Cambridge: Cambridge University Press).

Spinellis, C., K. Angelopoulou and N. Koulouris (1996) 'Foreign Detainees in Greek Prisons: A New Challenge to the Guardians of Human Rights', in R. Matthews and P. Francis (eds), *Prisons 2000* (London: Macmillan).

Spitzer, S. (1975) 'Towards a Marxian Theory of Crime', *Social Problems*, 22: 368–401.

Steenhuis, D., L. Tigges and J. Essers (1983) 'Penal Climate in the Netherlands', *British Journal of Criminology*, 23 (1): 1–16.

Steffensmeier, D. and M. D. Harer (1991) 'Did Crime Rise or Fall During the Reagan Presidency?', *Journal of Research in Crime and Delinquency*, 28: 330–59.

Stephan, J. (2004) *The High Costs of Imprisonment in America*, NCJ-202949, US Department of Justice.

Stephan, J. (2006) *The High Cost of Imprisonment in America*, NCJ 202949, US Department of Justice.

Stephens, T. (2006) *Three Out of Four Swiss Prisoners are Foreign*, Swissinfo.ch, http://swisssinfo.ch/eng/politics/internal_affairs/three_out_of_four_prisoners_are_foreigners.htm.

Stevens, P. and C. Willis (1979) *Race, Crime and Arrests*, Home Office Research Study No. 58 (London: HMSO).

Sudbury, J. (2002) 'Selling Black Bodies: Black Women and the Global Prison Industrial Complex', *Feminist Review*, 70: 57–74.

Sudbury, J. (2004) A World Without Prisons: Resisting, Militarism, Globalised Punishment and Empire', *Social Justice*, 31 (1–2): 9–29.

Sutton, J. (2004) 'The Political Economy of Imprisonment in Affluent Western Democracies, 1960–1990', *American Sociological Review*, 69: 170–89.

Swyngedouw, E. (1992) 'The Mammon Quest: Globalisation, Interspatial Competition and the Monetary Order', in M. Dunford and G. Kafkalas (eds),

Cities and Regions in the New Europe: The Global–Local Interplay and Spatial Development Strategies (London: Belhaven).

Sykes, G. (1958) The Society of Captives (Princeton, NJ: Princeton University Press).

Sykes, G. and D. Matza (1957) 'Techniques of Neutralisation: A Theory of Delinquency', *American Sociological Review*, 22 (December): 664–70.

Tarling, R. (1993) *Analysing Offending: Data Models and Interpretations* (London: HMSO).

Tarling, R., T. Davidson and A. Clarke (2004) *The National Evaluation of Youth Justice Board's Mentoring Projects* (London: Youth Justice Board).

Tchaikovsky, C. (1991) 'Mixed Prisons: Misogynistic and Misguided', Prison Report (London: Prison Reform Trust), 16 (Autumn): 12–13.

Thomas, C. (1977) 'Theoretical Perspectives on Prisonisation: A Comparison of the Importation Model and Deprivation Models', *Journal of Criminal Law and Criminology*, **68** (1): 135–45.

Thompson, E. P. (1967) 'Time and Work Discipline in Industrial Capitalism', *Past and Present*, **36**: 57–79.

Thompson, E. P. (1975) *Whigs and Hunters: The Origin of the Black Act* (London: Allen Lane).

Thorpe, D., D. Smith, C. Green and J. Poley (1980) *Out of Care* (London: George Allen & Unwin).

Tomasevski, K. (1994) *Foreigners in Prison* (Helsinki: European Institute for Crime Prevention and Control).

Tonry, M. (1995) *Malign Neglect: Race Crime and Punishment in America* (New York: Oxford University Press).

Tonry, M. (1997) 'Ethnicity Crime and Immigration Comparative and Cross National Perspectives', *Crime and Justice*, Vol. 21 (Chicago: University of Chicago Press).

Tonry, M. (1999) 'Why are US Incarceration/Imprisonment Rates So High?' *Crime and Delinquency*, **45** (4): 419–37.

Tonry, M. (2001) 'Symbol, Substance and Severity in Western Penal Policies', *Punishment & Society*, 3 (4): 517–36.

Travis, A. (2004) 'Private Women's Prison Brigs in the Interior Designers', *Guardian*, 9 June.

Trickett, A., D. Ellingworth, T. Hope and K. Pease (1995) 'Crime Victimisation in the Eighties: Change in Area and Regional Inequality', British Journal of Criminology, 35 (3): 343–59.

Tumim, S. (1996) 'The State of the Prisons', in R. Matthews and P. Francis (eds), *Prisons 2000* (London: Macmillan).

Uchitelle, L. (2005) 'The New Profile of the Long Term Unemployed', *New York Times*, 24 May.

Useem, B. and P. Kimball (1989) *States of Siege* (Oxford: Oxford University Press).

von Hirsch, A. (1992) 'Proportionality in the Philosophy of Punishment', in M. Tonry (ed.), *Crime and Justice: A Review of Research*, Vol. 16 (Chicago: University of Chicago Press).

von Hirsch, A. (1993) *Censure and Sanctions* (Oxford: Clarendon Press).

von Hirsch, A. and J. Roberts (1997) 'Racial Disparity in Sentencing: Reflections on the Hood Study', *Howard Journal*, **36** (3): 227–36.

Wacquant, L. (1999) 'Suitable Enemies: Foreigners and Immigrants in the Prisons of Europe', *Punishment & Society*, **1**: 215–22.

Wacquant, L. (2000) 'The New "Peculiar Institution": On the Prison as Surrogate Ghetto', *Theoretical Criminology*, **4** (3): 377–89.

Wacquant, L. (2001a) 'The Penalisation of Poverty and the Rise of Neo-Liberalism', *European Journal of Criminal Policy and Research*, **9**: 401–12.

Wacquant, L. (2001b) 'Deadly Symbiosis: When Ghetto and Prison Merge', *Punishment & Society*, **3** (1): 95–134.

Wacquant, L. (2005) 'The Great Penal Leap Backwards: Incarceration in America from Nixon to Clinton', in J. Pratt, D. Brown, M. Brown, S. Hallsworth, and W. Morrison (eds), *The New Punitiveness: Trends, Theories, Perspectives* (Cullompton: Willan).

Wagner, P. (2005) *Eric Cadora Shows how Incarceration is Concentrated in Particular Brooklyn Neighbourhoods*, www.prisonersofthecensus.org.news/2005/01/241Cadora.

Walker, N. (1981) 'Feminist Extravaganzas', *Criminal Law Review*: 378–86.

Walker, N. and M. Hough (1988) *Public Attitudes to Sentencing: Surveys from Five Countries* (Aldershot: Gower).

Walklate, S. (1995) *Gender and Crime: An Introduction* (London: Prentice Hall/Harvester Wheatsheaf).

Walklate, S. (2004) *Gender, Crime and Criminal Justice* (2nd edn) (Cullompton: Willan).

Walling, A. (2004) 'Workless Households: Results from the Spring 2004 LFS', *Labour Market Trends*, **112** (11): 435–45.

Walmsley, R. (2005) *World Prison Population List* (7th edn) (London: International Centre for Prison Studies, Kings College).

Walmsley, R., L. Howard and S. White (1992) *The National Prison Survey, 1991* (London: Home Office).

Ward, D. and G. Kassebaum (1965) *Women's Prison: Sex and Social Structure* (London: Weidenfeld & Nicolson).

Wasik, M. (2004) 'What Guides Sentencing Decisions', in A. Bottoms, S. Rex and G. Robinson (eds), *Alternatives to Prison: Options for an Insecure Society* (Cullompton: Willan).

Waters, R. (1990) *Ethnic Minorities and the Criminal Justice System* (Aldershot: Avebury).

Webb, S. and B. Webb (1963) *English Prisons Under Local Government* (London: Frank Cass & Co.)

Weber, L. and B. Bowling (2008) 'Valiant Beggars and Global Vagabonds: Select, Eject, Immobilize', *Theoretical Criminology*, **12** (3): 355–75.

Weber, M. (1948) *From Max Weber: Essays in Sociology*, ed. H. Gerth and C. W. Mills (London: Routledge & Kegan Paul).

Webster, C. (2007) *Understanding Race and Crime* (Buckingham: Open University Press).

Weiss, R. (1986) 'The Reappearance of the Ideal Factory: The Entrepreneur and Social Control in the Contemporary Prison', in J. Lowman *et al.* (eds), *Transcarceration: Essays in the Sociology of Social Control* (Aldershot: Gower).

Weiss, R. (1987) 'Humanitarianism, Labour, Exploitation and Control: A Critical Survey of Theory and Research on the Origin and Development of the Prison', *Social History*, **12** (3): 331–50.

West, H. and W. Sabol (2008) *Prisoners in 2007*, Bureau of Justice Statistics, Bulletin NCJ 224280, US Department of Justice.

Western, B. (2006) *Punishment and Inequality in America* (New York: Russell Sage Foundation).

Western, B., J. Kling and D. Weiman (2001) 'The Labour Market Consequences of Incarceration', *Crime and Delinquency*, **47** (3): 410–27.

Whatmore, P. (1987) 'Barlinnie Special Unit: An Insider's View', in A. Bottoms and R. Light (eds), *Problems of Long Term Imprisonment* (Aldershot: Gower).

Wilkinson, R. and K. Picket (2007) 'The Problems of Relative Deprivation: Why Some Societies do Better than Others', *Social Science and Medicine*, **65** (9): 1965–78.

Williams, R. (1980) *Problems in Materialism and Culture* (London: Verso).

Wilson, W. (1993) *The Ghetto Underclass* (London: Sage).

Wilson, W. J. (1987) *The Truly Disadvantaged* (Chicago: University of Chicago Press).

Witt, R., A. Clarke and N. Fielding (1999) 'Crime and Economic Activity', *British Journal of Criminology*, **39** (3): 391–400.

Woolf, Lord Justice (1991) Prison Disturbances April 1990 (London: HMSO). Worrall, A. (1990) Offending Women: Female Law Breakers and the Criminal Justice System (London: Routledge).

Worrall, A. (1990) *Offending Women: Female Law Breakers and the Criminal Justice System* (London: Routledge).

Worrall, A. (1997) *Punishment in the Community* (Harlow: Longman).

Worrall, A. and K. Pease (1986) 'The Prison Population in 1995', *British Journal of Criminology*, **26** (2): 184–8.

Wray, R. (2000) 'The New Economic Reality: Penal Keynesianism', *Challenge* (September– October): 31–59.

Wright, K. (1989) 'Race and Economic Marginality in Explaining Prison Adjustment', *Journal of Research in Crime and Delinquency*, **26**: 67–89.

Wrong, D. (1994) *The Problem of Order* (Cambridge, Mass.: Harvard University Press).

Young, I. (1990) 'The Ideal Community and the Politics of Difference', in L. Nicholson (ed.), *Feminism/Postmodernism* (New York: Routledge).

Young, I. (1997) *Intersecting Voices: Dilemmas of Gender, Political Philosophy and Policy* (Princeton, NJ: Princeton University Press).

Young, J. (1970) 'The Zookeepers of Deviancy', *Catalyst*, **5**: 38–46.

Young, J. (1988) 'Risk of Crime and Fear of Crime: A Realist Critique of Survey-Based Assumptions', in M. Maguire and J. Pointing (eds), *Victims of Crime: A New Deal?* (Milton Keynes: Open University Press).

Young, J. (1992) 'Ten Points of Realism', in J. Young and R. Matthews (eds), *Rethinking Criminology: The Realist Debate* (London: Sage).

Young, J. (1998) 'From Inclusive to Exclusive Society: Nightmares of the European Dream', in V. Ruggiero, N. South and I. Taylor (eds), *The New European Criminology: Crime and Social Order in Europe* (London: Routledge).

Young, J. (1999) *The Exclusive Society* (London: Sage).

Young, J. (2003) 'Merton With Energy: Katz with Structure: The Sociology of Vindictiveness and the Criminology of Transgression', *Theoretical Criminology*, **7** (3): 388–414.

Young, P. (1992) 'The Importance of Utopias in Criminology Thinking', *British Journal of Criminology*, **32** (4): 423–37.

Young, R. and C. Hoyle (2003) 'Restorative Justice and Punishment', in S. McConville (ed.), *The Use of Punishment* (Cullompton: Willan).

Youth Justice Board (2001) *Guidance for Youth Offending Teams on Achieving Equality* (London: Youth Justice Board).

Zatz, M. (1984) 'Race Ethnicity and Determinate Sentencing', *Criminology*, **22** (2): 147–71.

Zedner, L. (1991) *Women, Crime and Custody in Victorian England* (Oxford: Clarendon Press).

Zedner, L. (1995) 'Wayward Sisters: The Prison for Women', in N. Morris and D. Rothman (eds), *The Oxford History of the Prison* (New York: Oxford University Press).

Zedner, L. (2004) *Criminal Justice* (Oxford: Oxford University Press).

Zedner, L. (2007) 'Pre-crime and Post-Criminology?', *Theoretical Criminology*, **11** (2): 261–82.

Zimring, F. and G. Hawkins (1991a) *Incapacitation: Penal Confinement and the Restraint of Crime* (New York: Oxford University Press).

Zimring, F. and G. Hawkins (1991b) *The Scale of Imprisonment* (Chicago: University of Chicago Press).

Zimring, F., G. Hawkins and S. Kamin (2001) *Punishment and Democracy: Three Strikes and You're Out in California* (New York: Oxford University Press).

Index

For enquiries or renewal at
Quarles Campus LRC
Tel: 01708 462759